ATLANTA UNBOUND

In the series *Urban Life, Landscape, and Policy,*
edited by Zane L. Miller, David Stradling, and Larry Bennett

Also in this series:

Scott Larson, *"Building Like Moses with Jacobs in Mind": Contemporary Planning in New York City*

Gary Rivlin, *Fire on the Prairie: Harold Washington, Chicago Politics, and the Roots of the Obama Presidency*

William Issel, *Church and State in the City: Catholics and Politics in Twentieth-Century San Francisco*

Julia L. Foulkes, *To the City: Urban Photographs of the New Deal*

John D. Fairfield, *The Public and Its Possibilities: Triumphs and Tragedies in the American City*

William Issel, *For Both Cross and Flag: Catholic Action, Anti-Catholicism, and National Security Politics in World War II San Francisco*

Lisa Hoffman, *Patriotic Professionalism in Urban China: Fostering Talent*

Andrew Hurley, *Beyond Preservation: Using Public History to Revitalize Inner Cities*

ATLANTA UNBOUND

Enabling Sprawl through Policy and Planning

CARLTON WADE BASMAJIAN

TEMPLE UNIVERSITY PRESS | PHILADELPHIA

TEMPLE UNIVERSITY PRESS
Philadelphia, Pennsylvania 19122
www.temple.edu/tempress

Copyright © 2013 by Temple University
All rights reserved
Published 2013
Paperback edition published 2015

Library of Congress Cataloging-in-Publication Data

Basmajian, Carlton Wade, 1973–
  Atlanta unbound : enabling sprawl through policy and planning / Carlton Wade Basmajian.
    pages cm. — (Urban life, landscape, and policy)
  Includes bibliographical references and index.
  ISBN 978-1-4399-0939-3 (cloth : alk. paper) —
ISBN 978-1-4399-0941-6 (e-book) 1. Urbanization—Georgia—Atlanta. 2. Urban policy—Georgia—Atlanta. 3. Regional planning—Georgia—Atlanta. 4. City planning—Georgia—Atlanta. 5. Atlanta (Ga.)—Population. I. Title.
  HT384.U52A824 2013
  307.1'21609758231—dc23
                                            2013007878

ISBN 978-1-4399-0940-9 (paperback : alk. paper)

♾ The paper used in this publication meets the requirements of the American National Standard for Information Sciences—Permanence of Paper for Printed Library Materials, ANSI Z39.48-1992

Printed in the United States of America

013015P

Contents

Acknowledgments | vii

1 | Introduction: An Intentional Region? | 1

2 | Building the Atlanta Regional Commission | 15

3 | The River and the Region: The Chattahoochee River and the Atlanta Regional Commission | 47

4 | Projecting Sprawl? The 1976 Regional Development Plan of Metropolitan Atlanta | 85

5 | Growth Management Comes to Georgia | 111

6 | Atlanta's Transportation Crisis and the Battle of the Northern Arc | 137

7 | A Regional Story | 173

Notes | 187

Index | 253

Acknowledgments

This book would not exist without the inspiration and support of family, friends, teachers, and colleagues over the last decade. My gratitude cannot be adequately expressed in the pages here.

Scott Campbell, Robert Fishman, Matthew Lassiter, and Joseph Grengs oversaw this project from its beginnings as a dissertation. From the moment I first considered the University of Michigan for graduate school, Scott has been an invaluable resource and mentor. As an advisor, he was always willing to take time to talk about coursework, research, career, and life. Robert was remarkably encouraging as the project took form, offering insight and constructive critique at a number of extremely important moments. His scholarship has been the model that I have tried to follow throughout, though I am still far from reaching the standard he has set. As a fellow Atlantan, whose work on the transformation of the postwar urban South helped provide a framework for my study, Matt played a critical role in encouraging me to expand the original scope of the research to include a much longer time frame. He was a precise blueprint of what an outstanding instructor and advisor should be. Joe asked insightful and timely questions that helped me improve the focus of the project in its early phases. He also generously offered his friendship and advice over the years, which included some rather interesting music trading.

That this project got off the ground owes a great deal to my classmates at Michigan. Thank you for making Ann Arbor more fun than it had any right to be. Though at the time the hours spent in the windowless interior rooms of the Taubman College seemed almost endless, the conversations, arguments, and gripe sessions proved to be worth more than I can even begin to describe. Chris Coutts and Sanjeev Vidyarthi have my deepest gratitude for making Room 2208I not only a place to get a little work done but also a refuge and a space in which brutal honesty could be mixed with ridiculousness (and impromptu interior design projects). With them, happy hours were frequent, Friday cookouts were the highlight of the week, and friendships will last a lifetime. For Dan Spiess, heartfelt thanks for making the difficult transition to graduate school and southeastern Michigan bearable and, more than that, fun. Images from our numerous adventures are permanently burned in my mind. I owe Raju Mann for bringing a healthy dose of skepticism to all our Ph.D. bullshit and for a bit of Detroit magic when it was needed. Elijah Davidian offered unconditional friendship and an amazingly optimistic outlook on life. Nina David became a good friend and has become a good coauthor to boot. I thank Neha Sami and Anirban Adhya for commiseration, food, drink, and a forgiving form of friendship. I also thank Caroline Low, Taejung Kim, Phil D'anieri, and Xiaoguang Wang for lively hallway conversations, resource sharing, and advice.

The generosity of numerous people and institutions made the research this book is constructed on possible. The Georgia Archives staff, now scattered, deserve special acknowledgment for making a huge amount of obscure state government documents available. The papers in those boxes of materials form a critical foundation of this book. Despite operating on the stingiest of budgets and in an environment in which the fate of the institution itself was in doubt, the staff made Georgia's primary archival repository (a treasure for the people of the state) a relaxing place to do research. I am especially in debt to Renate Milner and Amanda Mos. Both endured my seemingly endless requests with good grace and made the days upon days spent in the frigid air of the Government Documents Reading Room not only productive but pleasurable. I thank them for advice on finding my way through the voluminous collection that documents Georgia's history, occasional lunches in Jonesboro, and gossip. It is not every day that a researcher meets a gang of archivists so unfailingly helpful and so warm and welcoming. Erica Danylchak at the Atlanta History Center was a huge help during my many months there. She provided insight and access to the massive Atlanta Regional Commission collection, still in the midst of processing, that was critical to this project. I commend the efforts of Sue VerHoef and Paige Adair, who provided guidance through the process of securing digital reproductions. Likewise, Helen Matthews provided guidance to the Atlanta History Center's vast collections at several critical moments. The staff at special collections in the Woodruff Library at Emory University deserve mention for their help during the earliest phases of the project. The staff at Georgia State University's Special Collections and Archives also provided valuable help, pointing me to several important oral histories housed in the Georgia Government Documentation Project collection. Susan Grimes at the Atlanta Regional

Commission and Steven Engerrand at the Georgia Archives were hugely helpful with securing permissions to publish. I thank Brad Calvert for providing helpful maps and being a lifelong friend.

The good folks at Temple University Press have been exceptionally pleasant to work with. From my first contact with the press, I have felt that my inquiries have been answered expeditiously, my concerns taken seriously, and my work appreciated. Mick Gusinde-Duffy, the editor who took this project from prospectus to completed book manuscript, was delightful to work with and provided reassuring support throughout. Zane Miller, one of the three editors of the Urban Life, Landscape, and Policy series, who read the initial draft of the manuscript in its entirety, offered pointed questions and suggestions but also unfailing encouragement. It never ceases to amaze me when someone of his stature also turns out to be so approachable and helpful. Likewise, it would be just about impossible for me to thank Larry Bennett enough for his help in getting the manuscript through the revision process. He read every page with the sharpest of eyes, noting inconsistencies, pointing out gaps, and suggesting changes that made the work considerably better. In a business in which timeliness is too often lacking, Larry's promptness was refreshing. Janet Francendese and Stephanie Lang, who oversaw the manuscript through its move into production and publication, made that process seamless.

Without the support and encouragement of my colleagues in the Department of Community and Regional Planning at Iowa State, my academic home for the past five years, completing this book could have been considerably more difficult. I owe special gratitude to Douglas Johnston, an exemplary department chair and an especially helpful colleague. When I was the most junior of junior faculty Doug protected me from arduous committees and granted me valuable course releases at just the right moments. Francis Owusu, whom I cannot thank enough, has been tireless with his generosity, encouragement, and friendship. He became a mentor without ever having been asked to do so. Riad Mahayni likewise offered consistent encouragement as the manuscript moved from dissertation to book, providing helpful comments on drafts of chapters and offering timely advice. As a fellow traveler in the process of adjusting to life in central Iowa, Gerardo Sandoval was my fifth-floor friend and sounding board. Monica Haddad, Kimberly Zarecor, and Gary Taylor have become friends who make life inside and outside the College of Design consistently interesting. Jane Rongerude has, seemingly overnight, become an incredible friend, a willing coconspirator, and a wonderful coauthor. The students who have found their way to my office at Iowa State over the last few years have been the source of both joy and frustration, but never once have they been anything less than fascinating.

Finally, I owe my deepest gratitude to my family. My father has been a remarkably stabilizing presence, quick with encouragement and never once questioning why I chose this path. He has showed me the value of patience over and over again. My mother has been cheerleader and critic, often in the same breath. Perhaps more than anything she instilled in me a fighting spirit and helped me realize the value of casting a skeptical gaze at everything around me. Most of all, my wife has been beside me, always there to listen to my ramblings but never afraid to let me know the moment I veer into the absurd. Without her love and support, in no way would this have been possible. To you, Paola, this book is dedicated.

ATLANTA UNBOUND

1
Introduction

An Intentional Region?

In the summer of 1994, the renowned Brookings Institution economist Anthony Downs delivered what he called an unorthodox speech to members of the Atlanta District Council of the Urban Land Institute. Speaking to a room full of developers, real estate brokers, and politicians, Downs explained that rather than talking about "traditional land-use and real estate issues," he would instead consider "the major challenges facing all large U.S. metropolitan areas." Among the challenges he mentioned were the usual suspects: crime, poverty, racial segregation, failing schools, congestion, and low environmental quality. Though he noted that each was important, Downs posited that governance—namely, a "governmental structure that consists of many small and nearly autonomous local governments"—was the biggest challenge of all. If metropolitan Atlanta's fragmented governing bodies were the culprits for the region's host of problems, how did they become so? In words oddly complimentary yet condemnatory, he let slip that Atlanta's local governments, despite apparent disorder, had succeeded in "carrying out certain growth related policies" that conformed closely to an "unlimited low-density vision" of how "growth ought to occur." But he followed with the suggestion that the region's "unlimited low-density metropolitan growth [had taken] place through an uncoordinated, seemingly almost random set of local public policies and individual private actions carried out by separate governments and private parties." In other words, the issues facing Atlanta at the end of the twentieth century, and by extension other large urban regions, were the consequence of local governments having run amok but in some vaguely coordinated fashion.[1]

Regional planning in the United States has frequently been the target of just this sort of criticism, for being weak and disorganized and, more often than not, "a disappointment."[2] Residential segregation by race and income, sprawling road networks, degraded air quality, overtaxed water and sewer systems, and intergovernmental competition for resources are often cited as seemingly irrefutable evidence of the failure of the federal government and the states to develop and implement a strong system of coordinated, regional planning institutions. But as Downs also suggested, these effects appear to be the result of a vaguely coherent vision, however fragmented it might seem. In many respects, Downs was channeling a sort of received wisdom.

This received wisdom is part of the legacy of a once robust debate about the value of regional planning and its goals, a dispute that dates to the beginning of the twentieth century and occupied the intellectual heart of planning as it coalesced from its beginnings in the nineteenth century into a modern discipline in the 1930s.[3] Yet at the end of World War II this debate was effectively buried and forgotten, and over the second half of the twentieth century the publicly supported regional planning agencies, and the plans they produced, received little attention for their role in the transformation of American metropolitan areas.[4] It is this assumed irrelevance that I challenge, arguing that regional planning remained powerful during the second half of the twentieth century, strengthened by significant, albeit quiet, support from federal and state governments.[5] Indeed, from 1954 until 1981 federal "grants for . . . planning work in metropolitan and regional areas" were a mainstay of support for regional (and local) planning.[6] But because regional planning activities were included in the complex mandates accompanying dispersal of federal funds, they mostly avoided public notice, by the media or others. Lacking the headline-grabbing drama of political grandstanding, racial conflict, or environmental catastrophe, they also evaded much scholarly attention. In part because regional plans are products of intricate institutional relationships and span multiple layers of government, their analysis is difficult, and so is reaching clear conclusions about their impact. Perhaps the most cogent reason postwar regional planning escaped notice is that it tended to be technical, arcane, and unusually boring.[7]

If we can put the boredom of the planning process aside for a moment and instead consider regional plans as devices for structuring decisions about development, as expressions of how regulations should be applied, and as indicators of which organizations and individuals would be allowed to participate, we can begin to recognize the imprint of regional thinking in the ways that local and state governments, along with federal infrastructure policy, together managed the urban development process. We can also begin to see that the process of regional planning, what might be called plan making, as it has been carried out still reveals distinct echoes of debates about regionalism from the earliest years of the twentieth-century.[8] One purpose of this book is to reconsider the influence of regional planning in this light, as both process and institution, exploring the way it was conceived, structured, and executed, using metropolitan Atlanta as a case.[9]

The externalities of development appear to have fractured modern city regions, but urban decentralization in the second half of the twentieth century was the work of a network of highly coordinated public agencies. Working at different scales, these agencies designed a set of regulatory conditions that favored single-family homes, strip malls, and private automobiles. Once these conditions were in place, households that were able took advantage, moving en masse from central cities, small towns, and farms into outposts along an ever-expanding suburban edge. A second purpose of this book is to explore the connections among these agencies to understand how they influenced the process of regional development.[10]

Researchers who have examined twentieth-century Atlanta have largely set aside the issue of regional planning, and often the geographic region itself, preferring instead to focus on socioeconomic and political forces that conditioned the development of the city, extrapolating that these same forces also shaped the greater metropolitan area.[11] The bulk of this scholarship has used the politics of race and community power as interlocking analytic frameworks. Beginning in the early 1950s, the first studies of Atlanta's power structure concluded that a small set of corporate chieftains effectively governed the city. They commanded an army of middle managers, professionals, and local politicians to carry out their directives, which most conspicuously included sustaining their social and political power while trying to maintain control of the city's growing black electorate.[12] On the basis of this work, scholars subsequently advanced the notion that the delicate politics of race in Atlanta determines how power has been wielded and how the city has developed. Regime theorists updated the power structure argument, explaining how downtown corporate leaders and elected officials learned to cooperate with the city's black leadership to reach a truce that helped the white elites maintain control, even as the black electorate reached majority status.[13] Social and political historians studied the city's racial geography during the twentieth century as a major factor in explaining the shape of the physical and political landscape, from the siting of freeways and transit lines to the location of shopping malls, sports arenas, and office parks to the political affiliation of the suburbs.[14] Geographers and sociologists have seen in Atlanta's physical, economic, and social form an expression of an implicitly racist growth machine, one beholden to the spatial demands of modern capitalism.[15]

The politics of race, complicated by power and political economy, offers a good explanation of the process of development in the city of Atlanta and echoes issues and conflicts documented in other cities.[16] Yet limiting discussion to the city overlooks broader institutions that influenced how the region grew and are not necessarily identical to the ones that operated within the city. Focusing on the city tends to miss issues originating at the state and regional levels. Despite Atlanta being both the

Figure 1.1 "Statue, West Elevation, Georgia State Capitol, Capitol Square, Atlanta, Fulton County, Georgia," 1990, Library of Congress, Prints and Photographs Division, HABS GA, 61-ATLA, 3-176

largest city and the state capital, a somewhat uncommon condition, little scholarly literature substantially addresses the influence of state or regional institutions on the urbanization process, which I argue is critical to understanding why Atlanta grew the way it did. While respecting the insights developed in the literature, my purpose is to explore the evolution of metropolitan Atlanta. I do this by taking the urban region as the primary unit of analysis.

This project began with a broad question related to the issues Downs raised in his speech: Is American-style urban sprawl actually unplanned? Discussions of the low-density built form endemic to American metropolitan areas in the postwar period, of which Atlanta is an ideal example, almost inevitably end in a groaning indictment of the unwillingness of local governments to cooperate and usually conclude that "the most important future challenge for metropolitan areas will be to create some kind of effective regional governance for both central cities and their suburbs," to force meaningful cross-jurisdictional conciliation.[17] Sparked by this sentiment, which has become something of a platitude among planners, I sought to investigate Atlanta's alleged unplanned urban sprawl. Might the region's scattered strip malls, office parks, and subdivisions have been the result of a plan? Later, I narrowed the project to three questions about the influence of regional planning in Atlanta's postwar development. First, what did the public institutions engaged in Atlanta's regional planning process hope to accomplish? Second, how was the relationship among those public institutions constituted, and how did it structure the regional planning process? Third, if Atlanta's regional planning process was coordinated across political scales, why did it lead to such extensive decentralization? All three questions concern how regional policies spanned political boundaries and how ideas about what constitutes good regional planning framed local debates.

I argue that the idea of the urban region, as part of the mesolevel that buffers federal and local governments, played a particularly important role in Atlanta's postwar development. Beginning in 1947, but especially from the late 1960s, decisions about how the region should be developed have been much more highly coordinated and planned than previously recognized. For nearly forty years the close working relationship between the Atlanta Regional Commission (ARC)—Atlanta's council of governments and its designated metropolitan planning organization—a cadre of state and local politicians, and a subset of federal agencies created and sustained a regional agenda that appeared haphazard but was in fact quite coherent.[18] At first representing a five-county metropolitan region, by 2002 ARC's footprint had expanded to ten counties, covering 80 percent of Atlanta's urbanized area and 83 percent of the greater metropolitan population.[19] ARC's growth both reflected and directed metropolitan Atlanta's.

To understand how Atlanta's regional planning process functioned, I turn away from simple mechanical indicators and toward the rules that govern the behavior of public agencies (structure) and the language and procedures the agencies use (discourse). Training a sharper lens on organizational issues helps us understand how the structure of the regional planning process, its jurisdiction, sources of funding, and participating stakeholders establish which development issues receive attention and how responses to those issues are crafted. Paying close attention to the discourse that is the heart of the regional planning process, expressed in meetings, hearings, reports, special studies, maps, and media, allows us to see how the process unfolds from the inside. Together, structure and discourse exert significant influence over development decisions, yet they are not easily visible and usually receive little attention.[20]

Most studies of regional planning have focused on the fate of explicit policies, those formally adopted by regional planning agencies that are directed at controlling specific development externalities at the local level. Success or failure is often measured by whether local governments implement those regional policies within a relatively short time frame.[21] More often than not, these kinds of studies deem regional policies failures, a result that tends to downplay the power and effectiveness of regional plans and regional planning agencies while sidestepping the details of the regional planning process itself. Taking a longer view challenges such evaluations.

By looking across several decades and a connected series of planning events, I argue that the agencies, the plans, and most importantly, the process have been a major influence on the shape of Atlanta's growth. Toward this end, this book excavates the regional planning process during a period roughly between 1968 and 2002, years when metro Atlanta experienced its most dramatic growth in population, jobs, and geographic extent. Using a variety of archival resources directly related to the regional planning process, I examine, in order, the creation of ARC (1968–1971); the writing of a regional watershed management plan (1971–1972); the preparation of a regional development plan (1973–1976); the passage of a state law that mandated comprehensive local planning (1987–1989); and a battle over transportation, air quality, and a suburban freeway (1998–2002). The written record of the planning process provides an inside view of how the discourse shared between the professional bureaucracy and public officials helped structure decisions about development. The case of metropolitan Atlanta provides an opportunity to focus on the regional planning process in a single place during a period of significant political, economic, and physical transition.

The importance of the relationship of ARC and the state to this story derives from their position as de facto managers of the regional planning process, a role that allowed a changing cast of politicians and public administrators to exert power over the development of the region and to guide the implementation of federal policy. These two forces, the political and regulatory, consistently shaped and constrained the regional planning process. Until the late 1960s, Atlanta's governing regime was a creature of the city's corporate executives, professional class, and their political allies, a very small group that Floyd Hunter described as "persons of dominance, prestige, and influence" who are "able to enforce their decisions by persuasion, intimidation, coercion, and, if necessary, force."[22] In the late 1960s, this group began to dissipate, a result of the expansion of regional boundaries, changed demographics, and new federal laws. Public administrators, state legislators (including representatives from the rapidly expanding suburban counties), and county commissioners who coalesced around a shared interest in the region's development began to replace them. This emergent governing coalition maintained a surprisingly congenial relationship, which imbued the region with a sense of consensus that persisted for twenty years. At the beginning of the 1990s, however, the regionalist coalition broke down as political control of several county commissions and state legislative districts changed hands. Chaos ensued as a new, more contentious group of stakeholders fought for control of the regional planning process. By the early 2000s, leadership of the state, including the governorship and a majority of the legislature, had shifted from Democratic to Republican, and the population demographics of the region looked very different. The regional planning process, viewed across time, reveals how political changes affected regional development.

The Legacy of Regionalism

The importance of regional planning has been recognized since the birth of city planning itself in the late nineteenth century. Dramatized in documents like Charles Eliot's metropolitan park plan for Boston and Daniel Burnham and Edward Bennett's *Plan of Chicago*, the soaring imagery associated with early regional plans paid homage to the idea that the modern city could be designed in a single frame, just as one might design a building or a park. By the interwar period of the twentieth century, however, a decidedly more empirical form of regionalism had mostly replaced the design schemes of the previous generation. The ideas of Ebenezer Howard, Patrick Geddes, Lewis Mumford, and Howard Odum offered a more process-oriented but also philosophical vision of what regional planning could achieve. Bearing witness to the intense and often ugly industrial urbanization that transformed both the cities and the countrysides of the Anglo-American world in the late nineteenth and early twentieth centuries, Howard, Geddes, Mumford, and Odum stridently argued that comprehensive regional planning could solve the pathologies of modern life.[23]

Believing that the conditions in central London demanded systematic depopulation, Howard dreamed Garden City as a new kind of urban form, a self-contained city of limited size, cooperatively owned by the residents, and intimately connected to the countryside. With time and careful planning, he argued that a constellation of garden cities could emerge, linked by railroads but permanently separated by productive agricultural land. On paper, Garden City was crisp and clear and has transfixed planners ever since. Geddes too saw the British industrial city as problematic but reacted with the detached eye of a scientist who sought to understand it as much as change it. Rejecting political boundaries as arbitrary, Geddes conceptualized the region as the geographic unit where humans and nature most closely aligned. To gather evidence for his claims, he spent years literally looking out over Edinburgh, fastidiously surveying the physical, social, and economic patterns of the city, building a complex theory about the union of the natural region, economic activity, and folk life. By treating a region as the unit of analysis, Geddes suggested a new lens for viewing and correcting social problems. On the American side of the Atlantic, Mumford and Odum saw themselves as intellectual descendants of Geddes. Mumford combined Howard's normative prescriptions with Geddes's measured empiricism in his belief that the only way to save the United States from itself would be to transform it into an environmentally conscious, decentralized society living in planned urban regions. Odum adopted the Geddesian regional survey as a tool to modernize the American South while avoiding the kind of disruptive, high-intensity urbanization that big American cities in the Northeast and Midwest had experienced. Howard, Geddes, Mumford, and Odum influenced a generation of social scientists, planners, landscape architects, and civil engineers and indeed gave shape to planning's intellectual core over the succeeding decades.[24]

Arguably, the most complete American effort to produce a regional plan that reflected this tradition was the *Plan of New York and Its Environs*, a ten-volume, ten-year project funded by the Russell Sage Foundation that began in 1921 and included many of the most renowned planners and social scientists in the English-speaking world.[25] The New York plan advanced a vision of urban decentralization that borrowed heavily from Howard and Geddes yet also seemed to violate the revolutionary spirit of their ideas.[26] Yet the rigorous empirical approach to understanding and planning the New York region demonstrated by the plan, including defining the region as a unit of analysis, melded social science and policy to provide a depth and intellectual rigor that had never before been so clearly evident in the nascent planning discipline. The subsequent influence of the *Plan of New York and Its Environs* on federal policy during the New Deal and World War II helped provoke federal interest in regional, state, and indeed national planning as a tool for managing the country. Many of the academics and intellectuals working in Franklin Roosevelt's administration supported public sector planning, seeing it as a tool for reining in the excesses of unregulated capitalism. The desire to make some kind of national planning agency a permanent fixture of the executive branch ran high during Roosevelt's four terms, but the end of World War II and the beginning of the Cold War ended hope that centralized planning would have a permanent place in federal policy.[27]

As World War II drew to an end and the peacetime economy warmed up, gauzy regional plans, amalgams of ideas from a variety of prewar sources, became popular tools for promoting economic growth.[28] These plans were often spearheaded by local chambers of commerce interested in helping their members capture a share of the growing national wealth. Though they usually owed their existence to private organizations, many postwar regional plans were claimed by sponsors to be civic activities.[29] They outlined fanciful civic buildings, multilane freeways, futuristic urban transit systems, and spacious suburban neighborhoods along the urban edge, revealing a lingering belief that American cities were in need of rebuilding.[30] Beyond the publicity the plans hoped to generate, they also accomplished more concrete tasks. In many cases, the infrastructure schemes, parks, and renewal areas in privately financed regional plans later became part of public plans. The first publicly (locally) financed regional planning agencies also emerged in the years just after World War II. Beginning in the early 1950s, a series of new policies expanded and transformed federal support for urban infrastructure and bolstered regional planning in the process.[31] For example, Section 701 of the federal Housing Act of 1954 funded demolition and construction but also provided direct support for activities that would increase regional cooperation around issues of housing and urban development.[32] The Federal Aid Highway Act of 1956 outlined and paid for the Interstate Highway System but also financed regional planning agencies in their efforts to develop urban highway systems that were at least nominally coordinated with surrounding land use. The 1950s-era highway and housing acts together ensured that public regional planning agencies would become nearly ubiquitous features of the governing structures of virtually every large and midsized city.

As the highways, bridges, sewers, and airports that framed postwar metropolitan growth took shape, the externalities of urbanization became increasingly visible and difficult to ignore. Waves of regulation addressing the negative effects of the growth of the built environment emerged in response. First came the 1962 Federal Aid Highway Act, which mandated and funded the creation of a national system of regional planning agencies to deal with the human and environmental cost of blasting massive highways through urban neighborhoods.[33] Through these new metropolitan planning organizations, transportation plans were required to engage the public, address civil rights, relocate households displaced by road building, assess the environmental impacts of development, and coordinate land use. After Lyndon Johnson took office in 1963, federal laws governing the built environment and using the region as a primary geographic unit flooded in: air quality legislation in 1963, civil rights in 1964, water pollution and urban renewal in 1965, historic preservation and model cities in 1966, and intergovernmental cooperation in 1968. Richard Nixon inherited and signed broad environmental protection in 1969 shortly after taking office, updated air quality laws in 1970, and oversaw a major expansion of water pollution control in 1972.[34]

Though at times appearing at cross-purposes, expanded federal legislation in the 1960s established new constraints on local control over the built environment while enhancing the power of regional planning agencies. As the condition of the natural environment became part of a complex science of ecology, measurable standards emerged that were linked to planning and infrastructure. Federal transportation policy slowly shifted from expansion to mitigation, a subtle but significant change that required regional agencies to confront the broader impacts of their plans. Legislation to strengthen intergovernmental coordination forced local governments to work closely with regional agencies on planning projects. Requirements for metropolitan-level planning were attached to a wide range of federal domestic programs. Awareness of the negative externalities associated with rapid urban development had finally made its way up to the federal policy-making apparatus and then, in a newly codified form, flowed back down to state, regional, and local planning institutions for implementation.[35] By the early 1970s, these changes reconstituted the regional planning process into a much more complex set of rules and procedures and remade the core activities of regional planning agencies, making the urban region a prominent component of federal policy over the next three decades.[36] Regional agencies finally began to resemble the comprehensive governing bodies their nomenclature suggested.[37]

Post-1970 Sprawl

In the early postwar years (between 1946 and 1970), most suburbs remained relatively compact. People still went downtown to work and shop. Public transit systems made the switch from streetcars to buses but remained relatively well used, and a few federally funded regional rail systems began to appear. In the late 1960s, however, another wave of suburbanization emerged, which roughly coincided with the growing scope of federal control over planning and the built environment. The square footage of the average home began to expand, while the average number of people per household shrank; the percentage of work trips made on mass transit began to decline; and the average distance between work and home grew. As a result, the years after 1970 saw the urban edge flow deeper into the hinterlands. What began as urban decentralization in the 1950s turned into deconcentration in the 1970s. As the baby boomers, a generation raised amid postwar prosperity, began to enter the labor force, they took advantage of the spoils of the system their parents had created to move themselves farther from central cities and into spacious suburban subdivisions on the fringe.[38]

Atlanta demonstrated this process vividly. Up until about 1970, development at urban densities outside the city was largely adjacent to the city limits, the product of city dwellers moving to new suburban neighborhoods.[39] But by the mid-1970s, population growth well beyond the inner suburbs began to accelerate. In 1960 Atlanta contained half the regional population, and Fulton and Dekalb Counties together accounted for 80 percent; by 1970 the city still accounted for one-third of the region's total, Fulton and Dekalb just shy of three-quarters. But by 2000 the city held less than a tenth of the region's population, and the Fulton-Dekalb share had fallen to 36 percent. In 1900 the population density of what could be defined as metro Atlanta was nearly 6,000 persons per square mile. By 1960 this density had dropped by 50 percent. Density continued to decline over the following four decades, falling to just over 1,100 persons per square mile by century's end.[40]

By the late 1980s regulation of the built environment in Georgia was more clearly articulated than ever before.[41] But despite layers of new regulations, better data, and more sophisticated analytic tools, Atlanta's horizontal march across north Georgia seemed more rapid and voracious every year. Noticing the seemingly incessant growth of the fringe, observers consistently concluded that regional planning must be weak and in need of significant reform.[42] Their solutions called for more collaboration and for bigger, more powerful regional agencies to replace ineffective councils of government and metropolitan planning organizations. As Downs suggested in 1994, "Creating regional governance arrangements that can influence key land-use and transportation decisions over all the counties in the Atlanta region is absolutely essential to solving the region's pressing growth-related and social problems."[43]

Researchers have tended to view the regional planning process in the late twentieth century as focused almost exclusively on ends, yet the complexity of its structure suggests that means may be more important. Viewing ARC and the state of Georgia as an integral part of an ongoing regional planning discourse reframes metropolitan Atlanta's built environment as a by-product of regulated behavior by interpenetrated public agencies and private actors rather than random actions by unrelated entities. Indeed, ARC had been orchestrating the regional planning process in conjunction with the state since its creation, consistently playing an important role in the major development decisions that gave the region its spatial structure. The present shape of metropolitan Atlanta, lacking limiting topography, is largely a manifestation of a highly developed regulatory framework, with ARC and the state sitting at the center. The close relationship between ARC and the state—persisting for decades through water supply plans for the Chattahoochee River, a series of regional development plans, and growth management legislation before finally being upended amid a transportation planning showdown—demonstrates how the planning process worked to structure decisions. The sheer predictability of the outcomes of this relationship belies the image of a disconnected, balkanized collection of independent political fiefdoms, all pursuing their own ends regardless of the consequences.

Ultimately, what Downs and like-minded observers have not enunciated is that each seemingly independent planning decision also worked in conjunction with the ones before it and the ones after, creating a temporal and spatial coherence of surprising extent. Regional development policies and plans for the Chattahoochee River encouraged land conservation, water protection, and neighborhood preservation, but they also accommodated a far-flung, single-family housing stock built around a system of cul-de-sacs, setbacks, and stream buffers. Growth management brought the state power to enforce a set of standards for local comprehensive plans but also purposely ignored how those plans would shape development. Transportation plans focused on strengthening the urban core and reducing congestion by gradually expanding roads and building a commuter-oriented mass transit system, but good roads pushed the urban fringe farther from the central city, and a hub-and-spoke transit system could not accommodate a multinodal commute shed.

Exploring the nature of the relationships that sustained the regional planning process raises several important points about how regional planning has worked in the postwar period, points important to understanding how sprawling metropolitan areas like Atlanta have been created and sustained. First, infrastructure systems, the pillars of the built environment, are the result of a highly structured but also consistently negotiated agreement between public agencies operating at the regional scale. The balance in this negotiation teeters on the ability of regional planning agencies to build and manage alliances between public and private actors. Second, the intellectual legacy of regionalist thought continues to exert a strong influence on the ideology and practice of contemporary regional planning. While regional planning agencies are creatures of their temporal-spatial context, they owe just as much to the old regionalist tradition. Third, treating regional planning as simply a product of the spillover effects and negative externalities of local development decisions fails to appreciate the connection between regional agencies, states, and the federal government. The way ARC and the state operate reflects the close coordination of policy and ideas between levels of government, whereby the regional agency acts as much as a representative of state and federal interests as it does local interests.

Metro Atlanta Expands

Between 1970 and 2002 Atlanta's low-density sprawl expanded at a rapid pace but largely because it was planned that way. Though the vision of an ideal urban form remained surprisingly consistent, the intervening years witnessed significant changes in the politics and practice of regional planning. As suburbs absorbed people and jobs, turning northern Georgia into a continuous expanse of urbanization, the regional planning process underwent three important disruptions. The first came with the creation of ARC in 1971, when the balance of power in the regional planning process shifted from a small cadre of downtown businessmen to a larger coalition of state and local politicians and public administrators, representing both city and suburbs, who would work together for nearly two decades and settle into a collaborative middle ground from which they would govern. The second came in the early 1980s, when President Ronald Reagan slashed direct federal support of state and regional planning programs. The state of Georgia stepped in, instituting a series of new policies designed to fill the void left by the federal pullback. The third came in the early 1990s as reinvigorated federal urban policy forced significant changes to the regional planning process and changing political alliances displaced several of ARC's long-standing board members and state legislative allies, upending the balance of power on the commission. A new group of politicians, supported by the legions of suburban homeowners who had flocked to metro Atlanta during the 1980s boom, took control of the regional planning process and ushered in a period of turmoil. Openly hostile to regulations that supported coordinated planning, the reconfigured regional coalition turned its attention to protecting the low-density, single-family subdivisions that many believed gave the region much of its appeal. For the next decade, the regional leadership remained at odds with just about any attempt to institute new environmental protections, more aggressive land-use controls, or expansion of the mass transit network. Only when a battle over a new suburban freeway engulfed the region did the impasse break.

The postwar years during which so many regulations controlling land development were created have been well documented, but the effect of those regulations remains less explored. In the years after 1970, many of the externalities that were supposed to be controlled and mitigated by the expanded regulatory framework got worse, not better. Each new regulation contributed to a transformation of both the regional planning process and the institutions that supported it. Though, with a few exceptions, parcel-level decision-making authority (zoning and building permits) remained embedded in local jurisdictions, the increasing number of regulations requiring regional consideration gave regional agencies significant influence over the broader context in which small-scale decisions could be made.[44] By examining the material record left behind from the regional planning process in Atlanta, this book tells one part of the story of the creation of metropolitan Atlanta. Considering how regional planning was set up and how it actually functioned highlights the intertwined role of politicians and the public bureaucracy in the production of Atlanta's low-density built environment. Regional planning unfolded in the course of meetings, conversations, news reports, conferences, and public hearings, as well as through an array of written materials, reports, plans, and maps. These details of the regional planning process provide insight into the fluid but complicated relationship between levels of government, how a vision for regional development was sustained over time, and how an urban region served as a planning unit. I conclude that in Atlanta the essential story is about the cohesiveness of the region, rather than the city and its suburbs or the conflict between them.

To get back to Downs's assertion that metro Atlanta is indeed a model worth exploring, what kind of model is it? In many respects, Atlanta's regionalist legacy is almost completely at odds with that of a place like Portland or Minneapolis, the two American cities most often identified with good regional planning. While coordination among local governments was made possible by the relationship between ARC's political board and planning staff, the support of state government, and the relative lack of local government fragmentation, the ends to which that coordination was put bore little relation to the natural resource protection imperative in Portland or the attempts at a more equitable redistribution of public funds in Minneapolis.[45] Despite conditions favorable for a progressive regionalism, Atlanta appears to have pursued something else entirely. In many ways, this makes Atlanta a typical case, both regionally and nationally. The processes behind the region's transformation in the postwar period are important to understanding its embrace of regional planning as a growth strategy that was not about shaping or containing growth but increasing the amount of it. Hence we must ask toward what end, and for whom, was Atlanta's regional planning process working? Answering this question demands a careful look at ARC, the state of Georgia, and the planning process they presided over. That is where I begin.

2
Building the Atlanta Regional Commission

In 1971, by an overwhelming majority and with the strong support of Governor Jimmy Carter, Georgia's 131st General Assembly passed a bill creating the Atlanta Regional Commission (ARC). Responsible for developing regional growth policies, collecting data, and providing technical support to local governments, all while ensuring that local plans meshed with federal transportation and environmental policy, the new commission replaced three existing regional agencies. Building on Atlanta's legacy of publicly supported regional planning agencies, which had been in place in some form since 1947, ARC was larger and more sophisticated than any of the agencies it replaced and represented a leap forward in terms of its power to convene local governments to participate in the regional planning process.[1] The new commission represented a substantial reconfiguration of the state's relationship to local governments.[2] Its location at the crossroads between federal policy and the state and local political power structure almost guaranteed that it would become a major force in shaping metropolitan Atlanta's growth and development. As a result of its strategic position, the kinds of activities ARC was designed to engage in and support, the information it would generate and disseminate, and the techniques it would use to develop regional policies took on heightened importance. The birth of ARC marked an important moment in the development of the region, when a confluence of changes in local demographics, state politics, and federal policies opened the door to significantly expanded control over land development practices.[3]

More fundamentally, ARC's founding reflected the changing geography of political power in Georgia and, especially, in the Atlanta region. With the rising influence of suburban jurisdictions and the changing demographics of the city of Atlanta, the decision-making authority vested in ARC was distributed in a way that tended to undercut the authority of the old power elite that had held sway over the city's politics for several generations.[4] This shifting power structure engendered significant local turmoil and sparked questions about how the region would be governed in the future. As Jack Spalding, former editor of the *Atlanta Journal*, wrote in 1971, "This [new] Atlanta, for all its energy and wealth is not as strong as the old Atlanta. It is not as maneuverable. The old Atlanta was cohesive. When its captains gave the command the troops fell in. Simple as that. The new Atlanta? Its old captains and kings barely know the new lieutenants. Nor do the troops charge anymore when they hear the bugle from the Chamber of Commerce."[5] With power more equally distributed among local governments, ARC, and the state, the interests of the city elites were no longer paramount. Decisions about land development, infrastructure, or allocation of federal funds, all requiring ARC's participation, would be negotiated, not dictated.

The events leading to ARC's creation accord with the movement of the center of Atlanta's political power from the core to the periphery. Atlanta's emerging political leaders devised a new regional planning framework, negotiated the extent of its scope, and then worked closely with the state legislature to create a new agency to become the central node in the decision-making network that oversaw the region's development. Understanding this process and the motivation behind it helps us see how a mixture of new and old notions of regional planning were melded and codified into a stable governing coalition for the region in the early 1970s. This coalition would play a significant role over the subsequent two decades, particularly in restructuring the state's leading city into a metropolitan region and creating a cohesive regional identity.[6]

The growth of federal power in the 1960s related to the evolution of planning as a critical public function and its utility in helping devise and implement increasingly complex layers of regulations, which needed coordination. An era of action around issues of intergovernmental relations and coordinated planning began in the late 1960s.[7] Accordingly, many of the initial tasks delegated to ARC mirrored the acute national concern over how so many different regulations, spread as they were among different levels of government, should interact with one another.[8] One of the solutions, arrived at only after the new policies had added to the confusion over the federal-state-local relationship, was to bolster the existing system of regional planning agencies acting as points of contact between local, state, and federal agencies to ensure a basic level of cooperation.[9] In this respect, the founding of ARC represented but one example of a much broader expansion of public authority to regulate how the built environment would be planned.

Intergovernmental Relations and Federal Commissions

Publicly funded regional planning agencies have existed in one form or another in most U.S. metropolitan areas since the mid-1940s, helped by federal funding allocated for the support of area-wide planning activities that was included in the 1949, 1954, and 1961 federal housing acts.[10] With passage of the 1962 Federal Aid Highway Act, however, the focus of these agencies was narrowed. Almost overnight they became critical actors in building the national freeway system, because changes in federal road policy mandated coordinated regional planning "as a condition to receiving federal capital assistance funds." Through the mid-1960s, regional planning agencies were consumed by the demands of federal highway planning.[11]

But in the late 1960s these agencies were transformed again, this time by the combined effect of one temporary federal commission, one standing federal commission, and two new federal laws: the National Commission on Urban Problems (popularly known as the Douglas Commission), the Advisory Commission on Intergovernmental Relations, the Demonstration Cities and Metropolitan Development (Model Cities) Act of 1966, and the Intergovernmental Cooperation Act of 1968. Together, they exerted considerable influence on the interaction of federal policies, state laws, and local governments. While the commissions and laws operated independently, their effects tended to dovetail. Like the National Advisory Commission on Civil Disorders (the Kerner Commission), each sought to address the deep demographic, economic, and spatial transformations unfolding in metropolitan areas across the country that had been punctuated by urban revolts in the second half of the 1960s. Each also considered how to restructure the way urban areas were governed to heal the deep divisions those disturbances had spectacularly revealed. The efforts were ostensibly bipartisan and drew on the varied expertise of academics, bureaucrats, and politicians, but all coalesced around the idea of using federal funding as a tool for favoring coordinated metropolitan decision making over insular local politics.

Conceived as an impartial expert body to examine the mechanisms of government relationships, the Advisory Commission on Intergovernmental Relations (ACIR) provided its congressional audience advice regarding a wide variety of issues of governance. Although operating outside the public eye, the commission was nevertheless quite influential.[12] Created in 1959 by the Eighty-Sixth Congress at the urging of President Dwight Eisenhower and Senator Robert Taft (R-OH), ACIR entered the scene at a moment of increasing confusion about the boundaries between federal, state, and local government responsibility. The new commission was charged with researching and recommending solutions to problems stemming from friction over jurisdiction that had become more pronounced as the reach of the federal government had extended.[13] Composed of a twenty-six-member bipartisan group of senators, representatives, governors, mayors, county officials, presidential cabinet members, and private citizens, who were backed by a professional staff of salaried researchers, the commission fulfilled a unique role at the interface of the federal bureaucracy and Congress. Issuing well-researched reports on issues related to governance, the commission's publications introduced policies and programs that Congress enacted in the late 1960s.[14] The commission's work had a particular influence on the Model Cities and Intergovernmental Cooperation Acts. By tackling issues related to special planning districts, metropolitan income disparity, taxation, federal grant-in-aid programs, and urban infrastructure funding (transportation, water and sewer), the commission's 1960s reports also identified matters related to regional planning and coordination that would unfold during the 1970s.[15]

Conceived by a federal task force chaired by an MIT planning professor, the Model Cities Act was Congress's response to the perception that inconsistent objectives and poor communication were hampering the "delivery of national government programs to the [nation's] cities."[16] When President Johnson signed the Intergovernmental Cooperation Act into law on October 16, 1968, just over two years after the Model Cities Act's passage, he reiterated the need for better coordination, noting that "the great legislative enactments in recent years—in education, housing, law enforcement, and health—all depend for their success on the closest cooperation between Washington and our State and city governments."[17] The new laws were intended to improve the efficiency of the vast federal grant-making apparatus by bringing different programs into conversation with one another.

Together, the acts' chief innovation for smoothing application for and distribution of federal funds to state and local governments was requiring that regional planning agencies review grant applications. In 1969 the Office of Management and Budget (then known as the Bureau of the Budget) issued Circular A-95 to establish the steps for implementing the acts. Now mostly lost to history, the circular outlined a process that required virtually all local applications for federal funds to be reviewed by a regional planning agency to ensure consistency with regional development goals. Without support from the regional agency, an application faced significantly longer odds at being funded. Entertaining, if not abiding by, the regional agency's comments was considered smart policy. Although it was not without failings, during its thirteen-year life the circular created a federally supported framework for regional coordination, increased interactions among local governments, and focused significant resources on state and substate planning agencies.[18]

With the publication of its final report, *Building the American City*, in 1969, the National Commission on Urban Problems, chaired by Senator Paul Douglas (D-IL), brought focus to the governing tactics that appeared to have exacerbated the same set of urban problems identified by the Kerner Commission a year earlier. While many central cities were withering, and in some cases literally still smoldering from civil unrest, the nation's suburbs were booming.[19] Perhaps more significant than the movement of so many people from city centers to suburbs was the seemingly exponential increase in the number of suburban municipalities, special service districts, and authorities. As the Douglas report noted, "In 1967, our metropolitan areas were served by 20,745 local governments. . . . [T]his means 91 governments per SMSA [Standard Metropolitan Statistical Area]."[20] This astonishing number of independent governments had carved the political landscape into thousands of tiny pieces, the vast majority of which had 2,500 people or fewer. Having so many small governments could be viewed as a Tocquevillian idyll of civic life, in which government was close, accessible, and responsive. But because most small suburban cities and townships also had the right to regulate land development within their borders, coordinating major developments that affected multiple jurisdictions had become increasingly difficult. The jagged political landscape permitted small jurisdictions to use their police power to prohibit multifamily housing units, mandate minimum single-family-lot sizes, and redraw school boundaries, which excluded certain demographic groups, identified by race (nonwhite) and class (low income), from living within their borders.[21] This locked the doors to spatial mobility for many and, in effect, also locked the doors of economic and social uplift.[22] A few state legislatures passed legislation to counteract local government fragmentation, but most did not.[23] Indeed, the Douglas Commission bluntly concluded that "eas[ing] the tension between city and suburb, between rich and poor, and especially between black and white" had remained problematic for so long because "too few have recognized how these basic democratic issues are related to local government structure and finance, to zoning policies, land and housing costs, or to national housing policies."[24] Hence the commission suggested that the federal government and the states revise and expand the power of the public regional planning agencies that had been set up in the mid-1950s to better coordinate local decisions regarding urban development.

By 1970 the recommendations of the Douglas Commission and the advice of the Advisory Commission on Intergovernmental Relations had brought attention to regional coordination, and Circular A-95 had subjected most federal grant programs to regional review. While the goals of federal policy carried considerable weight, the immediate situation Georgia's elected leaders faced was shaped by political considerations. Any new agency that might be created had to be capable of addressing the regional coordination issues specific to the requirements established by the A-95 process, but it would also need to satisfy the emerging suburban political power that was rearranging Atlanta's old governing coalition. The bones of any future agency would be composed of federal policy, but the flesh would have to reflect the realities of state and local politics. That certain tasks mandated by the federal government had to be carried out was a given, but the state legislature would ultimately determine the structure of the new public body. Concerted effort by a few individual legislators and public administrators led to an agency that was in some ways more powerful than federal laws required, but resistance among the rank and file in the General Assembly also limited the new agency's control over urban form. This compromise turned out to be crucial to how ARC would fulfill its multipronged directive over the long term.

Origins of Metropolitan Atlanta

In 1837 the city that sits at the core of present-day metropolitan Atlanta came to life, when the state legislature authorized construction of a new railroad, the Western and Atlantic of the State of Georgia, that would connect the Midwest to the Southern Piedmont by following a path along a prominent north–south ridge that was then known as Peachtree Trail. Burned to the ground in 1864 during Sherman's March to the Sea, Atlanta reemerged during Reconstruction with a new identity when a few vocal politicians from the city convinced their compatriots in the General Assembly to relocate the state capital from Milledgeville in 1868.[25] By the end of the nineteenth century, Henry Grady, editor of the *Atlanta Constitution*, was wandering the country on the city's behalf, loudly proclaiming the birth of a New South, reassuring anyone who would listen that white supremacy was alive and well and the doors for outside investment were wide open.[26] At the turn of the twentieth century, the city of Atlanta had a population just under 90,000; what could be called the Atlanta region had not more than 150,000. When Asa Candler bought the formula for manufacturing Coca-Cola in 1888, Georgia's economy was still centered on agriculture, but Atlanta was rapidly developing a niche as a regional manufacturing, distribution, and transportation center, which would serve the soft drink maker well.[27] By the time the stock market crashed in 1929, the city had grown to 270,000 people.

Yet through the first decades of the twentieth century, Atlanta scarcely resembled a region on the brink of becoming a major metropolitan area or even the future leading city of the American South. Though an important distribution point, Atlanta was part of a constellation of inland southern cities of modest stature, like Birmingham, Nashville, and Charlotte, all somewhat inconsequential compared to the region's big coastal cities, like New Orleans, Baltimore, and Washington. In the 1920s the wealthiest segments of Atlanta's population had begun to migrate north from the city center along Peachtree Street, but the bulk of the city's working-class population, both white and black, remained housed in a collection of modest neighborhoods that ringed the central business district.[28] The largest towns surrounding Atlanta—Marietta, Decatur, and College Park—though connected by a regional interurban network, were still distinctly separate entities with small populations, and most of the hinterland in the unincorporated counties outside the cities was given over to cultivation, grazing, or reforestation. Many of Atlanta's central neighborhoods remained close to their cotton mill village roots, and land in the outer reaches of the city itself was essentially rural. The legacy of immigration, seen in the tapestry of ethnic neighborhoods and social networks in cities like Cleveland, Detroit, and Chicago, was barely visible in Atlanta. Pre-Depression migration to the city had been mostly intraregional and intrastate, whites and blacks coming from little Georgia towns with names like Tiger, Hahira, and Buena Vista.[29]

Beginning in the late Depression, Atlanta's long-term growth prospects took a series of small steps forward as the city began to accumulate branch offices of federal agencies. These included the Malaria Control lab (which became the Centers for Disease Control and Prevention), the Federal Reserve Bank, the Court of Appeals for the Eleventh Circuit, and later, the regional headquarters of many other agencies of the growing federal bureaucracy.[30] These federal offices created a stable economic sector, one that would play a significant role in supporting a black middle class and bolstering the region's ability to attract investment in other sectors.[31]

The end of World War II brought an influx of newcomers. Single-family neighborhoods of inexpensive Cape Cod cottages and ranches on quarter- and half-acre lots began filling in the empty land in the western and southern extents of the city, spilling over into adjacent unincorporated areas in Fulton, Clayton, Dekalb, Gwinnett, and Cobb Counties and small nearby towns like Smyrna, Forest Park, East Point, Chamblee, and Norcross. Long, narrow commercial corridors stretched out into the new residential areas. Thoroughfares like Memorial Drive, Stewart Avenue, Jonesboro Road, and Marietta Boulevard were characterized by modest, low-rise shopping malls and interspersed with warehouses, occasional small factories, broad parking lots, and setbacks of one hundred feet or more from the street. These thoroughfares not only carried commuters to and from work but became retail and employment destinations in their own right. Slowly the highway strip malls lining these corridors began to displace older neighborhood shopping districts and Atlanta's central business district as the centers of the region's retail economy, establishing a pattern that would be repeated again and again as the region grew outward. When the first segments of the Downtown Connector, the spine of Atlanta's future urban freeway system, were laid out in 1949, the region was just at the beginning of a long march into the countryside, one that could have been predicted only by the most wild-eyed boosters. But an inkling of the future shape of the region would soon become visible, finding expression in the structure and activities of a series of regional planning agencies that would guide the region's physical form.[32]

Birth of Regional Planning in Atlanta

Like many cities, Atlanta possesses no obvious natural boundaries—no ocean or mountains or swamp.[33] In a 1977 interview, Walter Douglas, a prominent transportation engineer involved in planning the Metropolitan Atlanta Rapid Transit Authority (MARTA), Atlanta's regional mass transit system, contrasted Atlanta with San

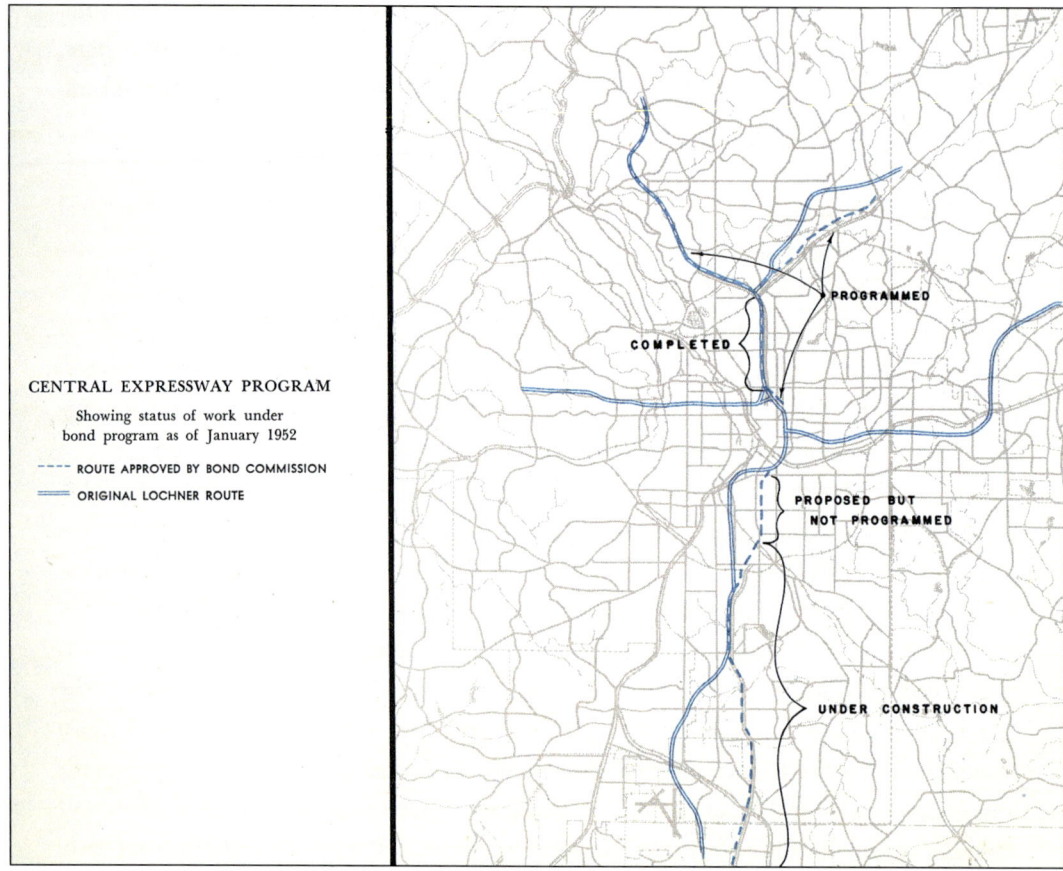

Figure 2.1 "Central Expressway Program," from Metropolitan Planning Commission, *Up Ahead: A Regional Land Use Plan for Metropolitan Atlanta*, February 1952, Atlanta Regional Commission Collection, Kenan Research Center, Atlanta History Center

Francisco (where he had previously worked on the Bay Area Rapid Transit system), saying, "Atlanta does not have the geography or topography to police its growth."[34] In other words, regulation laid the foundation for the region's low-density form, policy being the key factor in shaping the built environment rather than physical geography. The planning and building of postwar Atlanta can be traced back to the indirect influence of federal policy. But a more direct influence on Atlanta's built environment was the local development milieu, a product of politicians, businessmen, public administrators, and a succession of public regional planning agencies that first emerged in the immediate postwar period.

Atlanta's unofficial embrace of regional planning can be dated to 1937, when Thomas Reed, a political scientist who studied municipal governance, taught at the University of Michigan, and worked for the National Municipal League, was hired by the city to make recommendations for a regional governing plan for Atlanta. Written during the Depression, the Reed Report, as it came to be known, generated discussion among

Atlanta's political leaders but landed on a shelf when the war started.[35] However, the report had pointed out the necessity of collaboration between Atlanta and suburban Fulton County regarding delivery of city services to the county's urbanized but unincorporated areas and the need for the city to aggressively pursue annexation of land adjacent to its borders. Both issues came to a head a few years after the war when Mayor William Hartsfield oversaw the adoption of the Plan of Improvement in 1952, a contract that established parameters for the "sharing of services between [the] city and county governments" and annexed a large tract of unincorporated Fulton County into the city.[36]

In 1946 the Georgia Highway Commission hired the H. W. Lochner Co. to develop a transportation master plan for Atlanta, resulting in what could be described as a second protoregional plan. Largely an outline for an urban freeway system spanning the metropolitan area, the Lochner report offered a rough blueprint for the routes the Interstate Highway System would adopt in the 1950s.[37] More importantly, the report also suggested a high-speed road system as a structuring device for the metropolitan area.

Perhaps inspired by the Reed and Lochner reports, Atlanta's official embrace of a more permanent regional planning agency came in 1947, when a small group of Atlanta-area state legislators ushered a bill through the Georgia General Assembly to establish the nation's first publicly supported regional planning agency, the blandly named Metropolitan Planning Commission (MPC). Though its founding legislation charged the commission with writing "a master plan for the orderly growth of the district," it was given little formal authority and was constrained to "act in an advisory capacity only."[38] Supported from the general funds of Fulton and Dekalb Counties and the city of Atlanta, money for the commission was not guaranteed but depended on an annual negotiation between it and its constituent governing bodies. The Fulton and Dekalb County commission chairs, together with Atlanta's mayor, appointed the commission's board and were under no obligation to adopt or even recognize the commission's plans or policy recommendations. Despite possessing very little visible power, the commission proved to be quite influential over the long term, publishing several significant planning documents, including regional plans in 1952 and 1954, that were perhaps the first comprehensive visions of the future Atlanta as a low-density, garden-like metropolitan area.[39]

Though tasked with producing a master plan for the region, the MPC was never intended to be a regulatory or legislative body. Rather, the commission was conceived as a research organization for "continuous evaluation of key metropolitan factors" to allow development decisions to be founded "on data and projections resulting from this ongoing process."[40] But by the end of 1952, the commission released an ambitious regional development plan for Atlanta, *Up Ahead: A Regional Land Use Plan for Metropolitan Atlanta*. A culmination of nearly three years of inventory and analysis, the plan included a litany of recommendations regarding urban development. Proposing policies to sharply limit the horizontal growth of the region, *Up Ahead* suggested a planned population and geographic limit for the two-county metropolitan area, restricted to places adjacent to the central city and hemmed in by a circumferential greenbelt, an obvious reference to the London Greenbelt (an idea popular among U.S. planners in early 1950s) and, more distantly, Ebenezer Howard's Garden City.[41]

Maps produced as part of the 1952 plan categorized Atlanta's land according to development potential: development areas, mature areas, and renewal areas. To accommodate growth, the plan suggested a version of Clarence Perry's Neighborhood Unit as an appropriate organizing principle for the future residential subdivisions that would be constructed along the outskirts of the region.[42] Established suburban neighborhoods, especially those occupied by wealthier whites, would be preserved, but "older, centrally located neighborhoods which have so declined that far-reaching programs of rehabilitation and redevelopment will be required before they can be maintained as good close-in neighborhoods" would be subject to clearance and reconstruction.[43] Renewal, of course, would be largely directed toward black

Figure 2.2 "Facsimile Map of Proposed Regional Land Use Plan," from Metropolitan Planning Commission, *Up Ahead*

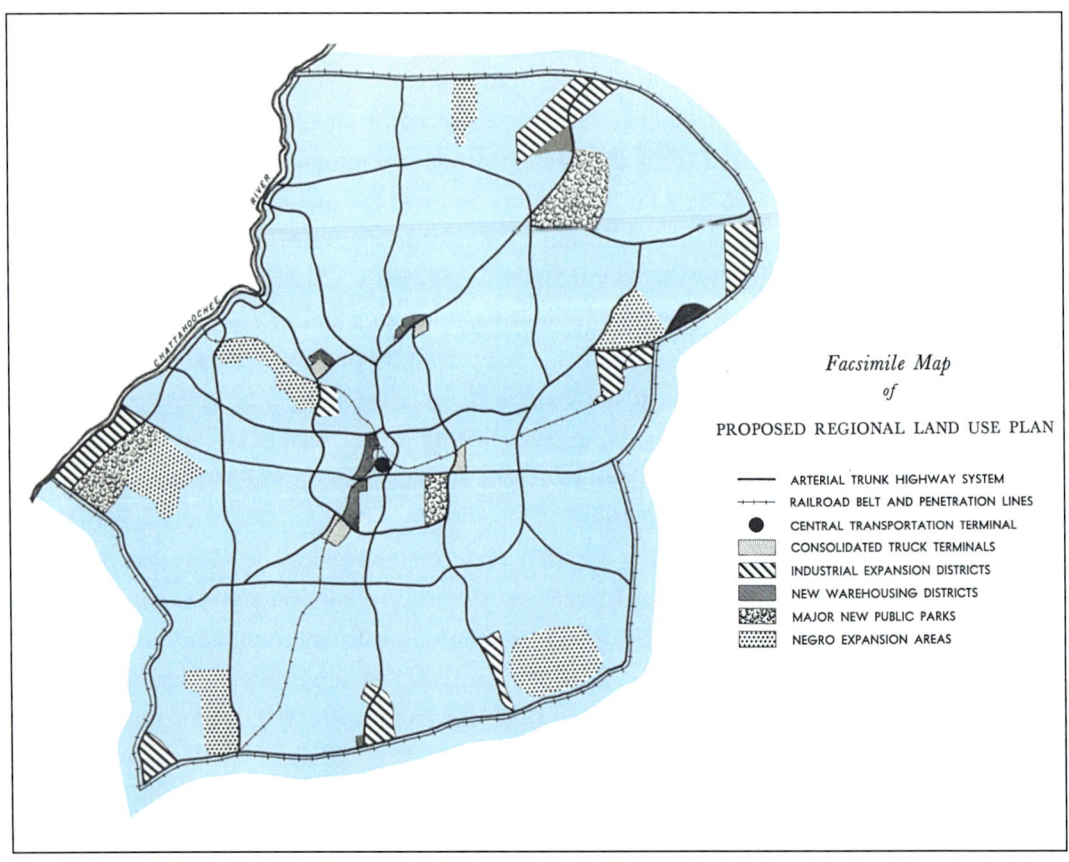

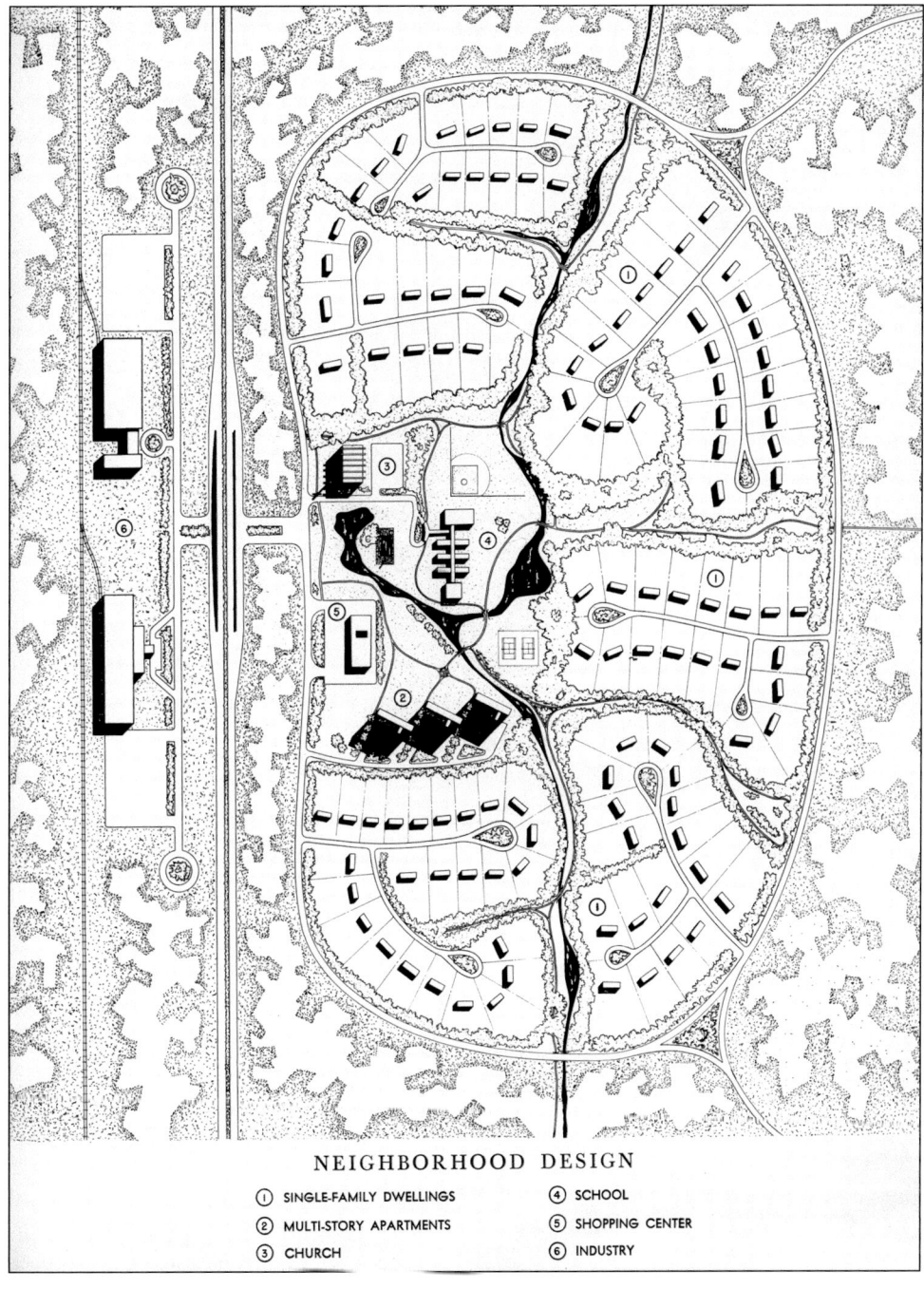

Figure 2.3 "Neighborhood Design," from Metropolitan Planning Commission, *Up Ahead*

neighborhoods that by the early 1950s had begun to push against the central business district on two sides.[44] To maintain residential racial segregation, the plan showed designated "expansion areas" inside and outside the city for housing the region's growing black population. While rising black political power had forced accommodation of some demands for new housing in the city, the plan served politicians' efforts during the 1950s to "control the black population's movement."[45]

In 1954 the commission released an updated regional plan, *Now . . . for Tomorrow*, that was largely a modification of the policies in *Up Ahead* and presented the first version of what would become a basic characteristic of Atlanta's regional planning process. While the classifications of development areas and preservation areas was retained, the major change introduced in the 1954 plan was that continuous population and employment growth would be the key policy trigger, the only question being when future growth would occur. The 1954 plan "suggested unlimited but planned incremental, concentric growth for the region," an adjustment made because "certain events had indicated that the basic objective of the 1952 plan was highly unlikely to be implemented." Those events included renewed faith in the all-growth-is-good maxim, but more directly the change in policy was a response to the need to provide space for the region's swelling white middle class and a reflection of the political reality that limiting growth to the urban core would not be well received by politicians, business leaders, or voters in the suburbs.[46]

Significantly, both the 1952 and 1954 plans echoed the Reed Report's urging for greater cooperation among the region's governments and included the schematic of a limited-access freeway system from the Lochner report. The two MPC plans also included the outline of a modest-sized heavy-rail transit system. Downtown Atlanta was at the center of the road and rail plans. Notably, the 1954 plan also deleted the references to establishing reserve areas for future segregated residential developments.

It was during the commission's most active years, 1952–1960, that development regulations, including zoning ordinances, subdivision regulations, and public facilities plans began to be widely adopted by municipalities around the region. Commission planners conducted municipal planning studies for member jurisdictions, wrote zoning and subdivision ordinances, and actively cataloged development regulations as they were adopted and implemented, activities supported in part by Section 701 of the Housing Act of 1954, which offered "federal planning assistance to state planning agencies, cities, and other municipalities."[47] The work of providing technical advice and writing ordinances demonstrated the emergence of an increasingly empirical regional planning practice.[48] While the five counties that composed the metro area had adopted zoning ordinances and subdivision regulations by the end of the 1950s, long-range development planning was less widespread. The handful of larger cities within the region, Decatur, College Park, East Point, and Marietta, tended to be more organized; all had undertaken long-range planning studies by the mid-1950s. But the unincorporated counties surrounding Atlanta had done little planning. Most jurisdictions outside Atlanta employed no professional planning staff and relied instead on assistance from the MPC or the small handful of local consultants in business at the time.[49] This vacuum of planning knowledge gave the commission (and the consultants) more authority than it might have otherwise had.

Through the late 1950s metro Atlanta's population grew steadily, but it remained by most measures a relatively small, compact urban region. Yet ideas about how much the region would grow were never in short supply. In a 1957 conference sponsored by the MPC and Georgia Power, the regional electric utility, dedicated to discussing planning and development in northern Georgia, participants projected that the Atlanta region would eventually span the eighteen counties within one hour's drive of the state capitol building downtown.[50] Fueled by continuing in-migration from rural counties and small towns around the South, the city reached a population of 487,000 by 1960, and the five-county metropolitan area, defined by Fulton, Dekalb, Cobb, Gwinnett, and Clayton Counties, nudged just passed the 1 million mark, though 80 percent of this total lived in either Fulton or Dekalb Counties. The city's population was 38 percent black and the region's just over 14 percent, though the distribution of households was not geographically even. The northern half of the city housed wealthier whites, while white working-class neighborhoods were spread around its far eastern, southern, and western flanks. Black neighborhoods were heavily concentrated immediately south and west of downtown, but a large number of small black residential enclaves were scattered throughout the region, following much older land settlement patterns characteristic of the Southern Piedmont.[51]

In 1960 the network of urban freeways that would speed cars to new suburban subdivisions was still under construction, and most outlying areas, even those within Fulton and Dekalb, lacked the basic infrastructure necessary to support development at urban densities. Employment in the region was still dominated by the central business district and a few close-in industrial areas, both of which saw impressive growth during the 1950s, though their dominance appeared to be increasingly threatened by the prospect of cheap land along the urban fringe becoming easily accessible by car. The region's first enclosed shopping mall, Lenox Square, had opened in 1959, and the perimeter freeway that would enable the rise of eight more malls in the next decade was not yet under construction. Yet even as the city's population was growing, the forces of decentralization had been operating for thirty years, and the pace of decentralization would only accelerate in the 1960s.[52]

Sparked by new planning requirements contained in the Federal Aid Highway Act of 1956 and included in a broader government modernization agenda pushed by Governor Ernest Vandiver, the General Assembly voted to abolish the Metropolitan

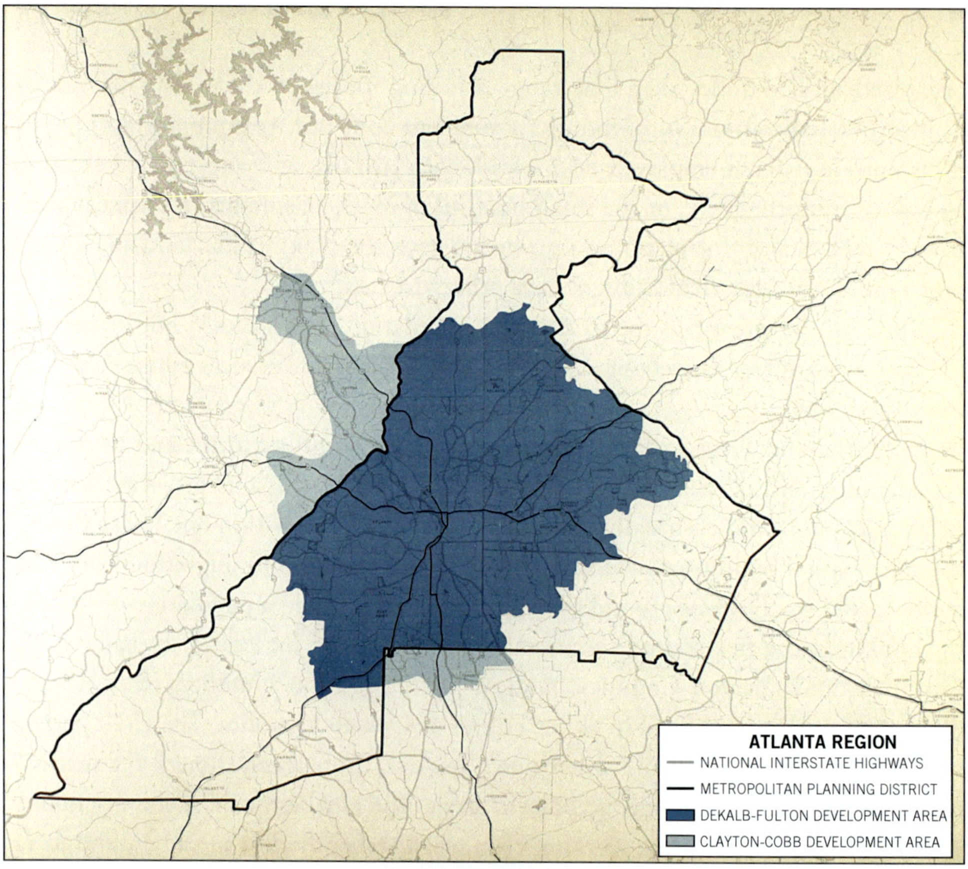

ATLANTA REGION
- NATIONAL INTERSTATE HIGHWAYS
- METROPOLITAN PLANNING DISTRICT
- DEKALB-FULTON DEVELOPMENT AREA
- CLAYTON-COBB DEVELOPMENT AREA

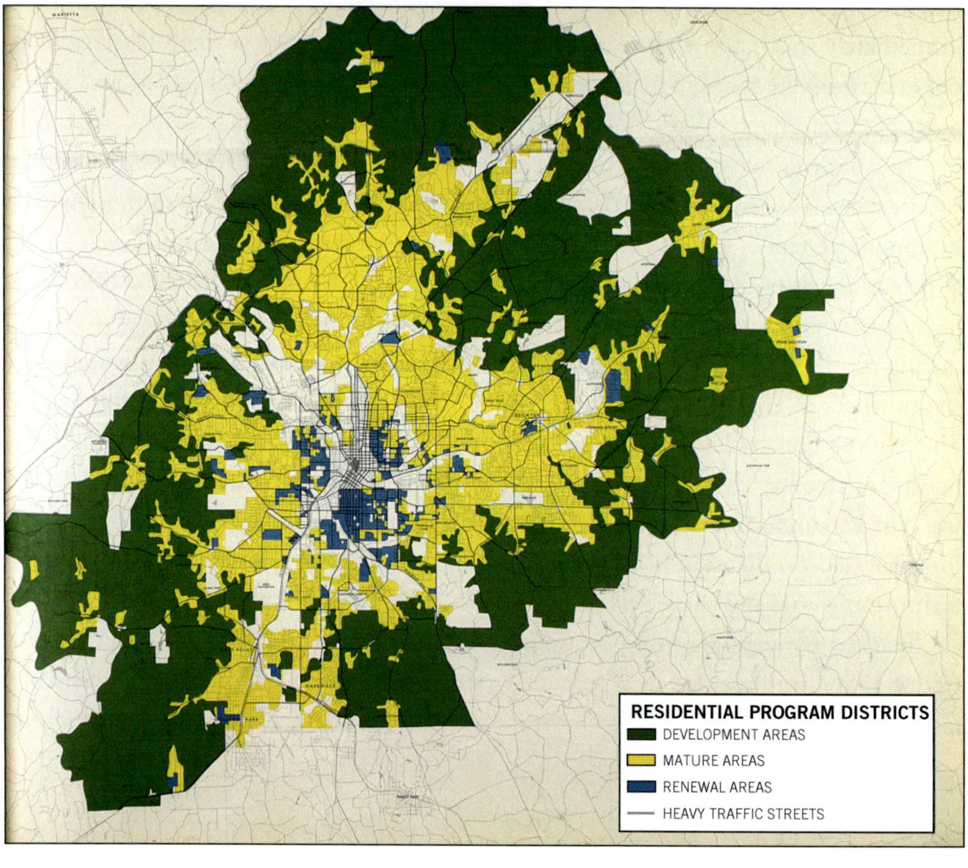

RESIDENTIAL PROGRAM DISTRICTS
- DEVELOPMENT AREAS
- MATURE AREAS
- RENEWAL AREAS
- HEAVY TRAFFIC STREETS

Building the Atlanta Regional Commission | 29

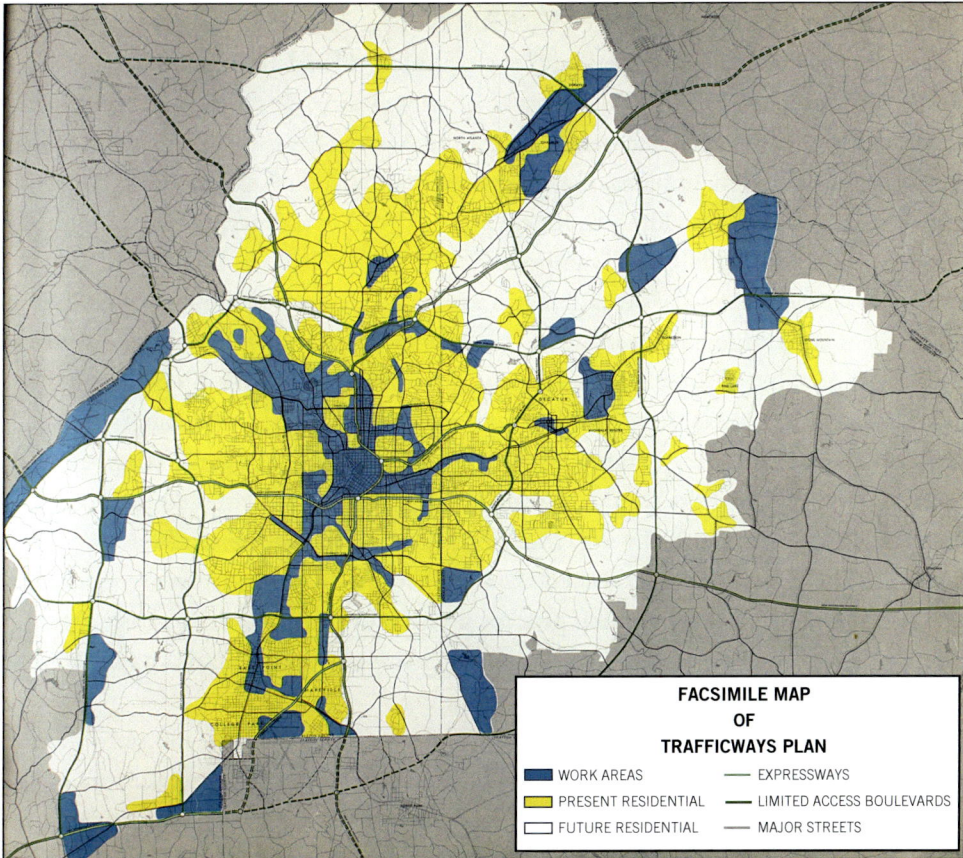

facing, top: Figure 2.4 "Atlanta Region," from Metropolitan Planning Commission, *Now . . . for Tomorrow: A Master Planning Program for the Dekalb-Fulton Metropolitan Area*, September 1954, Atlanta Regional Commission Collection, Kenan Research Center, Atlanta History Center

facing, bottom: Figure 2.5 "Residential Program Districts," from Metropolitan Planning Commission, *Now . . . for Tomorrow*

above: Figure 2.6 "Facsimile Map of Trafficways Plan," from Metropolitan Planning Commission, *Now . . . for Tomorrow*

Planning Commission in 1960 and replace it with a new and much larger regional planning body, the Atlanta Region Metropolitan Planning Commission (ARMPC).[53] A tight-knit and long-serving group of state representatives from Clayton, Cobb, and Dekalb Counties introduced the bill to create ARMPC in the Georgia House of Representatives during the 1960 session, framing it as a way to allow regional planning policy to keep pace with evolving federal planning requirements concerning urban transportation infrastructure. Passed by a unanimous vote in the house and senate, the bill was signed into law by Vandiver in the spring of 1960.[54] Intended to be a more comprehensive agency than the MPC, ARMPC had the same core tasks but moved into other facets of regional development planning. Hired from New York City, a young planner named Glenn Bennett was appointed director of the new agency, and an expanded professional staff was brought in to support him. Producing comprehensive regional development plans, making population estimates and forecasts, disseminating regional data, providing technical services, and coordinating federal highway planning all fell under ARMPC's purview.

Importantly, the agency's creation also expanded regional planning boundaries to make them coterminous with those of the Atlanta Standard Metropolitan Statistical Area (SMSA). First defined by the Bureau of the Budget in 1959, SMSAs were geographic catchment areas that identified coherent urban centers for demographic data gathering, analysis, policy making, and distribution of federal funds.[55] Beginning in the early 1960s, Congress would increasingly use these boundaries to determine financial allocations, especially for transportation infrastructure. Indeed, the 1962 Federal Aid Highway Act established the so-called 3Cs (comprehensive, cooperative, and continuing) highway planning process, an initiative that required a basic regional planning organization to be in place in all SMSAs with fifty thousand population or greater to continue to receive federal road funding.[56]

As it had done with the Metropolitan Planning Commission, the state limited ARMPC's regulatory powers. The power to zone land remained firmly in the hands of local jurisdictions, membership in ARMPC remained voluntary, and neither staff planners nor the governing board had formal power to review the content of plans adopted by local governments.[57] But under Bennett's leadership, ARMPC was able to cautiously extend its reach. Unlike the MPC, ARMPC took a more aggressive position on critical planning issues, writing subregional plans, lobbying the General Assembly, and advocating policies that would have a more direct impact on the physical shape of the region. One of the first reports ARMPC published, for instance, provided a detailed look at a four-line, hub-and-spoke mass transit system that would span all five counties in the SMSA. An expansion of the limited two-line system envisioned in the MPC plans of the 1950s, ARMPC's rail transit plan was published in early 1962. Coming at a moment when new regional heavy-rail systems were in the planning or construction phase in Cleveland, San Francisco, Washington, Toronto, and Montreal, the rail plan offered an aspiration for Atlanta's boosters. Yet only after the involvement of Atlanta mayor Ivan Allen Jr. and Governor Vandiver did the General Assembly finally permit a public referendum to change Georgia's constitution to allow the creation of a publicly supported regional transit authority. And only after the creation of the Urban Mass Transit Administration in 1964, which promised significant federal support for the development of new rail systems, did metro Atlanta's citizens get a chance to vote on a regional transit authority that could plan, fund, build, and operate a modern rail transit system.[58]

By 1964 ARMPC had begun contemplating future expansions of its jurisdiction, on the assumption that, barring any major changes to regional development policy, Atlanta's growth would stretch beyond the five-county area and that expanding its footprint would be necessary to maintain the agency's legitimacy.[59] In support of this idea, ARMPC produced two comprehensive regional development plans, in 1962 and 1968, which forecast significant physical expansions of metropolitan Atlanta. In response to federal highway planning requirements in the 1962 Federal Aid Highway Act (the 3Cs), ARMPC also initiated a process for reviewing local government applications for federal funds to build transport infrastructure against federal and regional criteria.[60] In 1965 ARMPC, in conjunction with the city of Atlanta and the state, wrote and adopted a regional airport systems plan, which set forth guidelines for the long-term consolidation of commercial air service in a single, large airport and for the first time brought airport planning under the regional planning umbrella.[61]

During the 1960s, municipalities around the region began to develop greater planning capacity. By the late 1960s, all the large local governments had adopted a zoning ordinance and development regulations, and most had adopted, or were in the process of adopting, long-range development plans.[62] The number of planners on municipal staffs increased, and as planning activities expanded so too had the engagement of ARMPC. Bennett, ARMPC's director, used his position to deliver the consistent message that planning for the region must be a high priority and when necessary draw from the collective expertise of the national planning community. With changing federal requirements for regional planning, more sophisticated planning technologies, new interest in the interaction of land use and transportation, concern about water and air pollution, and money available from programs administered by the Department of Housing and Urban Development, U.S. Department of Transportation (USDOT), and Urban Mass Transit Administration, pressure on urban jurisdictions to modernize planning regulations snowballed. Yet this pressure did not reach many of the smaller municipalities. While the larger communities that composed the core of the metropolitan area had adapted to the new demands, on the other side of the urban fringe even basic regulations like housing codes were still lacking, and enforcement of the codes that did exist was poorly executed. It would not be until later in the 1970s, after the creation of ARC, that all the local governments in the region would adopt a complete set of development regulations.[63]

Population and employment trends evident in the region in the 1950s largely continued through the 1960s. By 1970 the five-county region contained 1,390,000 people and 620,000 jobs, a nearly 40 percent increase over 1960. More importantly, growth was beginning to spill into areas outside the five metro counties, and the population of the central city was undergoing significant racial change.[64] Black migration to the city had continued apace, but middle-class whites had begun to leave the city in greater numbers, and legions of new white in-migrants were setting up house in the suburbs without transitioning through city neighborhoods first. The 1970 census also revealed that Atlanta's population had tipped toward majority black (51 percent), which finally forced transfer of political power from the old white establishment to a new black establishment.[65] The relative concentration of population within the city and Fulton and Dekalb Counties began to wane as more and more residential subdivisions sprouted in Cobb, Gwinnett, and Clayton Counties. Employment growth in all parts of the region remained strong, but a decreasing share of jobs in the central business district portended its declining significance. By 1970 Atlanta's central business district held only 15 percent of total regional employment, down significantly from a decade before. New employment clusters had emerged in northeast Atlanta, northwest Atlanta, the Buckhead neighborhood, and northwest Dekalb County, all located along the recently completed Interstate 285 perimeter highway. Though white-collar job growth was beginning to move northward, blue-collar employment remained strong on the south side, including in southwest and southeast Atlanta, College Park, Hapeville, and Forest Park, areas where manufacturing and distribution were heavily concentrated. The massive suburbanization of employment, to places like far northern Fulton County and northwestern Gwinnett County, had yet to happen by 1970, though signs were already pointing in that direction.

Much of the infrastructure that had been envisioned by the Lochner report and the MPC in the 1950s was completed during ARMPC's reign. The completion of the urban segments of the three interstate highways (Interstates 20, 75, and 85) that converged just south of Atlanta's central business district, as well as the perimeter highway that formed a sixty-mile asphalt band around the city, occurred between 1960 and 1970.[66] A massive new airport terminal, opened in 1961 eight miles south of downtown, expanded the accessibility and attractiveness of the region for economic development, though it did not by itself suggest where future growth would or should occur. MARTA was created in 1965, taking over transit responsibilities from the privately owned Atlanta Transit System.[67] Municipal water supply systems around the region steadily expanded.[68]

Accompanying this infrastructure boom were new regional shopping and commercial centers, sited at intersecting points along the new expressways.[69] As one after another of the new malls opened, retail sales increasingly shifted away from the old downtown department stores, continuing the long decline of the retail sector of Atlanta's central business district. Efforts to improve traffic flow and provide cheap and convenient parking had made downtown easy to drive to but did little to stem the decline in patronage, either real or imagined.[70] The attention the civil rights movement had put on discriminatory practices by retailers did little to help, as white shoppers fled the relatively public downtown stores for the more tightly controlled private spaces of suburban malls. Five Points, the historic center of Atlanta and anointed years earlier by boosters as the Times Square of the South, had begun to seem derelict by the late 1960s.[71]

Despite Bennett's efforts to expand ARMPC's reach by deepening its expertise and cajoling politicians to support its pleas for regional coordination, by the mid-1960s pressure from Atlanta's changing politics and increasing fragmentation of federal urban policy had begun to pull the agency apart. Though it remained the largest planning agency in the region, ARMPC's influence and support rapidly eroded. As the scope of federal urban policy expanded, the structural limits of ARMPC became apparent. With its all-citizen board of directors and small professional staff, the agency could not keep up with an increasingly complicated and overlapping set of federal urban policies. Further, the changing politics in Atlanta's suburbs made a regional agency that had been dominated by the interests of city politicians less acceptable to outlying jurisdictions. Attempting a quick fix, the General Assembly hastily created two regional coordinating bodies designed to correct ARMPCs's shortcomings: the Metropolitan Atlanta Council of Local Governments (MACLOG) and the Atlanta Area Transportation Study (AATS) in 1964.

Section 701 planning funds in the 1960s required central cities and their suburbs to come together to form a regional body. The need for 701 planning funds had made councils of governments (COGs) popular with state and local politicians.[72] With their voluntary membership that could include both citizens and elected officials, COGs were seen as the least threatening kind of regional planning agency.[73] When Congress began debating the Model Cities Act in 1964, the bill's language required local elected officials to have a greater voice in the planning process, which suggested that COGs would take on heightened importance in federal urban policy. MACLOG was Georgia's attempt to meet this mandate.[74]

The combined effect of the 1962 Federal Aid Highway Act and 1964 Urban Mass Transportation Act had broadened the definition of coordinated urban transportation planning from an exclusive focus on highways to one that included rapid transit systems. With ARMPC limited by its structure, a new organization was needed to bring Atlanta's regional transportation planning activities into compliance with the new standards.[75] In response, the General Assembly created the Atlanta Area Transportation Study. Under the "direction of the AATS policy committee," the new agency was supposed to help shift Atlanta's transportation planning process "from the originally highway-oriented planning effort to urban mass transit."[76] The quasi independence of the new agency helped direct attention away from highways and toward getting a mass transit system built but also clouded the question of leadership on regional planning issues.[77] Though the AATS promised to consolidate urban transportation planning functions in the region under the umbrella of a single organization, its creation sowed confusion about what the different agencies involved with transportation policy were supposed to be doing.[78]

Resolving an Impasse

Though ARMPC ostensibly oversaw both of the other agencies, the channels of communication among them were often clogged, and disagreements frequently arose about how resources should be allocated.[79] As the confusion created by having overlapping regional agencies intensified, a small group of public officials, including Glenn Bennett, ARMPC's executive director, and Dan Sweat Jr., chief administrative officer to Atlanta mayor Ivan Allen Jr., contracted the American Society of Planning Officials (ASPO) in 1966 to examine the condition of regional planning in metropolitan Atlanta and offer recommendations for change. In 1967 ASPO delivered a report that clarified many of the problems plaguing ARMPC, particularly the indefinite character of the relationship between ARMPC, the AATS, and MACLOG. The thrust of the report was to improve communication among Atlanta's regional agencies while maintaining ARMPC's status as the primary regional agency. Concrete recommendations touched on relationships, commission structure, policy development, implementation, and internal (staff) structure.[80]

The report suggested that ARMPC retain primary responsibility for coordinating regional planning, expand its role in providing professional staff to the other agencies, and continue to take the lead in disseminating planning information throughout the region. But it also recommended a reorganization of the ARMPC board into a set of "three standing committees: an executive, a planning, and an intergovernmental affairs committee," to make decision making more effective. The board would be supported by "ad hoc technical advisory committees for every major study it undertakes," with each technical committee including "specially qualified outsiders and top government officials" who could make ARMPC studies more authoritative. Increasing the size of the ARMPC board by adding members from the state highway and economic development departments and making membership in the agency mandatory for the existing governments were also recommended.[81]

To improve ARMPC's capacity as a policy-making organization, ASPO recommended that the commission "prepare a report assembling all policies and major recommendations" from prior "studies and plans," then "review . . . and official[ly] adopt" the policies "with which it agrees." Additionally, ARMPC "should concentrate on producing clear, specific statements of officially adopted development policies to guide the development of the region" and "summarize the policies and recommendations adopted by the Commission."[82] To aid policy implementation, the report suggested that staff study "all the means available to implement Commission policies." Research capacity was highlighted as ARMPC's greatest potential strength, and the report noted that ARMPC must work harder to establish itself "as a central headquarters for research and information on development problems and opportunities within the region."[83]

The report recommended that the agency spend less time on annual population and housing estimates, one of its longest-standing activities. ARMPC should communicate the criteria it used to evaluate local plan reviews and encourage local governments to collaborate more closely before and during the formal review. The ASPO report recommended regularly scheduled workshops to educate public officials about planning ideas, the importance of more interaction with the local media, and more intensive outreach to the public by commissioners (attending meetings, giving presentations, etc.). Providing technical assistance had been one of the hallmarks of the MPC and ARMPC, but ASPO suggested a significant reconfiguration of how such support should be delivered, shifting from direct contracts for service to more indirect, capacity-building tactics: model ordinances, personnel advice, and area studies. Finally, revisions to the agency's internal structure would divide staff into four sections, each dealing with one substantive area: regional planning, research, intergovernmental affairs, and transportation.[84] Beyond specific recommendations regarding organization and activity, the report heralded an important moment in the process of consolidating disparate regional planning activities within the confines of a single agency. The conclusions contained in the ASPO report raised questions about the fates of ARMPC, the AATS, and MACLOG.

During the same period, USDOT had also evaluated the regional planning process in Atlanta and found it lacking. On the basis of requirements in the 1962 Federal Aid Highway Act and 1964 Urban Mass Transportation Act, USDOT had concluded that metro Atlanta did not possess "a continuing, comprehensive, and coordinated transportation planning process under unified direction."[85] Direction was supposed to be provided by the ARMPC transportation coordinator, who was responsible for managing staff from the state highway commission who had been assigned to the AATS. The USDOT review found that the ARMPC transportation coordinator had failed to exert control over the day-to-day activities of the highway commission planning staff (who played an important role in providing transportation information to the AATS). That this staff arrangement had failed indicated that there was "no centralized direction over the transportation planning process in Metropolitan Atlanta." Without changes, the region's ability to receive federal transportation money would be compromised.[86]

The conclusions of the two reports sparked a wide-ranging debate about how to correct the problems confronting Atlanta's regional planning process in the 1969 and 1970 sessions of the General Assembly. The passage of the 1968 federal Intergovernmental Cooperation Act, the impact of Circular A-95, and ongoing demographic changes in metropolitan Atlanta added to the pressure on the assembly to act.[87] In an early salvo in this debate, a small contingent of state representatives from Cobb, Fulton, and Dekalb Counties, including Elliott Levitas, Gerald Horton, Harold Clarke, Robert Farrar, Sidney Marcus, and Howard Atherton, commissioned a report that highlighted the problems facing Atlanta and encouraged the state to take on a larger role in regional planning. In early 1969 Levitas and his allies presented their report to the General Assembly as a resolution. Their major conclusion was that the state's existing Planning and Programming Bureau, which should have been overseeing state planning and community development, was not "properly structured to carry out the functions and responsibilities of an effective community affairs agency" or "to carry out its [own] functions and responsibilities under the present law which created the Bureau," and it failed to meet the requirements of the recently issued Circular A-95.[88] The resolution argued that there was "a serious gap between the intensity of the problems facing local governments and communities and the state's willingness to address itself to those problems."[89] Noting that Georgia had become an urban majority state in 1960 and that "estimates indicate that the urbanization of the State is continuing," the resolution concluded with a call for a new state planning bureau.[90]

During the 1969 session, three bills were introduced to address the issues raised by the resolution. The first, to create a new cabinet-level community affairs agency to oversee planning and community development, was followed by two companion bills to enact city-county consolidations (Atlanta-Fulton and Decatur-Dekalb). The consolidation bills would have created two large urban governments at the Atlanta region's core, potentially resolving disputes between cities and counties over intergovernmental coordination issues. Though metro-area legislators and administrators generally perceived state involvement in planning and intergovernmental coordination as too timid, support from the majority of the rank and file in the legislature was weak, especially among rural legislators who feared the effects of a city-county consolidation, and all three bills failed in committee.

In the 1970 session, the Levitas-led group reintroduced the state planning bureau bill. Under increasing pressure to enact legislation that would meet A-95 requirements, the assembly this time passed the bill, which became Act 1066 and created the Bureau of State Planning and Community Affairs. Georgia's newest addition to the executive branch was "created to establish policy and direction concerning state planning and programming and community affairs for the development of the State's physical, economic, and human resources and to perform such other functions as may be provided by law."[91] A governing board comprising the governor, select members of the house and senate, and members of the Georgia Municipal Association and County Commissioners Association would set the policy direction of the new bureau, and a professional staff would manage day-to-day issues.

Among a range of specified activities, the bureau was directed to produce a State Biennial Development Program, which would "guide state programs and operations in order that such programs and operations shall make maximum contributions" to the development of the state. The governor would submit updates to the development program, along with his annual budget proposal, to the General Assembly for action. Act 1066 devolved day-to-day responsibility for state planning to a system of area planning and development commissions, whose boundaries and membership the bureau would be responsible for determining. The commissions would act as liaisons between local, state, and federal governments and would carry out much of the planning work of the state bureau, including A-95 reviews of local applications for state or federal funds, developing six-year capital improvement schedules, and preparing long-range forecasts of future population growth.

While the new bureau established a basic framework for state policy and for regional planning in rural areas, Atlanta's broken regional planning process remained unmended. As Levitas, Horton, and their allies strategized how to present a bill to reorganize Atlanta's regional planning agencies, James Aldredge, a regionally minded member of the ARMPC board and county commissioner from Fulton County, stepped in to help. Spending political capital, Aldredge spearheaded a small group of local elected officials (all ARMPC board members) who agreed to work with the legislators, as well as Bennett, Sweat, and Harry West, the young Fulton County chief administrator, to develop a reorganization plan for ARMPC that did not include city-county consolidation, which remained a hot-button issue. Their reorganization plan formed the basis of a bill Horton, Atherton, and Marcus introduced late in the 1970 session. Aimed at resolving Atlanta's regional coordination problems, the reorganization plan included most of the recommendations outlined in the ASPO report and identified during the USDOT review but also expanded citizen representation and granted ARMPC the power to review local zoning decisions.[92] The bill proposed shuffling the transportation program within ARMPC's organizational structure, putting all transportation-related planning activities under the control of a single coordinator. This coordinator would act by virtue of a signed agreement between the federal government, state highway commission, and ARMPC board.

This first version of the reorganization plan was attacked for handing too much control to bureaucratic agents and for giving zoning review authority to an intergovernmental commission without electoral accountability. Lack of support from most of the mayors and county commissioners in the region doomed its chances of passage, and the bill failed. Planning for another push in 1971, Horton, Atherton, and Marcus regrouped and quickly introduced a resolution to create a Metropolitan Regional Council Study Committee, comprising six members of the house, to complete a "thorough study of metropolitan problems and the coordination of possible solutions through intergovernmental cooperation." The study resolution signaled to the rest of the house that Horton and his allies intended to reintroduce a revised version of the bill in the next session.[93]

Picking up after defeat, Aldredge, Sweat, and West, now working with Don Mendonsa, chief administrative officer of Dekalb County, took the failed legislation back to the drawing table, reworking the bill to respond to criticism. The administrators held a series of meetings with local politicians and members of the legislature on the modifications to the reorganization plan, using these meetings to press the need for greater regional cooperation. They explained that demonstrating "unanimity among the local governments" around the Aldredge plan increased the chances of Horton's bill gaining support in the General Assembly. In its new guise, the balance of power on the board of the revised regional commission would give elected officials one more seat than citizen members, creating a majority, and review of local zoning decisions would no longer be part of the commission's authority. With the election of Jimmy Carter as governor in 1970 and his promise to prioritize administrative reform, the prospects for the regional planning bill increased significantly.[94] Horton, Atherton, and Marcus, now joined by Grace Hamilton of Fulton County, introduced the revised legislation as House Bill 84 at the beginning of the 1971 General Assembly session, backed by the vocal support of Governor Carter.[95] As the bill worked its way through the legislature in the spring, ARMPC's staff conducted an internal evaluation of their role in the conduct of regional planning in Atlanta in the 1960s. Comparing ARMPC to the MPC provided useful perspective. ARMPC staff characterized their work in the 1960s as a "piece-by-piece approach to detailing the regional plans (1962 & 1968) built on the assumption that the basic objectives defined during the fifties were essentially unchanged." Concluding that this tactic was no longer appropriate, staff recommended that the 1970s should begin with a thorough reexamination of the existing regional planning process because the "crisis response and piecemeal problem solving" of the 1960s could no longer address Atlanta's issues. Hence the staff suggested that the revised agency, whatever its form, should "again take the same type of comprehensive look at the region as [had been done] in the fifties."[96]

After receiving an affirmative vote from the powerful Local Government Committee, House Bill 84 passed the house relatively easily, but its trip through the senate was more contentious. A spate of amendments and amendments to amendments were proposed and voted on during the debate. Part of the controversy was who would have the power to determine which counties would belong to the new commission, the local governments or the General Assembly. The house version of the bill explicitly excluded language allowing municipalities to remove themselves from the authority of the regional commission, and voting in the senate on amendments addressing this relationship was close. One amendment would have required the General Assembly to remove any county or municipality from the commission if a resolution requesting removal was passed by a simple majority of the local governing body. This amendment failed, but a second was introduced and passed that allowed county commissions to petition the General Assembly to withdraw from the regional commission, though ultimate authority to make this decision remained with the legislature. Not everyone in Atlanta wanted a regional body that included suburban representation. The director of the Atlanta Urban League felt that the commission "would work against all inner-city residents, black or white, because it gives disproportionate representation to residents of unincorporated suburban areas."[97] In response to this criticism, right before the final up or down vote on the bill, a representative from Fulton County proposed an amendment to change the balance of membership on the new commission by giving the more populous counties proportionally more representation.[98] This, too, failed.

Despite the changes, and the failures to make changes, the final version of the bill that passed both chambers of the assembly retained much of the original bill's character. Removing zoning oversight was the most significant concession. More important were the victories, which were numerous. Having membership determined by the state legislature, establishing mandatory funding levels based on population, instituting the oversight of area plan reviews, clarifying responsibility for transportation planning, and consolidating all regional responsibility under one roof represented substantial changes from the existing situation. The tradeoffs brought Atlanta a planning commission that reflected the redistribution of decision-making authority over a much wider collection of local officials and a decided tilt toward greater state involvement.

As the General Assembly debated House Bill 84, ARMPC staff was busy distributing a report, "Regional Policy Development Process," to their constituent local governments. The document explained the work of the reconfigured regional agency, setting the stage for the new organization to provide the kind of comprehensiveness that many believed to be missing from ARMPC. Staff suggestions for the way the new agency should go about its tasks focused on the basic steps of the rational-comprehensive process—setting long-range goals, gathering data, executing analysis, and conducting periodic evaluation—and reinforced the recommendations in the ASPO report. The process would help the agency focus on pressing regional issues: intergovernmental cooperation, transportation, water and sewer infrastructure, open space, and land use. Long-range goals should be followed by policy standards, "unbiased and quantifiable comparisons of alternative plan proposals."[99] These policy standards would be used to develop more specific plans, which could be translated into discrete technical activities and short-range policies that would each accomplish one small part of the regional plan. Technical studies and reports would inform the major substantive issues the new agency addressed. This was rational planning at its best. While challenges to the assumptions at the center of comprehensive planning had been mounted from within the ranks of the academy, the dominance of the rational-comprehensive model in practice went virtually unchallenged in Atlanta.[100]

Passed midway through the 1971 session, Act 5, as it came to be known, created, "an [as yet unnamed] agency composed of offices of political subdivisions and private citizens to coordinate planning and development within each area of this State having a population of more than 1,000,000 according to the United States Decennial Census of 1970."[101] The act also eliminated ARMPC, the AATS, and MACLOG. The legislation consolidated functions divided among the three organizations but in a way that went beyond what the ASPO report had recommended four years earlier: the new commission would also take over regional law enforcement planning, public health planning, and human service planning.[102]

Following the boundaries of the existing five-county Atlanta SMSA, the new commission would be guided by a governing board comprising the chairman of the commission of each member county, one mayor from each county who would be elected by all the mayors of the municipalities within each county, the mayor of Atlanta, a member of the Atlanta board of aldermen, and eleven citizens, each representing a specially drawn district. The citizen districts would not be "concurrent with political boundaries but [would], instead, overlap city and county lines."[103] Local elected officials would recommend citizen representatives to the board. An executive director would be the interface between the professional staff and the board. As part of its regular duties, the commission would file an annual report with the Bureau of State Planning and Community Affairs, outlining the commission's budget, expenditures, planning activities, summaries of area studies, lists of applications for federal funds, local plans reviewed, and recommendations for new legislation. Act 5 required the commission to "prepare and adopt and from time to time amend, change, or repeal, after appropriate study and such public hearings as may be necessary, comprehensive development guides for its area."[104] Supported by the A-95 review process, Act 5 gave the commission authority to review any plan by a local government under its purview, "plan" being defined as "a written proposal that involves government action, expenditure of public funds, [and] use of public property . . . which affects the citizens of more than one political subdivision . . . and which may have a substantial effect on the development of an area."[105]

Local financing would come from mandatory yearly contributions by each member county and the city of Atlanta, to be based on annual population estimates (calculated by the commission). Gwinnett, Cobb, and Clayton Counties would contribute thirty cents for each person. Atlanta would contribute eighteen cents per person. Because Atlanta sits astride Fulton and Dekalb Counties, those counties were required to contribute twelve cents for each person living in the city in the county and thirty cents for each person living outside the city in the county. The counties and the city were each required to grant the commission an additional annual $2,000 bonus, over and above the population-based contribution. Provision was made for future per capita increases based on inflation.[106]

The basic framework of the commission provided a broad foundation.[107] Its size, breadth of function, and relationship with the state, reflected in its jurisdiction and funding, conveyed long-term security and stability. County and municipal membership was not optional; nor was the contribution of money toward the commission's budget. With authority derived from the A-95 review process, its status as the official transportation planning organization, and continuing funding from the Section 701 program, the commission had an important role in manipulating the flow of federal funds into the region. But like its predecessors, the new commission lacked explicit authority to operate a mass transportation system or co-opt municipal governing functions related to land use, specifically zoning.[108] Ultimately, the interplay of these factors would prove important when the administrators of the new commission began to carve out a bigger role for it in the regional planning and development process.

In January 1972, Charles "Charlie" Brown, the long-serving Fulton County commissioner, called to order the very first meeting of his fellow county commission chairs from Clayton, Cobb, Dekalb, and Gwinnett, the mayor of Atlanta, and a representative from the city's board of aldermen to initiate the new regional commission. The commission's board moved quickly to elect a chairman, choosing Ernest Barrett, commission chair of Cobb County and a champion of what he termed "regional statesmanship." It then established a process for electing a mayor representative from each county, chose citizen members, decided on a name (Atlanta Regional Commission), contracted a consultant to write human resource policies, and hired Dan Sweat Jr. as the first executive director.

Sweat had been deeply involved in the ad hoc committee that came up with the reorganization plan that created ARC. At the time of his appointment as executive director, Sweat was the chief administrative officer of Atlanta and had served as the city's staff liaison to ARMPC for several years. Through the 1960s, Sweat had worked in several positions close to the region's political elites, first as an assistant administrator of Dekalb County and later as executive assistant for Atlanta mayors Ivan Allen Jr. (1960–1968) and Sam Massell (1968–1971). Sweat had also been a vocal supporter of regional planning in metro Atlanta. During the 1960s, Dekalb County had been one of the fastest-growing counties in the United States, adding employment and population at a furious pace. Sharing a long border and a portion of the city of Atlanta with Fulton, Dekalb absorbed white and black migrants from both city and countryside. Sweat had played an important role in planning the county's growth, using water, sewer, and road infrastructure to create industrial and commercial districts and brokering the opening of undeveloped sections of the southern part of the county for new residential development.[109] Most of this growth was in unincorporated places. As a result, Sweat had overseen the county's transition to an urban municipality, offering an array of services much like a city.

As inaugural executive director of ARC, Sweat faced yet another arduous task: establishing ARC's foothold in the development politics of the region. Having spent his career as an appointed agent of the bureaucracy, Sweat was able to wield a powerful, behind-the-scenes influence on political figures instrumental in creating the new commission. Sweat's experience and connections helped reinforce the legitimacy of the infant ARC among local politicians, almost immediately extending its reach in ways that ARMPC had been unable to.[110]

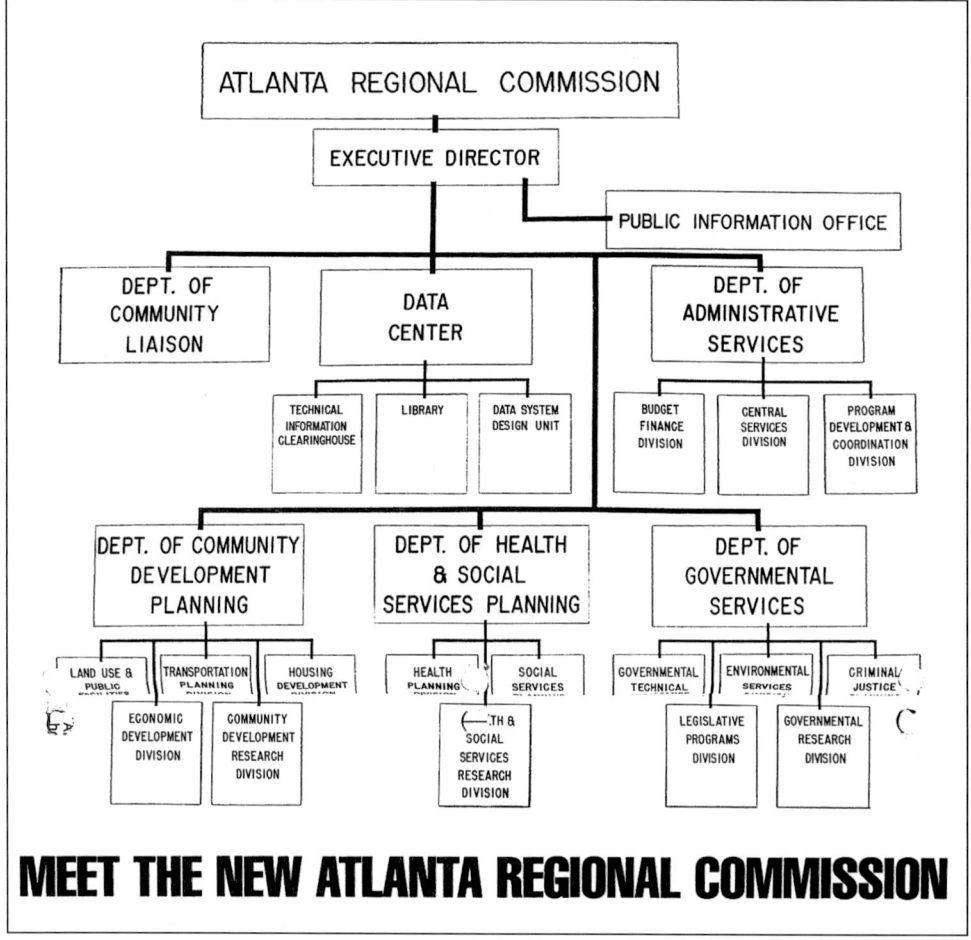

Figure 2.7 "Meet the New Atlanta Regional Commission," from Atlanta Regional Commission, *Annual Report*, 1972, Atlanta Regional Commission Collection, Kenan Research Center, Atlanta History Center

But Sweat did not operate by himself. The formation of ARC was the result of a collaborative effort by "a set of professional public administrators who worked together" on the ground, in constant communication with one another regarding governing issues.[111] The intellectual force behind the creation of ARC came from this small group of public administrators and planners and the county commissioners and state legislators who worked with them. The diffuse network that emerged, linking administrators, planners, and elected officials, provided a means for directly engaging the political system, affording the administrators considerable influence over legislation that would affect the new commission. Sweat reflected on these experiences in an interview near the end of his life, marveling at how he and his colleagues had managed to "wire [the government] together with baling wire and Scotch tape." This practical knowledge gave them a shared understanding and the ability to cut through the thorny politics of state and local government.[112]

During Sweat's tenure at ARC, funding for the commission grew rapidly. At the time, intergovernmental coordination was a national issue, finding significant support in Congress and the media.[113] Recalling ARC's early financial condition, Sweat remarked in 1996 that "money was not a problem. Money—we had money running out of our ears."[114] One of the first public regional planning agencies in the country to have a guaranteed local funding stream, ARC hired 135 employees over the course of its first two years in operation. Between the beginning of 1972, when the commission opened for business, and the end of 1973, when Sweat resigned, the annual budget grew from $1,711,000 to $2,862,000. By 1975 the yearly budget had reached $4.7 million.[115]

At The Doorstep of Great Change

The growth of metropolitan Atlanta represented the leading edge of Georgia's transformation from a rural to an urban state. With the 1962 *Baker v. Carr* Supreme Court decision effectively ending the county-unit system, Atlanta had rapidly gained political power during the late 1960s.[116] The 1970 census showed that the five-county metropolitan area had grown to 1.4 million people, 30 percent of the state's population. In response, the Office of Management and Budget expanded Atlanta's Standard Metropolitan Statistical Area to seven counties in 1973, and the state legislature promptly voted to bring the two new metropolitan counties, Douglas and Rockdale, into ARC's jurisdiction.[117] This growth had given credence to the idea that metropolitan Atlanta could reach 3 million people by the beginning of the twenty-first century.[118] Media hullabaloo over Atlanta's projected growth broadcast a message that mixed the old booster1sh vision of a vast metropolis with doomsayers' prognostications over the ecological inability of the region to house so many people. Stirring this debate was the fact that Atlanta had become majority black and was about to elect its first black mayor. During the 1960s the city's total population grew by just 10,000. But on its streets and across its neighborhoods, Atlanta experienced ten years of intense racial churning. With the end of legally segregated public facilities, working-class neighborhoods in the southern and western extents of the city began to transition from all white to all black. The public school system quickly resegregated, as white students all but disappeared.[119] Parallel to the demographic changes in the city was the population surge of Atlanta's suburban counties. Between 1950 and 1970, the five counties of metropolitan Atlanta added 670,000 new residents. As the largely unincorporated suburban counties grew, the relative concentration of the region's population began to fall, and the geographic distribution of whites and blacks became increasingly uneven. Though in 1970 the share of the total regional population living within Fulton and

Dekalb Counties still amounted to nearly 75 percent, that share was poised to fall rapidly in the coming years. The image of white suburbs surrounding a black city was more evident than ever before.

At the beginning of the 1970s, development along Atlanta's perimeter freeway (Interstate 285), the last segment of the region's Interstate Highway System to be completed, had begun to accelerate. New regional shopping malls spreading in an arc along the circumferential highway were beachheads for what would become major employment, residential, and retail nodes in unincorporated places like Dunwoody and Sandy Springs.[120] The region's first large-scale planned unit developments began popping up during the same period. Combining detached single-family houses, condominiums, and apartment buildings, these new subdivisions were the size of small towns, and though sitting in unincorporated parts of suburban counties, they required urban levels of service. These developments helped propel the growth of Atlanta's suburbs, which by this point was driven much less by out-migration from the city than by in-migration from other parts of the state and country.

At the same time, a commercial- and office-construction boom was occurring inside the city, though in a way that redistributed activity away from the central business district.[121] Fueled by a lingering urban renewal mentality, Central Atlanta Progress, a private downtown development agency associated with the city's business leadership, helped coordinate a series of major developments in downtown Atlanta that netted new hotels, convention facilities, stadiums, and tourist attractions but could not stem the out-migration of law firms, banks, accountants, and corporate offices or convince middle-class whites that downtown was a good place to shop.[122] Meanwhile, Atlanta's Midtown and Buckhead neighborhoods drew an increasing share of commercial property investment, supporting a boom in office space, shopping centers, and high-end residential development. As the regional economy that had been centered in downtown Atlanta became more distinctly multinodal and geographically dispersed, the balance of political power shifted as well. The structure of ARC reflected this.

Regional planning in Atlanta began as a relatively simple affair in the late 1940s but became increasingly complicated by the late 1960s. The first regional planning agency, the MPC, was limited to two counties, dominated by the city of Atlanta and its old corporate guard, and though supported with public funds, was forced to negotiate its small budget annually with its member governments. The primary legacy of the MPC lies in two long-range plans written in the 1950s. ARMPC arrived in 1960 with an expanded geographic scope and professional staff and new sources of funding. But the influence of the agency remained limited, and by 1964 political disagreements had fractured ARMPC, splitting its duties among three overlapping and at times competing regional planning agencies. With the founding of ARC in 1971, the state finally made an effort to reunite these functions and create a single, consolidated framework for regional decision making. By making membership mandatory and expanding funding sources, ARC brought the regional planning process back under one roof, a move that laid the groundwork for the commission to expand its power in the coming years.

Regional planning agencies do not by themselves create or inhibit population or employment growth, but they do have a hand in shaping where and how growth gets allocated. As conduits for information and money and political gamesmanship, regional agencies occupy critical ground between different levels of government.[123] The structure of these organizations, who they serve, how they represent political geography, where their funding comes from, and what tasks they are responsible for are all important. In the case of metropolitan Atlanta, efforts to institute a stable regional planning process, beginning with the founding of the MPC in 1947 and ending with the founding of ARC in 1971, had proceeded in fits and starts. But from 1971 forward, ARC exuded a stability, size, and complexity that far outstripped its predecessors. Over the next thirty years, with the strong support of the state, ARC would grow to occupy a central role in the regional development process, balancing an expanding number of federal policy directives against the region's often contentious politics.

3
The River and the Region

*The Chattahoochee River and
the Atlanta Regional Commission*

From its wellspring in the southern Appalachians to its mouth in the Gulf of Mexico, the Chattahoochee River has long been a critical resource for people in the southeastern United States. Through the nineteenth and first half of the twentieth centuries, cities along the river in Georgia and Alabama freely withdrew water for municipal supply and sent their (often untreated) waste downstream. Farmers drew the river's water for crop irrigation, and cotton and pulp mills and small hydroelectric dams harnessed the river's flow to produce fabric, paper, and electricity. Fishermen around Apalachicola Bay needed the briny conditions in the river delta for their oyster harvest. Under riparian rights, each group claimed its share of the river's water, and for many years these claims were easily accommodated.[1]

But the balance among claims shifted in early 1956, when the steel gates of the intake structure on Buford Dam in Gwinnett County, Georgia, first closed and the waters of the upper Chattahoochee began to back up into the wide but relatively shallow thirty-eight-thousand-acre Lake Sidney Lanier. Perhaps not inadvertently, a dam designed to regulate the flow of the entire river system, ostensibly for the equal benefit of all the users of the river, also created a more dependable water supply for metropolitan Atlanta.[2] The culmination of a long-standing plan by the Army Corps of Engineers to support navigation, generate power, and control flooding on the Apalachicola-Chattahoochee-Flint River system, the new dam also provided local politicians in Atlanta's burgeoning suburban counties concrete support for their dreams of economic growth. Local governments around the region leveraged municipal bonds and federal

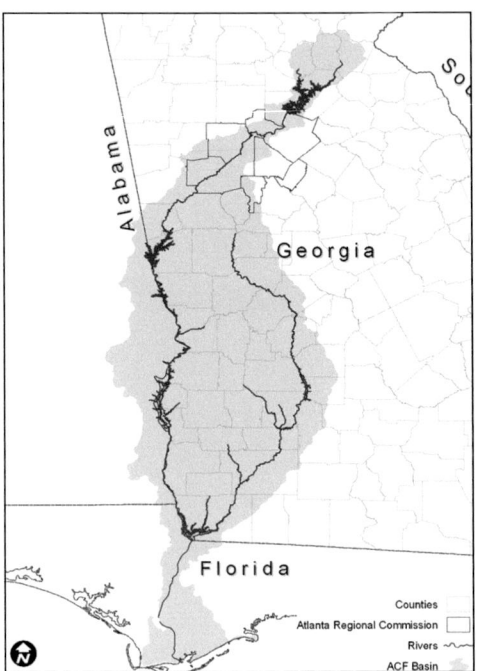

Figure 3.1 Apalachicola-Chattahoochee-Flint (ACF) River Basin

grants to build capacity to increase withdrawals of water to meet projections of future development and discharges of the wastewater such growth would inevitably produce.[3]

For much of the twentieth century, Atlanta's political leadership worried that the small size of the Chattahoochee would limit growth. Yet it was (and remains) the region's largest and most readily available source of water. Because the river was so vital, metro leaders understood that local governments could not by themselves manage the resource effectively.[4] Few local governments employed personnel who understood the complexities of water supply and wastewater management, and industries along the river resisted rules inhibiting production or profit. But by consistently failing to legislate regulations to protect the river from excessive pollution or decisively allocate withdrawals, the state had by default left the fate of the river to a motley collection of local politicians and industrial operators.

By the early 1960s, an uptick in water withdrawals by houses and office buildings sprouting along the riverbanks generated a host of problems state leaders could no longer ignore.[5] Angered by increasing pollution, downstream neighbors blamed the problem on unmanaged waste discharges from Atlanta and its suburbs.[6] A small handful of Georgia's politicians finally began to recognize that greater control over surface waters was critical to the state's economic growth, especially in metropolitan Atlanta. With competition for jobs and investment coming from nearby states, these officials worried about Atlanta's and Georgia's long-term prospects. Working hand in hand with state and federal agencies, Atlanta's political leaders spent the 1960s and 1970s restructuring Georgia's laws so that residential, commercial, and industrial growth could continue and the water supply so crucial to that growth could expand, regardless of downstream consequences. What had begun as an unfocused set of overlapping policies quickly evolved into a coherent agenda, one that clearly privileged the security of Atlanta's water supply over virtually every other use.[7] Pushed by changes in federal policy, the nascent environmental movement, and rapidly shifting demographics, the new Atlanta Regional Commission (ARC) adopted this perspective as its own.

By the end of 1972, a single land development controversy involving one of the founding members of ARC reframed how planning and development projects that touched the Chattahoochee would be carried out and shaped metropolitan Atlanta's overall water management strategy vis-à-vis its conflicts with downstream interests. Not until ARC's *Chattahoochee Corridor Study* did a coherent planning framework emerge to manage water supply and wastewater for metropolitan north Georgia.[8] Designed to control development along a forty-eight-mile stretch of the river between Buford Dam and the city of Atlanta, the Chattahoochee plan was the first of a series of ARC plans and policies that defined river use, influenced the development of the Atlanta region's primary water source, and galvanized a loose but coherent regional coalition around the problem of water resource planning.[9] The accumulated actions of ARC, the state, and the Army Corps of Engineers elevated the fight to control the Chattahoochee from a local squabble to an interstate battle with national implications.[10]

Figure 3.2 Map of study corridor, from Atlanta Regional Commission, *Chattahoochee Corridor Study*, 1972, State of Georgia Program and Budget Office Records, Planning Studies Folder, Georgia Archives, Morrow, Georgia

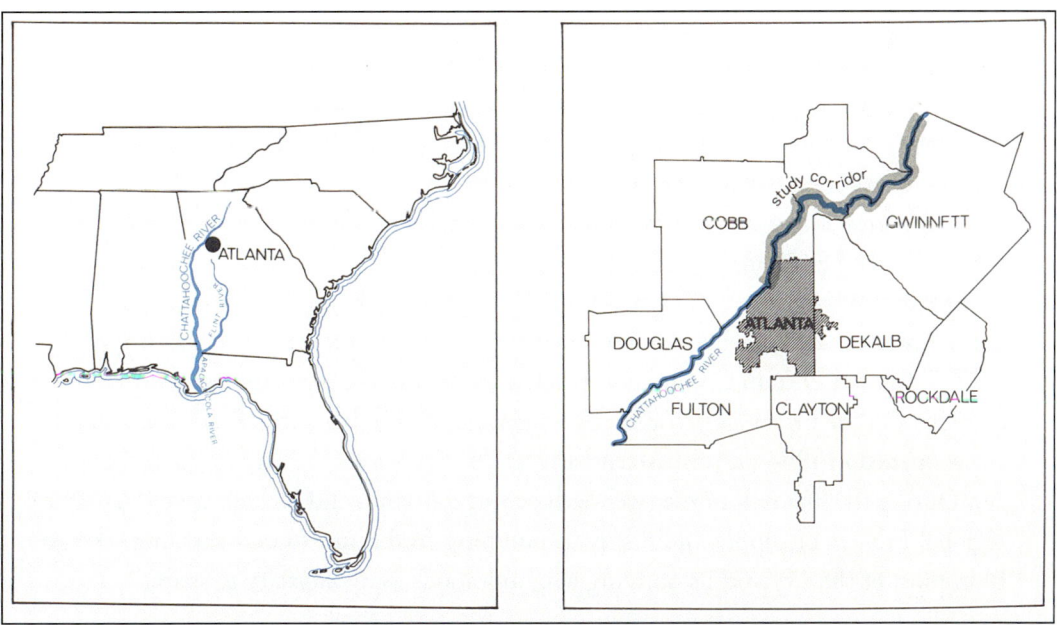

Received wisdom suggests that regional coordination around issues like water supply is an important tool for ensuring efficient resource allocation and for preventing sprawl.[11] In the case of Atlanta, however, regional water plans did just the opposite. Under the guise of cleaning up and protecting the Chattahoochee watershed, Atlanta's political leaders and planners used regional water policy, state law, and federal money to build an enormously complex and wasteful water supply system that became an engine for sprawl during a fifteen-year period beginning in the mid-1960s. How Atlanta's regionalists succeeded deserves exploration.

The River

Three primary rivers form the Apalachicola-Chattahoochee-Flint (ACF) basin, a major southeastern watershed that drains just over nineteen thousand square miles of Georgia, Alabama, and Florida. The Chattahoochee, the largest of the three, is small by many measures. Though rarely more than three hundred feet wide or twenty feet deep, its watershed spans nearly half (8,700 square miles) the total ACF basin, of which a small but significant portion drains the counties that make up metropolitan Atlanta.[12] As the river flows through Atlanta, separating the city from its northern and western suburbs, its banks display little of the intense industrial and commercial development often associated with major urban waterways. Over the years, residents and businesses along the Chattahoochee did not withdraw enough water to significantly impede its flow or return enough polluted wastewater to degrade the water available to downstream neighbors.

Beginning as far back as 1872 the Army Corps of Engineers conducted periodic surveys of the ACF basin.[13] During the later years of the nineteenth century, those surveys generated a range of plans for developing the river system for material gain, and boosters in Atlanta and Columbus, Georgia, tried repeatedly to marshal the Corps's support for federal aid to dredge channels and build dams.[14] Though the Corps's surveys consistently showed the infeasibility of a navigable channel to Atlanta, they supported a few dams to regulate river flow, primarily to control flooding and support limited economic development.

Despite its small size, the Chattahoochee has been the primary water source for the majority of Atlanta households since the city's first intakes were submerged in 1891. Suburban Dekalb County constructed its first intake pipe and pumping station in 1920, and the first major modern treatment plant in Atlanta, the R. M. Clayton facility, opened in 1934 on the eastern bank of the river along the city's western boundary. During the first half of the twentieth century, Atlanta and Dekalb were the major regional brokers of supply and disposal, pumping freshwater to and carrying sewage from most of the city and its outlying neighborhoods, with capacity to spare.

Although several Corps reports encouraged damming the ACF Rivers, through the first three decades of the twentieth century Congress consistently declined to allocate money for new dams on the system.[15] But during the Great Depression, New Deal programs offered increased support for infrastructure projects, including flood control and new sources of electric power. The Rural Electrification Administration, especially, sought power projects that would connect the underserved countryside to the national grid. In support of the Rural Electrification Administration's mission, in 1935 Congress directed the Corps of Engineers to thoroughly reevaluate harnessing the ACF Rivers system for rural electrification.[16] The resulting report, submitted to Congress in 1939, advanced a plan to construct six navigable locks and dams on the lower Chattahoochee, three hydroelectric dams on the upper Chattahoochee, and three hydroelectric dams on the upper Flint. The report concluded that the proposed dams and reservoirs would provide valuable flood control and navigation along the lower stretches of the river system, and cheap electric power would spur industrial development in the impoverished upper sections of the basin.[17]

Though the 1939 survey considered only a single dam on the narrow stretch of the Chattahoochee north of Atlanta, a 1942 resurvey of a short, forty-eight-mile section of the river that flows through Gwinnett County, Fulton County, and Atlanta recommended two northern dams instead of one: a major hydroelectric facility near the tiny town of Buford and a smaller, reregulation barrier near Roswell. The 1942 report argued that two dams would do a better job of regulating the entire ACF system, providing a steadier flow for generating electric power north of Atlanta while maintaining nine-foot navigable channels in the sections of the Chattahoochee and Apalachicola between Columbus and the Gulf of Mexico. But with federal money for major construction projects diverted to the war effort, the Corps declined to release the report to Congress.[18]

In late 1945, as the war was drawing to a close, Congress reauthorized a version of the Rivers and Harbors Act and included funding for a survey to explore the effect of the recently completed New Orleans–Apalachicola Inland Waterway on existing plans for the ACF basin. Transmitted to Congress in June 1947, the report questioned the financial viability of implementing all six impoundment projects originally proposed in 1939, but it noted that the original suggestion to build a single hydroelectric dam at Buford had received particularly favorable comments in a review by the Federal Power Commission. With the report calling the reregulation dam at Roswell too costly, Atlanta-area politicians and Georgia's congressional delegation embraced their only option, a single dam at Buford.[19] That the dam would create a large freshwater reservoir that could eventually be tapped as a municipal water supply was not lost on Atlanta's mayor, William Hartsfield, even though he declined to contribute city money toward its construction.[20]

Figure 3.3 Buford Dam, U.S. Army Corps of Engineers, South Atlantic Division, Mobile District

Congress approved construction of the dam at Buford in 1949, one of hundreds of postwar infrastructure projects intended to boost the nation's economy. Work was under way by March 1950. Six years later, the gates on the dam closed for the first time on a cold February day. Much to their delight, metropolitan Atlanta's political leaders saw their region's prospects for growth given a sudden, dramatic boost.

Without a sufficient tax base or in many cases access to the Chattahoochee, Atlanta's smaller suburban communities lacked the financial capital to construct water supply sources sufficient to serve substantial population growth. Through the first half of the twentieth century, only the city of Atlanta and Dekalb County water authorities possessed sufficient resources to build and maintain the infrastructure needed to underwrite extensive urban growth. As a result, suburban governments hungry for water to feed development were forced to negotiate agreements with the large systems.

The construction of Buford Dam promised to make the Chattahoochee's flow much more predictable and accessible. In response to the anticipated increase in water supply and as a reflection of their dissatisfaction with being forced to depend on Atlanta and Dekalb County for water, representatives from Cobb County convinced the 1951 Georgia General Assembly to establish a new water authority that could draw from Cobb County's stretch of the Chattahoochee. Establishment of Cobb's new water agency significantly increased withdrawals from the river, laying the groundwork for future growth and opening a market for the county to pump Chattahoochee water to small towns and unincorporated areas northwest of Atlanta.[21] This led to a jump in interjurisdictional contracts to buy and sell supply and treatment capacity across political boundaries and between adjacent governments. The result was an increasingly dense network of water and sewer mains, outfalls, and pumping stations, replete with "complicated cost-sharing calculations."[22] Though chaotic, the region's water web proved just stable enough to support the influx of population and industry that began in the 1950s.

By 1960 Atlanta, Cobb, and Dekalb provided the bulk of all municipal water in the region, with the vast majority of withdrawals and discharges depending on the Chattahoochee and its tributaries. Yet as the large water authorities grew, so also did small authorities dependent on interjurisdictional agreements. The zeal of county commissioners to use water supply to help finance growth pushed the major water authorities to sell increasing quantities of water to jurisdictions outside the Chattahoochee watershed.[23] These factors extended the geographic reach of the major regional systems but also expanded the volume of water withdrawn from the Chattahoochee and never returned.[24]

As late as 1960 most of the land along the Chattahoochee north of Atlanta's suburban fringe faced minor development pressure. Mountainous topography, poor soil, and spotty infrastructure kept the area in a rural, almost stereotypically Appalachian condition.[25] As a result, the Chattahoochee's water ran clear when it reached the outer edge of metro Atlanta, supporting a variety of flora and fauna, even a federal trout fishery, and providing the small communities along the way with a relatively high-quality water source.[26] The rural-dominated state legislature had consistently demonstrated little concern with the quality of the northern Chattahoochee's waters or the fate of land along its banks. As long as sufficient water was available to meet the needs of northern Georgia's small factories, farms, and towns, questions about the land bracketing the northern Chattahoochee had been left in the hands of local governments. However, when the degraded condition of the Chattahoochee's water began to emerge as an interstate commerce issue in the early 1960s, tension between local, state, and federal agencies over the most appropriate regulatory framework quickly developed. Conflict about how to control land development, which political jurisdictions should have access to withdraw water, and what management structure would best guide the use of the river's waters seemed hard to avoid.

Federal concern with water management had peaked during the Depression and then gone quiet during the war. Congressional debates about the appropriate federal role in allocating the waters of large rivers in the eastern United States returned after the end of the war.[27] With the need to move the nation's war economy toward peacetime activities, management of water infrastructure became an important cause. Concerns about infrastructure surfaced in several major congressional reports and legislative initiatives directed toward national and regional water policy.[28] Between 1946 and 1961 federal commissions broadly examined the nation's water resource planning and management efforts. The reports and plans produced by the commissions emphasized different sides of the water problem but shared an overriding concern with establishing a national water policy.[29] Ideas directed at managing the nation's waterways emerged from the work of the commissions, but the political disagreements over water allocation remained so intense that the water commissions never reached the national coherence they purportedly sought.[30] They did give rise, however, to several initiatives that attempted to address water management through a regional framework, which had significant implications for Atlanta and the Chattahoochee.

A bill introduced in the Eighty-First Congress in 1950, by Senator Robert Kerr (D-OK), would have created a plan for allocating eastern waters loosely modeled on the Colorado Compact.[31] Though Kerr's bill never reached a floor vote, a few local politicians following the debate from northern Georgia recognized the benefits a bill like Kerr's could have for securing metro Atlanta's future water supply. In 1947, before authorization of Buford Dam, Mayor Hartsfield had written the regional director of the Army Corps, explaining that "the City of Atlanta is now becoming genuinely worried over its future water supply."[32] Even after funds for Buford Dam had been allocated, Hartsfield and his political allies continued to seek assistance in securing water resources to support Atlanta's growth. They saw Kerr's bill as a possible path and after its failure urged Georgia's senior U.S. senator, Richard B. Russell, to introduce a scaled-down version of Kerr's bill.

Signed into law by President Eisenhower in 1958, Russell's bill created the U.S. Study Commission, Southeast River Basins. Though pitched as an experiment in planning for watershed development in the eastern United States, a goal it largely did not achieve, the commission nevertheless outlined several approaches that would influence the strategy metro Atlanta leaders would later use to consolidate their control over allocation of the Chattahoochee's water.

Focusing on the major river basins in the southeast, including the ACF basin, the commission's 1963 report noted that the increasingly urban land-use patterns in the ACF watershed would introduce new demands on management of the region's water resources.[33] Arguing that "activities in all parts of the basins are rather closely related to the existence, development, and use of the Chattahoochee, Flint, and Apalachicola rivers," the report stressed the need for better area-wide cooperation between jurisdictions that shared the watershed.[34] The commission also highlighted the paucity of reliable information documenting land and water conditions in southeastern river basins and brought attention to the challenge of writing water resource plans without accurate information.[35] Significantly, the commission found that the Chattahoochee was "grossly polluted for about 100 miles below Atlanta."[36] At the time the report was published, the largest water and sewer authority in the region, the Atlanta Water Resources Commission, still maintained an extensive system of combined sewer overflows (CSOs). This was also the situation in many of Atlanta's suburban jurisdictions.[37] As a low-tech system for managing urban runoff, CSOs, during major rain events, allow raw sewage from overloaded pipes to mix with storm water, creating a polluted stew dumped directly into the region's rivers and their tributaries. Even worse, smaller suburban cities with old, poorly managed, or nonexistent treatment facilities simply dumped untreated wastewater directly into surface waters. Moreover, by the early 1960s most of metro Atlanta's treatment plants were already approaching overload.[38]

Perhaps most portentously, the commission report identified a looming conflict between neighboring governments over pollution and the fair use of ACF basin water under the southeast's existing riparian rules. Though the report suggested several changes in laws to clarify the expectations of the constituencies sharing the ACF basin, the states made little effort to reach an agreement about how to deal with this problem.[39] The region's surface water management problems, compounded by projections of significant population growth over the next three decades, appeared to be on the verge of getting completely out of hand.

The early 1960s also brought pressure from the growing environmental movement on the federal government and the states to revise existing water quality laws.[40] In light of this, Georgia's politicians understood the politics of demonstrating that they were taking the Chattahoochee pollution problem seriously, especially if the state were to avoid federal intervention, which might threaten ongoing industrial development efforts and the growth potential of metro Atlanta. In response, the Georgia General Assembly passed the Water Quality Control Act in 1964, creating the state's first independent water quality control board to address general issues of water pollution in Georgia's rivers, streams, and wetlands.[41] The new water quality legislation promised to clean up the discharge coming from Atlanta and its suburbs. The act specified that by 1975 all municipal and industrial sewage treatment facilities (point sources) would provide secondary treatment before discharging waste into any of the state's surface waters. On the basis of data gathered for the 1963 commission report, the Water Quality Control Act required all municipalities and major industrial interests along the Chattahoochee to show how they would achieve pollution abatement by the 1975 deadline.[42]

In 1965 Congress passed the National Water Resources Planning Act and the Water Quality Act, and in early 1966 it passed revisions to the Water Pollution Control Act (also known as the Clean Water Restoration Act).[43] The National Water Resources Planning Act, another attempt to forge a national water policy, was designed to "encourage the conservation, development, and utilization of the water and related land resources of the United States on a comprehensive and coordinated basis." It established the Water Resources Council and river basin commissions and provided financial aid to states to increase water planning activities.[44] The Water

Resources Council required states to develop pollution standards for interstate waters, because "the banks of a river may belong to one man or even one industry or one State, but the waters which flow between those banks should belong to all the people."[45] The Water Pollution Control Act amendments directed the newly established Water Resources Council to "conduct a comprehensive study of the effects of pollution" on U.S. waterways. A study report would be due to Congress in three years.[46]

Almost as soon as the new federal water pollution laws took effect, officials from the newly created Federal Water Pollution Control Administration (FWPCA) turned their attention to reports of interstate pollution problems, including complaints from jurisdictions within the ACF system.[47] Despite Georgia's 1964 pollution law, by mid-1965 discharges from municipal sewage plants and industry into the Chattahoochee around Atlanta had become severe enough to bring formal complaints from officials in Alabama and Florida. By the end of 1965, pollution in the Chattahoochee downstream from Atlanta had brought complaints from residents as far south as Apalachicola, Florida, who spoke of "the river being polluted to the extent that it was killing fish as far down as Lake Seminole."[48]

Though "Georgia's executive in charge of cleaning up polluted waters [claimed] federal authorities [were] intent on muddying the waters of the state's anti-pollution program," officials at FWPCA took the complaints about the Chattahoochee seriously and generally brushed aside contrarian pronouncements from Georgia's officials.[49] Moreover, the national media had begun to pick up on the emerging crisis of polluted surface waterways, thrusting the issue before a broader public. This added attention helped push the FWPCA to deal with problem rivers around the country, a move that industry worried would leave them "stuck with a major share" of "the cost of reversing pollution of the nation's streams," then estimated to be upwards of $75 billion.[50]

Despite intensive lobbying by industry and states to reduce the power of the FWPCA, its administrator appeared to take seriously his mandate to clean up the nation's waterways and convened pollution enforcement meetings around the country. Because Atlanta's pollution had impaired an interstate water body, the Chattahoochee River, the FWPCA administrator called two bistate enforcement conferences to discuss pollution in the river, the first in 1966 and a follow-up meeting in 1970. The enforcement conferences brought together businesses, media, politicians, and bureaucrats from Georgia and Alabama and representatives from several different federal agencies to address pollution stemming largely from municipal treatment plants, textile mills, and poultry processing factories.[51]

Designed to be public discussions about how to solve the Chattahoochee's pollution problems, including both heading off a bigger squabble and developing a workable plan for abating existing sources of pollution, the conferences grappled with the technical and political scope of urban water management. Noting that the city of Atlanta, Dekalb and Cobb Counties, and the industries within represented the largest users of the river for water supply and the biggest polluters, federal officials pointed out that these jurisdictions alone contributed more than 60 percent of the total bacterial load entering the Chattahoochee. Specifically, the major portion of the downstream pollution load was linked to three wastewater treatment plants operated by Atlanta: R. M. Clayton, Utoy Creek, and Sandy Creek. During the enforcement conferences, federal officials reiterated that the problem was exacerbated by dividing the administration of water policy across metro Atlanta among more than twenty political subdivisions. After hearing testimony about "notable severe lapses" in completing upgrades to the problem treatment plants, the FWPCA administrator expressed frustration at the slow progress of Georgia's reform efforts. Noting that "from 1966 to 1970 is a pretty long time," the administrator criticized the state's leaders for their failure to secure "positive assurance that there is going to be compliance" from local water management agencies and reminded them that "these are the cases we have trouble with."[52] Concluding the conference, he explained that the region's existing treatment facilities were "inefficient, uneconomical and poorly operated with respect to the water quality problems of the entire region," which provided clear evidence of a dire need for more vigilant "area regulatory planning."[53]

In 1967, between the two pollution enforcement proceedings, the Atlanta Region Metropolitan Planning Commission (ARMPC) had hired an engineering firm to evaluate existing water supply and sewer systems around metro Atlanta. The engineers issued a report in 1968 that detailed the poor (or in some cases nonexistent) state of much of the region's water infrastructure and facilities and the complications caused by the web of agreements between the region's water and sewer systems. The report echoed the findings of the U.S. Study Commission, Southeast River Basins, and the 1966 pollution enforcement conference.[54] A few months after the release of the engineers' report, ARMPC published a regional water management report based in part on the engineering study. Noting that the water problems "are incapable of solution without the concerted action of many governments," the report concluded that creating a metropolitan level water and sewer authority would be the best solution.[55] It attracted little public notice.

Despite the issues raised during the enforcement conferences and in the ARMPC report, neither state officials nor metro Atlanta's local governments sought significant changes in state water policy. The state's chief water official continued to chafe at federal authority, referring to federal water quality directives as "bureaucratic dogma."[56] He also complained that directives designed to prevent further degradation were "obnoxious" and in violation of "the spirit and the letter" of federal water quality laws.[57] In the meantime, as Atlanta's population grew and industrial activities expanded, complaints continued to roll in about the "gunk" and "raw sewerage" that were being dumped into the Chattahoochee.[58]

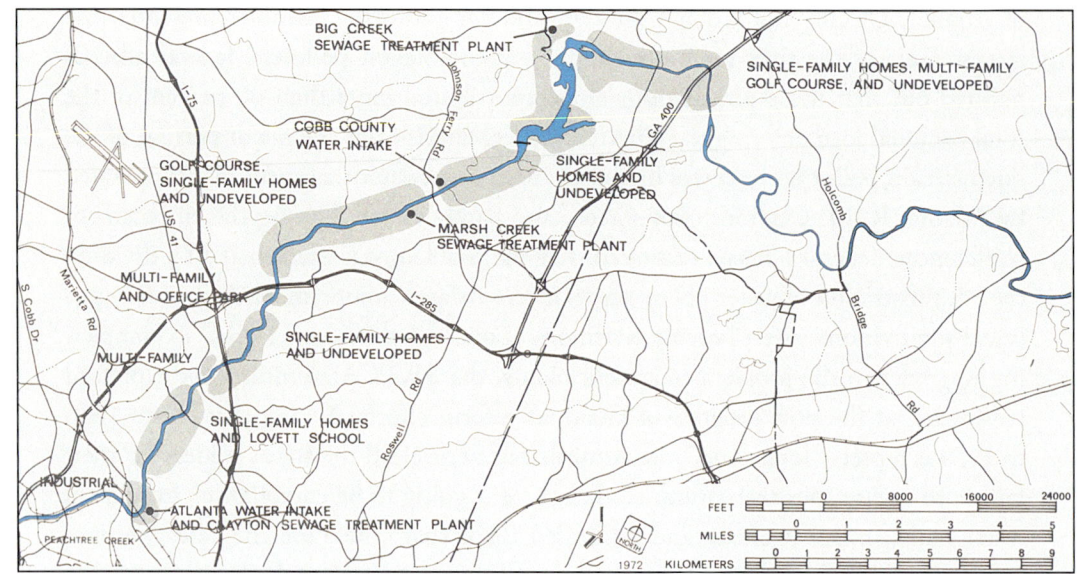

Figure 3.4 Chattahoochee Corridor Study, north, from Atlanta Regional Commission, *Chattahoochee Corridor Study*, p. 7

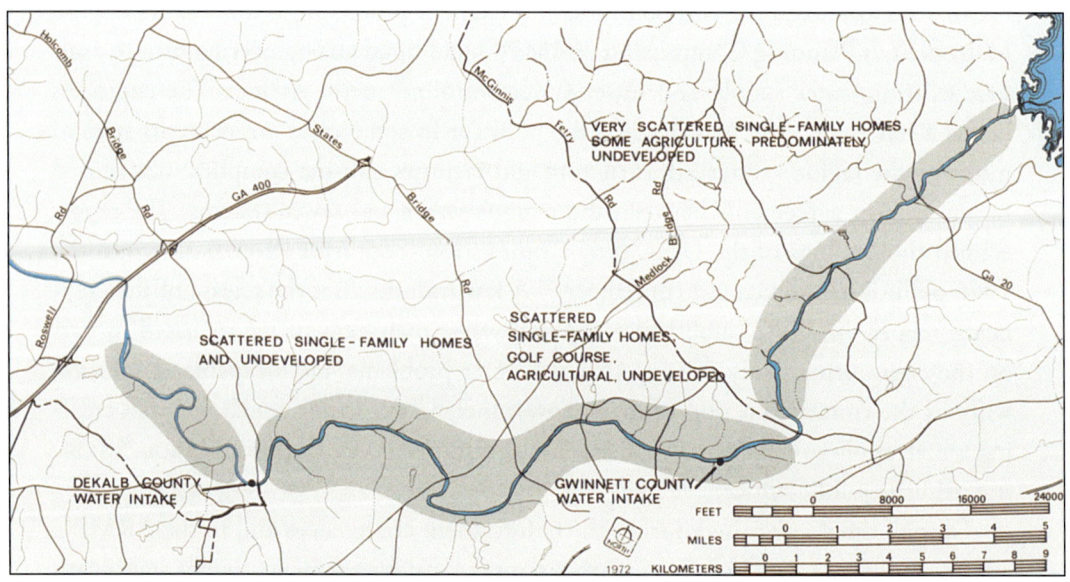

Figure 3.5 Chattahoochee Corridor Study, south, from Atlanta Regional Commission, *Chattahoochee Corridor Study*, p. 8

The *Chattahoochee Corridor Study*

In 1967, just before ARMPC issued its report calling for metropolitan coordination, a local developer with a history of turning the red clay of north Georgia into strip malls and apartment complexes had proposed a moderately sized multifamily residential development on a five-acre parcel adjacent to the Chattahoochee. Lying near a bridge that carries Interstate 285 across the river in an unincorporated section of north Fulton County, the development would have included a mixture of commercial and multifamily residential structures surrounded by green space to be held in permanent reserve. Because of the site plan's size and the intensity of use it proposed, the project had generated a muted outcry among local environmental activists. Apparently seeing few political repercussions from doing so, the Fulton County Commission paid little mind to the opposition, ignored concerns of neighboring jurisdictions, and approved the project. Site preparation work was under way by the middle of 1969. In mid-1970, the developer went back to the Fulton commission to request exemptions to the original site plan, allowing use of the protected land for additional commercial structures. While the developer "was successful in getting the . . . county commission to grant exceptions to covenants that allowed them to grade away at a green belt and bulldoze down a knoll," the decision did not come easily.[59] Only after lengthy deliberation did the Fulton commission grant the request, this time over much louder public protest, which now included accusations of cronyism by members of the commission.[60]

Just as the controversy over rezoning along the Chattahoochee River found its spark, federal water policy was shifting in a way that would further shake up metropolitan Atlanta's water management scheme, a result of Congress creating the National Water Commission in 1968.[61] Initially directed to catalog, analyze, and organize the increasingly onerous and complex water issues facing the nation, the commission would help propel passage of the federal Clean Water Act in 1972, which would give the Environmental Protection Agency (EPA) a powerful new tool for regulating pollution in the nation's waterways.[62]

In early 1971 a new water authority in Gwinnett County, which had frontage along the Chattahoochee and potential access to Lake Lanier, joined the region's three major systems, Atlanta, Cobb, and Dekalb. Envisioning a future in which commerce and industry would take advantage of the county's cheap land and good highway access, boosters hoped to grow Gwinnett's economic footprint. They realized that they would need to significantly expand the county's water withdrawal capacity to do so. The county commission convinced the state legislature to authorize the creation of new water and sewer authorities and immediately began selling bonds to finance the construction of intakes large enough to not only supply water to existing and future residents and businesses but also sell water to adjacent municipalities.[63] Unheeding of the recommendations of the pollution conferences and ARMPC's report, the state's willingness to continue to allow local political decisions to drive expansion of interbasin transfers further complicated the process of allocating water and exacerbated the existing pollution problem.[64]

Thus, by the time the Georgia General Assembly voted to establish ARC in 1971, pressure on metro and state leaders to develop a more coordinated regional water planning program was flowing down from the federal level and bubbling up from the local level. The growing thirst of municipal water systems coupled with interbasin transfers, runoff, and siltation helped keep attention focused on the declining condition of the Chattahoochee watershed. Rezoning cases that several years earlier would have escaped notice flashed into major controversies. The implications for Atlanta's future growth in leaving these issues unchecked did not go unnoticed.[65] Local media coverage of the water pollution problem in the region had increased sharply. Editorials decrying the failure of the state, local governments, and regional agencies to adequately address problems stemming from land development along the river amplified demands for change.[66] Federal oversight had been augmented, but still missing were aggressive state policies, good data, and political will.[67]

At first glance, the Fulton County Commission's rezoning decision appeared to be the lever for finally changing water management policy in Georgia. The uproar captured the attention of the new governor, Jimmy Carter. In the late spring of 1971, Carter stepped into the fray by requesting that the Fulton County Commission issue a temporary moratorium on rezoning all parcels abutting the river, which would have stopped work on the controversial project. Ignoring again the controversy and this time the governor, the commissioners permitted the developer to push ahead. Fed up, a group of residents and environmental organizations based in northern Fulton County filed an injunction request with the Fulton Superior Court to stop all additional work on the parcel until a resolution could be reached. The court granted the injunction in July, but controversy raged through the winter as the Fulton County Commission continued to hear rezoning applications for other parcels along the river.[68]

At the beginning of 1972, little progress had been made in dealing with the rezoning controversy. The politics surrounding the river, however, had grown even more complicated. Early in the new session of the Georgia General Assembly, Robert Walling, a state senator from Dekalb County, introduced a bill to create an independent five-person board to oversee all rezoning requests along the controversial stretch of the Chattahoochee north of Atlanta, but his effort ran headlong into "the newly established Atlanta Regional Commission" and its desire to "place itself in the forefront of the Chattahoochee issue."[69] Even before Walling had introduced his bill, Dan Sweat, the executive director of ARC, had realized that power to review development proposals along the river would be crucial to his agency's long-term legitimacy.[70]

To this end, in February Sweat convinced the members of the fledgling ARC board to accept a resolution opposing Walling's river bill. Immediately after voting for the resolution, the ARC board passed a second resolution declaring that development along the river represented a cross-jurisdictional issue and therefore fell under the area-plan-review powers the commission had been granted by its founding legislation.[71] Opposing Walling's bill was a strategic move. Without the support of ARC, the bill was immediately buried in a state senate committee, which bought the commission enough time to develop a comprehensive strategy that would bring the Chattahoochee under its control. By the middle of 1972, ARC staff had written a draft plan for the Chattahoochee corridor that would make good on Sweat's desire that ARC have a prominent voice in development decisions along the river.[72]

The ARC board formally adopted the *Chattahoochee Corridor Study* in late 1972. By establishing ARC's authority to review all proposals for development on land within a one-mile-wide buffer along the contested segment of the river north of Atlanta, the plan set the stage for ARC to intervene in the still simmering Fulton zoning controversy.[73] When members of the Fulton County Commission at first resisted ARC's claim of authority to review development proposals, Sweat filed a lawsuit in Fulton Superior Court alleging that the commissioners had violated the state law that required ARC to review all development proposals with area-wide impact.[74] Though ARC lacked explicit zoning review authority, Sweat effectively bluffed the Fulton commissioners into believing that ARC was prepared for a long court battle. Thus, after months of controversy, the Fulton commission finally relented. While the contested project ultimately went forward, the settlement solidified ARC's right to review future project proposals in the river corridor and helped allay fears that the river would be ruined by development.

In its final version, the *Chattahoochee Corridor Study* outlined ARC's jurisdiction as a two-thousand-foot swath on each side of the river for forty-eight miles, from directly below Buford Dam to a point on the far southwestern side of Atlanta. Within this buffer, the plan required all development proposals to be consistent with ARC's regional policies and measured against a system of land vulnerability standards. Seven graduated vulnerability categories, based on distance to the water's edge and flood hazard potential, were outlined and defined land clearing and impervious surface ratios allowable for parcels in the river corridor.[75]

The gracefulness of the plan was perhaps most apparent in the corridor maps that accompanied it. The simplicity of the regulations and the clarity of the map proved a useful tool for exercising control over land development. Showing that mapping something is part of controlling it, the corridor map provided a crisp representation of the spatial relationships among individual parcel boundaries, existing land uses, water and sewer infrastructure, and topography.[76] The map also detailed the vulnerability zones; projected where future development might go, including land that should

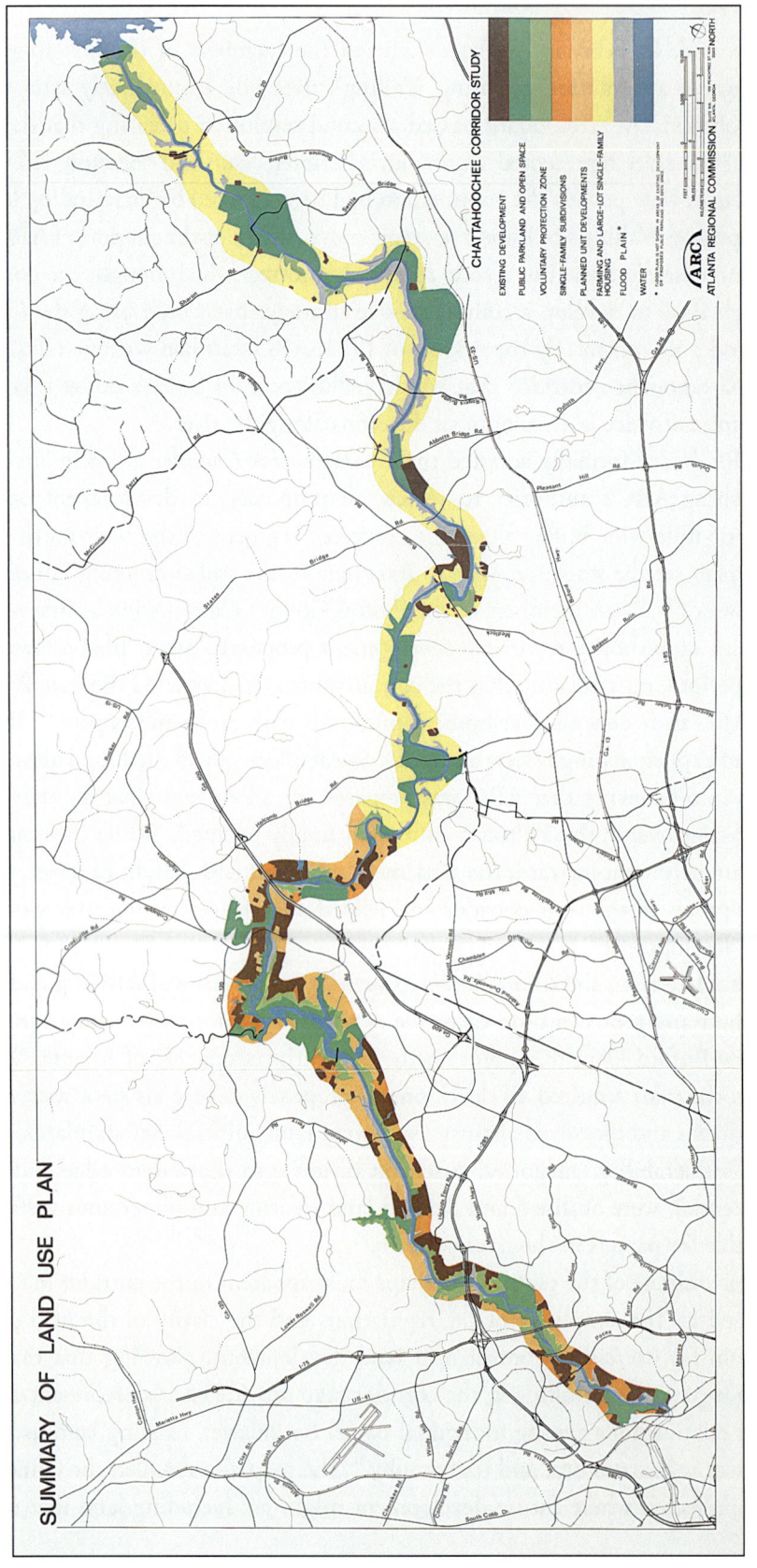

Figure 3.6 "Summary of Land Use Plan," from Atlanta Regional Commission, *Chattahoochee Corridor Study*

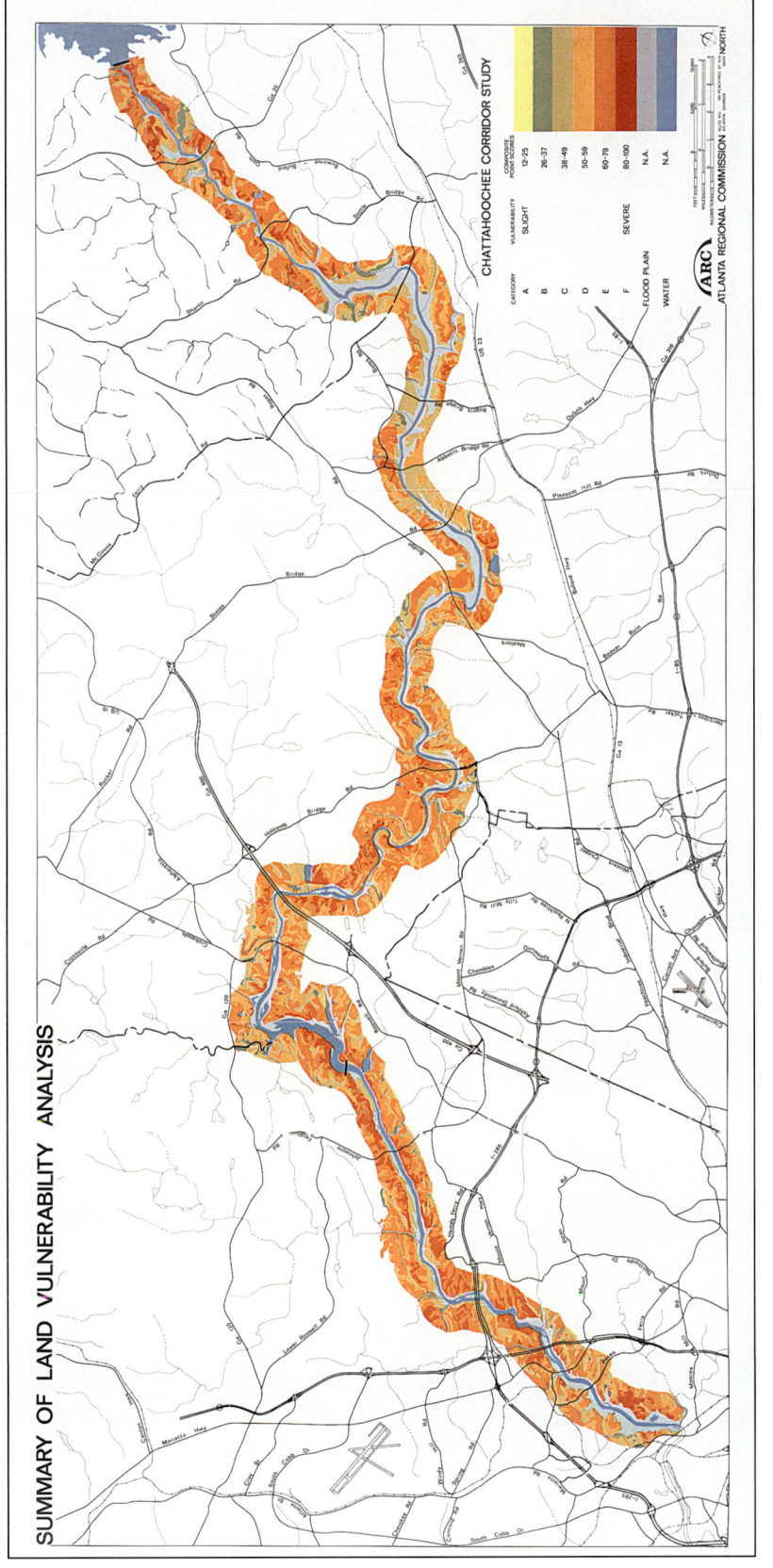

Figure 3.7 "Summary of Land Vulnerability Analysis," from Atlanta Regional Commission, *Chattahoochee Corridor Study*

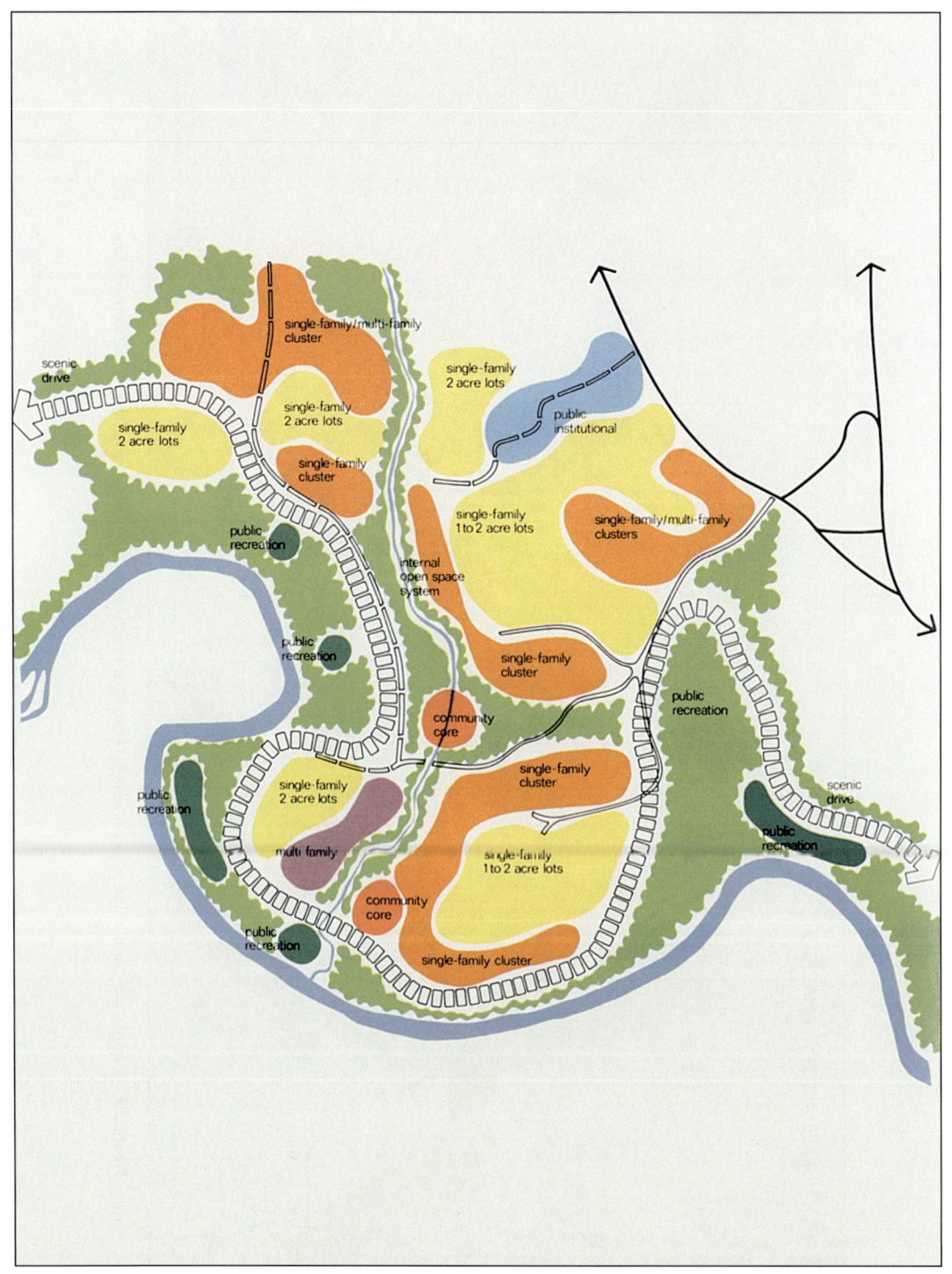

Figure 3.8 Land-use schematic diagram, from Atlanta Regional Commission, *Chattahoochee Corridor Study*

Figure 3.9 Model subdivision design, from Atlanta Regional Commission, *Chattahoochee Corridor Study*

be reserved as permanent green space; and even suggested a model landscape design scheme for future riverside subdivisions.

Among its achievements, the *Chattahoochee Corridor Study* identified several mechanisms that would be used in subsequent efforts to institute regional water management coordination and further legitimized the power of the fledgling ARC. Gathering detailed site and grading plans, calculating land vulnerability ratings, describing

Figure 3.10 "River Corridor Plan" diagram, from Atlanta Regional Commission, *Chattahoochee Corridor Study*

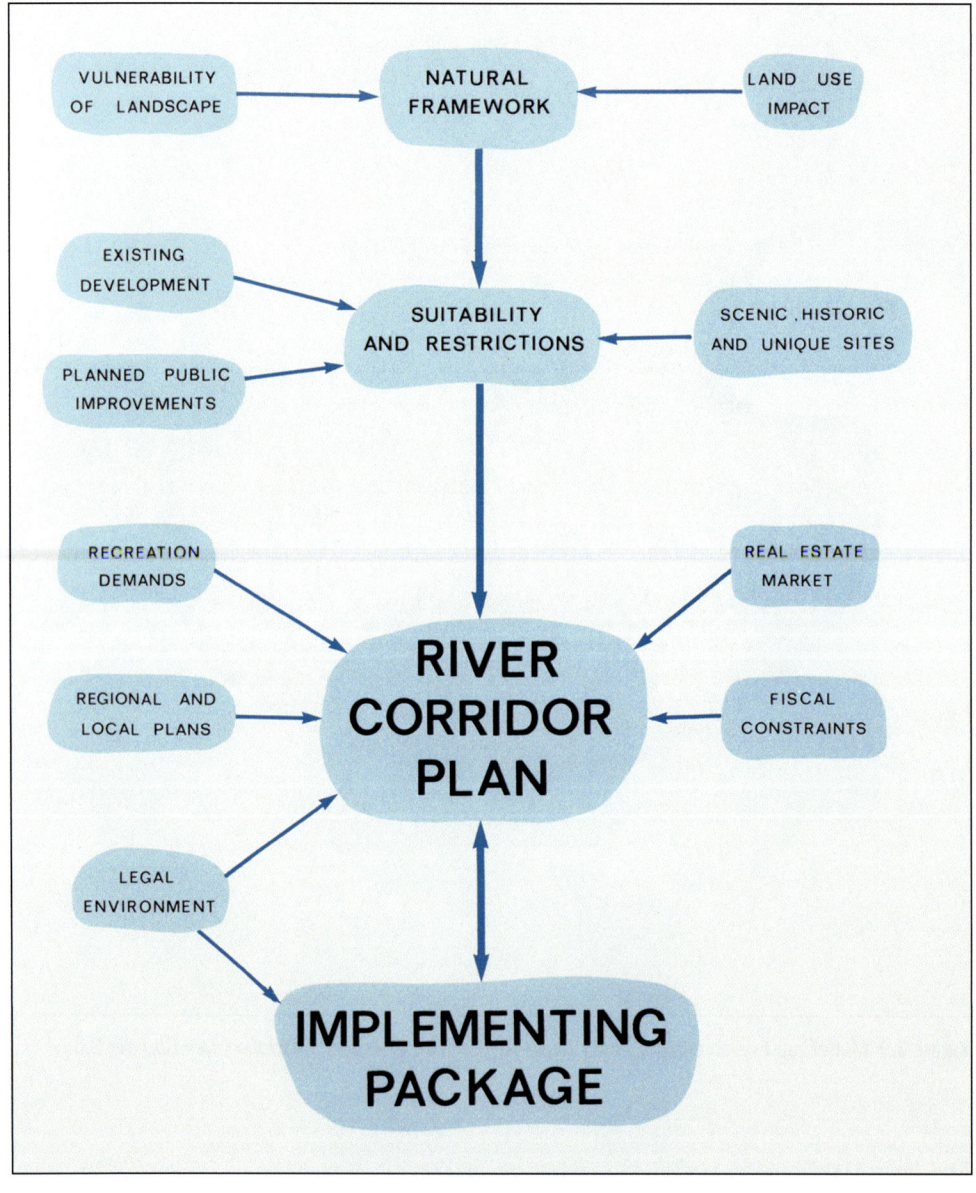

existing vegetation, and establishing erosion control measures all required substantial effort by developers. This opened avenues for informal negotiation and enforcement well before a site plan got to the stage of a formal hearing.[77] Perhaps most importantly, the Chattahoochee plan received significant support from the state, all the way up to the governor's office, which gave ARC the ability to informally pressure reluctant local governments in ways they could hardly afford to ignore.[78]

While ARC was completing the Chattahoochee plan, the bill that would become the Clean Water Act of 1972 was winding its way through Congress. Signed into law in October, one month after the plan was adopted, the Clean Water Act called for significant federal investment in unit process wastewater treatment technology and infrastructure solutions to water pollution in urban areas to improve the nation's befouled waterways.[79] Establishing a formula that allocated to local governments 75 percent of the cost to build new or upgrade existing municipal wastewater treatment facilities, the Clean Water Act was expected to greatly improve the quality of the nation's rivers and streams through a set of increasingly stringent standards. With an initial allocation of $18 billion to be distributed over the course of ten years, the Clean Water Act put substantial financial resources toward a massive rebuilding of the nation's wastewater treatment capacity.[80] Many hoped the Clean Water Act would become the long-desired coherent national water policy.[81]

The Clean Water Act directed two federal agencies, the Army Corps of Engineers and the EPA, to oversee water pollution control. Before the 1970s, wastewater systems had mostly been planned and funded at the local level. The Clean Water Act changed that. Authored during the peak of congressional enthusiasm for direct federal support of state and regional planning activities, the Clean Water Act contained an important clause—Section 208—that made metropolitan cooperation an important part of rebuilding the nation's wastewater infrastructure. Section 208 mandated that all federal agencies involved in the implementation of Clean Water Act projects in metropolitan areas work through established area-wide planning agencies.[82] Though many states had begun to institute new water quality regulations in the 1960s (as Georgia had in 1964), creating statewide pollution commissions and water quality boards, Section 208 required governors to designate regional agencies to develop metropolitan-level wastewater plans for urban regions with populations greater than fifty thousand. Designed to work with the existing A-95 review program, area-wide water plans were intended to establish policy guidelines and a process by which applications from municipal and county governments seeking wastewater infrastructure funding would be reviewed.[83]

Thought to better comprehend local issues than statewide commissions, regional planning agencies were in many ways ideal water planning bodies. They were large enough to span significant portions of urban watersheds, and they could provide valuable perspective on how water demands from different jurisdictions influenced water conditions in the region. They were also information repositories with access to data and expertise to assist in the examination of complex water issues. And because of the existing A-95 review program, regional agencies possessed experience with intergovernmental negotiation around federal funding.[84] Many regional agencies had ongoing transportation planning programs that held important implications for the condition of the natural environment. Adding water issues to their tasks seemed comparatively easy.[85]

As part of developing implementation strategies for the Clean Water Act, the report of the National Water Commission suggested that federal agencies that dealt with water infrastructure, such as the Corps of Engineers, "deemphasize their construction operations and replace them with planning and management functions."[86] Following this recommendation, Congress directed the EPA and the Corps to experiment with region- and watershed-wide water resource planning activities in a few demonstration cases. By redirecting some of the Corps's efforts toward "software (nonconstruction)" roles, Congress hoped that useful precedents would emerge that could be applied broadly.[87] These regional water studies were intended to create connections between wastewater, water supply, and regional context, demonstrating how water systems and watersheds could be planned together. The Corps drew up an initial short list of sites for pilot funding, but Atlanta was not included.[88]

At the urging of a small group of Atlanta-area politicians, Georgia's senior U.S. senator, Herman Talmadge, convened a meeting in September 1971 with several high-ranking officials from the Corps of Engineers and the EPA to "discuss long range planning of water resources for the Chattahoochee River Basin."[89] The following March, Talmadge coerced members of the Senate Public Works Committee into adding Atlanta to the pilot study list. In May the Corps announced that its "Urban Studies Program would provide for developing a comprehensive water resources management plan for Atlanta."[90] By the end of 1972 a congressional appropriation had been secured and the Corps and the EPA, in conjunction with ARC and the state of Georgia, initiated a multiyear water resource planning project in metro Atlanta (officially named the Metropolitan Atlanta Water Resources Management Study but usually referred to as the Atlanta Study).

When ARC released a draft version of the Chattahoochee plan in the summer of 1972, discussions about the upcoming Atlanta Study were just getting under way, but the outlines of a water resource planning strategy had already begun to emerge. After the ARC board approved the Chattahoochee plan in September, its procedural requirements were widely circulated among local governments and the state, though local support lagged. But by the close of 1972 ARC had signed a memorandum of agreement with the Corps of Engineers, the EPA, and the state setting up the Atlanta Study, a step that pressured reluctant local governments to formally adopt the procedural requirements of the Chattahoochee plan.[91] Once the authority of the

Chattahoochee Corridor Study had been established, ARC could leverage its power over regional water management. Over the following nine years, ARC would work under the umbrella of the Atlanta Study to manage conflict over the disputed northern segments of the Chattahoochee River and to determine what purpose Lake Lanier should serve in the long-term development of the ACF system.[92] Together, the *Chattahoochee Corridor Study* and the Atlanta Study helped ARC and its political allies push legislation through the General Assembly granting metro Atlanta politicians even more far-reaching power over the river's fate.[93]

At ARC's urging, a revised version of state senator Walling's 1972 river protection bill was introduced early in the 1973 session of the General Assembly. The new bill, cosponsored by Dekalb County senators Elliott Levitas and Paul Coverdell, would become the Metropolitan River Protection Act. With strong support from ARC and Governor Carter, the bill faced scant opposition and passed quickly through the legislature and to the governor's desk.[94] As part of the bargain that had been struck when ARC was created in 1971, local control of zoning decisions remained paramount to legislators from virtually every county in the state. Many believed that giving a regional body like ARC zoning review power was the first step in a larger usurpation of zoning power by the state. Beholden to its constituents, and needing to keep rural legislators at bay, the ARC board resisted including zoning review authority as part of the river protection bill.[95]

Intended to "provide a flexible and practical method whereby political subdivisions in certain metropolitan areas may utilize the police power of the State consistently and in accordance with a comprehensive plan," the Metropolitan River Protection Act further codified ARC's role in regional water management.[96] Though it left zoning review on the table, in many ways the Metropolitan River Protection Act could be seen as "Georgia's first substantive piece of land-use legislation," in terms of governing development in the critical Chattahoochee corridor.[97] The act made into state law the requirement that governments adjacent to the river submit all proposals for development on parcels lying partly or completely within the corridor to ARC for review against the regional policies set forth in the Chattahoochee plan.[98] During the review, local government staff and typically the applicants themselves were encouraged to meet with ARC staff to discuss and revise the proposal before final action was taken. For a local governing authority to issue a certificate allowing land-disturbing activities, a proposal had to be found consistent with the river corridor plan (by vote of a simple majority of the ARC board) or else it was revised to meet stipulations set forth by ARC staff review (and then affirmatively voted by the board). Under the act, ARC's recommendations could be overridden only by a majority vote of the full membership of the local governing council (a quorum vote was not enough). Though the act considerably broadened ARC's role in regional water management and underscored the importance of the *Chattahoochee Corridor Study*, it preserved local zoning power and sharply limited the use of tools for shaping the physical form of land development.

Almost before the ink dried on the Metropolitan River Protection Act, reports emerged alleging lapses in its administration. In late 1973 a General Assembly investigative committee suggested that ambiguity in the new legislation would make evaluating development proposals for compliance difficult and argued that ARC lacked the staff to detect violations of the act. With the Clean Water Act demanding dramatic improvements to the quality of the state's surface waters, especially the section of the Chattahoochee in metro Atlanta, the investigative committee concluded in its report that the protection act as written would prove insufficient to the task of cleaning up the river.[99]

Compounding this problem was the fact that the state had yet to designate ARC as Atlanta's Section 208 wastewater planning agency, a necessary step for the region to begin receiving Clean Water Act funding for wastewater treatment infrastructure. But even before ARC could get its application for Section 208 funds together, Georgia's ranking water resource administrator had already begun complaining to the EPA that the requirements of the Clean Water Act "produced confusion and frustration for state administrators and denied any administrative flexibility for solving local and state problems."[100]

In December 1973, ARC finally submitted its initial request for financial support from the EPA to prepare its Section 208 regional wastewater plan. The EPA promptly rejected the request. In a letter to ARC's executive director, the Atlanta-based EPA regional administrator identified three reasons for denying the commission's request for 208 funds: overlap between the Section 208 requirements and the ongoing Atlanta Study; no official designation of Atlanta by the governor as a 208 area; and ARC's enabling legislation not meeting Section 208 requirements that local governments relinquish their right to apply directly to the EPA for wastewater infrastructure funds.[101]

Two months after being rebuffed, ARC began addressing the problems the EPA administrator had identified. The chairman of ARC's board submitted a formal request to Governor Carter to identify metropolitan Atlanta as an area "with substantial water quality control problems," to designate the boundaries of the area to "coincide with ARC's planning area," and to "designate ARC as the single representative organization . . . capable of developing effective areawide waste treatment management plans." He noted that Section 208 funds were needed because "a major portion of ARC's 1974 work program proposed for EPA joint funding provides essential input to the [Atlanta Study] which is not duplicated by the study."[102]

But the ARC chairman also urged Carter to try to sidestep the third requirement the regional administrator imposed by making the 208 designation so as to allow the region's local governments to avoid having to agree in advance that "a single management agency" would be the "best approach to plan implementation."[103] After consulting with the EPA administration in Washington, the director of the Georgia Department of Natural Resources advised Carter that he could identify Section 208 boundaries but "non-designate" those areas until the affected local governments "understand and accept" the requirements that designation would impose. This loophole would still allow Carter to "maintain [the] option" to redesignate 208 areas in the future.[104] When Carter notified the EPA secretary, Russell Train, that he had identified seven areas in the state as "eligible 208 planning areas," including ARC's jurisdiction, he noted that he had decided "to non-designate" the areas for the time being because of his disagreement with the regional director's stipulation that local governments must agree to adhere to the plans instituted by area-wide agencies. He justified his action by claiming that "only part of the Section 208 regulations have been promulgated by EPA" and thus the regional director's stipulations should not be mandatory.[105] As a result of Carter's complaint, the secretary allowed ARC to negotiate an agreement with the regional EPA office to waive the requirement that local governments relinquish their right to apply directly for federal money. With the agreement in place, Carter designated ARC as the official Section 208 planning agency for Atlanta in late 1974. The commission moved to begin the Section 208 planning process.

With the opening gavel of the 1975 General Assembly only a few weeks away, ARC used its status as the Section 208 planning agency to address some of the perceived weaknesses of the existing laws protecting the Chattahoochee. To accomplish this, the ARC board put its weight behind two bills that would be introduced at the beginning of the new legislative session. One was a bill sponsored by Senator Levitas to create a comprehensive erosion and sedimentation policy for the entire state.[106] The second was a bill amending the Metropolitan River Protection Act. With the rezoning controversy in Fulton County still fresh in the minds of many legislators, prospects for the new bills were strong going into the session, and momentum generated by the *Chattahoochee Corridor Study*, the Atlanta Study, and the Clean Water Act helped the bills pass both chambers of the Georgia legislature by a comfortable margin. The new governor, George Busbee, signed the bills into law in the spring of 1975.[107]

The Georgia Erosion and Sedimentation Act mandated "a statewide comprehensive soil erosion and sediment control program" that would "protect land, water, air and other resources of the State."[108] The new act required the governing authorities of every county and municipality in the state to adopt "a comprehensive ordinance establishing the procedures governing land-disturbing activities which are conducted within their respective boundaries."[109] Thereafter, any property owner proposing land-disturbing activities would be required to secure a permit from the local governing body, which in turn would submit the permit application to the district office of the state's soil conservation service for review.[110] The strengthened Metropolitan River Protection Act gave additional authority to ARC's development review

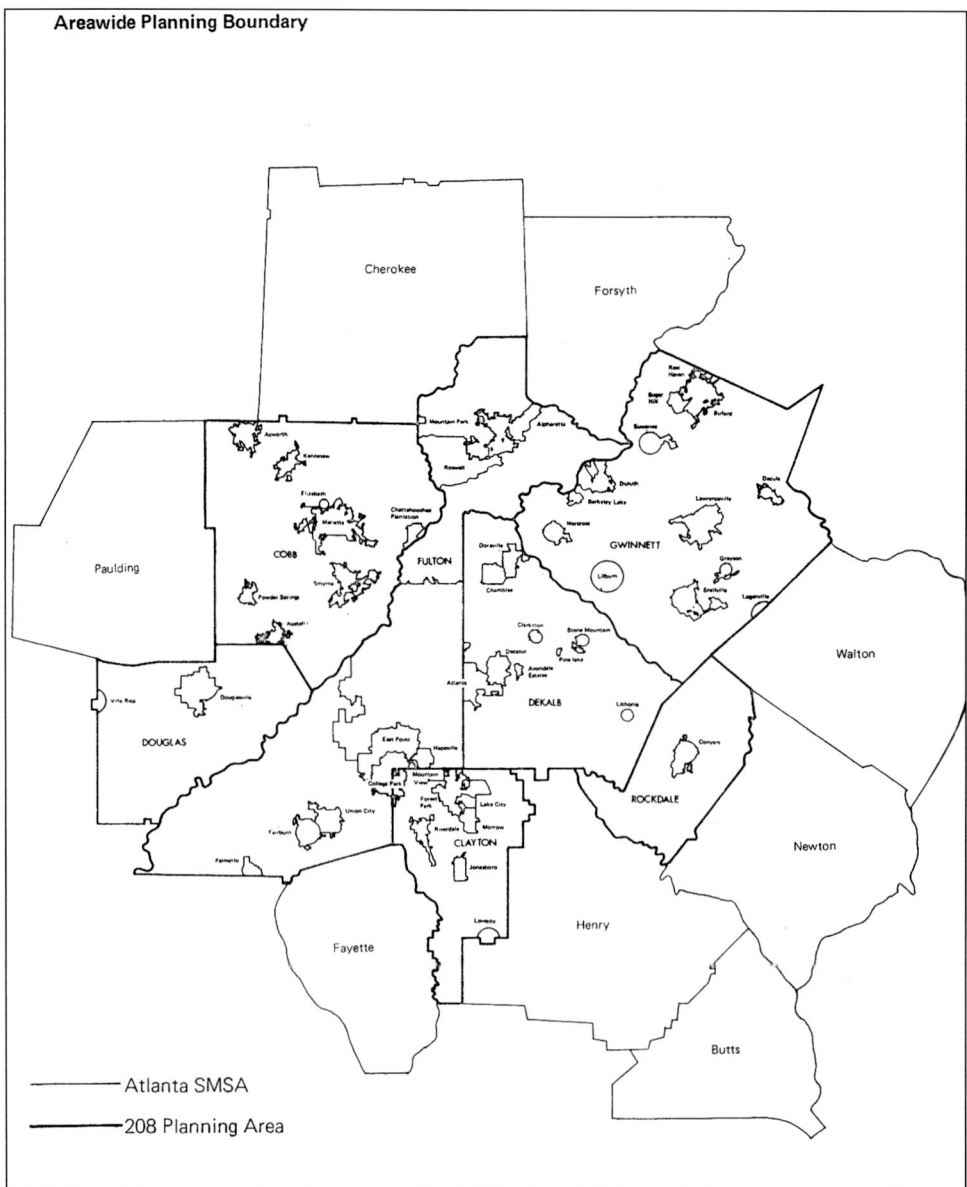

Figure 3.11 "208 Planning Area," from Atlanta Regional Commission, *Atlanta Region Areawide Wastewater Management Plan*, October 1978, Atlanta Regional Commission Collection, Kenan Research Center, Atlanta History Center

process by making willful noncompliance by local governments considerably more difficult.[111]

The new laws helped forge a closer relationship between ARC and some of the state's most powerful politicians. They also, like the policies preceding them, sought to encourage more negotiation between stakeholders rather than to ban development practices that damaged the state's surface waters. Though the legislature's decision to require local erosion control ordinances and permits indicated an ongoing change in the perception of water management, this shift could as much be traced back to changes in federal law as it could to genuine support for water resource management. While ARC's influence had clearly grown, the commission still operated under constraints. Though senators like Levitas and Walling realized that more centralized control over surface water would improve state water quality, their support for tougher regulations was tempered by the political realities of the state.

Even with the limited reach of Georgia's water protection laws, by the middle of the 1970s the local media had begun reporting positive changes in the quality of northern Georgia's lakes and rivers, changes that were often attributed to the combined efforts of ARC and the state.[112] In March 1974 the *Atlanta Journal-Constitution* reported that "federal environmental experts predict that antipollution measures currently in operation or under construction . . . will adequately free streams and rivers from pollution [by] the mid-1980s."[113] Despite anticipated improvements in the water quality of the northern stretch of the Chattahoochee, pollution remained a significant problem for many of the region's smaller tributaries and especially for communities downstream of Atlanta. In late 1975, for example, the *Atlanta Constitution* reported that in the middle of the previous summer up to 90 percent of the water that flowed down the South River, which drains portions of Atlanta and Dekalb County and is a major a tributary of the Ocmulgee River, was post-treatment plant effluent.[114]

As the designated Section 208 wastewater management agency for metropolitan Atlanta, ARC had to develop a regional wastewater plan that demonstrated compatibility between its regional wastewater policies, the local plans of constituent governments, and Clean Water Act requirements.[115] Because of the exception the EPA granted to ARC's Section 208 status, the regional wastewater plan also had to respect existing local plans. To write a plan within these constraints, ARC staff used an approach that might best be described as bottom up. Constructed by cherry-picking policies from a cross section of existing local plans, the regional wastewater plan was essentially an amalgam of local policies, most of which relied on technological fixes rather than behavioral changes or controlling land development. The policies included updating infrastructure to improve wastewater treatment, expanding the area available for land-based filtering of wastewater, consolidating smaller and older treatment facilities, increasing cooperation among area governments, and expanding sewer service areas.[116]

At the same time, ARC staff also developed a regional water supply plan, meant to be a companion to the wastewater plan. Since water supply was outside the purview of the agreement that hamstrung the Section 208 plan, the commission took a more top-down approach that emphasized behavior modification and development restriction. The water supply plan included exhaustive documentation of existing water sources, projections of future demand, and calculations of the amount and potential sources of water needed to sustain the region's anticipated growth. Recommendations included reducing water consumption through conservation, improving connections between supply systems (redundancy), exploring new groundwater sources, expanding off-stream storage capacity, and limiting land development near critical water supplies.

In 1976 ARC published the pair of plans. The *Water Supply Plan for the Atlanta Region* and the *Atlanta Region Areawide Wastewater Management Plan* described a significantly expanded role for ARC in region-wide water resource planning activities, in hopes of confronting the way that "for so long [Georgia's leaders] thought of water as being unlimited, and now [they] find it's not."[117] The plans reiterated an idea ARMPC had advanced back in 1968: since waste and supply share a small source in Atlanta—the Chattahoochee River system—waste and supply systems should be planned together. "That the problems are most complex is evident. That they are incapable of solution without the concerted action of many governments is equally obvious," was

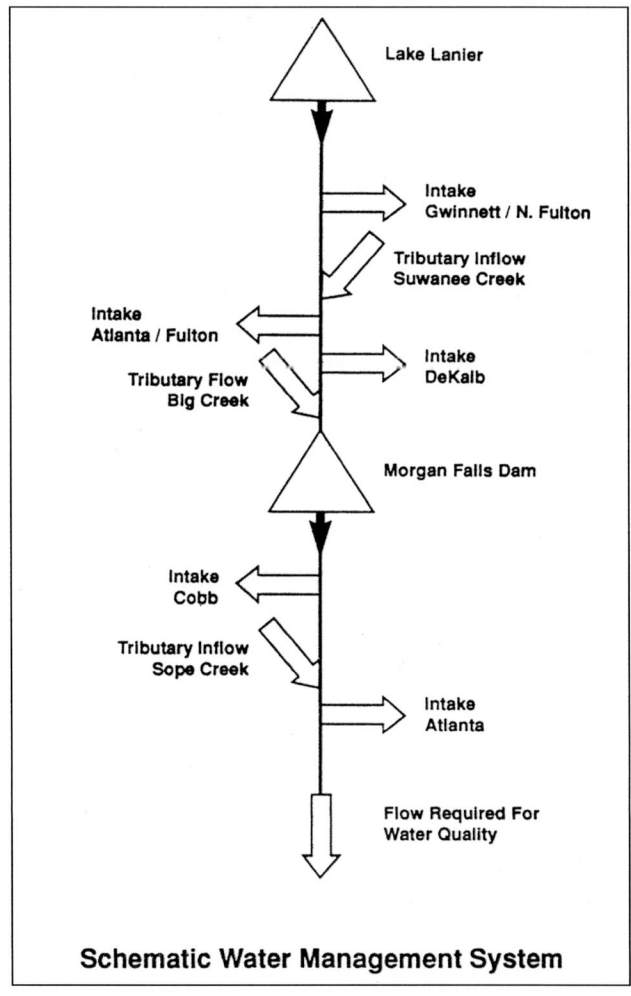

Figure 3.12 "Schematic Water Management System," from Atlanta Regional Commission, *Atlanta Region Areawide Water Supply Management Plan*

the sentiment of the 1968 ARMPC report that also coursed through ARC's plans.[118] Using data provided by the Atlanta Study, the two plans cataloged a wide range of issues related to water resources, many of which previously had been identified but not thoroughly documented, described, and juxtaposed, and concluded that improved regional cooperation was critical to Atlanta's future.

In late 1976 the Georgia Department of Natural Resources and ARC reached an agreement that the state would "concur" with the Section 208 regional wastewater plan. This designation "would not be construed to foreclose the possibility of amending the plan" but did mean that the state would begin issuing water pollution permits and certifying "grant applications to the Environmental Protection Agency that are consistent with the Plan," opening the Clean Water Act funding pipeline to metro governments.[119]

The water management plans spurred additional state action to control water withdrawals, however. In light of the "serious problems in the metro area" related to the state's "dwindling" supply of surface water and the recent decision by the Department of Natural Resources to accept Atlanta's new regional wastewater plan as the basis for issuing pollution permits, a bill was introduced in the 1977 General Assembly that would become the Georgia Surface Water Management Act. Though it faced significant opposition from legislators "from the counties that operate their own water authorities" and from rural politicians who perceived the bill as a kind of "statewide zoning," the bill was strongly supported by Governor Busbee.[120] Though most major industries and municipal authorities were swept up in the legislation, the bill's framers overcame resistance by including language that allowed each withdrawal permit to be negotiated on a case-by-case basis, giving water users the power to bargain with the state's Environmental Protection Division administrators over the amount of water they would be allowed to withdraw. In its final form, the act established the state's authority over all withdrawals from surface waters exceeding one hundred thousand gallons per day. As a corollary to the wastewater permitting process, the act required large water users to apply for withdrawal permits from the Environmental Protection Division. The law gave Environmental Protection Division administrators the authority to deny an application for new or increased withdrawals if they determined that a water source was oversubscribed.[121] While ARC's 1976 regional water supply plan had received no formal state certification, Environmental Protection Division administrators entered an agreement with ARC acknowledging their plans "to use the water supply plan as the basis for issuing the surface water permits" under the Surface Water Allocation policy established by the Surface Water Management Act.[122]

A New National Recreation Area

The final piece of the regulatory puzzle surrounding the northern Chattahoochee would come in 1978, two years after Jimmy Carter moved into the White House.

Through his involvement in the controversy surrounding riverside rezonings as governor in the early 1970s, Carter appreciated the importance of managing the river, and he understood the Chattahoochee's importance for Atlanta's long-term water supply. Achieving permanent protection for the remaining undeveloped parcels of land along the river had been a goal for many of Atlanta's environmental organizations. Over the years, joint local-state-federal efforts to set aside selected parcels of land along the river for permanent protection from development had met with piecemeal success, but the prospect of creating a large, contiguous natural area had seemed out of reach.[123]

In late 1972 a grant from the National Park Service's Land and Water Conservation Fund allowed the Georgia Bureau of Outdoor Recreation to acquire a 377-acre parcel along the river to establish the Chattahoochee Palisades State Park. In January 1973 at the urging of Governor Carter and the Georgia Department of Natural Resources, Senator Sam Nunn (D-GA) introduced legislation in Congress that would provide $60 million for the purchase of land for a new national park along the upper Chattahoochee, covering the same area as ARC's *Chattahoochee Corridor Study*, north of Atlanta and south of Buford Dam. While a national park was popular with the public, local politicians in areas along the river corridor could be expected to resist relinquishing so much prime developable land. Many perceived federal ownership as an unwelcome intrusion. ARC's executive director Sweat protested directly to Nunn that introducing federal legislation "could have detrimental effects on the momentum and spirit of cooperation" that ARC had struggled to build with land owners and developers.[124] Asserting that the *Chattahoochee Corridor Study* "represents the optimal balance of developed land and park land along the river, and that the developers and land owners feel confident with the plan," Sweat's appeal to Nunn revealed the delicate balancing act ARC faced: trying to maintain legitimacy with its local constituents by avoiding the appearance of putting any real restrictions on development while relying on state and federal support for its livelihood.[125] After additional consultation with the governor, Nunn agreed to withdraw the bill.

In mid-1973, shortly after Carter signed the Metropolitan River Protection Act into law, the Georgia Power Co. donated another 162 acres of river land to Fulton County to expand the palisades park. The county leveraged Georgia Power's gift to win another grant from the Land and Water Conservation Fund to purchase 15 additional acres of land to add to the park. Later that year, the state allocated $500,000 in matching funds to secure another grant from the Land and Water Conservation Fund to purchase 66 acres to establish the Island Ford Natural Area, a point in the Chattahoochee corridor near one of the largest islands in the river. In September 1973 the state again came up with a match for Land and Water Conservation funds to acquire land to develop a new trout hatchery just south of Buford Dam. In March 1974 a grant from the Land and Water Conservation Fund was combined with a one-time grant from ARC to implement the fish hatchery plan.[126]

Coupled with ongoing federal concern with urban watershed pollution problems, support from a variety of local river advocacy groups, and Jimmy Carter's 1976 presidential election victory, the prospects for a more comprehensive, federally funded effort to protect the Chattahoochee corridor, in the form of a new national recreation area, were running high. The ARC board had finally embraced the idea, despite a vocal minority of suburban politicians remaining opposed to a large federal park in Atlanta's suburbs. In late 1976 Andrew Young (D-GA), representing Georgia's Fifth Congressional District, moved into the fray by introducing a bill in the House of Representatives to create a long, spindly national recreation area that traced the Chattahoochee River from Buford Dam to Atlanta. The federally protected area would be more or less coterminous with the forty-eight-mile stretch of river governed by the *Chattahoochee Corridor Study* and the Metropolitan River Protection Act.

Young's bill met immediate resistance in the House from one of his fellow Georgia delegation members, Larry McDonald, a Republican who represented a wealthy corner of Cobb County that coveted land along the river for private development. Sticking by his conservative base, McDonald scuttled the river protection bill in the House Rules Committee. Known for his extreme antigovernment positions, McDonald opposed Young's bill in prepared testimony submitted to the House Rules Committee: "Homeowners along the river will be deprived of the value of their land." The *Atlanta Constitution* noted that McDonald also had previously "objected to the cost of the river park," asserted that the "state, not the federal government, should pay for it," and declared "that he does not believe the US Constitution provides for federal ownership of park land." The refusal of the chairman of the House Rules Committee to call to quorum members whose votes were needed to put the bill on the House calendar effectively buried Young's bill for the 1976 session. Young claimed that many of the rules committee members "did not object to the Chattahoochee bill" and that he remained "confident" about the bill's future, hoping that it would be the "first bill signed by President Jimmy Carter."[127]

Indeed, after Young had left the House for an ambassadorship, Elliott Levitas, the new Fifth District representative, reintroduced the Chattahoochee recreation bill in early 1978. With President Carter vocally supporting the legislation, both chambers passed the resolution, and the president signed it into law on August 15. The new Chattahoochee River National Recreation Area created a federally protected, nine-thousand-acre preservation area that snaked right through the heart of Atlanta's northern suburbs.[128]

Settling Up: The Final Draft of the Atlanta Study

Two years later, in August 1980, the draft final report of the Metropolitan Atlanta Water Resources Management Study was circulated among metro-area politicians and planners. The report presented three scenarios (named, simply, Plans A, B, and C) for managing Atlanta's water resources into the future. Plan A called for the construction of a reregulation dam six miles downstream from Buford Dam. While a second dam would flood part of the newly created Chattahoochee National Recreation Area, it would improve flow for the benefit of Atlanta's water supply and its downstream neighbors. Plan B suggested reallocating some of Lake Lanier's storage capacity for municipal water supply. Plan C would reallocate a smaller portion of Lanier's storage capacity but also dredge Bull Sluice Lake, a small impoundment dating from the early twentieth century that had silted up, to add on stream storage capacity. Not surprisingly, each scenario included a set of financial, environmental, and administrative costs to the state, the federal government, and downstream communities, and each included significant benefits for Atlanta's water supply.[129]

In agreement with Atlanta's political leaders, the key public agencies participating in the Atlanta Study—the Corps of Engineers, the EPA, ARC, and the Department of Natural Resources—settled on Plan A. But beginning with two public hearings in early September, the proposal to construct a reregulation dam immediately became the "focus of a turbulent public debate." Citizens and local environmental groups attending the hearings charged that the "study was done by an agency whose priority is building dams," that the "study reflects a serious bias toward structural solutions," and that it "reflects a political as opposed to objective solution."[130] Other groups noted that the EPA's support of a reregulation dam "appears to be completely opposite of our understanding of EPA's role in protecting the environment."[131] The owner of a trout fishing lake in the vicinity of the reregulation dam complained that the dam was based on "deliberately falsified costs and benefits" and would have a "disastrous effect on the present recreational use of the Chattahoochee River."[132] Even the Florida Department of Environmental Regulation chimed in, observing, "We do not believe that the report adequately serves Florida's interests or the interests of regional water resource management."[133]

Perhaps most significantly, the U.S. Department of the Interior (DOI), the National Park Service, and the Fish and Wildlife Service sharply questioned the conclusions of the study. Evaluating the report, the regional Fish and Wildlife Service administrator pointed out that while "mitigation is a crucial factor in determining project effects on fish and wildlife values," in the draft final report "mitigation receives only limited mention." Without a mitigation plan, the Fish and Wildlife Service objected to the "finalization of the study report in its present form."[134] The DOI complained that the scenarios outlined in the draft final report had the potential for "seriously impacting the Chattahoochee River National Recreation Area" but that Interior agencies have "had little opportunity to participate in [the] planning study," and thus the "document does not contain sufficient information to assess the impact . . . on our program areas of interest." Absent better coordination and more complete data, the DOI refused to evaluate the scenarios presented in the draft report. Noting that "it makes little sense to place two Federal agencies in an adversarial relationship because of the lack of coordination and problem resolution," the DOI "strongly recommended [the study authors] take positive steps to consult with and involve appropriate staff of the National Park Service and the Fish and Wildlife Service in preparing the final study document."[135]

Atlanta's prodevelopment political establishment quickly lined up supporters to speak out in favor of the reregulation dam scenario. The outpouring was overwhelming. In admitting that the dam "will cause environmental problems during construction/initial operation," the regional director of the EPA suggested that these problems should be understood as simply a "*change* in environmental conditions" and not unfairly construed as negative.[136] The Southeastern Power Administration noted "the additional power costs associated with the reregulator" but nevertheless concluded "that the proposed Plan A best meets all the overall objectives of water supply, flood control, recreation, and power in an environmentally acceptable manner."[137] Suggesting that "the Chattahoochee National Recreation Act was passed with the clear intent that the necessity may occur to construct a re-regulation facility" and that "this alternative is the most feasible," Ed Jenkins (D-GA), representing the Ninth Congressional District, reassured the regional Corps of Engineers director of his support for the conclusions of the Atlanta Study.[138]

Forming a unified front, a contingent of the most powerful politicians from metro Atlanta offered strong support for the reregulation dam scenario. In a letter to the Corps of Engineers signed by the governor, mayor of Atlanta, and county commission chairmen of Cobb and Gwinnett Counties, the elected officials contended that "this study of the need for a reliable water source was under way prior to the establishment of the [Chattahoochee] park," and thus the "detrimental impact of a critical water shortage . . . on the social and economic welfare of the Atlanta area . . . makes it . . . essential that we move forward at this time with a plan."[139] Regional planning and water management agencies, most importantly ARC, all expressed "preference for the re-regulation dam alternative."[140] The president of Georgia's main electric utility, Georgia Power, wrote in support of the reregulation dam because it "would increase the peaking power of Buford Dam" and threatened that "this additional peaking power would otherwise have to be provided by peaking plants using nonrenewable resources such as coal, gas, or oil."[141] Even the Georgia Department of Natural Resources, ostensibly responsible for protecting the state's environmental resources, "concur[ed] with the preferred alternative of the re-regulation dam," expressing concern only that "additional evaluations will be made and/or clarification provided to resolve concerns expressed by the State related to the trout hatchery and the trout fishery," an investment the state had only recently made.[142]

However little they seemed to matter, public comments were divided over the new-dam option. Residents around Lake Lanier tended to support the dam, "warn[ing] against adoption of any of the Corps' proposals that would hurt boating and fishing in Lake Lanier by tampering with the water level."[143] Comments from most Atlanta-area residents, however, strongly opposed the reregulation dam but split over the other alternatives, with many advocating the outright rejection of all three plans.[144]

Pushing forward with apparently little regard for the controversy the draft final report had generated, in February 1981 the Corps of Engineers released the final Atlanta Study report.[145] Beyond being an encyclopedia of local water issues, the report endorsed the preference of Atlanta's political leadership and recommended building a reregulation dam six miles downstream of the existing Buford Dam. The report also made several other suggestions related to managing the region's available water resources. The most important was that "recreation, water supply, and water quality control be acknowledged as full project purposes at Lake Lanier . . . and that all of these purposes be fully considered in future decisions affecting the use or operation of Lake Lanier." This reading of Lanier's originally legislated purpose was at odds with many of Atlanta's downstream neighbors. Intended to provide oversight until a long-range plan could be developed, the report also suggested a new "short-term operational plan for the Lake Lanier/Chattahoochee River system" that would "include raising the normal pool of Lake Lanier one foot and increasing offpeak releases from Buford Dam."[146] Less controversial suggestions included more carefully regulating the Chattahoochee's flow to provide a reliable water supply for the jurisdictions in four counties immediately south of metro Atlanta and studying the feasibility of building new impoundments on several smaller rivers in northern Georgia.[147] The report concluded that the Chattahoochee-Lanier complex "should continue to be a major water supply source, with additional smaller local sources maintained or developed where feasible" and should meet Atlanta's water demands until 1990 or even 2000 and perhaps beyond.[148]

Despite broad support from Atlanta's politicians, the Corps of Engineers, the EPA, ARC, Georgia Power, and various state agencies, the fate of the reregulation dam hinged on the willingness of Congress to allocate nearly $20 million to fund its design and construction. The region's most convincing political voices descended on Congress to lobby on behalf of the project. In testimony before the U.S. House Subcommittee on Water Resources in July 1982, Michael Lomax, chairman of the Fulton County Commission, ARC board member, and rising political star, described the "wide range of support" among local organizations for the conclusions of the Atlanta Study report. Arguing somewhat disingenuously that there are "no apparent adverse environmental impacts of [the reregulation dam] that cannot be minimized, avoided or mitigated," Lomax "urge[d] Congress to include authorization of the re-regulation dam in the 1984 Federal budget."[149] Coming amid a recession, Lomax's testimony was not enough to overcome the mood in Congress and the Reagan administration's hostility toward costly and controversial infrastructure projects.

In early August, Rep. Bo Ginn (D-GA), from the First Congressional District, wrote to Lomax that because of "the controversy surrounding this particular project" and because the Reagan administration remained "strongly opposed to the authorization of any new water resource projects," he "did not believe [the reregulation dam] will be approved this year."[150] Congress finally authorized a reregulation dam in 1986 as part of the Water Resources Development Act, but no funding was allocated. Ultimately, the dam ended up idled by its cost and the political difficulty of impounding a major urban river in the late twentieth century.[151]

Recommendations aside, the publication of the Atlanta Study report represented the output of fifteen years of water resource planning. Though the study had convened various stakeholders around the issue of water management, supported a large-scale data-gathering effort, and spawned multiple spin-off studies, plans, and policies, it had done little more than reinforce the existing presumption among metro Atlanta's elected officials that growth should not be imperiled by water supply restrictions.[152] Despite its promise to develop a rational plan for cleaning up the river and ensuring its water could be shared by everyone with a fair claim, the study and all the planning that had gone into it had simply crystallized the position of Atlanta politicians: ensuring sufficient water supply and wastewater capacity to realize a grandiose vision for metropolitan Atlanta, regardless of environmental cost.

A Continuing Thirst

By the middle of the 1980s, the Corps of Engineers, ARC, and the state of Georgia had entered into an agreement for forecasting short- and long-term water demand in the Atlanta metropolitan area. As part of the Atlanta Study, ARC had developed a short-term-demand model to "calculate the minimum weekend and weekday releases from Buford Dam . . . [to maintain] water supply and water quality." Short-term projections of demand would be transmitted every week directly from ARC to the Corps of Engineers, which would use the projections to release enough water from Lake Lanier to maintain flow in the Chattahoochee to meet Atlanta's water needs.[153] The agreement also permitted ARC's forecasts of population growth and water demand to continue to be used to guide the state in issuing water withdrawal and waste discharge permits on the Chattahoochee between Buford Dam and Atlanta.[154] At the same time, the Corps of Engineers, again in conjunction with ARC, the EPA, and the state, permitted the thirsty Gwinnett County Water Authority to lay intakes directly into Lake Lanier.[155]

With this agreement in place, politicians from metro Atlanta, working hand in hand with state and federal agencies, had managed to implement a set of policies that allowed them to effectively take over the Chattahoochee River and by extension the entire ACF system. Since securing water supply was a critical factor in the region's growth, managing this agreement became an important part of ARC's work. In an interview in the late 1990s, Dan Sweat reflected on ARC's history, remarking, "The one thing I take the most pride in is the *Chattahoochee Corridor Study*. We sort of rolled the dice. . . . The developers had discovered [the river]. It was and still is our water resource . . . and we felt we had to move fast to do something or we would lose the Chattahoochee River, because it was just too ripe for development."[156]

By virtue of its wedge position between federal regulations, state laws, and local politics and its consistent level of federal and state support, ARC maintained wide influence over how Atlanta's regional water management scheme unfolded in the 1970s and 1980s. As the agency representing the aspirations of metro Atlanta's political leaders, ARC worked closely with the regional offices of the EPA and the Corps of Engineers to prepare plans that projected growth and largely disregarded the physical limits of Atlanta's primary water supply source and the needs of downstream neighbors. These plans reshaped Georgia's water laws, putting Atlanta's desire for water above pollution, conservation, or fair use. Increasing withdrawals from the lake and river met Atlanta's water demand, but the volume of wastewater dumped back into the river continued to degrade the quality and quantity of water flowing to cities and counties downstream.[157]

Regulating the river's flow did not, however, address the problem of overreliance on the Chattahoochee. Though a few small reservoirs were constructed to help stabilize water supply in counties in the far southern reaches of the region, Atlanta's big northern suburbs remained largely chained to the Chattahoochee and Lake Lanier. On more than one occasion during the late 1980s, the Corps of Engineers increased permitted withdrawals directly from Lake Lanier so that local water authorities could continue to grow their supply.[158] Those decisions conflicted with a strict release schedule needed to ensure that downstream flow would meet the needs of other water users that depended on the river to feed their intakes, not to mention the needs of the river's rich aquatic life.[159]

Throughout the 1970s and 1980s, metro Atlanta added people and jobs at a furious pace.[160] Water use by new faucets far outstripped water savings from better fixtures or less leaky pipes. Water management planning in the wake of the Clean Water Act became a technically complex endeavor that community-based groups could not easily control. Activists were forced to carefully pick their battles, homing in on only those issues that were visible, resonant, and close to home. Rainfall varied from year to year, but there was no significant source of groundwater authorities could turn to in a pinch.

Explanations of how the Chattahoochee with its limited flow could accommodate so much demand include technology, politics, and luck. Advances in infrastructure design helped improve the efficiency of water and wastewater systems. New water pipes suffered fewer leaks and less frequent breeches. Advances in water treatment technologies helped clean up point-source discharges. New building standards at the local, state, and national levels required lower-flow water fixtures, and federal laws governing the manufacture of common water-using appliances stipulated greater efficiency.[161] This helped hold per capita water usage in the region relatively stable, even as overall demand grew.[162] The activities of citizen groups and conservation organizations that sprang up to support preserving different uses of the river can also be credited with influencing how the Chattahoochee was managed. The efforts of these groups helped publicize pollution issues facing the river and draw public attention to the river as a precious amenity.[163] Finally, luck helped northern Georgia avoid a multiyear, extended drought that would have reduced water flow in the Chattahoochee to a trickle, drained Lake Lanier, and turned downstream surface waters into pure effluent.

Water resource engineers, climatologists, and economists recognized the fragility of Atlanta's water supply and the potential environmental and economic devastation an extended drought would bring.[164] Plans for networks of new reservoirs were laid, but few of the dams were built.[165] Despite periodic seasonal droughts, rainfall always seemed to rebound. While individual drought events tested the limits of the region's water supply, public memory proved incredibly short. Major policy changes that would sharply curb water-hungry development never saw the light of day.[166]

Nevertheless, as a result of efforts in the 1970s, by the mid-1980s linking water resources to state planning policies had achieved a significant measure of support among influential metro-area state legislators.[167] One of them would be elected governor in 1982. The elevation of Joe Frank Harris to the governor's mansion marked an important moment in the state's incursion into land-use policy, even as the Reagan administration was simultaneously undermining many of the federal planning programs and regulatory frameworks erected just a decade earlier.[168] By January 1990, in part because of the quest for water supply, Georgia had entered the ranks of growth management states, a distinction seemingly at odds with its image as a land developer's paradise.

The unwillingness of state politicians to enforce aggressive conservation tactics and the ability of regional and state officials to negotiate increased withdrawals from their only source of water helped keep Atlanta's seemingly endless thirst on a path for conflict with its downstream neighbors.[169] In efforts to improve the condition of the Chattahoochee, the difficulties of intergovernmental coordination surfaced again and again. These difficulties would extend two decades into the future[170] and eventually escalate into an all-out legal war over the Chattahoochee.[171]

4
Projecting Sprawl?

The 1976 Regional Development Plan of Metropolitan Atlanta

By late 1972 the Atlanta Regional Commission (ARC) had emerged as a principal institution in Atlanta's metropolitan governing structure. The *Chattahoochee Corridor Study* had demonstrated ARC's influence in the regional planning process. Leveraging his deep connections to Atlanta's political elites, ARC director Dan Sweat had pushed the commission to take on an expanded role in the politics of regional development, somewhat beyond the tasks included in the commission's founding legislation.[1] Supported by new federal regulations that required designated regional planning agencies to review a wide range of local government applications for federal funds, ARC's position between federal policy and local politics granted it significant influence.[2] Against this backdrop, staff planners at ARC began writing a new regional development plan (RDP) as "an expression of how the Atlanta Region should grow and change in order to achieve the region's goals for the future." The RDP would also help fulfill the commission's responsibility to oversee development activity in the five counties that formed the metropolitan area.[3]

At the close of 1975 ARC would adopt this new RDP, a significant achievement in many respects but not without controversy. Intended to be a comprehensive statement about the future physical shape of the Atlanta region, the RDP formed a second moment in ARC's expansion of its reach among different levels of government while operating within a context of ostensible political difference. In writing the RDP, ARC adopted an urban model—a set of mathematical equations that represent the process of land development—to produce region-wide population, employment, and land-use projections. Initially presented as merely background for an open planning process to derive regional policies, the model ended up co-opting the process, helping suppress public discussion and providing justification for a rather narrow analysis and a limited slate of policies. The quasi-scientific certainty of the model lent it legitimacy within the region's development discourse. But most importantly, the model submerged a set of predetermined outcomes that supported continued low-density growth of the metropolitan area. These outcomes, jointly determined by federal policy, state politics, and local regulations, were built into ARC's structure and thus ultimately reflected in the policies contained in the RDP.[4]

Considered by many planners to be useful tools for extrapolating growth and development trends into the future, large-scale urban models first emerged in the 1950s. Despite nearly two decades of refinement, by the early 1970s the models were capable of handling only a limited number of easily quantifiable variables and could be difficult to calibrate to conditions on the ground.[5] Even with these limits, models provided planners with a way to combine basic demographic and transportation data to create an image of how an urban area might be expected to develop. In part because of their computational complexity, the models appeared sophisticated and scientific, though the growth projection techniques buried in them often had well-documented problems with accuracy. And as with other planning tools, the results of the models were subject to political manipulation by actors interested in using the projections for their own gain.[6] In the instance of Atlanta, only just before the RDP was officially adopted did anyone begin to recognize how the model had shaped the plan, privileging policies that matched projections of sprawling growth while hiding meaningful alternatives.[7]

The process of writing the RDP operated according to an internal logic but also engaged a regional political culture that maintained a permissive attitude toward development and remained mostly uninterested in tackling race or class inequity.[8] Yet the region's political leadership had been roiled at the start of the 1970s by Atlanta's shifting growth during the previous decade. Marked by an almost schizophrenic combination of enthusiastic declarations of what the coming decade would bring in the way of new development and fear that the region was doomed to a fate of racial and economic polarization, the editorial boards of Atlanta's two major newspapers seemed to obsess over what recent demographic changes portended for the fate of the city and the region.[9] Perhaps influenced by the media attention, the vision in the 1976 RDP's words, tables, graphs, maps, and renderings reflected the conflict between the standard progrowth politics of the region and concern with the implications of demographic change. Yet the RDP also revealed the strictures of the urban model that justified the major policy statements.[10] Managing the intersection of these forces within the RDP was important to the success of the plan but also to growing ARC's influence.

Through its first five years, a small cadre of politicians who were quite familiar with one another governed ARC. Through meetings, seminars, training sessions, and reports, ARC built connections among its stakeholders and provided a secure place for decision makers to discuss big-picture development policy. The model was a critical input to these discussions, since a great deal of ARC's influence derived from its capacity to gather, translate, and disseminate technical information related to the condition—past, present, and future—of the region and to convene stakeholders around this information. Though generating and distributing information had been on the agenda of Atlanta's various regional planning agencies since 1947, never before had it been as important as it was to ARC as it began the RDP process.[11]

As Robert Fishman points out, in the 1960s "American regional planning . . . underwent the collective equivalent of a near-death experience," being salvaged only after planners and policy makers began to understand that the urbanism of Jane Jacobs and the environmental ethic of Ian McHarg were not mutually exclusive planning goals.[12] Perhaps inspired by these ideals, regional planning reemerged in a new form at the end of the 1960s, becoming an important part of federal urban policy and influencing development decisions in metropolitan areas around the country. Yet the ends toward which the revitalized practice of regional planning led were not necessarily those that Jacobs or McHarg would have advocated. Federal requirements attached to regional transportation plans, support from Section 701 funds of the federal Housing Act of 1954, and the continuing implementation of the A-95 review program provided a tremendous boost to the power of regional planning agencies, virtually ensuring that they would play an important role in determining metropolitan development patterns.[13] The problem was that these regulations provided little ostensible guidance regarding urban form, and well-funded regional agencies, even with the wind of federal policy at their backs, did not always limit sprawl or alleviate spatial inequality. The 1976 RDP helped ARC, sitting at the confluence of federal policy and state and local politics, cement its status as Atlanta's key agency in implementing federal urban policy, the moderator of regional planning politics, and the main source for planning knowledge.[14] But the RDP did not produce a blueprint for compact or environmentally sensitive development. In fact, ARC and its 1976 RDP illustrate how federal policy merged with state and local politics to create a regional planning agenda marked by a self-fulfilling prophecy of sprawl.[15]

The Problem of Growth

In 1970, at the beginning of the state legislative session, the January 18 edition of the *Atlanta Journal-Constitution* included a special section dedicated to reminiscing about the city and the region, from its origins as a railroad crossing to its current status as a growing regional center. Atlanta's dailies had long been downtown institutions, allied with the interests of the city's business elites, and their portrayal of the region's character had begun to emphasize the potential threat recent changes might portend.[16]

Specifically, by the end of the 1960s there was a "significant shift in population balance" in the city, as upwards of sixty thousand whites left and seventy thousand blacks moved in.[17] Even before the city's black majority was made official by the census, a special issue of the *Atlanta Journal and Constitution Magazine* in the autumn of 1969 had wondered whether "Atlanta [will] become an ungovernable hodgepodge of conflicting political interests, black on the inside and white around the edges, with development and design falling apart at every municipal border, every county line."[18]

Debates in the 1968, 1969, and 1970 legislative sessions of the Georgia General Assembly aired worries about how demographic changes in the city would affect the metropolitan area more generally and what this meant for the balance in power between urban and rural political bases. Politicians recognized that the looming redistricting following the 1970 census would significantly change this balance in both branches of the legislature, and with those changes metro Atlanta would carry greater relative weight in state government. Georgia was now an urban state, dominated by urban concerns, and its major city, Atlanta, had been remade into a sprawling metropolitan region where the distinctions between city and suburb were both sharper and blurrier. As one editorial writer put it, "The old Atlanta was self-contained. The new Atlanta spreads and spreads."[19]

As middle- and working-class whites moved suburbanward and lower-income blacks moved into the southern and western quarters of the city to replace them, Atlanta was gaining an increasing concentration of the region's poorest households. The spatial inequality identified over and over in reports issued by the Advisory Commission on Intergovernmental Relations, the Kerner Commission, and the Douglas Commission seemed to be intensifying. Yet growth along the urban fringe was not without its own problems. Residential development in places like Gwinnett and Cherokee Counties brought an influx of newcomers expecting urban services that rural local governments were ill prepared to provide.[20]

Even with the churning, the total population of the city had increased by only 2 percent, a sharp drop from the previous decade's rate, and the areas of greatest growth in the regional labor market were well outside the central business district. While downtown Atlanta remained the largest single employment node in the region, other employment nodes, especially those in the northern reaches of the city and the northern suburbs, began to catch up.[21] With much of the benefits of recent employment gains going to the suburbs, the fate of the central city, and especially the old central business district, appeared to be imperiled. While they encouraged the fears of the white middle class, the editors of the *Journal* and *Constitution* also sometimes challenged misconceptions, highlighting the breadth and scope of new development proposals slated for the central city, trumpeting the region's overall population growth, and generally projecting "a more populous and economically prosperous" future.[22] Both papers often reminded their readers that amid political bluster about suburban rebellion and city decline "there remains a spirit of cooperation between Atlanta and its sister cities . . . [because] Atlanta's problems are their problems, for they are, in a sense, Atlanta itself."[23] Thus while by some measures the divide between city and suburbs was stark, strong links remained, particularly among a few state-level politicians, county commissioners, and public administrators. Nowhere was this cooperation more important in the early 1970s than in the circle of legislators and public administrators who controlled ARC.

The founding board of ARC had been guided by a small group of elected officials, most of whom had enduring ties to the places they represented, operated within a stable one-party political environment, and had personal connections with one another. The executive director, Dan Sweat Jr., had been the chief assistant in the administration of Ivan Allen Jr., Atlanta's popular but controversial mayor, and by the time Sweat took the reins at ARC he was an old hand at dealing with the region's political leaders. This tightly knit group understood the impact the region's demographic changes would have on planning and development. The early leaders of ARC recognized the importance of framing this discussion and that ARC could establish its role in the regional planning process only by engaging major regional issues, like the control of the Chattahoochee. They clearly understood that the placement of infrastructure—namely, water and roads—would determine where and when future development would happen.

At the outset of the RDP process, ARC signaled its transition from the timid demeanor of its immediate predecessor (the Atlanta Region Metropolitan Planning Commission) to a forward-looking professional agency. Recalling the optimistic plans of the 1950s, particularly the Metropolitan Planning Commission's 1952 plan *Now . . . for Tomorrow*, the ARC board emphasized the need for a rebirth of grand, comprehensive visions, guided by the availability of state-of-the-art data analysis techniques and broad thinking.[24] Changes in federal policy in the late 1960s meant that the new regional plan would have to include policies for overseeing federal grant programs related to transportation, wastewater, the aging population, policing practices, and public hospital administration.[25] By virtue of its scope, the new plan would involve a lengthy process of data collection, analysis, and outreach. Benefiting from advances in technology and the support of a much stronger regional planning agency, the new RDP process represented a significant break from its predecessors in terms of size and budget but also in the scope, expectations, and reach of its investigation.[26] The RDP would allow a deeper-level description and analysis than ever before. In short, the new RDP would represent a new beginning.

In late 1972 the ARC board took the first steps. The board set a schedule that anticipated an adopted plan by the end of 1975. By explicitly connecting the new plan to the regional plans of the 1950s, ARC sought to reinforce a sense of continuity and, perhaps more importantly, to avoid being targeted by politicians looking to score political points.[27] Touting the RDP to constituent local governments as a "benchmark in an ongoing planning process," commission members hoped that the new plan would counter latent public suspicion that their new agency represented an expansion of state and federal power, or a Marxist government, by framing the new plan as an outgrowth of a tradition of regional planning in Atlanta.[28] The RDP process was thus presented as a community-building exercise that would guide and inspire the development of the region, even though the content of the RDP would closely adhere to a specific set of substantive planning areas required by federal policy.[29] The new RDP would project a twenty-five-year horizon, though staff expected a useful life of at most ten years.[30] It would take nearly three years to complete.

Choosing a Model

In early 1975, only a few months before the RDP was officially adopted, ARC staff released a short report subtitled *Framework for the Future*. In its first pages staff outlined the results of a recent multifaceted analysis of the Atlanta region's future population, employment, and land use. The analysis had been based on the assumption that "an additional 2 million people will live in the 7-county Atlanta Region in year 2000."[31] In retrospect, this assumption was the first clue that the urban model had profoundly shaped the RDP process. The origin of the assumption, however, lay in the early 1950s. In 1954, before the widespread application of advanced urban models, the Metropolitan Planning Commission had suggested that regional plans abandon static urban boundaries or policies that restricted growth and instead engage in "a continuous planning process" using periodic projections of future development based on population growth. Only a germ in the mid-1950s, the idea of population growth projections serving as the framework for regional development planning throughout the country gained ground during the 1960s, helped along by changes to federal policy, advances in technology, and new ways of thinking about planning.[32]

The first large-scale urban models were developed and tested in the United States in the mid-1950s. The 1954 Detroit Metropolitan Area Traffic Study was the first comprehensive region-level transportation study, though it was methodologically unsophisticated. A year later the Chicago Area Transportation Study (CATS), under J. Douglas Carroll's direction, became the first complex quantitative model of an entire metropolitan area that incorporated "computers, trip distribution, traffic assignment, and benefit-cost analysis."[33] Publications and reports documenting CATS found a ready audience among city and regional planners who recognized the study's transformative potential, and by the early 1960s cities across the country undertook regional studies using large-scale urban models. When Congress approved the 1962 Federal

Aid Highway Act, instituting the so-called 3Cs (comprehensive, cooperative, and continuing) highway planning process, regional models became part of the normal operating procedure for every metropolitan area with over fifty thousand population.[34]

By demonstrating how data from different sources could be processed with predefined mathematical algorithms, CATS produced "a landmark transportation related land use study" that offered vivid representations of urban development scenarios.[35] At the most basic level, the output was a set of growth forecasts. On the basis of an assumed total regional population and transportation infrastructure, the model would distribute future population and employment within predetermined geographic areas. It would then project what traffic and land-use patterns might look like if different development policies were pursued. While CATS and its derivatives reduced the complexity of a metropolitan region to a comparatively small set of variables, perhaps a necessary step in modeling complex social systems, their popularity lay in their ability to provide seemingly precise, objective projections of the distribution of population, employment, and land use at defined intervals of years with apparent objectivity.[36]

Optimizing resource allocation, a fundamental concern of government policy, motivated quantification and measurement of urban conditions. "Computerized models of the metropolitan area promised to increase planners' understanding of the urban development process," which encouraged their widespread adoption.[37] Another motivation was changes in planning education and planning's relationship to the emerging science of policy analysis. These changes supported the idea that planning should be a rational, predictable activity. Urban models offered a tool that could make a complex modern metropolis seem eminently manageable.[38] Advances in computing power made working with large data sets easier. Improvements in techniques for gathering and analyzing population and economic data had increased models' accuracy and reliability.[39] Quantitative tools to solve social problems were growing in popularity, and large-scale urban models held promise for better, more precise policies that replaced some of the art that had previously characterized the planning process.

By the late 1960s the regional planning process and large-scale urban models had begun to evolve together. The technical prowess of the models produced a level of presumptive veracity, an extremely useful impression when dealing with politically sensitive decisions. Among the first and most important activities a regional planning agency would undertake in preparing a plan were population and employment projections, critical inputs to the model. Federal support for planning-related activities bolstered this approach, and the use of quantitative models in the regional planning process grew. Regional planners learned to depend on the sophistication of these analytic tools for validation of the planning process itself. By the time ARC emerged in the early 1970s, urban models had been an accepted part of regional planning for a decade.[40]

Though the power of urban models to dictate the regional planning process was significant, the tedium of such highly technical procedures prevented them from garnering much public attention.[41] Thus, in early 1972 the ARC board approved the staff's selection of an urban activity allocation model without much debate. The urban model ARC adopted, known as EMPIRIC, was "designed to provide estimates of the future year levels of population, employment, and land-use variables for each of a series of 290 subareas or districts."[42] Essentially a derivation of the model developed by CATS in the 1950s, EMPIRIC would do what urban models before it had: quantify changes in population and employment and tie them to changes in different land-use patterns.[43]

While the use of an urban allocation model was pushed by federal policy and encouraged by trends in planning thought, the prominence of the model in the Atlanta RDP process was not predetermined at the outset. Initially pitched as background to the plan, the modeling exercises over time shifted to center stage.[44] During the course of developing the plan, the results of the allocation model became a nearly sacrosanct image of the region's future. The quantitative, numbers-don't-lie character of the model played a significant part in determining future development scenarios. Regard for the model's output increased further because it focused on critical infrastructure—roads, transit, and wastewater systems—around which development would accrete. Infrastructure was tightly bound to federal support for regional planning and was one of the basic inputs to the model. Stakeholders in the RDP process focused on infrastructure because it had significant financial implications but could also be manipulated.

Prepping the model, which included data gathering and cleaning, calibration, and transforming outputs into usable information, fit neatly into ARC's role of producer of regional information. With its extensive data inputs, complicated calculations, and spreadsheet outputs, the model was presented as part of a "continuing series of analytic planning efforts" that affected an air of impartiality and certainty.[45] Moreover, ARC's mastery of EMPIRIC allowed it to effectively monopolize the market for regional data analysis.[46] No other agency operating in the region, aside from the state or one of the public universities, possessed the resources to adequately evaluate this work. Only just before publication of the final draft of the RDP did anyone involved in the planning process challenge ARC's use of the model.

Fitting the Plan to the Projections

Looking back, the second clue that the planning process might come to be built around an urban model appeared in 1962 with the publication of *Atlanta Silhouettes*, a slim volume written by the staff of the Atlanta Region Metropolitan Planning Commission. Adumbrating *Framework for the Future*, *Atlanta Silhouettes* was a succinct numeric description of what the region would look like in twenty-five years. At the time, the commission's computing capacity still lagged behind its aspirations, and the projection methods used in *Silhouettes* were quite basic. Nevertheless, wide distribution among local governments and state officials helped *Atlanta Silhouettes* demonstrate to the region's politicians how several simple data variables could show the connection between existing conditions and anticipated growth.[47] By the time ARC appeared ten years later, computing capacity more closely matched aspirations, and the enhanced sophistication of extrapolation methods could more convincingly ground future policies.

In mid-1972, ARC staff released the first of several iterations of a working paper, *Study Design for Development and Application of EMPIRIC Activity Allocation Model*, that outlined how EMPIRIC would be adapted and calibrated to fit Atlanta's conditions.[48] Though widely known among modeling experts, details about how urban models worked remained mysterious to almost everyone else. The explanations that ARC staff offered, laid out in technical language, could hardly be described as clear. A short quote from *Study Design* attempting to explain how family income was included as a variable in the model provides a glimpse of the complicated wording to which ARC staff resorted:

> The most severe adjustments for the Atlanta application usually fall upon the structure type submodel. Within the forecast process, the simultaneous equation module values of family income are transformed into structure type measures for evaluation. Included in this process is the row-factoring of the structure type submodel values to district control totals from the simultaneous equation module.[49]

The challenge of interpreting the model was underscored when an ARC planner, interviewed by an *Atlanta Journal* reporter in late 1973, could be no more precise than saying, "We have all of this included in a mathematical model of the region. As we get proposals from people, we will feed the suggestion into the computer and it will tell us how it will affect the various living patterns throughout the region."[50] His elliptical acknowledgment of the opacity of the model revealed just how much of a black-box operation the process remained. While *Study Design* described in detail how EMPIRIC operated, it did so in a way that most participants in the planning process, especially the politicians and the public, would be hard-pressed to understand. With no access to explanations of the calculations in simpler or disaggregated terms, nonspecialist stakeholders could not know the parameters included in the model.

Once the model was calibrated, ARC used EMPIRIC for three discrete tasks: forecasting the distribution of population, employment, and land use; developing a set of scenarios of alternative policy decisions; and assessing the impact of these scenarios.[51]

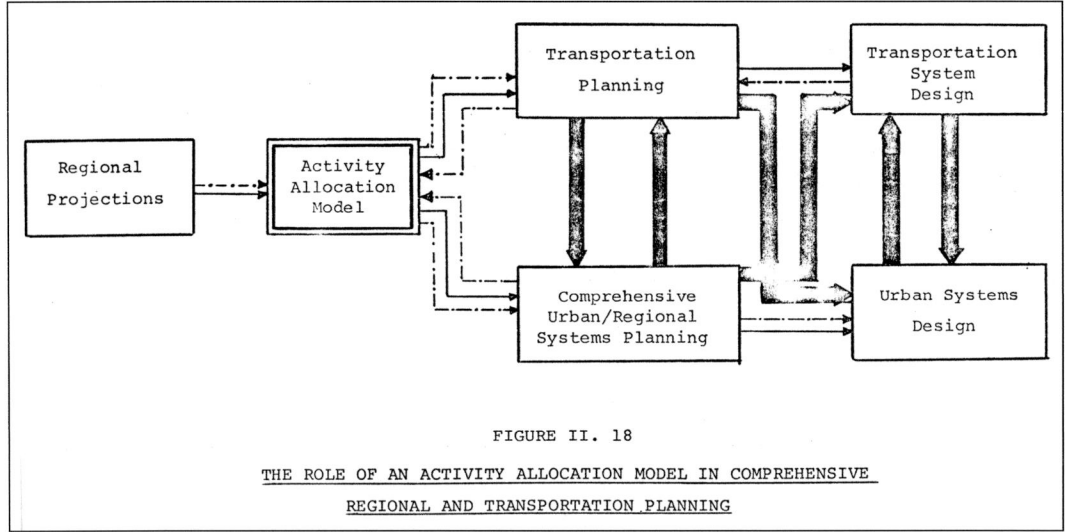

Figure 4.1 "The Role of an Activity Allocation Model in Comprehensive Regional and Transportation Planning," from *Study Design for Development and Application of EMPIRIC Activity Allocation Model*, prepared by Peat, Marwick, Mitchell, and Co. for Atlanta Regional Commission, December 1972, Atlanta Regional Commission Collection, Kenan Research Center, Atlanta History Center

ARC staff fed information into the model regarding transportation infrastructure, water and sewer improvements, zoning regulations, and the amount of developable land, and the model churned out a rudimentary measure of population carrying capacity for small geographic units within the region based on the assumed future total regional population. On the basis of this carrying capacity, the model distributed population and employment projections for the years 1980, 1990, and 2000 by dividing the metropolitan area into 290 districts and 34 superdistricts (aggregations of districts). The district boundaries were either 1970 census tract boundaries or traffic analysis zone boundaries (which are in most cases subdivisions of census tracts).[52] Which boundaries were used depended on location and population density. Traffic analysis zones were smaller and better suited for denser central areas; census tracts were larger and were used in the lower-density fringe areas of the region. The model used two baseline data points, 1961 and 1970, as its projection base years. Data for these years included total population and employment, existing land use, and number of new housing and demolition permits issued by jurisdictions within the region.[53]

Starting from an assumed total regional population of 3.5 million (2 million more than in 1970), the model first projected superdistrict-level changes in the distribution of employment and population using a simple technique known as share of growth.[54] This technique calculated future change in the population and employment of a superdistrict on the basis of that superdistrict's past share of the total population of the region. Thus, how a superdistrict had fared in the recent past, factoring in carrying

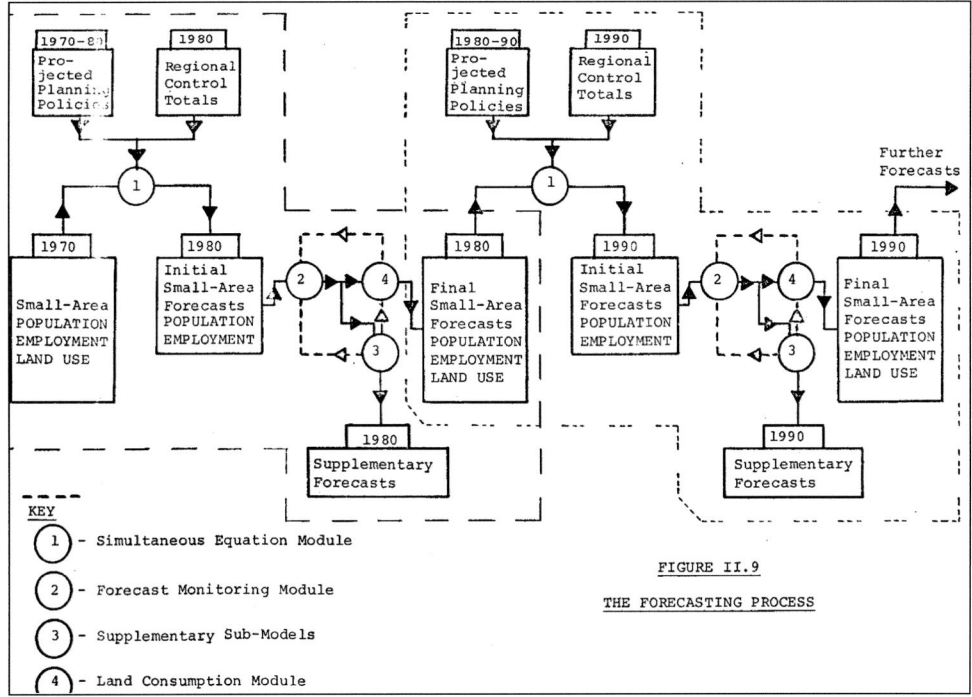

Figure 4.2 "The Forecasting Process," from *Study Design for Development and Application of EMPIRIC Activity Allocation Model*

capacity and transportation infrastructure, determined how the model would distribute population to that superdistrict in the future. Later, the superdistrict projections were disaggregated into districts according to the same share-of-growth formula.[55]

Once projections were allocated down to the district level, each district was assigned to one of four development categories (core, mature developed, rapidly developing, and satellite). The categories were based on the existing mixture of land-use types, anticipated levels of population growth, and the expected mixture of future land use. The categories also designated each district's capacity to absorb new population. In other words, each category would receive a predetermined development density in the future, based on its existing land use and anticipated carrying capacity.[56] The categories were meant to be a simple way to visualize the region's future built environment.

As part of calibrating EMPIRIC to Atlanta's particular regional geography, ARC staff created three alternative policy packages, which "featured three different transportation systems along with the existing land use policies prevalent in the region."[57] The extent and type of transportation infrastructure was the biggest differentiating factor in each scenario. Other policies, zoning or other development controls, were similar across scenarios, a step that automatically narrowed the possibilities of future development.[58] The first scenario presumed growth and development trends would continue unabated and existing policies and regulations and transport infrastructure

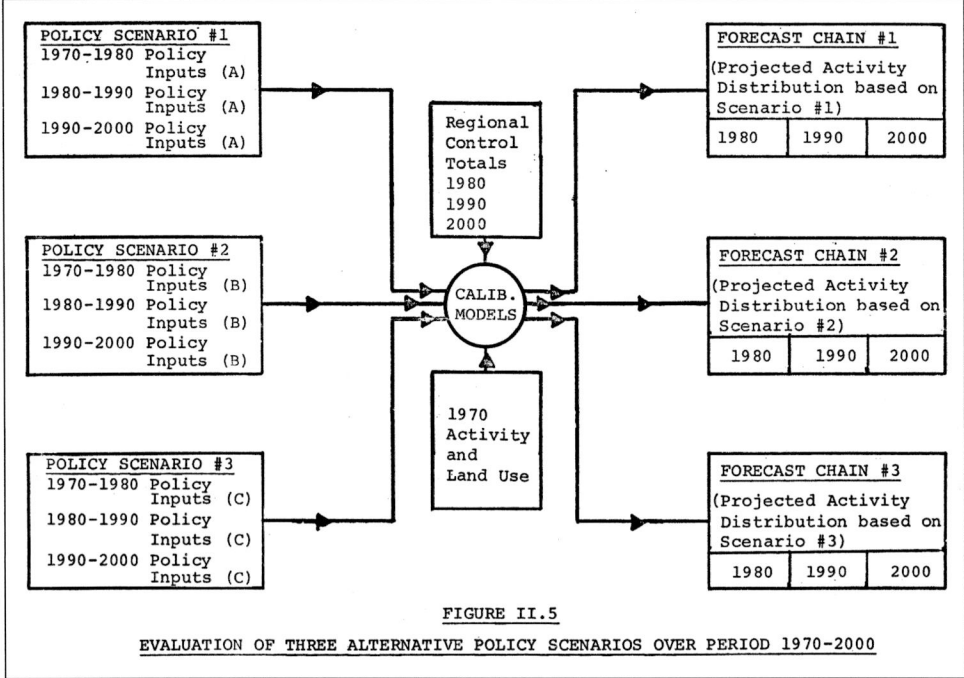

Figure 4.3 "Evaluation of Three Alternative Policy Scenarios over Period 1970–2000," from *Study Design for Development and Application of EMPIRIC Activity Allocation Model*

remain unchanged. The second envisioned the construction of an extensive mass transit system with comparatively little development of the freeway system beyond what existed in 1970. The third envisioned a limited rail system and a highly developed highway and collector road system. Each scenario was carried through the steps of the modeling process, until selection of one for official endorsement by the ARC board.[59]

Though the scenarios were largely similar, embedded within each were small policy levers that controlled transportation mode split, developable land, water service availability, and permissible building densities. These levers allowed staff planners to tweak the model at different points in the projection chain, changing a few development standards midstream, releasing or removing developable land in different years, and testing the effect of the construction of new towns or other major regional developments on the distribution of population and employment around the region.[60] But because the policies were tested only in bundles, tied to one of three basic transportation infrastructure scenarios, there were in actuality far fewer possible outcomes than the number of variables suggested. Bundling constrained the effect that entering or removing individual policies would have on the model outputs.[61]

While share-of-growth projection methods can be used in small areas with a history of slow growth or decline, in the case of metro Atlanta, with its uneven growth and vast geographic scale, the calculations produced noticeably divergent results. Sub-areas that had grown a little faster than the region as a whole in the past showed tremendous gains through year 2000, and those that had grown more slowly than the region overall showed significant decline. For instance, policies that restricted the acreage of developable land produced large declines in population in particular districts. Yet changing density limitations to offset changes in the total amount of developable land did not provide a correction.[62] The combined effect of altering policies within the model produced uneven and confusing results and a high degree of error. Gains or losses projected by the model in some areas of the region violated common sense. The model suggested that one of the largest population and employment nodes in the region, Buckhead, would decline in population over the projection period, despite generous development regulations, high-density ceilings, high property values, and otherwise favorable development conditions.[63]

Seemingly bizarre outputs aside, buried in the text of a 1975 U.S. Department of Transportation report, *Introduction to Urban Development Models and Guidelines for the Use in Urban Transportation Planning*, had been a surprisingly clear and prescient statement about the vision the RDP would offer:

> Since EMPIRIC is calibrated using data points experiencing both growth and declines, its coefficients are strongly influenced by the characteristics of declining areas. When used in a forecasting mode, the model will, over time, tend to project this decline in inner areas and in effect produce a "doughnut" with a ring of highly concentrated population around a steadily declining core.[64]

Stripped of its technical details or its political context, EMPIRIC, by design, presented a stark picture of the direction the region's growth would take: a seven-county region of rapidly growing suburbs surrounding a deflating core.

EMPIRIC's results held a fine line between believable and outrageous, resulting in part from the model's internal structure and in part from the rigidity of a narrow set of transportation scenarios. Specific policies to relieve traffic congestion or conserve residential land or increase building density could be evaluated only as part of a larger package. Land-use policies could not be isolated for separate consideration. This suggests that even if a wider set of possible growth policies or different assumptions about population growth had been used, the model would not have significantly changed outputs because of the way it chained together forecasts.[65] With the parameters it was given, the only future the model could show was one that stuck closely to the past.

The decision to base the regional planning process on EMPIRIC, a narrow model further constrained by a small set of possible scenarios, meant that ARC's leaders had effectively decided that only a very few regional development outcomes would be possible. The apparent objectivity of the model hid the critical linkages between the

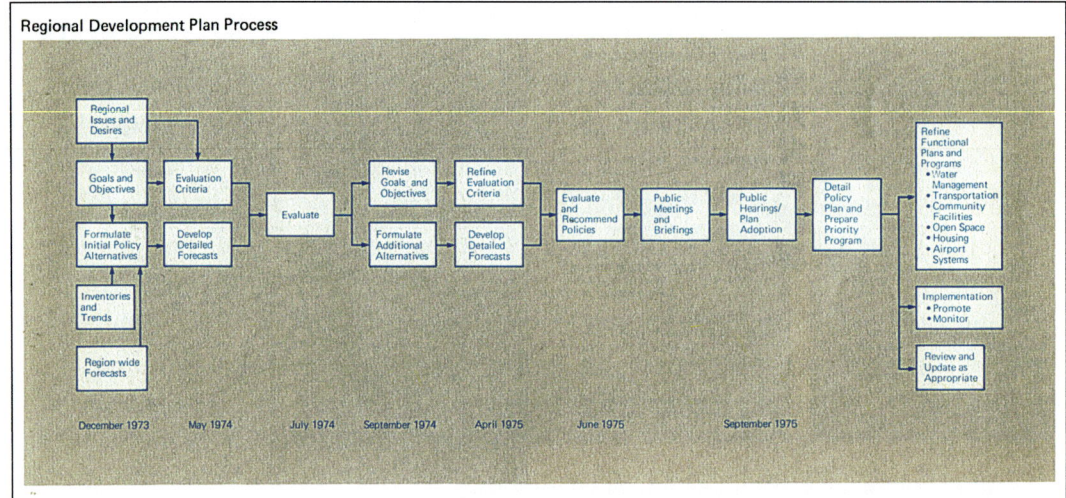

Figure 4.4 "Regional Development Plan Process," from Atlanta Regional Commission, *Regional Development Plan of Metropolitan Atlanta*, 1976, Atlanta Regional Commission Collection, Kenan Research Center, Atlanta History Center

allocation model and potential outcomes.[66] Instead of decisions being made after open discussion and detailed policy debate, they were preordained.

After two years of building and running scenarios, ARC staff released the first draft of the EMPIRIC outputs in mid-1974.[67] After an additional six-month period of comment and debate, a set of revised figures was published in early 1975 in *Framework for the Future*. Following several more months of internal discussion, ARC's governing board officially adopted scenario three as the guiding framework for the RDP, a decision supported by a brief staff report that argued that scenario two was politically untenable and that the difference between scenarios one and three in terms of the built environment would be negligible. The final draft of the RDP was published a few months later.

Predetermined Outcomes?

Decentralized growth, including population, employment, and land development, provided an overarching theme for the final draft of the RDP. Widely distributed growth—first in assumptions about future total regional population, later in the model's specifications, and finally in the policies included in the RDP—was central to the process. This followed an ideology of growth as a worthwhile end and the old regional planning goal of a decentralized urban population. As an ARC staff report put it, decentralized urban growth was simultaneously policy and vision, the "heart of the planning process."[68] In some ways, ARC's interest in growth projections adheres to the growth machine John Logan and Harvey Molotch describe in *Urban Fortunes*. The preoccupation with population and employment expansion of many of those involved in the RDP was surely related to their desire to effect an increase of "aggregate rents and trap[ping] related wealth for those in the right position to benefit," even if they did not articulate it.[69] Yet the primary group of supporters of sprawling growth was not limited only to land-holding elites.[70] The enthusiasm for growth also was one of the tenets of American regional planning, which had viewed the deconcentration of urban population as a basic goal, though the best means to achieve this end, and what it should look like, has been disputed.[71] That Atlanta's planners and politicians basically agreed on the desirability of low-density development suggested that enriching a few landowners was not necessarily the only motivating factor behind a plan that championed decentralized growth for the region.[72]

Displaying characteristics derived from both the legacy of regionalism and the growth machine, ARC's orchestration of the RDP process was further complicated by local conditions. The legal context of Georgia, for example, affected the process. At the outset ARC staff were instructed to ignore ideas for policies without strong legal precedent in Georgia, regardless of whether those policies had been adopted in other states or described in the planning literature. As a result, an explicitly slow-growth scenario with artificial growth boundaries or building-permit limitations, which might have put policies before projections, was never seriously considered. In a working paper explaining the origin of the scenarios, ARC staff carefully worded the case for this exclusion: "There is little or no point in constructing scenarios—involving for example the withholding of large amounts of land from development—if no realistic mechanisms exist for implementing them in the real world." Thus if a scenario included regulations that had not been tested in Georgia or represented a substantial leap from existing policies, it was excluded.[73] Judging potential planning policies by virtue of precedents only within the state filtered out innovative ideas.

The single largest portion of ARC's budget in the early 1970s was dedicated to "data and information." When it was created, ARC was expected to be "a resource tool for making meaningful improvements in the future of the Atlanta metropolitan region," using among other things the "[quantitative] evaluation of the probable implications of alternative public policies." One precursor to evaluating the potential effect of any policy was building a base of information about the region. This included annual estimates of the region's current population and employment.[74] Most federal urban development programs tied the distribution of funds to population. Moreover, ARC's founding legislation required each member county to make an annual contribution for basic operating expenses. Those contributions were based on a per person rate. Population estimates determined ARC's financial support. Models and projections made regional planning indispensable, and measuring growth became an important preoccupation of commission planners. Entrenching data analysis and the EMPIRIC model at the center of the RDP process served ARC quite well.

As the process unfolded, debates consistently started and ended with the model: how much growth it indicated and where this growth would occur. The final version of the RDP revealed how this happened. Noting that "it is necessary to prepare long-range population and economic forecasts for the region as a whole so that they may be used as a quantitative basis for comparing alternative plans for the future and also for subsequently refining and amending the adopted plan from time to time,"[75] the RDP translated EMPIRIC's projections into visual evidence of how the model and policies together produced a comprehensive image of the region consistent with the prevailing political culture. With some creative interpretation, the nearly inscrutable data tables from the raw model outputs were transformed into vivid images of future growth and development. In a progression from regional maps to renderings of an ideal neighborhood, the RDP visualized a low-density urban landscape.

Projected changes in population and employment were presented in simple choropleth maps that highlighted districts and superdistricts where growth would likely occur. As the warnings about EMPIRIC had predicted, the maps showed consistent decline in the urban core and growth in the outer stretches of suburban counties. More startling were detailed renderings of what the RDP's combination of growth, infrastructure, and land-use policies might look like at the neighborhood scale. Easily the most telling visuals in the entire document, these images showed a hypothetical progression of land development patterns that moved from a classic urban grid to disconnected, suburban cul-de-sac subdivisions.[76] It was residential planning that would ostensibly preserve the quality of the region's surface water while expanding road infrastructure to reduce congestion and bringing new residential areas closer to the countryside.[77] The design of these neighborhoods was only implicit, a function of the confluence of transportation and the environment. The graphics showed a low-density, suburban landscape defined by roads and waterways, populated by single-family houses, and shopping malls.[78] Undercutting the idea of the model as an impartial analytic tool, the outputs suggested specific areas of the region where growth should occur, where future infrastructure investments should be directed, and what form growth should take.[79] It was a near perfect rendering of the sprawl that would unfold over the next three decades.[80]

Contesting the Plan

As the final outputs of the EMPIRIC model and draft policies for the RDP circulated among members of the local planning and development community in mid-1975, the model finally began to attract scrutiny. A few observers questioned the model's

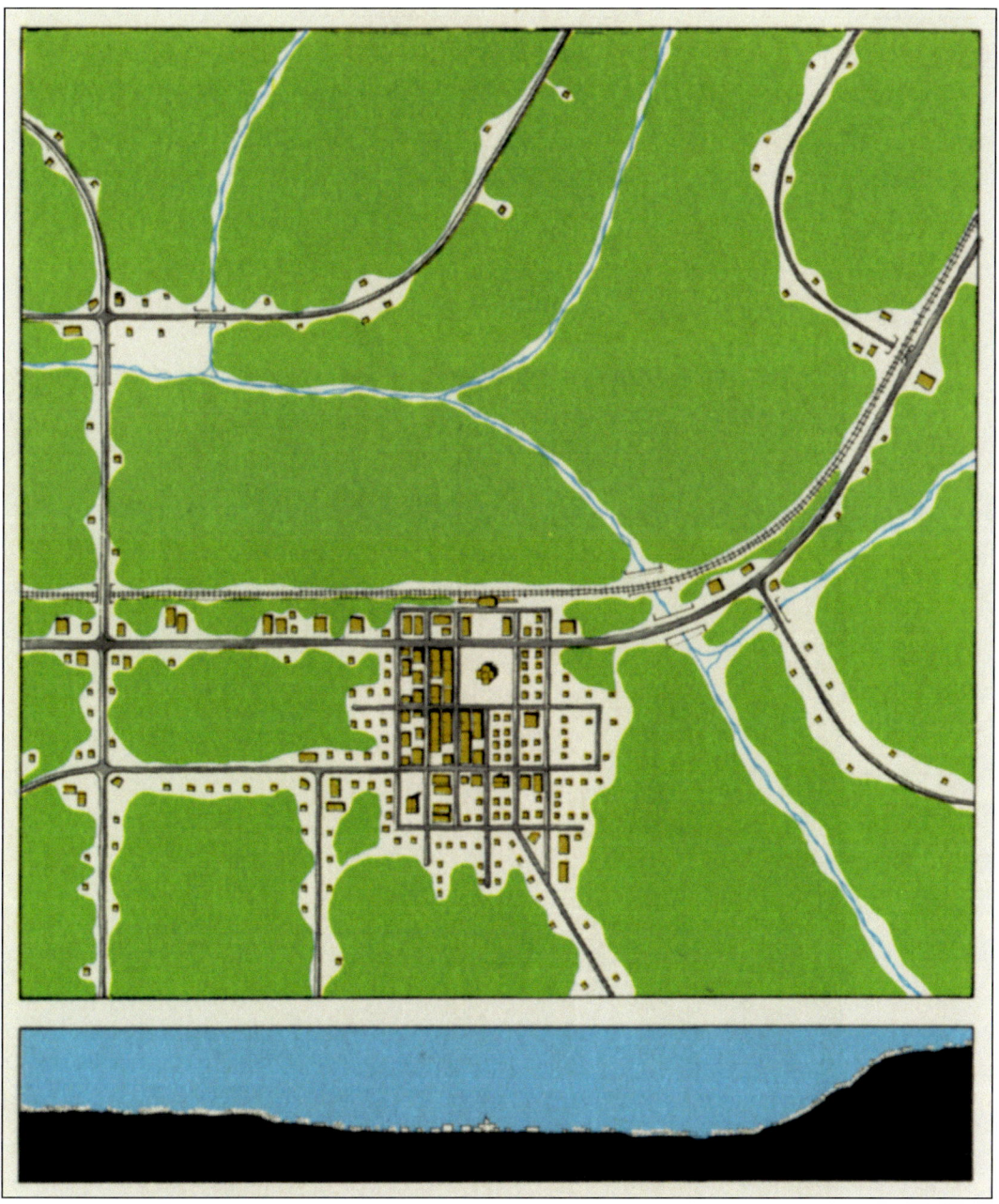

Figure 4.5 "A Typical Area of the Atlanta Region about to Undergo Accelerated Development," from *Regional Development Plan of Metropolitan Atlanta*, the figure, which continues on the next three pages, shows the progression of development in the area

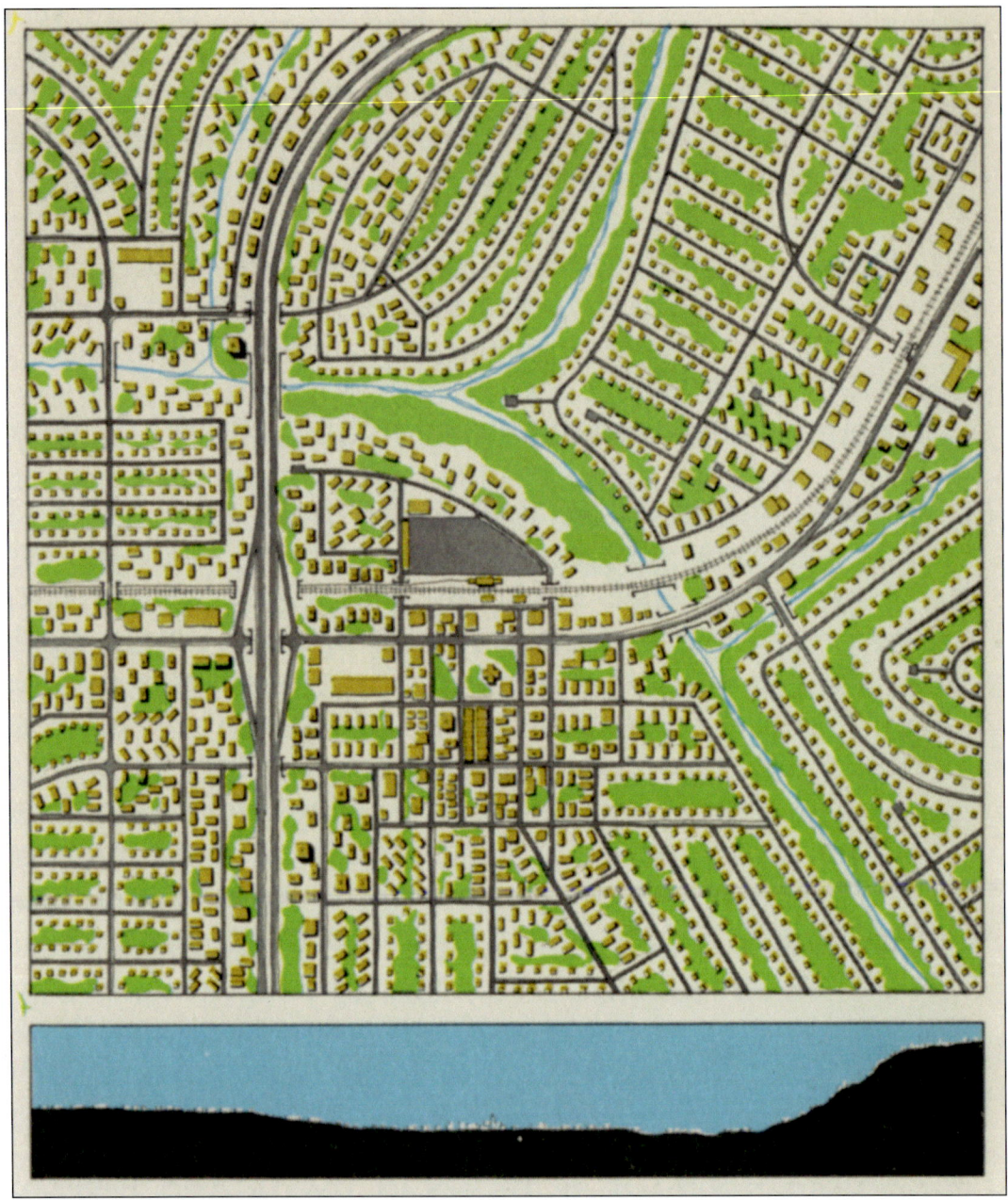

Figure 4.5 (*continued*)

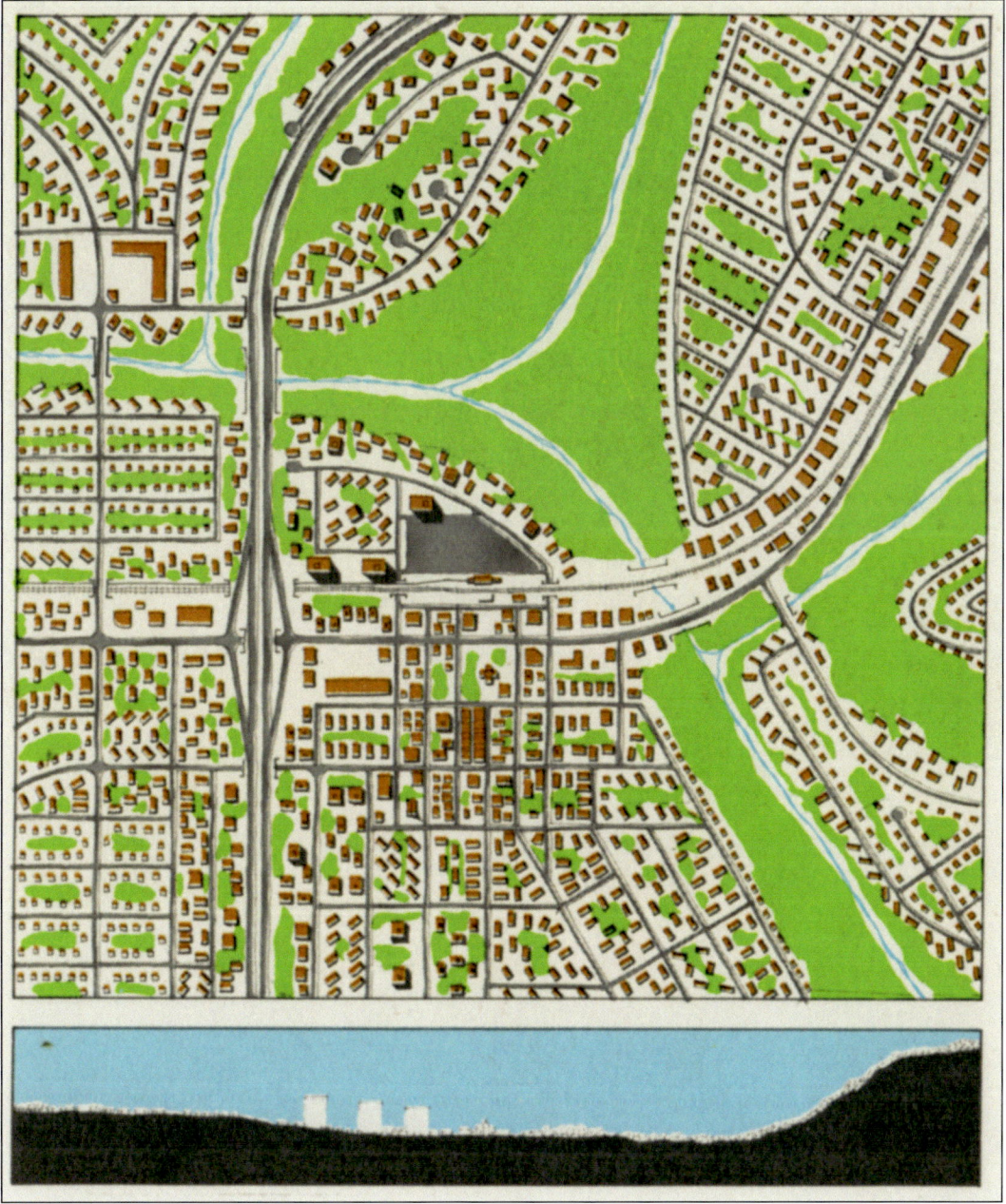

Figure 4.5 (continued)

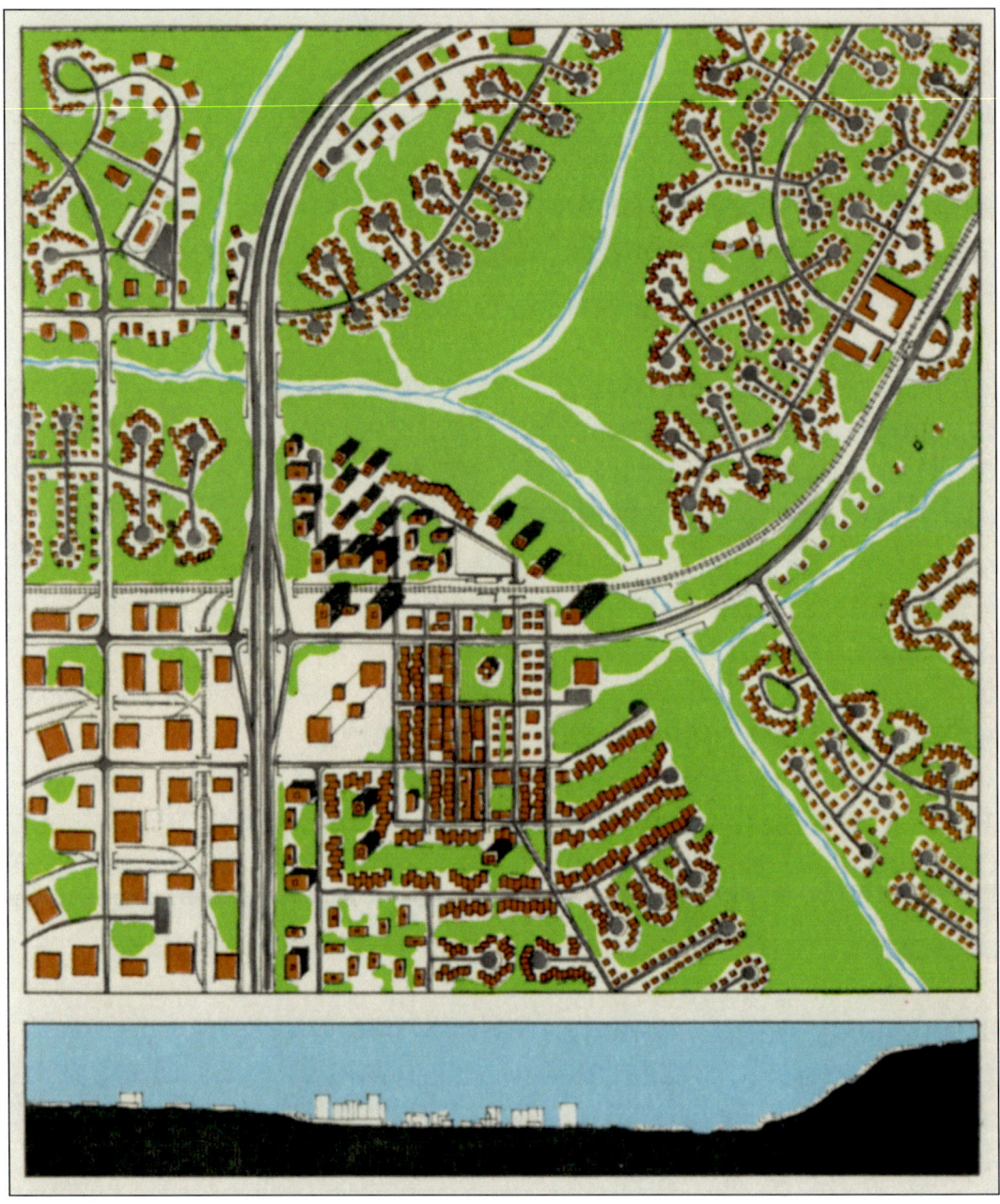

Figure 4.5 (*continued*)

influence on the RDP and the vision it suggested for Atlanta's future, asking whether the model outputs had played an outsized role in decision making and had been used to justify the transportation, environmental, and land-use policies described in the plan.[81] But broader recognition of the influence of the model took time. At the beginning of the planning process, a few prescient stakeholders had suggested that the model might distort the results. In an ARC board meeting in 1972, one of the citizen members had suggested that the urban model might be problematic to the policy-making process because "it seemed all ARC was doing was accommodating growth rather than guiding it."[82] Yet his criticism fell on deaf ears. Only when the plan was a few months from completion three years later and the projections were set to be adopted as official guidelines for the region were concerns more stridently voiced about how development policies had been generated and approved, what role the model played, and who had participated in the process.

The presentation of RDP policies during board meetings and public forums in the summer of 1975 brought the model and the process into the daylight. Supporting documentation released with the draft policies hinted at how the model had been used and how its outputs had affirmed the goals of state and local officials. Angered by the proposed policies, a small group of professional organizations and community groups, including the local chapters of the American Institute of Architects and the League of Women Voters, began to coordinate their complaints that ARC had used the model to turn the regional plan into a recipe for sprawl. Concluding that the RDP was merely "accommodating growth," they charged that ARC's governing board was not concerned with guiding growth.[83] During the short period of public comment in June on the EMPIRIC outputs and draft RDP policies, they alleged that the RDP was hiding an "unconstrained growth policy" that would lead to "continued, uncontrolled growth" because of the "selection of transportation as the chief modifier of future growth patterns."[84] Criticizing the data collection and modeling activities of ARC that dominated the planning process, the Georgia Conservancy, a probusiness environmental organization, cut to the core of the complaints, claiming that "alternatives to growth and development should be the result of planning, not the basis for planning."[85] A report released by one of ARC's own subcommittees suggested that the board had so tightly controlled the planning process that dissent from a growth agenda had been nearly impossible.[86] In fact, the Community Development Advisory Council, an ARC group charged with overseeing citizen input in the RDP process, did not formally request "that staff should explain in layman's terms the implications of each alternative" until June 1975.[87] Criticism of the model and the RDP came too late. The fear that the regional planning process had catered to political desires turned out to be well founded. That ARC's leaders had bent the RDP process to fit their goal of using infrastructure to encourage development became apparent.

The EMPIRIC outputs became the region's official population projections for federally supported planning programs when the ARC board formally adopted the RDP in December 1975. Yet for the next several years ARC was forced to defend its projections, rebuffing accusations that the model had played an inappropriate role in the RDP process and had produced an inaccurate picture of the region's growth. When planning for new wastewater treatment plants began in 1976, the RDP projections were challenged by the EPA, which threatened to withdraw the region's grant money due to it from Section 208 of the 1972 Clean Water Act if the numbers were not revised downward. In 1978 Atlanta's mayor and a local transportation advocacy group upbraided ARC for producing projections that were "too high" and "not in our ballpark."[88] Grudging settlements between ARC and its critics avoided dustups, and each time ARC's projections were allowed to stand.[89]

Nonetheless, as the process to produce the a new RDP geared up in the early 1980s, the critics looked to have been correct. In a staff review of EMPIRIC's performance, significant problems emerged. Mostly, they involved the quality of the data used in the model and the way the region had been divided for analysis. Many of the allocation districts were unevenly sized, the projection base was mismatched to the projection horizon, and there were "errors in the exogenous regional activity totals input to EMPIRIC," which included overforecasting family households and multicar households and underforecasting nonfamily households and households with one or no cars.[90] Individually none of these errors would undermine the model, but together they could produce large errors in predictions of where future development would occur. This meant that calibrating the model—fitting it to the specifics of Atlanta—had been mishandled. The results of those mistakes had been adopted in the RDP.

Charting the Power of the RDP

Writing the RDP crystallized a close relationship between federal policy, state interests, and the ARC and reinforced expectations by politicians that uninhibited growth would continue. Over time, the process initiated by the RDP helped sustain relationships between key regional actors (state and local politicians, bureaucrats) in key policy areas (federal transportation and environmental issues, infrastructure), lending credibility and inevitability to a pattern of growth and development that was, after all, a choice. The technical specifications of the RDP process, determined by a combination of regulations and standards of professional planning practice, were manipulated to meet the demands of a regional political culture that saw growth as a positive and unavoidable end.

Though the RDP was designed to span a broad topical range, the combined pressures of state law, federal policy, and local politics turned the plan almost entirely toward infrastructure.[91] Hard-infrastructure policies, those with direct funding implications, tended to be the most specific and least flexible. Soft-infrastructure policies—land use, housing, and the like—were discussed in broad terms, vague enough to allow local municipalities flexibility in adopting or rejecting different policies as they saw fit.[92] In the end, the RDP focused mostly on issues with clear implications for major projects related to roads, transit, and water.[93]

In this sense, the influence of the regional plan could be seen in the circular logic it created: setting a projection horizon and creating a set of policies that encouraged infrastructure development that would accommodate new development according to the need expressed in the projection and policies. A 1981 report by ARC staff that looked back at lessons learned from the 1976 RDP explained exactly how this process worked, using the example of transportation policies: "The ARC resolution adopting the RDP as a development guide [did] not specify transportation polices" but rather "provide[d] a detailed list of recommended transportation projects and actions," thus "when the RDP document was assembled around the adopted resolution, ARC staff formulated a set of transportation polices that 'fit' the adopted projects."[94] This process allowed growth projections to acquire undue influence. The full implications of the way the RDP was written would reveal themselves only over the ensuing years.[95]

To avoid the potential problem of dissonance between policy goals and on-the-ground development, RDP policies were written to allow interpretative flexibility. The projections, however, were intended to be mostly immune to modification. If development projects approved by state or local governments appeared to conflict with RDP policies, there was room to assert that the project actually did fit the spirit of the plan, since very few polices in the RDP suggested restrictions on specific practices.[96] As a result, both official forecasts and developments could be used to justify where and when policies should be modified or infrastructure constructed, even though ARC staff recognized that the problems inherent to the urban model were so significant that major changes had to be undertaken for future projections. The immediate effect of this kind of planning is neither dramatic nor wholly apparent but accumulates over time.[97]

Leaving a Legacy

In total, the RDP process produced over one hundred studies, reports, papers, public meetings, and hearings. In one way or another, each detailed some small piece of the planning process. Guiding these studies were local, state, and federal interests, visible in the topics the studies covered as well as in the analytic methods deployed. Policies originating at different governmental levels and from different agencies often required different kinds of data, used different measures of performance, and measured compliance using different standards. Every regulation and requirement helped shape what information was considered in the process, how that information was analyzed, and how the results were presented. The final plan reflected an amalgam of demands from different directions. In a single document, ARC attempted to address the demands of its enabling legislation, satisfy its local political constituents, and integrate an array of federal transportation and environmental regulations.

Of the things that ARC could do, managing the regional planning process was perhaps the most important. Because land was developed and infrastructure built piece by piece, the overall shape of the region's development was hard to track, particularly in the context of a single regional plan. This has given rise to the temptation to suggest that the milieu in Atlanta produced random, unplanned, or uncoordinated decision making. The RDP process challenges this conclusion, revealing that the power of ARC to coordinate decisions arose from its orchestration of the less visible side of planning: deciding who can participate, determining what data are admissible, specifying which methods of analysis to use, and adjudicating what policy precedents to include. Hence the power of the commission largely depended on its capacity to manage the planning process, and like the *Chattahoochee Corridor Study*, the RDP helped ARC's effort to build this capacity. The paper trail left by the RDP revealed how extensive, complex, and fluid ARC's effort was.[98]

While the decision to produce forecasts was dictated by policies at the federal level, decisions about forecasting methods and how their results would be used were left in the hands of politicians and the professional bureaucracy.[99] Since ARC's charter vaguely stated that the agency would "engage in a continuous program of research," the specialized, technical tasks of the RDP process fell to the staff.[100] Though this permitted staff considerable leeway in shaping the flow of the planning process, including selecting the urban model, state and local politicians, who tended to support weak regulations, ongoing infrastructure investment, and as much population and employment growth as possible, were permitted to establish the ultimate outcomes of the regional planning process. Staff responded by calibrating the model to project growth outward from the urban core and then writing policies that encouraged the realization of that growth. These steps happened quietly and remained behind the scenes and beyond the purview of most observers, except those deeply involved in the planning process. The little media reporting about the model and its projections presented them as technical details best left to the experts.[101] This enabled forging the regional plan without much public scrutiny.

The 1976 RDP was the second step of a long-term effort to devise a more coordinated regional planning process. The influence of the RDP on the way regional planning was practiced in metropolitan Atlanta in the 1970s extended through the next two decades.[102] Writing the plan helped ARC's effort to become the conduit for the aspirations of Atlanta's political leadership and helped maintain an atmosphere in which growth was both a positive end and a framework for regional planning.[103] The projections at the heart of the plan would help the state and local governments secure federal funding for new infrastructure projects, just as the framers of ARC had intended.[104] And in the coming decades, writing periodic regional development plans would become one of ARC's highest-profile activities.[105]

5
Growth Management Comes to Georgia

> *The smart money says that Georgia is a bad bet for any kind of growth management. We're a pro-business bastion. We're probably home rule heaven. Nevertheless, in under two years, a new growth management strategy went from the gleam in some dreamer's eye to the law of our state.*
> —John Sibley III, "How the Georgia Growth Management Plan Enhances Local Preservation"[1]

When the ballots had been counted in the 1980 presidential election, Ronald Reagan had won the popular vote by nearly 10 percentage points. In defeating Jimmy Carter, Reagan had carried all but six states, leading to a landslide victory in the Electoral College and dealing Carter a painful defeat. Georgia's "conservative and progressive" president was sent packing back to Atlanta, and Reagan kicked off his New Federalism revolution on January 20, 1981, with his now infamous inaugural address broadside on government.[2]

As Reagan began his ideological battle to free states and local governments from federal oversight, early returns from the 1980 Census of Population and Housing confirmed that the demographic shifts that had begun to restructure urban life in the United States in the 1960s had continued unabated through the 1970s. Though migration of blacks out of former Confederate states and into urban centers in the Northeast and Midwest appeared to be slowing, the draining of middle- and working-class whites from large central cities showed little indication of reversal.[3] With the completion of the final urban segments of the Interstate Highway System, people and jobs had continued to leave central cities at a startling rate.[4] In most places there was little to stop them and indeed much to encourage them. New houses on the periphery remained affordable and accessible to those with sufficient means. Automobile commuting remained relatively painless, having not yet succumbed to the gridlock that would come to characterize the life of the hapless suburban commuter.[5] With jobs, housing, shopping, and a collection of social institutions for nearly every need, picking up an entire household and reconstituting it along the urban fringe without missing a beat was easier than ever. The suburbs and exurbs ringing America's large central cities boomed.[6]

As these spatial-demographic shifts unfolded, in addition to political and economic controversies, the 1970s had witnessed a range of policy innovations that profoundly influenced local, regional, and state planning. Perhaps most significantly, the federal A-95 review program had established an interlocking set of metropolitan-level regulations for coordinating the actions of local and state governments with federal policies. The mandates of the A-95 review process became an important part of federal urban policy in the early 1970s and led to regional coordination clauses being included in other federal programs.[7] Section 208 of the 1972 Clean Water Act mandated the development of regional water plans.[8] The 1970 and 1977 Clean Air Act amendments established regional air quality guidelines.[9] Amendments and reauthorizations of the Federal Aid Highway Act in 1970, 1973, and 1975 broadened the role of regional planning agencies to include more consultation between federal, regional, and local agencies and finally opened the Highway Trust Fund to mass transit expenditures.[10]

During the same period, innovative new state- and region-level planning policies emerged in different parts of the country.[11] Driven by the growing power of the environmental movement, visible in the national land-use bills being debated in Congress, these planning initiatives, later dubbed a "quiet revolution," opened conversations about the shape future land development policy should take.[12] While a national land-use bill never became law, the debates surrounding the bills highlighted issues important in subsequent state-level efforts to enact land-use planning laws.[13] These state planning policies arrived in two waves, one from the late 1960s to the late 1970s and a second from the early 1980s to the late 1980s.[14] First-wave programs, in Oregon, Florida, and Vermont, were responses to heightened public concern over environmental decline and increased federal support for intergovernmental coordination activities.[15] Second-wave programs in New Jersey, Maine, Rhode Island, Georgia, and Washington appeared to be driven by a more disparate set of issues, which included environmental protection but also the need to spark job growth and fill gaps left by Reagan's attempts to rescind direct federal support for planning and infrastructure.[16] Both waves of state-level planning initiatives capitalized on growing citizen discontent with urban development's effect on quality of life but also were motivated by the utility of comprehensive planning as an economic development tool.[17]

The introduction of state comprehensive planning legislation in Oregon in 1973 offered perhaps the most complete demonstration of this new stance toward planning. Oregon's law, with its relatively strict top-down requirements, presented a compelling model for how states might take a strong role in the control of land development, one oriented toward preserving valuable agricultural land, constraining urban sprawl, and ensuring the protection of fragile surface waters. The reach of the Oregon law exempted no county. Every jurisdiction was required to prepare a comprehensive plan and submit it for state approval.[18]

On the heels of Oregon's land-use law, Georgia embarked on its own lengthy journey to mandate state and local planning. In the early 1970s, Governor Jimmy Carter pursued a wide-ranging effort to reorganize the state's bureaucracy, in the process creating new departments and state agencies. At the same time, he created a short-lived commission charged with developing ideas for a state land-use planning law.[19] Although Carter's planned growth commission failed to produce workable legislation, the idea had long legs.

Georgia has rarely been lauded for its efforts to regulate land development.[20] During the 1970s and 1980s, state leaders had done just about everything in their power to encourage rapid population growth and urban sprawl and had done little to imperil local land-use control. Yet fifteen years after the demise of Carter's planned growth commission, the Georgia General Assembly almost unanimously enacted a package of laws that not only strongly encouraged local land-use planning but also established a three-tiered system of intergovernmental coordination that linked local governments, regional planning agencies, and the state.[21] After years of debate, comprehensive planning legislation was finally signed into law in the summer of 1989.

As with Oregon's and other first-wave programs, concern about protecting natural resources provided the initial rationale for the state to extend its authority over local planning. However, two important characteristics of Georgia's growth management system make it distinct from other states. First, because Georgia's politics in the 1970s and 1980s had become increasingly dominated by the concerns of metropolitan Atlanta, politicians had begun to see the fate of the entire state through the lens of the region. The governor, public administrators, and legislators responsible for introducing state planning legislation and ushering it through the General Assembly had close connections to the metropolitan area, and they devised growth management laws that privileged infrastructure, land development, and job creation to benefit the state's leading urban region. In effect, the growth policies conflated natural resource protection and coordination with securing Atlanta's water supply, expanding its transportation network, and building its economy. Second, Georgia's leaders conceived growth management as a way to standardize the local and regional planning process to make a better environment for development without shaping physical outcomes. Thus, similar to policies in other states, Georgia's growth management scheme restructured land development decisions and regulated the planning process. But unlike other states' planning systems, Georgia's encouraged growth with few restrictions or controls on location. Hence planning as a tool to rein in abusive land development practices, hatched as part of the government reforms of Governor Carter in the early 1970s, had been repurposed by the end of the 1980s to support an agenda of infrastructure investment, land development, and economic growth.[22]

Jimmy Carter and the Initial Push for State Planning

Jimmy Carter won the 1970 gubernatorial election in Georgia in part by casting himself as an old-fashioned Southern conservative. Despite winning a plurality of the state's white working-class vote by appealing to their racial fears, Carter would model his single term on the progressive tradition of former governors Ernest Vandiver and Carl Sanders, the latter whom he beat in the Democratic primary before dispatching a forgettable Republican challenger. When the newly elected governor delivered his famously blunt inaugural address in 1971 to the Georgia General Assembly, he tipped his hat to the changes in Georgia's politics created by the federal civil rights legislation of the 1960s and signaled his belief that changing the way government decisions were made would confront, and he hoped bury, the ugly legacy of discrimination.[23] Carter's emphasis on civil rights was also an acknowledgment of the changing demographic characteristics of the Georgia Democratic Party's political base. He sought not only to come to terms with Georgia's racially polarized past but also to project a vision for the state's future that hinged on a major reorganization of the public bureaucracy. Though less newsworthy than his public remarks on civil rights, Carter's agenda of organizational reform had equally far-reaching effects.[24]

Embarking on "comprehensive government reorganization" as his main legislative effort, Carter first took a hatchet and then a needle and thread to the state's Byzantine governance structure. Cutting and consolidating, Carter cobbled together large departments and administrative units out of existing small ones.[25] He oversaw the creation of the Georgia Heritage Trust and the total reorganization of the Departments of Transportation, Natural Resources, and Community Affairs. He spearheaded an effort to amend the Georgia constitution in 1972 to grant counties legal authority to provide urban services on the same footing as municipalities and laid the groundwork for the creation of the Chattahoochee River National Recreation Area. Like Vandiver and Sanders before him, Carter understood the importance of institutional structures and the art of public relations and was well aware of how much a governor could influence the success or failure of new policies and agencies.[26] Yet the full effect of Carter's modernization effort would be fully realized only years later. By streamlining and professionalizing state agencies, he helped consolidate power in the governor's office, in the process creating a political environment that supported greater regulatory involvement by the state in issues that had previously been the domain of counties and municipalities and in many instances ignored.[27]

In early 1973, near the end of his major administrative reforms, Carter turned his attention to land-use planning. Public awareness of the problems created by land development practices in metropolitan Atlanta had recently intensified, particularly with respect to the Chattahoochee River. Pushed by planning requirements in the A-95 review program, Section 208 of the recently enacted Clean Water Act, and the likelihood that one of the national land-use bills then being debated in Congress would become law, Carter created the Commission on Planned Growth to explore legislation to make local land-use planning and protection of vital natural areas mandatory across the state.[28] The commission comprised a small group of his legislative, business, and bureaucratic allies. Carter appointed as chairman Joel Cowan, the local developer behind Peachtree City, the state's sole successful postwar new city.[29] Other members included Joe Frank Harris, a state senator from northern Georgia who would later become governor; Howard Atherton, Atlanta-based leader of the urban caucus in the state senate; and Paul Coverdell, who would go on to hold one of Georgia's seats in the U.S. Senate.

The planned growth commission set out to develop a strategy, and Carter hoped a legislative proposal, to tighten controls on the way land was regulated in Georgia. The commission was also supposed to support the work of the Vital Areas Council. Itself a product of the 1973 legislative session, the council had been set up to "identify and develop standards for the protection of certain areas of the State of vital concern," a formal mechanism for protecting the parts of Georgia's natural environment deemed "most critical to [the] immediate future."[30] When the planned growth commission released its report at the end of 1973, less than a third of the state's 159 counties had zoning or development regulations in place and far fewer had comprehensive land-use plans. Most of Georgia's local governments went their own way, either ignorant of or not caring about their neighbors' concerns. Moreover, the rural electoral bloc in the Georgia General Assembly had for years blocked policies permitting more aggressive state regulation of land development.[31]

Predictably, perhaps, the final report stopped well short of the commission's original goals, noting meekly, "We were relieved to find it unnecessary to recommend immediate vast new State regulations."[32] In deference to the reticence of many state legislators to endorse any policy that might be perceived as limiting growth or usurping local control, the report merely stated that "a policy of 'no growth' is not viable in Georgia."[33] Instead, the report identified and described land-use issues facing the state. To many observers the commission reflected the fear of challenging home rule and the state's prevailing "strong bias toward independent and powerful local government."[34]

Despite being hamstrung by legislative politics, the Commission on Planned Growth laid out a few strategies to protect natural resources and discourage sprawl. Noting that most of Georgia's recent growth was "haphazard, chaotic and random because of inadequate planning," the commission recommended establishing a system of regional coordinating agencies as organizational elements of a future growth management policy.[35] It also outlined "19 actions by the state and local governments to end past land abuses in Georgia and accommodate an upsurge in growth expected over the next several decades." Among those actions were better "control of densities," "preservation of adequate open space," establishing a statewide "coordinated land use planning process," and offering a program of "economic incentives" to spur development in rural areas of the state.[36]

The political will to implement growth management lagged far behind the commission's ability to initiate a conversation about state planning. In the years following the planned growth commission's final report, local interest in and support for substate planning and coordination began to decline. Part of this decline stemmed from the confluence of an anemic economy and increasing inflation and part from the failure of Congress to produce workable national land-use legislation.[37] Yet perhaps the biggest reasons were the timing of the commission, Carter's fleeting interest in the issue, and his national political ambitions. Together, these factors left little room for the planned growth commission to have much impact on Georgia's planning or political culture.[38]

As Carter turned his attention to the 1976 race for the White House and left his gubernatorial term behind, the suggestions of his planned growth commission were pushed to a back burner. The new governor, George Busbee, a long-serving Georgia House of Representatives Democrat from Albany known for his quiet manner (campaigning as "a workhorse, not a showhorse"), took leadership of the state at a moment when the national economy was sluggish and discussions about the political and economic imbalance between the "two Georgias," the urban core centered on Atlanta and the rural remainder, were becoming heated. In response to the mood, Busbee tried to conduct a palliative first term, focusing most of his energy on fiscal responsibility, a restrained approach to state regulation, promotion of economic growth, and early childhood education.[39]

Early in his second term, however, Busbee slowly began to reengage with the issue of state planning. Inspiration arrived in late 1978, when James Hunt, the new governor of North Carolina, established a balanced growth board to guide a growth policy for his state.[40] Hunt's hope was to develop a policy framework that would support "economic growth and job opportunities throughout the state, at the same time maintaining . . . dispersed population."[41] The result was the Balanced Growth Policy Act, which he signed into law in 1979. While not statewide growth management per se, on paper North Carolina's law engaged many of the same issues—environmental protection, intergovernmental cooperation, and urban growth centers—and tried to address them within a statewide system of regional planning agencies.[42] A state with similar aspirations to Georgia's and a fierce regional competitor for investment, North Carolina's strategy offered a model of regulation mild enough to suit Busbee's taste and weak enough to avoid offending anyone. North Carolina's policy was duly noted among Busbee's executive staff, though a move to develop a balanced growth policy in Georgia would not come for two more years.[43]

When Reagan took office in 1981, direct federal aid to states, regional agencies, and local governments came under renewed assault as the president "set forth a sweeping agenda of budget reductions, tax cuts, personnel freezes, block grants, and deregulation initiatives—all intended to dramatically lower the fiscal and administrative profile of the federal government."[44] Reagan's rhetoric of reducing federal intervention specifically targeted infrastructure funding, financial support for planning activities, and the level of federal oversight of urban development activities. Though it is not clear that Reagan's assault on federal support for planning and infrastructure was the primary motivation for Busbee's action, in early 1982 the governor finally took more decisive steps toward a state planning law. Presiding over his last General Assembly as governor, Busbee successfully pushed through the legislature a bill creating the Georgia Commission on State Growth Policy. His timing could not have been better.

On July 14, 1982, barely a month after the Georgia General Assembly wrapped up its session, Reagan issued an executive order rescinding Circular A-95, sweeping away a symbolically important federal policy supporting coordinated planning, leaving the states to pick up the slack. Under the new order, federal agencies were directed to actively discourage "the reauthorization or creation of any planning organization which is Federally-funded," to create a "strengthened federalism."[45] Though the clearinghouse function of the A-95 review process had not produced the kind of coordinated substate planning it had originally promised, the program had nevertheless been able to "ensure a process of discussion" among adjacent local governments, evidence of the "regional intelligence" necessary to fostering genuine cooperation.[46] Yet Reagan's intent was quite clear: the federal hand should recede and states should handle intergovernmental coordination and substate planning on their own.[47] Barely a month after Reagan ended the A-95 program, Busbee issued his own executive order tasking the state's new Commission on State Growth Policy with finding ways to "improve coordination and cooperation among the state and its local governments . . . [to] give proper attention to the preservation of Georgia's natural and human resources, and to promote improvements within the intergovernmental system to assure cost effectiveness in the delivery of governmental services to the people of Georgia." Charged with developing a strategy to prevent some of the "helter-skelter development" befalling Georgia, the commission parroted many of the ideas enunciated in North Carolina's growth policy.[48] However, Busbee was less than four months from leaving office by the time commission members were appointed in September, and without much support from the lame-duck governor, the commission was idled.

Busbee's successor, Joe Frank Harris, initially seemed an unlikely candidate to take up the cause of pushing Georgia toward an embrace of state planning. Before entering politics, Harris had run a wholesale concrete business he inherited from his father. Though he had represented only a small district in rural north Georgia for eighteen years when he won the 1982 gubernatorial election, his profile among his colleagues in the General Assembly was far from obscure. A close confidant to the powerful Speaker of the Georgia House of Representatives and for six years chairman of the Appropriations Committee, Harris had amassed considerable capital among his fellow legislators, a significant factor in his winning the Democratic nomination and general election. Generally considered quite conservative, Harris spent most of his first term recruiting new industry, though he flashed previously unknown ambition when he pushed legislation through the General Assembly to overhaul Georgia's moribund public education system.[49] After winning reelection in a landslide in 1986, Harris surprised many of his former legislative colleagues by not only revisiting the issue of statewide planning but pushing it to the top of his second-term legislative agenda.[50]

Several surrounding events likely contributed to Harris's motivation. President Reagan continued his push to shift the balance of power in the federal-state-local relationship. Neighboring Florida restructured its growth management laws in 1985 to strengthen the state's hand, forcing local governments into greater vertical compliance with an overall state plan and boosting protection for critical environmental resources.[51] An extended drought in northern Georgia through the spring and summer of 1986 had put water management issues foremost in the minds of the state's leaders, who were always on the hunt for ways to ensure adequate water supply to feed Atlanta's expansion. Ongoing population and employment growth in metro Atlanta continued to strain smaller suburban governments' ability to deliver a full range of urban services. Increased competition from North Carolina, Florida, and Tennessee had brought added attention to the effect unchecked growth in Atlanta might have on the state's ability to attract new investment.[52]

State planning, however, had been on Harris's mind for years. Having served on Jimmy Carter's short-lived planned growth commission in 1973, Harris had been party to the commission's original charge to build a case for statewide growth management as well as witness to Busbee's eight years of ignoring the issue. Shortly into Harris's first term, his administration had quietly begun working to reconstruct Busbee's languishing balanced growth commission, creating a new advisory body that also included pieces of Carter's more far-reaching reform effort from a decade earlier.

The Realization of State Planning

The beginning of the effort that would finally produce a state planning policy lies somewhere around the middle of 1983, when Jim Higdon, the commissioner of the Georgia Department of Community Affairs, drafted a memo to Harris recommending that the governor petition the state legislature to "extend the life of the Commission [on State Growth Policy]" by an additional year and "change the principal mission of the commission from advising on intergovernmental relations to advising on ways to promote sound economic growth and development in Georgia."[53] With Higdon's help, Harris's executive staff set about removing several incumbents on the dormant commission who were "obtrusive" or who failed to "grasp the Commission's purpose." They were replaced with individuals more amenable to the governor's vision.⁵⁴ In a memo to Harris in the summer of 1984, after the new commissioners had been installed, Higdon put forth a strategy for developing growth management legislation in Georgia. This strategy would shape the entire process that followed and prove critical to transforming state planning from a way to control substandard land-use practices into a strategy for economic growth.⁵⁵

The crux of Higdon's vision was that, rather than confronting "the evils associated with urban decay and urban sprawl" or exploring "radical forms of regulation," the new commission should work to develop a strategy that would make "jobs available for all Georgians" and also provide additional state services without the imposition of "new taxes." Perhaps most significantly, Higdon asserted that a new "growth policy or development strategy should *not* be designed to direct growth to certain areas." Rather, state efforts to provide "direct funding for various purposes, to transportation links, to tax policy," should be based on an "early warning system" that would allow "necessary infrastructure development [to] keep pace with private development decisions" and not the other way around.⁵⁶ With this, the idea behind Carter's statewide planned growth commission had been transformed.

Both Higdon and Harris recognized that the organization, composition, and leadership of the growth commission that would develop legislation would be the most critical part of the entire process. Hence Higdon recommended the commission be made up of "influential business people who will have the ability to bring the private business community into full partnership with the state in the developmental phase of growth and development strategies." He reasoned that the presence of high-visibility corporate leaders "will also make it possible to surface issues that need to be raised, but perhaps not by the Governor or his staff directly." Urging a short time frame "to prevent protracted debate about insignificant issues," Higdon believed the proposed strategy should allot "limited time" to the commission to force it to "face policy issues." The proposal for the reformulated growth commission strongly endorsed moving "beyond an analysis of the issues" and toward "propos[ing] an action plan" that could be "presented to the Governor and General Assembly for implementation." Thus, a planned growth commission full of prominent political and business leaders would provide Harris instant credibility and also political cover, because some rural legislators might see the legislation as a power grab by the governor. Thus, by the time Harris was reelected in November 1986, a strategy for developing a progrowth management policy for the state was in place.⁵⁷

On January 13, 1987, in his second inaugural address, Harris spoke mostly about his first term's accomplishments: education, job growth, and "responsible management of our state's fiscal resources." But at the end of his speech Harris slipped in a few words about state planning. Noting that despite the state's recent good fortune, the "responsibility is great to protect the natural resources God has given us" and that "our existence is linked to the future of our land, air and water," he declared that "a 'growth strategy' for the future must be developed to ensure that improvements to our infrastructure are wise and productive." While acknowledging that "local government officials . . . must help to meet this economic development need," Harris reiterated his belief that the state should provide "strong assistance" in this effort.[58]

The seriousness of his proposal for a new state growth policy proved difficult to discern at first. One editorial writer for the *Atlanta Journal-Constitution* ventured an "English translation" of Harris's comments, explaining that "developers will not be allowed to rush in and throw up subdivisions and shopping centers willy-nilly. The proper infrastructure must be in place. . . . The state wants to see to that, if local government will not."[59] While many observers recognized that Atlanta's breakneck growth might be a threat to the region's quality of life and its economic competitiveness, few expected Harris to do anything about it. But by the time Harris's allies in the Georgia house presented a resolution urging the governor to create a new growth commission, the notion that "comprehensive and state-wide growth planning is essential" to the state's future had become more widely accepted.[60] That the state would "force rural counties into zoning and land use planning" began to be seen as a potential outcome of whatever growth management policy Harris eventually proposed.[61] The big question was how far the governor would go toward making rural counties adopt "land use standards and adhere to them" and what the political cost of that decision might be.[62]

Mandatory local land-use planning, a hallmark feature of the state planning policies adopted in the 1970s, had been part of the conversation around the Georgia capitol since the late 1960s.[63] The legislation that created the Atlanta Regional Commission (ARC) in 1971 had initially included a land-use-plan requirement for all Atlanta-area governments, though this had been dropped when the legislation reached the General Assembly.[64] Similarly, Governor Carter's planned growth commission had recommended a "coordinated land use planning program to develop broad guidelines for land use in Georgia" and had even suggested a "constitutional amendment" to allow the General Assembly the "right to set uniform criteria in establishing goals and standards for zoning decisions" across the state.[65] In the intervening years, the General Assembly had considered a series of planning bills, though acting on none. Even as the Harris administration was working behind the scenes on its strategy for state planning, a bill that would require local land-use planning had been introduced in the 1986 and 1987 sessions by Rep. Terry Lawler from Clarkdale. Without the governor's support, the bill failed both times to generate enough support to make it out of subcommittee.[66]

In April 1987 Harris made perhaps his single most significant decision regarding his growth commission by naming Atlanta attorney John Sibley III as staff director. Son of John Sibley Jr., who had chaired the Sibley Commission, a group of Atlanta leaders who devised the plan to desegregate Atlanta's public schools in the early 1960s, the younger Sibley had been practicing law in Atlanta for fifteen years and was well connected in Atlanta's political and social circles when Harris tapped him to direct the growth commission.[67] During his first week on the job Sibley defined procedural strategies the commission would pursue, a structure for how the commission should be organized, and a mold into which potential members should fit.

Following Higdon's original recommendation that members of the commission be individuals "who can move opinion and redefine turf" and suggesting that the goal of the commission should be "long-range strategies for 'quality growth,'" because "no one opposes quality growth," Sibley designed a preemptive strike to head off the major counterarguments the commission would likely face from its critics ("quality growth" also became part of the commission's name). In a key memorandum, he explained to Harris there were "three distinct points of view from which different constituencies approach quality growth: economic development, resource management, and governance," and though these different views often contest one another, they "do not present irreconcilable conflicts." Hence if the governor allowed the commission to focus on one viewpoint at the exclusion of the others, the commission would likely be perceived as "distort[ing] the issue." Thus, Sibley recommended that "all three points of view should be kept involved and in balance at every step" during commission deliberations. He suggested that Harris use a "more general" sounding executive order to shape the commission, one that would "leave room to search for new and creative strategies" as the commission went about its work.[68]

Sibley framed the commission's work so that all policy recommendations would flow through his office first and thus could be worded so that they did not offend the rural legislators whose support would be needed. Recommending the formation of "technical advisory groups" to "develop position papers" on issues related to growth, he suggested the commission avoid "conventional topics" and "conventional answers." To accomplish this, Sibley advised that the technical advisory groups be organized around substantive topics "that really determine whether or not quality growth will happen." The resulting advisory reports would seek "creative alternatives, not answers," including inventories of existing conditions and "alternative strategies for getting from where we are to where we want to be." As part of this approach, Sibley suggested an aggressive public outreach program that would "take . . . the Commission to the people" and "listen to the whole state." Extensive outreach would create acceptance for a constitutional amendment that seemed likely to be necessary to implement statewide planning.[69]

On June 16, 1987, Harris issued an executive order creating the Quality Growth Commission. Reducing several years of backroom strategizing into a one-page statement, the order reflected the advice of Higdon and Sibley to use the power of state planning to support economic growth, especially in metro Atlanta. Declaring that "economic development and its full benefits can only be realized if Georgia's physical infrastructure facilities . . . are adequate to support development," Harris's executive order assured lawmakers that the commission's work of "defining growth strategies" would respect Georgia's "tradition of local autonomy" in matters of planning.[70]

Harris and Sibley named mostly reliable political allies to the commission. Though no nominee was known for strident partisan politics, hints about the expected direction the commission would take could be gleaned from the names on the list, which, following Higdon's advice, included some of the state's most powerful and influential individuals. Membership was strongly tilted toward Atlanta, including representatives from Atlanta's biggest corporations: Coca-Cola, Citizens and Southern Bank, and Southern Bell.[71] Several legislators were appointed, three of whom were considered future gubernatorial candidates, and the chairman of the commission was politically connected Atlanta developer Joel Cowan, an old friend of Harris's who had also chaired Jimmy Carter's growth commission fifteen years earlier.[72]

The publication of the commission roster raised hackles in several quarters. Over the following weeks, complaints rolled in, many reflecting fears that the commission was tilted too much toward the "professional planning community, banking institutions and trade organizations."[73] A jilted county commissioner from Albany, in southwest Georgia, complained that "practically all appointees are from Atlanta or north Georgia," which he took to be the governor's "obvious discrimination" against southern Georgia. The president of the Dahlonega-Lumpkin County Chamber of Commerce wrote to express his concern: "We perceive . . . a lack of adequate representation of the North Georgia mountain communities on the commission," where critical surface waters originate.[74] A state representative from Atlanta active in planning and zoning issues in the General Assembly, Kathy Steinberg, blasted the governor for not naming her to the commission, remarking in an interview with the *Atlanta Constitution*, "I'm very angry, even if it's not appropriate to say so."[75] Other complaints came from industry associations miffed at being excluded and small-town politicians eager for a bigger stage.[76]

Harris and Sibley moved quickly to get the new commission up and running. Harris told commission members at their swearing-in ceremony in late June, "Your challenge will be to identify the issues that must be addressed in Georgia now, to find the best strategies for dealing with those issues, and to define the steps for implementing those strategies." Noting that the commission had "the opportunity to develop a continuing capacity in Georgia to anticipate needs and plan for future growth," the governor reminded the members that he saw the commission as "a priority of my second term" and that no initiative is as "important to the future as this is."[77] The *Atlanta Journal* optimistically deciphered Harris's charge as "developing a plan to change the state from a collection of bickering political fiefdoms into a unified cooperative" and concluded that the most important outcome "will be the creation of an atmosphere of consensus" rather than a written plan.[78]

While commission members tended to cite "coordinated economic development" as their highest priority, when the commission convened for its first meeting in mid-July, other priorities surfaced and clashed, most conspicuously around the "two Georgias" divide.[79] The mayor of Thomson, a small town in eastern Georgia, said that finding ways to "disperse economic growth throughout the state" was surely a bigger problem than conserving land. A commissioner from Atlanta seemed genuinely surprised that "protection of 'open spaces' and natural attractions" was a "lower priorit[y] than economic issues" among her colleagues from outside metropolitan Atlanta. Other participants pessimistically predicted everything from a "confrontation" between the state and local governments over the authority to zone to a flat-out rejection of the state's authority to implement any planning standards whatsoever.[80] Yet over the coming months, Harris and Sibley gently pushed members of the commission to coalesce around a small group of common issues.

They accomplished this by hiring a team of facilitators from the University of Georgia to create a process plan for the commission. The facilitators designed a process that divided the commission into four working groups, each tasked with developing a separate list of issues, goals, and policy options related to a specific substantive area: important facilities and infrastructure, economic development, land use, and natural resources. Though Sibley admonished the commission and the working groups to "use a process that [was] grounded in actively involving the affected constituencies at every level of the process," the facilitation plan also called for convening two expert panels to provide general advice to the commission and supplying a professional staff of advisors to the commission and each of the individual working groups.[81]

The expert panels were tasked with explaining the state of the art in growth regulation and planning.[82] Composed of academics, representatives of nongovernmental organizations, and state bureaucrats, the expert panels identified substantive topics, explained them to the commission subcommittees, and transmitted their findings directly to the office of the staff director. Though the process design tried to confine the role of the panels and the staff "to issues of expertise," it placed "the Staff Director of the Commission in a position to act for the [entire] Commission in monitoring and directing the process."[83] By early autumn of 1987, input from the expert panels had been gathered, compiled, and reported back to Sibley, who transferred a summary to the working groups, which would decide which issues to include in the final report to the governor. The issues ranged widely, from the nomenclature of growth to the legal limits of local governance, to endangered environmental resources, to the dominance of roads in Georgia. A few essential issues were quickly identified, and by February 1988 the working groups were reporting their results. As the ideas refined in the working group meetings were transmitted by the commission staff, Sibley worked to determine the legal and financial feasibility of the issues, develop an implementation strategy, and perhaps most critically, build acceptance in the state's political establishment. In almost every case, the group reports simply underlined the positions Harris, Higdon, and Sibley had staked out months or years earlier.

The natural resources task force identified monitoring and public education as important tasks and highlighted protection of the state's surface water resources from "contamination, unwarranted channelization, and diversion," but their emphasis was on "manag[ing] these watersheds as the most basic contributor to growth."[84] The land-use task force recommended a program of "statewide comprehensive planning" based on minimum standards, "coordination and consistency among plans," and review by "regional authorit[ies]" of plans with "interjurisdictional fiscal/physical impact." But at the same time the task force also "reaffirmed its conviction that zoning decisions should remain in the hands of local authorities" and that there should be no "state takeover" of local zoning power.[85] Recommendations from members of the economic development task force focused on finding "new methods of financing businesses in Georgia," increasing the involvement of the state university system in economic development efforts, and "sorting out the relations between state agency planning and statewide planning."[86] Finally, the capital facilities task force zeroed in on water supply infrastructure, concluding that Georgia needed a system of new reservoirs to ensure long-term water supply for metropolitan Atlanta.[87]

At the end of February, Sibley reported to the governor that the working groups agreed on four basic points. The first was that the state should do "everything possible to accommodate growth" in existing high-growth areas (that is, Atlanta). Second, the commission's plan should seek to "stimulate and enhance the quality of life in low-growth areas." Third, the state must ensure "coordination among state agencies" and "cooperation between existing governmental bodies" to reduce the cross-jurisdictional "impact" of development decisions. Fourth, the state should devise a "three-tier governmental process" to connect state, regional, and local planning and development efforts.[88]

In early March 1988, in an interview with *Georgia Trend Magazine*, Quality Growth Commission chairman Cowan pulled back the curtain on some of the commission's deliberations. Suggesting that the future recommendations of the commission would be "very controversial," Cowan highlighted how the commission had concluded that the "state [should] ha[ve] a role in planning" and would likely recommend "some [form of] mandated planning." Cowan also revealed that the commission had contemplated recommending an amendment to the Georgia constitution so that "the state is empowered to mandate standards and procedures for land use governance."[89]

Following up on his plan to "tak[e] the commission to the people," in the early spring of 1988 Sibley organized a series of public hearings around the state to showcase the findings of the working groups.[90] With the main point of the hearings being to publicize the work the commission had already accomplished, they were to be highly structured events. Commission members were warned that "proper planning and discipline" were necessary to keep the meetings from becoming "counter productive," since different "interest groups have learned to 'pack' the audience." Commission staff was instructed to intervene if necessary to prevent the meetings from becoming "too democratic." Presentations should be "clear, well-rehearsed, and highly visual," and commissioners were implored to stick to very brief explanations of the process, the goals of the commission, and the findings.[91]

From late March through early May, Sibley, Cowan, and a rotating cast of commission members convened fifteen public meetings around the state to gauge, but also shape, public reaction to the task force recommendations. An analysis of the comments of the roughly 1,200 people who attended at least one of the meetings noted that "comments . . . generally fell into five subject areas on which numerous comments were received" and that by a significant margin "the majority of speakers supported the basic thrust of the Commission." The five areas receiving the most comments were education, natural resources, economic development, land use and zoning, and transportation, though opinions tended to cluster around a smaller collection of key issues: greater "state role in economic development," the belief that "planning and zoning should be left to the local level to decide," and "more protection of resources" for future water supply.[92] Perhaps most importantly, "only a handful [of comments] expressed complete dissatisfaction with any and all aspects of the Commission's work."[93]

Resistance had been expected from rural residents and certain members of the General Assembly.[94] But reports of the demeanor of the public meetings, which almost always included state representatives, found little opposition to even the commission's most far-reaching recommendations, and the displeasure that was expressed was as much a result of miscommunication as genuine anger. Addressing what appeared to be the only source of major concern with the public, the commission's proposal to implement coordinated land-use regulation, the most conservative editorial writer at the *Atlanta Journal* reminded readers that under the task force's recommendations "property rights are not under assault, local zoning control is assured."[95] In an April interview with the *Atlanta Constitution*, Cowan remarked that he "had been surprised that no organized opposition has so far emerged."[96] It appeared as if the breadth of interests represented on the Quality Growth Commission, the fact that its members were drawn from "Georgia leaders," and that the recommendations were "extremely pragmatic" were indeed paying off.[97]

By May the working groups had wrapped up, and Sibley began moving the commission toward adopting an implementation program, the final step in preparing a legislative package for the 1989 session of the General Assembly. Privately, Sibley urged the governor to give his visible support during the transition period, suggesting that Harris consider a well-timed and "strongly supportive press release" to allay lingering fears among commission members and "some key groups" that he was "not really likely to support the recommendations of the Commission."⁹⁸ In early July, Sibley reported back to Harris that the reception of an interim report outlining the work of the Quality Growth Commission among state agency directors had "generally been very favorable," with one notable exception: the Georgia Department of Transportation (GDOT). In a pointed letter addressed to Sibley, the GDOT commissioner complained that the commission's recommendations were "too soft," would create a "big and unnecessary new bureaucracy," and that the report was "written without an opportunity for comment from department heads." A few weeks later, after a private meeting with the governor, the GDOT commissioner became quite contrite, writing to Sibley to express his willingness to work with the commission to ensure "mobility and accessibility" for the state's citizens.⁹⁹ Several of the most powerful state lobbies, including the Georgia Municipal Association, the Georgia Development Alliance, and the Association of County Commissioners of Georgia, came out in full support of the growth commission's interim report.¹⁰⁰

By the end of July, Sibley had an outline of the implementation process complete. He convened a small working group of commission members and charged them with "flesh[ing] out" a short section of the interim report on "comprehensive, coordinated, and continuous planning and management" to divide implementation responsibilities among, local, regional, and state agencies.¹⁰¹ Recommending a "bottom-up planning process," the group outlined a "legal and institutional framework for a comprehensive, coordinated three-tiered" planning strategy. Their report suggested splitting responsibilities for the statewide planning process among local governments, regional agencies, and the state and creating a governor-appointed state planning commission to oversee the entire process, including devising statewide goals, planning procedures, regional boundaries, and minimum standards for local plans. Local governments would develop "local growth management plans" that met standards established by the state. Regional agencies would review local plans to identify "areas of conflict." State agencies would establish long-range plans for their operational jurisdictions and seek ways to cooperate.¹⁰² Sibley released a short report describing the implementation process for public comment in August and scheduled four public hearings over three days in mid-September.¹⁰³

Apparently learning lessons from the Carter commission's failure and Busbee's inaction, Harris, Higdon, and Sibley recognized the importance of "condition[ing] target audiences to accept the Commission's goals and objectives" if the recommendations were to evolve into workable legislation.¹⁰⁴ During the previous spring, as the commission working groups were finishing up, Sibley had pulled together an ad hoc Quality Growth Commission subcommittee to devise strategies for tailoring communication about the commission's work to key stakeholders.¹⁰⁵ This subcommittee's priority was to "inform and educat[e] the Georgia General Assembly" about the "broad support" among the public for adopting the Quality Growth Commission recommendations. The resulting strategy included taking a "personalize[d] approach" to influential legislators, without "inundat[ing]" them with detailed policy prescriptions. This approach included a video that gave an overview of the commission's work and "four or five case study examples" that illustrated different recommendations, as well as a "slick summary report" of the process. The video and report would be distributed to assembly members with a "cover letter signed by Governor Harris, Speaker Murphy, and Lt. Governor Miller . . . encouraging the legislator to consider the merits of the Commission's recommendations." Other politically important groups—state department heads, local government lobbying organizations, leaders of the state's larger local governments, and business organizations—would also receive videos and summary reports to distribute to their constituencies.[106]

The effort to tightly control the message of the commission paid dividends. By late summer, the Georgia Conservancy, the business-friendly environmental nonprofit that had been generally supportive of the state's growth management efforts, had issued a press release supporting the recommendations of the commission, and the Georgia chapter of the Sierra Club voiced tentative optimism about the commission's work.[107] The Georgia Municipal Association and Association of County Commissioners of Georgia went so far as to launch a coordinated attack on the *Atlanta Journal*, writing in letters to the editor that they "continued to be appalled at the editorial comments made by the Atlanta newspapers" that assumed that their organizations would automatically oppose the commission on the grounds that the commission recommendations "threaten local autonomy." The letters noted that, "quite to the contrary," both organizations "continue to feel good about the direction of the commission's work."[108]

By early autumn, Sibley had begun shaping the commission's recommendations into a final report. In several memos Sibley told the governor he was "trying to accelerate the Commission's timetable to produce a final report before the pre-legislative forum," and he reiterated the necessity of the governor and members of the commission using a "standardized message to cover as many stops on the rubber chicken circuit as possible." He also detailed the "key products" of the commission requiring legislative action and incurring new costs. These included legislation to permit the state to take a stronger role in coordinating planning, build and manage a system of regional reservoirs, and fund a solid waste and water and sewer construction program. The estimated cost of these programs varied, from $300,000 to study regional reservoirs to $3 million to $4 million to fund activities supporting coordinated planning, to millions of dollars for new roads.[109]

Sibley and his staff worked through October to finalize the wording of the Quality Growth Commission recommendations, secure advanced support from friendly stakeholder groups, and exert damage control among interest groups dismayed with the commission's findings. In mid-October, Harris and Sibley pulled together an informal legislative "implementation committee" comprising state politicians, local government officials, and a few "private interests" that would sell the merits of the growth commission's report to remaining holdouts in the legislature. This committee laid out a one-year timeline in which legislation would be introduced to the General Assembly, signed into law by Governor Harris, and take effect.[110] By the eve of the public release of the Quality Growth Commission's report, details about the proposed regulations and the time line for implementation had been widely reported. Stories in the media highlighted new requirements for coordinated regional planning, mandatory local land-use plans, and plans for regional reservoirs. They raised questions about whether the "time honored doctrine of home-rule" would be eroded by the new planning requirements. They asked whether rural governments would vigorously enforce new mandates for local land-use planning and the oversight authority given to agencies of "regional and state control." And they worried that local resistance would turn the commission's recommendations into a "toothless wish list."[111]

The final version of the commission report, *Quality Growth Partnership: The Bridge to Georgia's Future*, was released to the public November 2, 1988. The recommendations the commission had developed over the previous eighteen months became a "nine point strategy" for guiding growth in Georgia, appropriately symbolized with an image of a bridge. Recommendations were grouped by substantive area: human needs, infrastructure, environment, economic development, and coordination. Each recommendation included a brief description of the strategy followed by a few suggestions for implementation. Most recommendations eschewed depth and detail, the exception being the section on coordinated planning, which outlined in some detail a "three-tiered partnership for planning" and a new "framework for planning." Front and back covers included, the entire report was only sixteen pages.[112]

The timing of the report's release was strategic. Just seven days after it was published, Governor Harris used his keynote address at the General Assembly's annual prelegislative forum to kick off the public phase of selling the commission's recommendations. With the opening of the 1989 session of the General Assembly barely two months away, Harris began to condition the legislators. Declaring that he "could not be more pleased with the depth and breadth" of the report, he touted the recommendations as a "detailed blueprint" for Georgia's future. He expounded on the report's emphasis on the importance of human resource development, intergovernmental cooperation, natural resource protection, and access to capital for businesses in the state. Initially greeted with applause, the report was read by most of the Atlanta media as announcing important new powers for the state. Especially promising was the idea of "withholding state public improvement grants from governments that fail to plan adequately for growth," a suggestion that portended the state "ensur[ing] that metropolitan governments cooperate with each other" around infrastructure issues to

Figure 5.1 "The Bridge to Georgia's Future," from Governor's Growth Strategies Commission, *Quality Growth Partnership: The Bridge to Georgia's Future*, November 2, 1988, Governor, Legal Division Subject Files, 1984–1990, Growth Strategies Commission Folder, Georgia Archives, Morrow, Georgia

avoid "overtaxed water and sewer systems, crowded schools, and jammed highways." The *Atlanta Constitution* opined that "the [Quality] Growth . . . Commission has done a superb job of identifying problem areas" and that the commission has "performed a valuable public service."[113]

But the state forcing hundreds of local governments to write and adopt comprehensive plans seemed almost too good to be true. Once the report had been made public, doubts about the fate of the commission's recommendations emerged from two directions. Predictably, a handful of rural legislators criticized the proposed regional coordinating bodies for amounting to "double taxation," creating "another tier of government," and infringing on home rule.[114] Fears that the state might fail to fully fund the mechanisms needed to implement the recommendations were also voiced.[115] Directors of existing planning agencies worried about their status in a new system that appeared to emphasize state and regional control. Yet consternation from the other end of the spectrum was more pronounced and focused on the lack of enforcement provisions in the report. Observers questioned the willingness of a majority of the members of the General Assembly to vote to give state and regional planning agencies "genuine enforcement power." Without despotic power, the commission and its work was in danger of becoming "largely a waste of time."[116] Others worried that getting this legislation through the General Assembly would test the governor's ability to "talk, cajole, threaten, and plead as he has never done before."[117]

In fact, the problem of enforcement had been raised at many junctures before completion of the final report. Around the time the commission's interim report was released in the summer of 1988, questions had emerged about how powerful a new land-use law could actually be, given the political culture of the state. Joel Cowan, the Quality Growth Commission chairman, had acknowledged that the commission's "strategy ha[d] been to avoid getting too ambitious" to ensure "that the commission produce[d] something by its November deadline that the General Assembly [would] pass." To some, Cowan's words telegraphed that the commission tried to make proposals that did not "leave room for anything that anybody could possibly object to," creating in effect a "toothless tiger," which led one Georgia Institute of Technology planning professor to regard the gentle approach as designed to fail, another indicator of Georgia's "bankrupt" planning culture.[118] In the end, the commission avoided recommending the creation of an independent state planning agency, limited discussion of a tax increase to support state planning, and sidestepped the issue of zoning review.

In late October, just days before release of the final report, Department of Community Affairs director Higdon wrote to Governor Harris that a "majority of experts" had agreed that "a Constitutional amendment would be necessary" for the state to "mandate the coordinated planning process without violating local governments' home rule powers." But in a clear wish to avoid political backlash, Higdon argued instead for legislation that would "accomplish the same result by requiring planning as a condition to being eligible for certain state grants."[119] Sibley, his staff, and a few members of the Quality Growth Commission spent November "rethinking their plan to push for a constitutional amendment that would force local governments to participate." They came up with a recommendation for an administrative rule requiring state agencies to withhold funds if a local government failed to adopt an acceptable land-use plan. By early December, the idea of amending the state's constitution to require local governments to participate in the new land-use planning process was dead.[120] By the end of December, even the "legal requirement that state agencies withhold public improvement grants [from local governments] that fail to adequately plan for growth" had been dropped from the state planning legislation.[121]

In place of mandates or funding cuts, local governments that did not adopt a comprehensive plan would be only ineligible to apply for several extra state grants to support planning and infrastructure development. Disciplinary action against local governments that failed to plan would be decided by a group of state agency directors convened by the governor at a later date. While Cowan rationalized this tactic, saying, "The end result will be the same, I just think it might take longer without a law than with one," it had become painfully obvious that the draft legislation represented a compromise before the real battle had begun.[122] On the other hand, as a compromise to get to a bill that would pass, the trade-off could also be viewed as "shrewd politics on Harris's part." The palatability of a bill that provided extra money if a plan was adopted was hard to contest, and it seemed unlikely the assembly would object to "local governments deciding they want a grant." What one commentator called a "carrot with teeth" was also the art of the possible, a bill that could get through a gauntlet of recalcitrant legislators suspicious of the governor's motives.[123]

As the General Assembly convened in 1989, Sibley and Cowan orchestrated a minor publicity blitz. In an extended interview published in the January 1989 edition of *Georgia Trend Magazine*, the president of the Business Council of Georgia, a member of the Quality Growth Commission, discussed the growth commission's final report at length, concluding, "I think it's very good."[124] In an op-ed written for the *Atlanta Journal-Constitution* the Sunday before the session opened, Cowan detailed Georgia's rapid but geographically uneven growth and reminded legislators that "the key to carrying our success to every community is to implement the recommendations of the Governor's Growth Strategies Commission."[125] In a January 3 editorial, after noting that the proposed legislation "is not zoning," the *Augusta Chronicle* declared that what the growth management legislation "does propose is revolutionary" and that "for the first time . . . all levels of government" would be required to work together.[126]

When the opening gavel of the 1989 General Assembly fell on January 9, "few legislators or lobbyists had openly criticized the growth strategies plan," and the commission's "pragmatic approach" and robust publicity strategy appeared to have secured the fate of the legislation. The recommendations of the Quality Growth Commission report were introduced in four bills, each addressing one issue. One bill authorized the Georgia Department of Natural Resources to plan and construct a system of "regional water supply reservoirs to provide water to local governments beyond their short-term needs." A second bill bolstered existing erosion and sedimentation laws and "strengthen[ed] [state] control over land disturbing activities" to prevent "unnecessary sedimentation of state waters and adjacent land." A third bill, the so-called planning bill and the major piece, established a framework for "coordinated and comprehensive planning on a statewide basis," created the Governor's Development Council, reconfigured the Department of Community Affairs, and set up new regional planning agencies. A fourth bill, the narrowest of the bunch, gave the Georgia Environmental Facilities Authority new powers to "fund solid waste projects for local governments."[127]

The chairmen of the committees in the Georgia house and senate that the growth management bills would be assigned to publicly voiced their support from the beginning, one going so far as to predict on the first day of the session, "You're going to see the legislation pass." When the powerful Speaker of the Georgia House of Representatives communicated his support for the legislation at the end of the first week of the session, its success was virtually sealed.[128]

Anticipated resistance to the erosion and sedimentation, land-use, and solid waste bills was largely absent. In fact, during the State Planning and Community Affairs Committee hearings on House Bill 215, the planning bill, the only motion put forward that would have substantially "weaken[ed] the measure" died from failure to find a motion to second, prompting the chairman of the committee to exclaim, "I thought we'd have more opposition than this."[129] Despite Harris's efforts to presell the need for new reservoirs, the water supply bill was the only one to face vocal resistance.[130] The director of the Georgia Conservancy worried that the water supply plan "does not require those who build the reservoirs to compensate for damage to wetlands or wildlife habitats."[131] The *Atlanta Journal* editorial page feared that the water bill "creates a monster" and puts "near total control of Georgia's most precious natural resource in the hands of one department with powers so broad it can act independently," a prospect that was, "in a word, horrifying."[132] Though the water bill passed, the debate over its content raised enough concerns that later attempts to allocate funding for specific water supply projects would run into stiff opposition from legislators, regulators, and environmentalists concerned about cost and environmental impacts.[133]

By the end of January, the House State Planning and Community Affairs Committee had endorsed House Bill 215, the centerpiece of the legislative package.[134] During the floor debate, modifications were comparatively few. The final version of the legislation reflected almost everything the Quality Growth Commission had suggested and, more importantly, what Harris, Higdon, and Sibley had plotted years prior.[135] Agreement was reached on the final wording of the planning bill on March 15. Despite having to trade a bit of increased oversight by the General Assembly for votes, on March 16 Sibley wrote to Quality Growth Commission members that the legislation as passed was "just as strong as [their] recommendations." He applauded the effort of the commission, declaring, "Georgia has stepped to the forefront among the states" with its new planning process.[136] Harris signed all four bills into law on April 18, 1989. At the signing ceremony Harris remarked, "Units of government will work together as never before," and predicted, "We have together planted seeds that" will "ensure a rich harvest of prosperity for Georgia in the 1990s and on into the next century."[137] Lingering confusion about exactly what changes would be in store for local governments did not quell public enthusiasm for the new laws.[138] As the assembly session drew to a close in late April, Harris began collecting accolades for his "direction and influence" in pushing a collection of laws that "will have a greater impact on the positive future growth and development of Georgia than anything else in its past."[139] With Harris's signature, Georgia joined the short list of states with state planning laws on their books.

As the dust settled in the summer of 1989, standards for local plans remained undefined, and tools for financing the plans were not yet in place.[140] Nonetheless, recognition arrived quickly. Sibley and Harris spent much of the rest of the year touting

Georgia's newfound status as a "national leader in the second wave of growth management initiatives" in lectures, interviews, op-eds, and feature articles.[141] In early 1990 members from the Georgia chapter of the American Planning Association (APA) nominated Harris for the association's national Distinguished Leadership Award, the highest honor the association bestows on a public official. In giving the award to Harris, the association's awards committee noted that "it's unusual for a Governor to take such a broad view." The association lauded Harris's political acumen, because "Georgia appeared to the APA awards jury an unlikely setting for a balanced growth strategy."[142]

Expanded State Control

In its final version, running nearly one hundred pages, the State-Wide Planning and Development Act, unofficially the Georgia Planning Act, accomplished much of what Governor Harris, Higdon, and Sibley had intended, erecting a program that standardized the planning process across the state and strongly encouraged local governments to embrace comprehensive planning. In six sections, the act prescribed a program for mandatory statewide planning and development, created the Governor's Development Council, and forged new, concrete connections between the Department of Community Affairs and the Department of Natural Resources.

Part one of the act established the Governor's Development Council, which was to be a permanent executive branch body comprising the commissioners of the major administrative divisions of the state along with a few extra members appointed by the governor. The council was charged with supervising and reviewing long-range planning efforts of state agencies, particularly the design and construction of public facilities.[143] The council was to help the different fragments of the public bureaucracy learn to work together in designing the state's future. Part two redefined the responsibilities and powers of the Department of Community Affairs. As a result of the act, the department would serve as the primary liaison between local governments and the state and function as the state's principal agency for managing comprehensive development planning. Part two also stipulated that the department would provide planning assistance to local governments; develop and manage a detailed land-use database; devise a statewide rural economic development plan; maintain a program of research on planning, development, and government affairs; and serve as staff support for the Governor's Development Council in developing a comprehensive plan for the state. The most important of these activities, what might be considered the "carrot with teeth" part of the legislation, was that the department would be responsible for developing a set of minimum planning standards against which all local plans would be evaluated and had the authority to grant special funds to local governments whose plans met those standards.[144] If local governments produced plans that met the standards of the

Department of Community Affairs, they would be designated as qualified local governments, allowing them to apply for grants to fund infrastructure construction and support economic development activities.[145] The planning standards applied to every county and every city with a population over 2,500. Updates to local plans would proceed according to schedules established as part of the standards.[146] In time, the minimum standards system would go a long way in defining the character and quality of local plans, which would in turn help determine how effective the state's effort at growth management would be later judged.

Part three of the act established a system of regional development centers across the state. Modeled after ARC, the new regional development centers were to be intermediaries between local governments and the state. Thus, every county and municipality was assigned to a regional development center and required to pay annual membership fees to support it. As ARC had been, the centers were to be engaged in brokering local planning issues, including writing and adopting regional development plans, assisting local governments with plan preparation, serving as intergovernmental coordinating bodies, and supplying information to the state's new planning and land development database. But here, too, the most important function had to do with the implementation of the minimum planning standards for local comprehensive plans. The regional development centers would be the front line and responsible for reviewing and commenting on all local comprehensive plans, comparing them against the state's minimum standards, and rendering judgment on a plan's quality.[147] In many respects the centers would operate as miniature versions of ARC.[148]

Part four of the act amended state code to expand the power of counties and municipalities in the state to write and adopt comprehensive plans, capital improvement plans, and regulations appropriate to carrying out policies in their comprehensive plans. Part four also assigned each county and municipality to a regional development center, set annual fees, and directed local governments to participate in developing a state land development database.[149] Part five outlined the role of the Department of Natural Resources in the comprehensive planning process. The law required that the department develop its own set of watershed standards to protect the public water supply. These standards included buffers around rivers, streams, and wetlands and land development density stipulations for lands that abut or otherwise affected surface and groundwater resources.[150] Part six tied up odds and ends resulting from the changes in state code wrought by the act, corrected conflicts with existing legislation, clarified and strengthened procedures for reviewing development proposals on lands regulated by the Metropolitan River Protection Act, and set up new requirements related to rural economic development and the modernization (digitization) of local land records.[151]

Implementing the planning policies contained in the new legislation would be another struggle. Only a few years earlier, Florida had begun implementing its growth management legislation, which had been passed into law in 1985, and reports about the twists and turns in that process were not encouraging. Florida's law, a bundle of regulations much like Georgia's, required every county to adopt a comprehensive plan and identify critical environmental resources that deserved extra protection. But Florida's law allowed little room for negotiation between the state and local governments, having laid the burden of proof on local officials to demonstrate that their plans included adequate infrastructure (roads, water supply) before new development would be approved. Resistance from local governments had been strong, and half the plans submitted to the state for review were initially rejected. Four years later Florida's growth management laws were beginning to take hold, as local governments became accustomed to the planning standards.[152]

In some ways, Georgia's road to implementing its new land-use laws faced fewer likely roadblocks. Local governments had more standing in the process, more authority to negotiate with the state, and thereby more control over how the laws would work on the ground. Moreover, the state's role was less commanding and more accommodating. The laws' structure made negotiation, consensus, and incentive the preferred strategies for ensuring compliance rather than punishment. If a local government failed to produce an adequate plan, it failed to qualify for certain state funds but probably would not be taken to court or dragged before an executive committee to explain its decisions. Minimum standards for local plans, to be set after the bill, would have to go before the General Assembly for final approval, giving hesitant politicians assurance that they would be able to vote on the standards at a later date. The balance in Georgia's state planning scheme cleared a path for legislative approval that might otherwise have been blocked.

If the political careers of Roy Barnes and Johnny Isakson, state legislators who were influential members of the Quality Growth Commission, are any indication, Georgia's statewide growth management laws grew out of the same Atlanta-centric planning milieu that ARC had been building for nearly two decades. Both politicians were products of Cobb County, and the differences between them at the time appeared to be largely a matter of party affiliation.[153] Barnes belonged to the state's Democratic majority and had cut his teeth in Jimmy Carter's "conservative and progressive" faction of the party, which had made strides in moving past its roots in massive resistance to desegregation. Isakson positioned himself as a centrist among the state's growing Republican Party, a probusiness politician focused on jobs and economic expansion rather than divisive social issues. Barnes and Isakson worked closely together during their General Assembly days to get Harris's growth bills through the necessary committees. Both were outspoken in their support of state and local planning as a tool to support and encourage, rather than restrict, growth. Barnes and Isakson, perhaps more than any other state politicians of their generation, represented the strange dichotomy of Georgia's land development politics in the 1980s, in which fundamental agreement just below the surface belied an outwardly contentious relationship. Both would go on to higher office, Barnes becoming governor and Isakson rising to the U.S. Senate.

The laws put into place during the 1989 legislative session were a significant step in state oversight of land development. In virtually every respect, Georgia's growth management laws were another moment in a long-term effort to increase the authority and scope of the state's control over local governments while supporting development potential in metro Atlanta. The incrementalism built into Georgia's statewide planning legislation, a page lifted from ARC's two decades of experience dealing with local governments in metro Atlanta, should be measured as much by its clear-eyed understanding of political reality as by its timidity.

6
Atlanta's Transportation Crisis and the Battle of the Northern Arc

> "That Northern Arc has had a life of its own," said Atlanta City Councilman Doug Alexander. "Every time we've tried to stop it, it keeps coming back to life."
> —"The Northern Arc Must Justify Itself," Atlanta Constitution, July 9, 2001

At the beginning of 1990, resistance to the state's power to regulate land development, a posture long popular among many of Georgia's rural and suburban politicians, appeared to have softened. The Georgia Planning Act, successfully pushed through the General Assembly by Governor Harris, had significantly increased the state's oversight of land development decisions and had made local comprehensive planning a new priority. In mid-1990, the Department of Community Affairs finally issued the planning standards that local governments would have to adhere to in preparing their comprehensive plans. By the end of 1991, the first wave of local plans up for compliance review were delivered to the planners working in regional development centers around the state. As the Atlanta Regional Commission (ARC) marked its twentieth birthday, it appeared to be at the peak of its influence. Over the previous two decades, ARC had made itself into the de facto planning intelligence center of the Atlanta region and effectively for the entire state. The commission's position at the center of the regional planning process, as the conduit connecting local governments, state government, and federal agencies, had become indisputable.

Through the 1970s and 1980s, despite periodic recessions, population and employment growth in Atlanta maintained a heated pace. The 1990 census counted just over 2.5 million souls in ARC's nine-county region. During these decades "nearly 70 percent of the region's population growth spread out north of the Atlanta core," which tilted the population balance ever more toward the two largest north suburban counties, Gwinnett and Cobb.[1] Over this period, Gwinnett averaged population gains of nearly 8 percent per year, and Cobb routinely hit 4 percent per year. Between 1970 and 1990, these two counties alone gobbled up 55 percent of the region's total population growth and ranked as two of the fastest-growing counties in the United States. Despite the counties' overall growth, the percentage of nonwhite population in Gwinnett and Cobb dropped steadily during those decades, the effect of thousands of whites filing into the new subdivisions popping up across the counties' nearly eight hundred square miles of mostly unincorporated territory. Even with the massive influx of whites, metro Atlanta's overall population grew more racially diverse.[2] In the 1990 census, nearly 32 percent of the region's population self-identified as nonwhite.[3]

By 1990 an increasingly visible socioeconomic divide was apparent.[4] While the experience of this divide lay in the everyday tactics of individual households that created and reinforced unofficial boundaries in Atlanta's residential geography, its roots lay in economic class. The north–south divergence in the region was clearly visible in the built environment. City councils and county commissions across the region permitted hundreds of new residential developments, strip malls, office buildings, and industrial parks. The effect of this building boom, like population growth and income, was far from equally distributed.[5] The accumulated effect of these conditions was that by 1990, even a marginally keen observer could identify a concentration of high-income whites (and a few wealthy blacks), upscale malls, and high-end office parks in pockets around the northern suburbs and an alternative world of lower- and middle-income whites and blacks, modest subdivisions, and a motley collection of warehouses and distribution centers scattered across the southern suburbs.[6]

Simultaneously, the federal Department of Housing and Urban Development's Hope VI program was beginning the long process of demolishing Atlanta's massive system of public housing, putting intense pressure on the supply of affordable housing in the city.[7] With planning for the 1996 Olympic Games came a huge number of ambitious redevelopment projects in the region and their possible exacerbation of the effects of the uneven distribution of growth.[8] At the same time, the regional planning process seemed only to reinforce the north–south divide by continuing to direct the majority of the region's total transportation dollars to major infrastructure projects designed to relieve congested roadways in the northern suburbs. Yet in retrospect, a regional pattern of segregation that had been building for three decades peaked in the late 1980s.[9] By the mid-1990s, the rate of black out-migration from the city to the suburbs had accelerated, and these movers had been joined by thousands of blacks, whites, Asians, and Latinos moving to Atlanta's suburbs from other parts of the country. This redistribution of population would turn metro Atlanta's two biggest suburban counties, Cobb and Gwinnett (the epitome of white suburbia), into its most racially and economically diverse.[10]

What united the region during the 1970s and 1980s was the consistent lack of density in its built environment. With amazing speed, rural, unincorporated places on every side of the city had been inundated with single-family houses on large lots, big-box shopping centers, one-story warehouses, and low-rise office parks. As a result, the density of metro Atlanta in 1990 registered barely 1.5 persons per acre, making Atlanta one of the least dense large urban areas in the country.[11] As much as Atlanta's overall growth suggested prosperity, the conditions created by this growth would spark an attack on the regional planning process in the mid-1990s.

The early 1990s also witnessed two significant changes to federal transportation policy that would make Atlanta's regional planning process especially vulnerable: amendments to the Clean Air Act in 1990 and the passage of the Intermodal Surface Transportation Efficiency Act (ISTEA) in 1991. These regulations, among the major pieces of urban policy enacted during George H. W. Bush's presidency, marked an about-face in terms of federal support for state and regional planning and offered new tools aimed at transforming the standard practices of state and regional planning agencies.[12] Essentially reversing the Reagan administration's eight-year effort to undercut direct federal support for state and regional planning activities, the new controls promised to reshape regional decision-making processes, moderate Reagan's New Federalism, and pull some of the power that had been passed down to state and local governments back to the federal level.[13]

Congressional approval of the 1990 Clean Air Act amendments set new ambient air quality standards that lowered the threshold of acceptable levels of several common pollutants in urban areas. Overnight, the amendments increased the number of metro Atlanta counties out of compliance with federal air quality standards and forced communities along the urban fringe that had previously escaped regulation to acknowledge their contribution to the degradation of the region's air.[14] The amendments also required state and regional planning agencies to clearly demonstrate how their transportation plans would improve air quality (rather than merely prevent further decline). Signed into law by President Bush in 1991, ISTEA revised the regional planning process and altered the criteria for how state transportation departments and metropolitan planning organizations would allocate transportation funds. The law required regional transportation plans to take a more comprehensive view, one that included an explicit consideration of land-use and environmental policy and that reflected a more equitable balance between expenditures on roads and on other transportation modes. The Clean Air Act and ISTEA focused on the critical nexus of infrastructure and metropolitan development patterns, and both used language that emphasized coordinated regional decision making, which was a response to criticism that the existing regional transportation plans did not adequately consider land use, the environment, alternatives to automobiles, or the voice of the public.[15]

Complaints about the federal transportation planning process ignoring land use or the public's preferences, however, were nothing new.[16] Beginning in the late 1950s, federal interstate highway projects had faced well-organized protests that exposed the complex intermingling of the political, bureaucratic, and private interests that manipulated the shape of the national highway system in ways at odds with the public interest.[17] These conflicts typically exploded around plans to introduce multilane freeways into central-city neighborhoods—perhaps no instance more dramatic than the showdown between Robert Moses and Jane Jacobs over the proposed Lower Manhattan Expressway.[18] Atlanta itself was the site of several skirmishes from the 1960s through the early 1980s.[19]

Major battles over suburban roads, however, have been far less frequent. Yet in the aftermath of the new federal air quality standards contained in the Clean Air Act amendments and ISTEA, metro Atlanta experienced just such a road battle, centered on a proposed freeway (nicknamed the Northern Arc—a reference to its shape and location within the metropolitan area) that would have carved a path primarily through forests and pastures, twenty-five miles beyond the urban core.[20] The showdown over the Northern Arc was the culmination of a much larger planning crisis that buffeted the region for nearly a decade. The difficulty of producing a plan that conformed to the mandates in the Clean Air Act and ISTEA led to an unusual fracturing of Atlanta's political leadership and eventually a meltdown of the regional planning process. The meltdown played out in the ARC boardroom, the governor's mansion, and the courts, the result of conflict among a group of newly elected county commission chairmen who joined ARC in the mid-1990s, the governor of Georgia, the Atlanta business community, and a coalition of environmental and social justice nongovernmental organizations. In the end, the fight to reform Atlanta's transportation planning process unfolded as part of a larger dispute between advocates of local control and the federal, state, and regional agencies charged with regulating development.[21]

A Regional Transportation Network

From its inception, Atlanta's urban freeway system followed a wagon-wheel periphery-to-center design.[22] The region's highways more or less followed a set of routes laid out in 1946, ten years before the Federal Aid Highway Act of 1956 was signed into law and twenty years before the Interstate System would be completed.[23] By 1970 Atlanta's urban freeway system comprised five major roads, two that ran north–south (Interstates 75 and 85), two that ran east–west (Interstate 20 and Lakewood Freeway), and a ring road (Interstate 285, the Perimeter) that tied the north–south and east–west freeways together.

As the suburban counties surrounding Atlanta grew through the 1970s and 1980s, large subregional employment and retail nodes developed along the busy freeway corridors crisscrossing the region. These nodes were especially concentrated in the triangle north of the city formed by the intersection of Interstates 75, 85, and 285.

In this triangle, five enclosed shopping malls opened between 1970 and 1990, each positioned along the same segment of Interstate 285 (which was rapidly becoming a decidedly unquaint Main Street for the north side of the region). First came the associated retail and commercial operations that tend to colocate with anchor shopping centers, later the corporate back offices, and finally the front offices.[24] These nodes attracted increasing numbers of people (commuters and shoppers) from all directions but particularly from the northern suburbs. With the seemingly endless new development in the 1970s, traffic congestion in the northern suburbs had become a significant issue by the middle of the 1980s.

Moreover, changes in transportation behavior—increasing multiple-car households, increasing numbers of middle-class women entering the workforce, and declining public transit ridership—were testing the capacity of the road system.[25] As the region's employment and population base further decentralized, "downtown [Atlanta's] share of the area's total employment shrank to 7.4 percent from 10.4 percent between 1980 and 1990," while "its work force grew only 11.7 percent." At the same time, "employment along the Georgia 400 [a toll road through the upscale Buckhead neighborhood] corridor in north Fulton surged nearly 300 percent, and jobs in south Cobb grew 53 percent."[26] Commuters traveled increasingly longer average distances between work and home, and households were pulled in multiple directions: to the central business district or from one suburb to another, with the latter being more frequently the case. Without the option of crosstown mass transit or a major east–west freeway on the north side, the wheel-like shape of the transportation network forced the vast majority of commuters to drive significant distances, and most chose to do so alone.[27] The only high-capacity connection between Cobb, north Fulton, and Gwinnett Counties was Interstate 285.

As traffic on the northern stretch of the sixty-mile Perimeter increased, the road, which had been designed as a bypass for traffic moving through the region, not as an urban arterial, became a magnet for intensive commercial development. By the late 1980s, Interstate 285 had come to resemble exactly the kind of urban arterial it had been designed to alleviate. Drivers used the road to run errands, shop, and drive between suburban homes and suburban workplaces. Interchanges functioned almost as surface street intersections. Buildings at first huddled at the corners of overpass bridges, but higher-rent office towers later fronted the stretches of road between interchanges, as if overlooking a picturesque promenade or river. The buildings crowding the road helped push the volume of vehicles traveling it steadily upward, which clogged traffic lanes and pushed gridlock onto the arterial routes that crossed the highway.

To make matters worse, metro Atlanta's arterial and surface street system tended to follow the vagaries of topography rather than the straight lines of surveyors. Major thoroughfares, most of which were old local routes, wound their way along the region's predominant north–south ridgelines, curving and twisting with the landscape. Many of these roads were part of the state's system of arterial highways, which subjected them to Georgia Department of Transportation (GDOT) control. The region's surface streets, smaller in scale and controlled by local governments, tended to follow the same ridgelines and be underengineered for the volume of traffic they carried.[28] For many years, counties in Georgia had no standardized system for acquiring and planning future public rights-of-way.[29] Though towns in the state had established street grids in advance of land development, unincorporated counties lacked the legal authority to do so. Because so much of metropolitan Atlanta's development in the second half of the twentieth century happened in unincorporated areas of large, quasi-rural counties, a significant portion of the region's local and neighborhood streets were planned and constructed by developers and turned over to county government control only after the roads were graded and the lots platted. The majority were designed to serve single residential subdivisions, which meant that the bulk of the region's street network tended to be self-referencing and disconnected. Adjacent subdivisions rarely connected.

While federal money to add road capacity had been available through the 1970s, Reagan's agenda in the 1980s included curtailing funding of new infrastructure in favor of better management of existing systems, a stance that made finding money to expand the network of local roads that much more difficult.[30] GDOT picked up some of the slack, but much of its focus was on building and maintaining arterials. This meant that most counties were left with little alternative but to accept new residential roads as "gifts" from private developers. As a result, a dense network of through routes never emerged. In other words, the grid so common in most U.S. metropolitan areas never existed in metropolitan Atlanta, a condition that squeezed traffic into a system of arterials and freeways without any redundant relief routes. During the 1970s ARC produced transportation plans that attempted to deal with the region's growing traffic problems, but these plans mostly reinforced old patterns of periphery-to-center connectivity, maintaining the accessibility to Atlanta's original central business district that was thought necessary to ensure the region's overall health.[31]

Regulating Air Quality

The history of federal interest in urban air quality extends at least back to 1955, when Congress passed the first Air Pollution Control Act. The law provided money to support pollution research but did not specify measures of control. In 1963 Congress passed a revised version, the Clean Air Act, setting up the framework for later amendments that would shape transportation plans. The 1963 act established a goal of pollution control and set the first emissions standards for large stationary sources.

In 1967 another round of revisions produced the Air Quality Act, which expanded the scope of federal involvement beyond setting stationary source standards to include regional ambient air monitoring stations (Air Quality Control Regions) and point-source inspections, as well as state implementation plans for controlling future pollution.[32] While mild in its language, in part a reflection of the imprecision of environmental science at the time, the 1967 revisions took the critical step of identifying long-term environmental side effects that the nation's burgeoning automobile-oriented transportation system was creating. Major revisions to federal air policy came again in 1970, coinciding with the burgeoning popular support for environmental issues and the beginning of the national land-use debates in Congress.[33] The 1970 Clean Air Act amendments sharpened the regulatory tools in the law, establishing National Ambient Air Quality Standards that urban regions would be expected to meet, forging much more explicit links between state and regional transportation plans and environmental quality, and redefining the goals of state implementation plans.[34]

With 1977 came another round of congressional revisions, this time expanding the states' role in meeting air quality goals, toughening the requirements for urban areas to remain in compliance with the National Ambient Air Quality Standards, and setting deadlines for regions to demonstrate improvements in ambient air quality. The 1977 amendments required states and regional planning agencies to cooperate in adopting a state implementation plan that set out specific steps for managing urban transportation systems to avoid increases in emission of several atmospheric pollutants. The amendments also established a system to classify counties according to their relative pollution levels, helping determine allocation of future federal transportation funds.[35] Once adopted by the state, the state implementation plan had to be sent to the EPA for final approval. If accepted by the EPA, the plan would become a binding agreement between the region, the state, and federal agencies.[36]

The 1977 Clean Air Act amendments delegated responsibility for managing each state's air quality program to a designated state agency, which in Georgia was the Environmental Protection Division (EPD) of the Department of Natural Resources. Since the heavily populated counties in the Atlanta region made the biggest contribution by far to the state's vehicle emissions, the focus of the state's air quality planning was centered there. With the introduction of the new air quality rules, new levels of cooperation among ARC, the EPD, and GDOT were necessary if they were to negotiate a state implementation plan. An acceptable state plan meant that the existing regional planning process in Atlanta would have to change to incorporate the new air quality requirements.

As in other large metropolitan regions, Atlanta's declining air quality related to the way the region's transportation system had been planned. The rapidly expanding number of single-occupant automobile and truck trips, necessitated by a sprawling built environment, caused a steady deterioration of the region's air quality.[37] Nevertheless, the initial measurements of metro Atlanta's ambient air quality in the mid-1970s found marginally acceptable levels. Thus, the first state implementation plan, written and approved in 1980, presented only a few suggestions for changing the existing trajectory of regional development. Its major contribution was to outline a plan for a region-wide vehicle inspection program. The inspections would gather data to establish a baseline against which the state could monitor changes in automobile emissions over time and develop a strategy for further reductions in the future.

But just two years later, in 1982, an updated set of air quality measurements revealed that a significant portion of metro Atlanta exceeded the minimum threshold levels for ground-level ozone, one of the two air quality indicators the EPA adopted to enforce the provisions in the 1977 Clean Air Act amendments. As a result, the EPA moved ten metro Atlanta counties from the marginal to the serious category. This change in designation meant that the EPD, GDOT, and ARC had to revise the region's transportation plans, comparing them to an air pollution model of the relationship of road infrastructure, travel behavior, and various climatic conditions. Because Atlanta's air quality slid into the serious category, existing long-range plans for new transportation projects would have to demonstrate that ARC and its state partners were making a good faith effort to reduce emissions and meet air quality standards. The lapse also meant that all subsequent updates to the region's transportation plans would have to be tested against the EPA's air quality standards.[38]

Over the next seven years, Atlanta's air quality failed to comply with established ground-level ozone standards an average of five days a year. During that period, the EPA consistently approved minor changes to regional transportation plans. Despite those regular approvals, carbon monoxide and ozone levels slowly but steadily rose across the region.[39] Some portion of the region's air quality decline could be attributed to the simple increase in cars and trucks on area roads. Another part could be attributed to Atlanta's humid climate and the happenstance that comes with how, when, and where air samples are taken.[40] But the number of miles all those vehicles were driven and their average speed also reflected an increasingly complex and congested road system. Thus, an important part of the decline could be directly connected to the regional transportation plans but more insidiously to the structure of the regional planning process. This was the critical connection the EPA asserted in its interpretation of the Clean Air Act regulations. Regional planning agencies were required to use specified urban simulation models to project air quality based on changes in population, transportation infrastructure, and land use. The EPA used the outputs of the models to determine whether a region's planning efforts were on track to meet preestablished air quality standards. Though an increase in population would not necessarily lead to an increase in automobile trips or an increase in the length of the average trip, because of how plans were written in Atlanta, it did.[41]

The Outer Perimeter

If ever there was proof that bad ideas never truly die, one need look only as far as Atlanta's Northern Arc, which began life with a more literal name: the Outer Perimeter. The idea for a two-hundred-mile, limited-access highway encircling metro Atlanta first appeared in a state highway commission plan from the late 1960s, near the end of the halcyon days when Congress still regularly allocated money for big new infrastructure projects. The earliest incarnation of the road, imagined in 1968 as a future congestion relief route for the still incomplete Interstate 285, was scuttled before detailed plans were prepared.[42] In mid-1971 the idea for another, slightly different version of the outer loop emerged from a General Assembly transportation study committee, though it gained little traction with state highway department officials or metro Atlanta's political leadership and quietly disappeared. A 1973 ARC staff report issued during the process for the 1976 regional development plan again broached the subject of the road and even offered the possibility that an outer ring road might be necessary if the region met the RDP's long-term-growth expectations.[43] In each instance, arguments in favor of building the road hinged on the need to reroute long-distance truck traffic away from the center of the region; providing an additional high-speed, east–west linkage; and boosting the economic development potential of the rural, Appalachian foothill counties north of Atlanta.[44] Arguments against the road cautioned that its ability to relieve or reduce traffic would likely be limited, the exorbitant cost might jeopardize funds for other transportation projects in the state, and its impact on the natural environment would be enormous. By the mid-1970s Atlanta's urban freeway system had been completed. The attention of the region's political leaders turned toward finalizing the design and beginning construction of the region's heavy-rail transit system, which helped keep the Outer Loop off the list of long-range transportation projects.[45]

Despite the millions invested in the new rail system, Atlanta's automobile congestion problems persisted, and the public's demand for new road investment remained high. By the early 1980s, just as the region's air quality was showing serious decline, another push for the Outer Loop was poised to begin. In addition to recommending a state growth management policy, Governor Harris's Quality Growth Commission had suggested establishing a program to develop the state's highway system. The 1989 bill that became the Georgia Planning Act also set up the Governor's Road Improvement Program, which was designed to use state gasoline tax revenues for planning and building highways in nonurban counties to support economic development.[46] Almost all the territory targeted for new road investments was outside the purview of ARC and thus not subject to its review or federal air quality standards. In fact, many of the strongest supporters of growth management viewed the expansion of rural highways as an important part of the state's overall planning strategy.[47]

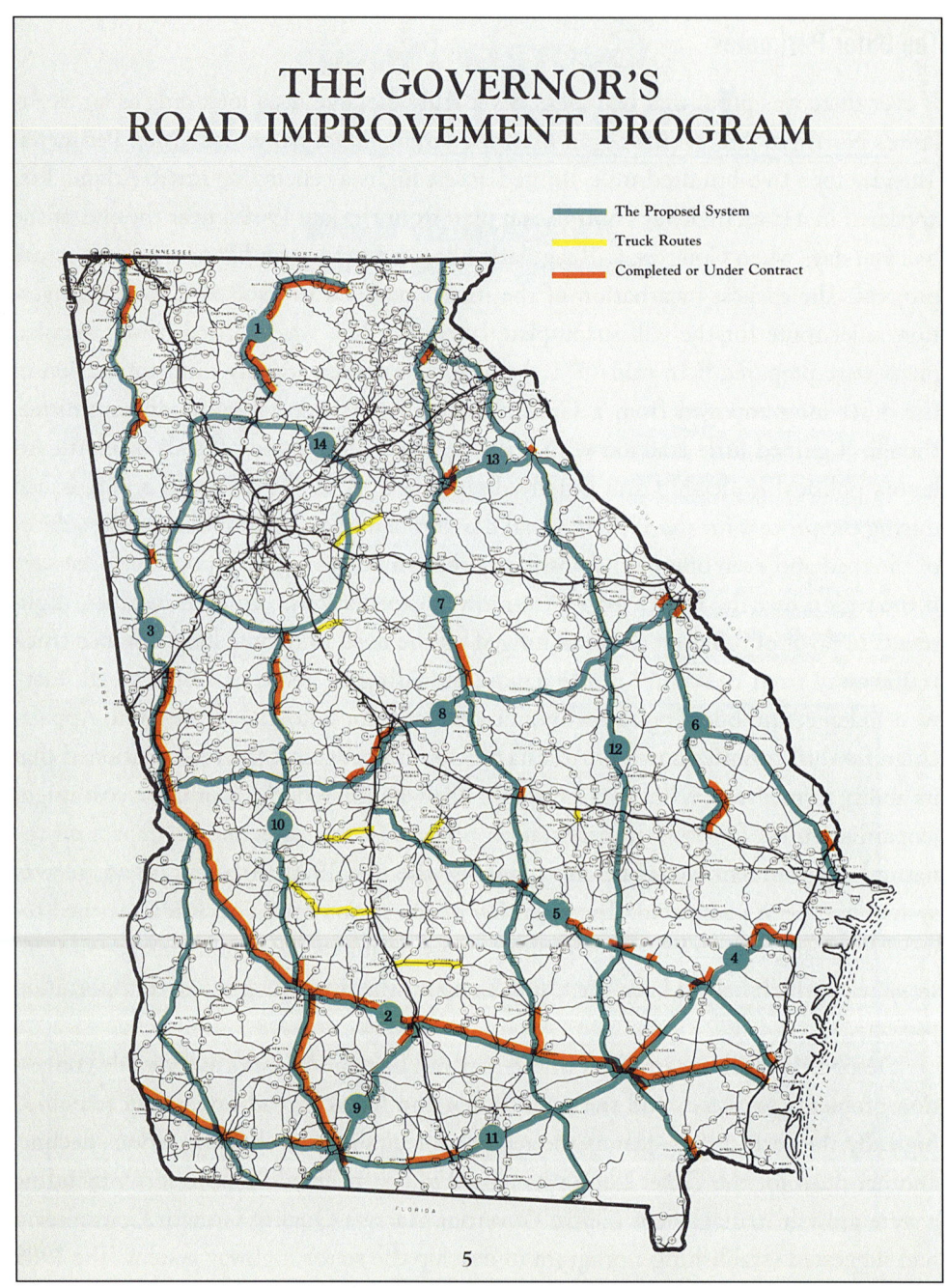

Figure 6.1 "The Governor's Road Improvement Program," from Governor's Growth Strategies Commission, *Quality Growth Partnership: The Bridge to Georgia's Future*, November 2, 1988, Governor, Legal Division Subject Files, 1984–1990, Growth Strategies Commission Folder, Georgia Archives, Morrow, Georgia

Although it was discussed in annual budget sessions in the General Assembly during the 1980s, the Outer Perimeter had never captured the attention of anyone with enough political muscle to push the project forward. Expecting support from the General Assembly if the new state road program was approved, GDOT included a modified version of the Outer Perimeter as part of the initial proposal for the road-improvement system. The cost of this incarnation of the Outer Perimeter was estimated at more than $1 billion, a price far beyond what the Governor's Road Improvement Program could possibly finance with gasoline taxes without significant federal support. Though it had little prospect for receiving federal funding, the road nevertheless remained in GDOT's active list of transportation projects for the state.[48] Even after the legislation passed and projects included in the program began to move into the planning and design pipeline, the Outer Perimeter failed to find support in the legislature. Moreover, because a few sections of the road fell just inside Atlanta's air quality noncompliance area and would be subject to a mandatory review of air quality impact if federal funds were involved, building the road would require ARC and EPA approval. Only the sheer magnitude of the project had kept the road publicly visible, intermittently appearing in the pages of the *Atlanta Constitution* and the *Atlanta Journal-Constitution* as a curiosity.[49]

When Congress passed the 1990 amendments to the Clean Air Act that targeted mobile source emissions in the nation's largest cities, the EPA directed state governments and regional planning agencies to come up with new ways to address their urban air quality problems. The amendments lowered acceptable levels of the two major pollutants, ozone and carbon monoxide, and required noncompliant urban regions to revise their transportation plans to clearly show how they would reduce those pollutants by 15 percent between 1994, when the new regulations took effect, and 1996. From 1996 to 1999, the act required a further 3 percent per year drop. In 1999 a reevaluation of pollution thresholds would occur. Without updates to existing state implementation plans that reflected the new air quality standards, the EPA would refuse to approve further updates to regional transportation plans.[50] Regions without updated and conforming transportation plans would be ineligible for funding for capacity-adding projects—namely, roads. Therefore an approved state implementation plan was a critical step if Atlanta expected to continue receiving its full share of federal transportation funds. If ARC, GDOT, and the EPD failed to produce a qualifying plan by the end of 1993, the state would be left in a difficult position, subject to loss of funds for capacity-adding projects (though it was uncertain whether the EPA would enforce these provisions).[51] As a result of the 1990 amendments, thirteen counties (up from ten) in metro Atlanta were deemed out of air quality compliance when the new air quality standards took effect in 1991.

The election of Zell Miller as governor in 1990, another in a procession of pro-growth, New South legislators who cut their political teeth riding the coattails of

Jimmy Carter, promised several more years of leadership eager to use the state to support economic growth but reticent to regulate the externalities of that growth. A scion of the Democratic faction that had run the state since 1970, Miller indicated not long after taking office in 1991 that he did not intend to challenge the practices that had pushed the last twenty years of development in metro Atlanta. Indeed, after suffering through two years at the beginning of his first term when the "threat of shrinking revenues and rising unemployment overshadowed concerns about Georgia's air, water and tree cover," Miller helmed the state through a subsequent "unprecedented stretch of uninterrupted economic expansion."[52] By the time he was well into his second term, this robust growth had exacerbated the planning problems facing Atlanta. Yet Miller steadfastly refused to assign a role for the state in "curbing Atlanta's sprawl and its reliance on single-occupant automobiles," telling the *Atlanta Constitution* that "the state Constitution is clear that local governments have the responsibility for planning and zoning."[53] Only in retrospective appraisals of Miller's two terms as governor did the fact that he "completely ducked the tough issues around Atlanta's smog, congestion and sprawl" emerge as a major blemish on his record.[54]

Despite the real threat from traffic congestion and dirty air, the governor's disinterest in the issue and the political winds blowing through the region's local governments stalled any serious discussion of new regulations. In the fall of 1992, retirements and primary defeats upended an entire generation of local politicians, many of whom shared a base of experience and a regional perspective that had been critical to ARC's functioning and ability to coordinate its members. "Nearly a fourth of the regional planning and research agency's 36-member board [would] not return" in 1993, and particularly significant was the retirement of Manuel Maloof, the long-serving chief executive officer of Dekalb County and chairman of ARC.[55] As the *Atlanta Journal* noted, among all the departures "the greatest loss [might have been] Mr. Maloof, a founding member of the Cassandra Society, a prophetic futurist whose missionary work preaching cooperation and regional solutions to common problems—water, waste, transportation—focused an entire region."[56] Losing so many members of ARC at one time, particularly ones who had spent years working together to build cooperation and trust, provoked "some local leaders, ARC staff and [board] members [to] wonder whether the group's generally cooperative manner [would] be ripped apart" by new members who might be more selfish or more narrowly focused on the concerns of their local constituents.[57]

Even though the governor tried to ignore Atlanta's growing air quality problem, Atlanta's business leaders were increasingly focused on what deteriorating air quality might do to the region's economy if left unchecked. At the same time, ARC staff began the multiyear process of updating the region's long-range transportation and development plans, a task made more difficult by the confusion created by the turnover in leadership.[58] Beyond bringing together disparate interests around a single table,

ISTEA and the Clean Air Act amendments required ARC to completely redesign the regional planning process to make it more collaborative, give more weight to public input, and more carefully consider the interaction between land use and transportation. To meet the new air quality standards, ARC would have to work even more closely with GDOT and the EPD to update Georgia's state implementation plan, which needed to be submitted to the EPA for review by mid-1993.

After several months of work, a draft implementation plan was submitted to the EPA, which quickly ruled that the plan did not show how metro Atlanta's nonattainment counties would meet air quality standards by the 1999 deadline and sent the plan back for revision. One of the primary reasons the EPA cited for the failure of the draft plan was the Outer Perimeter (which GDOT had never removed despite lack of public support for the road). Frustrated by the EPA's decision, in late 1993 the ARC board, by now filled with new members, directed the planning staff to prepare an independent analysis of the Outer Perimeter.[59] For what was supposed to be an exhaustive study of the road's feasibility, staff were instructed to examine a no-build scenario as well as several different versions of the road, varying by extent (some were not complete circles) and radius from the central city. Individual segments of the road were to be examined separately.[60] The analysis sought to explore the cost of acquiring land and the construction costs of different versions of the road, project the daily average of vehicles that would use different segments of the road, and ascertain likely air and water quality impacts.[61]

As part of the process of updating the regional development plan, ARC organized several dozen public events around the region and included the Outer Loop as one of the topics of discussion. During the meetings, the Outer Loop drew a significant number of comments, delivered by a few proponents and many vehement opponents. Out of more than a thousand comments received, only 21 percent "said they favored construction of the entire loop." An additional 5 percent supported a northern segment, and 25 percent supported "some portion of the road" along with other transportation investments. Perhaps not unexpectedly, "the road's most robust support came from the north side . . . [b]ut even there, opposition outweighed support about 2-to-1."[62] As ARC's public outreach effort unfolded, the *Atlanta Journal-Constitution* asked for readers' opinions about the costs and benefits of the Outer Loop. The responses the paper received were decidedly mixed. Negative ones pointed out that the road would "chew up more of Georgia's beautiful land," that it would be a threat to "rivers and streams that give [Atlanta] life," that it "would cause more traffic and congestion for the outlying areas," and that it "would be a terrible waste of money." Positive responses tended to be more focused on the benefits of alleviating traffic and congestion, emphasizing that the loop road could provide an alternative truck route that would "free our expressways of traffic into the city," would be a way to "relieve our two-lane highways of North Georgia," and would allow the continued expression of "individual choice and freedom."[63]

Issuing a report in late 1994, ARC staff argued that no version of the entire Outer Loop would be suitable, measured against congestion relief, cost, or negative environmental externalities.[64] More specifically, the study suggested that the loop "would generate development pressures on environmentally sensitive areas," that it would "tend to redistribute the overall growth and development of the region from the existing suburban area to the exurban area," that "the loop would not significantly reduce traffic on I-285," that "the loop would worsen emissions and overall air quality," that it "would likely compete with other needed transportation improvements," and that "viable alternatives" should be pursued.[65] However, staff noted that one part of the road was potentially feasible: the northernmost segment, a sixty-mile stretch between Interstates 85 and 75 that would provide a new east–west route and would potentially lead to an overall reduction of traffic in the most congested part of the Atlanta region.[66] This was the same segment that drew the most positive comments during the public meetings. Far from endorsing the segment, staff concluded that further study could be warranted. Thus was born the Northern Arc.

The conclusions of the Outer Loop study, considering the road's negative impact on the state implementation plan, generated controversy within ARC. As drafts of the staff report circulated among ARC's members, disagreements arose about precisely what recommendations the board should issue. Evaluating the road on a segment-by-segment basis, the staff report indicated that certain sections of the loop were more viable than others, yet the entire road was clearly not viable. While most members of the ARC board could easily dismiss the feasibility of the entire road, members came to different conclusions about what policy to craft. Some wanted the entire road deleted from regional transportation plans and hoped it never returned, and others wanted to include the most viable northern segments of the road for future study without including any others. A few, however, wanted the Northern Arc segments pushed to the top of the list of long-range transportation projects and wanted to develop plans for completing the remaining segments of the road in the future.[67]

Support for the road broke along geographic lines, though not cleanly. Representatives from the city of Atlanta and Dekalb County were firmly against the entire Outer Loop or any segment, with the mayor of Atlanta calling the road "an environmental nightmare and a financial sinkhole."[68] Also opposed was the county commission chair from Cherokee County. The Cobb County and Rockdale County Commission chairmen supported the Northern Arc, but neither supported the Outer Loop. The only intense, and unabashed, support for the entire Outer Loop came from Gwinnett County Commission chairman Wayne Hill and representatives from GDOT. A majority of the Gwinnett commission "remain[ed] convinced the Outer Perimeter is a stopgap, if not the ultimate solution, to future congestion," and Hill assumed the role of the road's chief cheerleader at ARC. As the *Atlanta Journal* noted, "Gwinnett leaders are fast emerging as central backers in the Georgia Department of Transportation's vision for building the road—expected to be the biggest public works project ever in the state."[69]

Considering the conclusions of the staff report and the widely varying opinions of its members, the ARC board faced a formidable challenge in developing a single recommendation. If any segment of the Outer Loop was included in long-range plans and the state implementation plan, this much was clear: the road would have to be run through EPA-approved transportation models to determine its impact on air quality before moving forward. With an unapproved state implementation plan hanging in the balance, ARC's decision had serious implications.[70] The decision to include or exclude the road from regional development plans seemed likely to determine the region's eligibility for federal transportation funds.

When ARC's board gathered on November 23, 1994, to vote on a final recommendation, positions had been staked. Subcommittee and staff reports had been presented, the *Atlanta Journal-Constitution* had warned that "the project is simply too expensive," and the Atlanta business community had weighed in with only "limited and lukewarm" support for the road.[71] After a rather spirited discussion, the board voted twenty to ten to pursue the Northern Arc. With a motion introduced by the ARC chair, Randy Poytner of Rockdale County, who had been a weak supporter of the entire Loop, staff were directed to undertake a more detailed analysis of a sixty-mile northern segment of the road connecting Interstate 75 to Georgia Highway 316 (a newly constructed freeway in the northeastern section of the metro area) to understand its potential impact on the region's air quality. The northern segment of the road selected for study had a radius stretching a little more than thirty miles from downtown Atlanta. It would connect the region's two major north–south routes, Interstates 75 and 85, and two major state freeways. This step would also better position ARC and state transportation officials to search for outside (federal) sources of financing.[72]

The compromise also authorized further study of the effect of adding an additional segment (twenty miles) of the road, on the eastern side of Atlanta, connecting Interstates 75 and 20. The motion eliminated any further consideration of other segments of the loop road. Staff was instructed to look for transportation alternatives to building the other segments of the Loop.[73] Finally, the motion directed staff to take up the immediate tasks related to the study of the northern segment's feasibility, so that it could be included in updates to regional transportation plans, a step that would allow the project to be modeled for its impact on air quality and move immediately into the design and engineering phase, if funding ever became available.[74]

Despite the ARC board's vote, there was scant possibility that money would be available to build the Northern Arc. Given the estimated price tag of $1 billion-plus and that only very preliminary work had been done on securing land for the route, the road's future seemed dim. While ARC's decision to include the Northern Arc in the region's long-range plans opened the door to eventually allocating funds toward

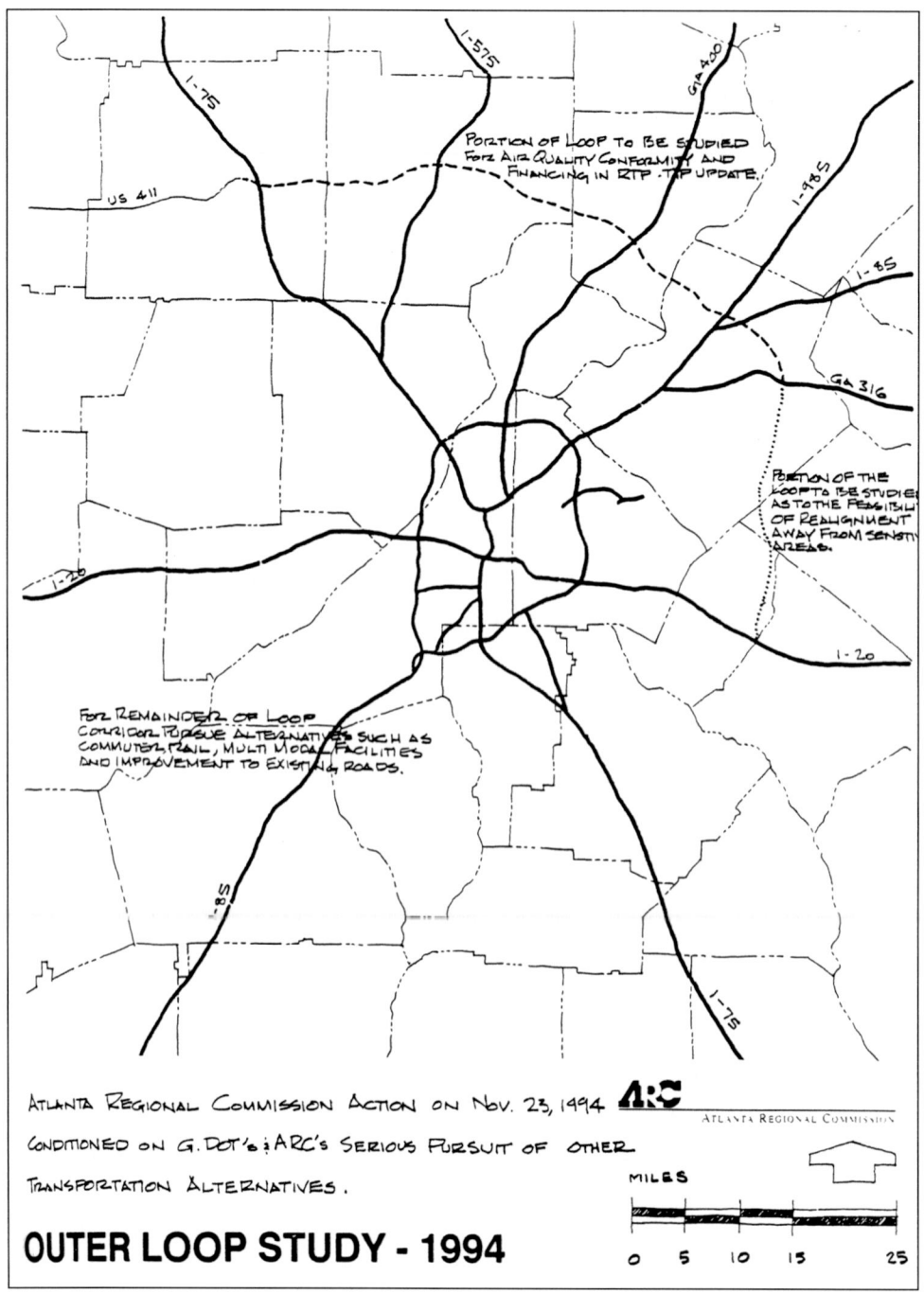

Figure 6.2 "Atlanta Regional Commission Action on Nov. 23, 1994," from Atlanta Regional Commission, *Outer Loop Study/Conclusions*, November 1994, Atlanta Regional Commission Collection, Kenan Research Center, Atlanta History Center

design and construction and certainly signaled a new level of seriousness, the road remained mired in controversy over its impact on the region's air quality and sprawl.[75]

The vote ushered in two years of back and forth among ARC, GDOT, the EPD, and the EPA over the status of the state implementation plan and whether the road projects included in the plan, particularly the Northern Arc, could ever put the region on a path toward reduced emissions. Between 1994 and 1996, the EPA granted ARC a series of extensions to give planners time to revise regional plans to find the mix of projects that could pass the EPA's compliance test. During this extended period of negotiation, compromises between the EPA and ARC allowed federal transportation funds to continue to flow to the region even as the plans that were supposed to show how the region would conform to ambient air quality standards remained unsettled.[76] Finally, in June 1996, ARC, GDOT, and the EPD agreed on a revised implementation plan. The plan, submitted for testing against the EPA's air quality model, failed. Despite planners' efforts to come up with a plan that stakeholders in the region were willing to accept, the EPA's "computer models show[ed] the latest road plan would hurt rather than help" the state's effort to reduce emissions, "busting the caps on harmful emissions by up to 10 percent."[77] In fact, the revised plan showed air quality getting significantly worse by 1999, a result of the road projects that remained in the plan. Metro Atlanta's regional planning process seemed to be moving even further in the wrong direction.

After the revised plan failed to pass the air quality test, EPA representatives signaled in late June that they would stick to their earlier promise of, beginning in early 1998, restricting federal funds for projects that added road capacity. In August 1996 Douglas Neely, the EPA's Atlanta branch air protection chief, sent a letter to ARC explaining that "there would be no quick fix for the problem" and that "ozone air pollution in the region cannot be solved without addressing and reducing emissions from motor vehicles."[78] The message seemed clear: federal support for capacity-adding road projects would be revoked until ARC produced an implementation plan that passed the EPA's air quality test, though projects supporting nonmotorized infrastructure or improving the management of existing infrastructure would retain eligibility for funding. Nevertheless, GDOT continued to push ahead with "preliminary work" on the Northern Arc, including buying land and hiring consultants to write environmental impact studies for the road.[79]

The EPA's message that it intended to hold fast on suspending Atlanta's access to federal road money was a wake-up call for many of the region's business and political leaders, who either had assumed a compromise would be reached in the nick of time or lacked understanding of how the regional planning process had changed in the wake of ISTEA and the 1990 Clean Air Act amendments. Media reaction to the possibility of a showdown with the EPA was swift. The *Atlanta Constitution* editorialized vehemently, pointing out that Atlanta's leaders "continued to act as if that law would never be enforced" and refused "to invest in alternatives to the automobile, even though they knew the region was approaching federal pollution limits." Noting that the "head-in-the-sand attitude caught up with them," the state's failed plan represented an indictment of state and regional transportation officials and the broken transportation planning process they presided over.[80]

The EPA's decision and the pressure from the publicity it generated forced ARC and its partners to immediately revisit both the state implementation plan and the region's long-range plans with a renewed sense of urgency. As they began revising the plans, they had to walk a fine line between necessary and politically feasible actions. Several suburban counties announced their intention to develop local sources of road funding that would not be subject to federal review, providing a backdoor for capacity-adding projects to go forward, but the overwhelming cost and complexity of planning and building roads squashed these efforts before they got off the ground.[81] Thus began a haphazard process of pulling road projects from the transportation plan to get to a list that could pass air quality tests but still remain politically popular enough to appease everyone at the state and on the ARC board.[82] Despite its obvious harm to Atlanta's air quality, the Northern Arc remained on the list of favored projects. And GDOT continued to keep the part of the Outer Loop outside ARC's jurisdiction on its list of developmental highways deemed "critical to the state's transportation future."[83]

In late 1996, ARC and the state settled on a concrete step toward future air quality improvement. In addition to removing road projects from the region's long-range plans, ARC suggested a major expansion of the regional auto emissions testing program. Under this scheme, mandatory every-other-year testing of all private vehicles would be expanded from the region's four core counties to all thirteen in the nonattainment area.[84] This expansion of the scope of the vehicle inspection program would be accompanied by a lowering of acceptable emission thresholds. Measuring tailpipe emissions was a politically easy sell, since it required virtually no change in travel behavior and could be accomplished by a rule change that did not need the approval of the General Assembly. Moreover, it shifted the costs of compliance onto individual drivers. Projects like sidewalks, bike lanes, and intersection improvements remained eligible for federal funding, so ARC pushed its constituent governments to add non-capacity-adding infrastructure projects to the implementation plan.

ARC and its partners continued to deliberate over revisions to the regional transportation plans during the waning days of 1996, though in an increasingly confused and acrimonious way.[85] Compromise among board members was proving to be nearly impossible, in part "because the problem defies political boundaries and the solution means improving everything from power plant emissions to the behavior of more than 1 million drivers." The region struggled "to find a single person or entity to take full responsibility for fixing it." As the director of ARC noted, "It's an invisible enemy, [and] you can't even get some people to agree there's a problem."[86] Despite widespread acknowledgment of the need for a solution to the air quality problem from just about everyone involved, Governor Miller refused to take up the issue, creating a major leadership void.[87]

With no gubernatorial leadership, little regional agreement, and ineffective "pleas for less driving in greater Atlanta to meet clean air laws," an effort emerged, led by ARC and GDOT, to try to circumvent Clean Air Act rules in such a way that funding could be preserved for several politically popular road projects that would otherwise have to be removed from the plan because they would worsen the region's air quality.[88] This effort was based on language in the 1990 Clean Air Act amendments that permitted the grandfathering of budgeted transportation projects if they also had complete, approved environmental impact statements by the time a funding freeze went into effect. Under the grandfathering exception, these projects could move forward even if the state and region failed to develop a transportation plan that demonstrated conformity to air quality regulations. But for grandfathered projects to move forward, both the U.S. Department of Transportation (USDOT) and the EPA had to agree, signing off that necessary due diligence had been accomplished in good faith. This "loophole in the law would allow state DOT officials to build projects on the expired list as long as they [had] done some preliminary work and completed environmental studies" by the time the freeze went into effect. "To make those projects eligible, the DOT [was] working frantically to meet those criteria on as many of the more than 100 projects [included in the plan] as possible, DOT officials said."[89] In early 1997 ARC and GDOT agreed on a list of thirty-three capacity-adding road projects that they would request be grandfathered before the freeze in federal transportation money took effect. Attempting to use an expedited approval process to rush through the required environmental impact statement process, their grandfathering plan would "ensure at least some needed projects [could] be built," even if the updated state implementation plan "again fails to pass federal muster." As the chairman of the Gwinnett County Commission acknowledged, "This is just the insurance, in case we can't adopt a plan."[90] The Northern Arc did not make this short list, though it remained in long-range plans.

In June 1997 President Bill Clinton's administration announced new ground-level ozone standards for urban regions, which made compliance for metropolitan areas like Atlanta that much more difficult.[91] The change in air quality guidelines pushed the ultimate target further out of reach, but because of Atlanta's ongoing struggles, the new rules turned out to be "a mixed bag for Georgia." "We're generally where we were before," said the chief of air protection for the EPD.[92] Through the rest of the summer, ARC continued to work on a long-range plan that would allow the implementation plan to meet targets for reduced emissions by the end of the year.[93] Yet a broader vision that considered the relationship between land use and transportation infrastructure, which ISTEA had made a policy priority, continued to be missing. Most of the emphasis of the long-range plan entailed figuring out a combination of road projects that could be plugged "into a computer model that will calculate how well they bring Atlanta and its suburbs into compliance with air-pollution regulations" in anticipation of having the ARC board vote on a list of projects by late October.[94] The ARC board justified pursuit of this piecemeal strategy because of the need to preserve "home rule—local government's power to determine planning within its own county or city limits." Coming to a regional vision for how to reduce emissions was complicated by the political posturing of a few influential board members. Bill Byrne, chairman of the Cobb County Commission and a new ARC board member, for instance, at one point declared, "Land-use planning is a function of economics," and predicted, "Any kind of concept that comes forward that is not free-market driven will fail."[95] By casting long-range, regional planning as a simplistic choice between "Georgia's tradition of market-driven growth [and] a heavier-handed approach to land-use regulation," Byrne and his allies hamstrung ARC, complicating the commission's ability to develop a coherent regional plan that demonstrated a commitment to improving Atlanta's air quality. Ignoring increasingly urgent concerns of the Atlanta business community, consistent editorializing by the *Atlanta Journal* and the *Atlanta Constitution*, and shifting public opinion, a few members of the ARC board appeared to be digging their heels in and putting the region on a path to a showdown with federal officials.[96]

A month before the updated long-range transportation plan was due to be presented to federal officials for review, the Environmental Defense Fund wrote a letter to USDOT alleging that ARC and GDOT were "abusing [the grandfather] provision by seeking to grandfather more than $1 billion worth of highway expansions" into the region's long-range transportation plan. Arguing that "what's happening in Atlanta in transportation is of national significance," the Environmental Defense Fund's barely veiled threat of a lawsuit got the attention of federal officials.[97] USDOT opened a formal review of the road projects on ARC's grandfather list, which raised new questions about the legitimacy of the environmental impact statements for the grandfathered projects. Even as the list of grandfathered projects was being scrutinized, ARC's board plowed ahead, and "over some protests that it might make it harder to clean up Atlanta's air . . . passed an 'interim' spending plan that included 54 highway widening and new road construction projects," many of which were still under environmental review.[98] Though a deal between the EPA, the Federal Highway Administration, and USDOT permitted Atlanta to continue federally funded work on grandfathered projects under the interim plan, the EPA's restriction on the use of federal funds for other capacity-adding roads in the region took effect in early 1998.⁹⁹ As a result of the funding freeze, the ARC board directed staff to turn their full attention to resolving remaining problems with the region's long-range regional transportation plan so that full conformity with air quality standards could be achieved by a self-imposed April 1998 deadline and eligibility for all federal funds could be restored. One of those problems was the Northern Arc.

By March, ARC staff had completed an initial revision of the long-range transportation plan. Yet including the "$15 billion worth of road, rail and other projects [the board had] called for in the plan," along with the projected growth in the region's population, computer models forecast "more people driving greater distances in ever-worsening congestion, with declining air quality." In brief, "the surge in mileage driven by the projected 4.5 million residents of the 10 counties in the region would offset technological improvements in vehicles and cleaner fuels in only a few years." The ARC board had assumed the plan would be ready for finalization, but the results of the air quality models sent staff "back to the drawing board."¹⁰⁰ In July, still without an approved long-range transportation plan, ARC adopted an updated interim plan to keep money flowing to ongoing transportation projects. This did little to quell the firestorm over the future of the regional transportation planning process.¹⁰¹ As the *Atlanta Journal* editorialized shortly after the interim plan was presented to the public, "There is no more perfect example of a broken process than the Atlanta Regional Commission on transportation planning."¹⁰² Nonetheless, under the agreement between the EPA and USDOT, the interim plan, with its list of contested projects, was allowed to go forward.

By the middle of the summer of 1998, Atlanta's air quality noncompliance had become a major part of the political conversation heading into the November gubernatorial elections. A series of summits sponsored by the Metro Atlanta Chamber of Commerce, meant to introduce the candidates and the public to issues the chamber believed important, focused on quality-of-life problems that threatened the region's economic competitiveness. Out of these meetings came the Metropolitan Atlanta Transportation Initiative, an organization of business executives and elected leaders that agreed to "try to forge a political consensus on sticky issues such as creating a regional transit system, [and] introducing cleaner fuels and better management of development." Its goal was to "deliver a package of recommendations to the newly elected governor in December," in hopes of breaking the logjam that had upended the regional planning process.¹⁰³

As the gubernatorial race heated up in the early fall, ARC and GDOT's failure to produce a transportation plan that would pass federal air quality tests emerged as a front-burner issue. The *Atlanta Constitution* contended that the gravity of the situation meant that "unless the next governor of Georgia makes reform of [ARC and

GDOT] his top priority upon taking office, no amount of studies or good intentions or public meetings will make any difference whatsoever to this region's future." The new governor might have to oversee a complete redesign of these agencies for them "to solve the problems they helped to create."[104] Roy Barnes, who by many accounts had been a rising star almost from the moment he was first elected to the General Assembly in 1974, emerged early on as the leading contender for the Democratic nomination. As the controversy surrounding transportation in Atlanta dragged on, Barnes clearly recognized the significance of Atlanta's planning problems and promised, if elected, to "immediately introduce legislation to authorize a regional transportation authority, and a similar agency to oversee water and sewer treatment."[105] In November Barnes won the race to succeed Zell Miller, defeating a well-financed but uninspiring Republican. Though enormously popular, Miller left office having completely failed to address Atlanta's regional planning crisis.[106] In a state increasingly dominated by metropolitan Atlanta but with a rapidly declining Democratic majority, Barnes maintained a connection to Georgia's old political guard but had a sensitivity toward suburban issues and a mild environmentalism that resonated with the urban electorate.

Though young, Barnes arrived at the doorstep of the governor's mansion as a relatively old legislative hand. By the time he was elected to the state's highest office, he had served twenty-two years in the General Assembly, six in the house and sixteen in the senate. Perhaps more importantly, he had been a member of Joe Frank Harris's Quality Growth Commission and one of the legislative floor leaders during the 1989 session when the bills to create Georgia's growth management laws were ushered through the General Assembly. Having helped craft that legislation, Barnes was well versed in the power of planning and the challenges of political bargaining. He had experienced firsthand the politics of finessing rural and suburban legislators to accept greater state control of land development practices and understood the importance of supporting the growth agenda of Atlanta's political and business leaders.

Almost immediately Barnes had to draw on his political capital. A few days after his election, ARC ran into the most forceful challenge yet to its efforts to write a conforming plan when a coalition of local environmental groups, including the Georgia chapter of the Sierra Club, the Georgia Conservancy, and Georgians for Transportation Alternatives, together represented by the Southern Environmental Law Center, filed "a notice of intent to sue the U.S. Department of Transportation . . . the Georgia Department of Transportation . . . and the Atlanta Regional Commission."[107] Emboldened by President Clinton's 1994 executive order that directed federal agencies to make "achieving environmental justice part of [their] mission," the groups asserted that Atlanta's regional planning process had violated federal law.[108] The threatened suit was an attempt to "stop the [grandfathered] road projects from going ahead until they [were] part of a federally required 20-year plan that meets emissions targets." The local media would later dub this group the Roadblockers. The coalition alleged that, by allowing the existing transportation planning process to continue even as the grandfathered projects remained under review, ARC, GDOT, the EPD, USDOT, and the EPA had violated the spirit and the letter of the pollution laws designed to clean up the nation's air.[109]

Jolted by the suspension of federal road money and now facing the possibility of a major lawsuit, the all-growth-is-good sentiment that characterized the regional planning process in Atlanta had come completely unraveled. While Barnes appeared to believe his election had given him a mandate to get the regional planning process back into conformity, the task would not be easy. Ensuring local governments that continued growth could be balanced with cleaning up the region's air demanded a level of finesse few politicians possessed.[110] Barnes had suggested during his campaign that Atlanta needed a new regional planning authority, one that could remedy ARC's weaknesses with a significantly expanded palette of land development controls.[111]

In the years since its creation in 1971, the power and influence of ARC had been part of an ongoing discussion among regional stakeholders and state legislators. Changes in federal policy in the 1970s had expanded the number of programs under ARC's umbrella and the counties under its jurisdiction. Concomitantly, the General Assembly had gradually expanded the scope of ARC's review powers.[112] Yet under Reagan direct federal support for regional planning had eroded, and local politicians had grown more hostile to the idea of regional governance. Thus, as the region's transportation crisis heated up in the mid-1990s, many observers felt that ARC lacked the credibility to effect the changes necessary to restore stability to the regional planning process. The *Atlanta Constitution* referred to the commission as "little more than a talking head, blabbing away but without arms, hands, legs or feet to implement its decisions."[113] Many believed only a new agency could really shake up the regional planning process.

A regional body with the power to issue bonds and veto local zoning decisions was not a new concept for Atlanta. The initial proposal for ARC in the late 1960s had included zoning review and revenue-raising authority, but because of resistance from rural legislators, none of those powers made it into the final version of the legislation. Similarly, when the Metro Atlanta Chamber of Commerce had convened a group of business and government leaders to discuss ideas for solving the region's transportation crisis the summer before Barnes was elected governor, the Metropolitan Atlanta Transportation Initiative that emerged was a throwback to the original vision for ARC. And when the chamber of commerce proposed a new agency to Barnes shortly after he was elected, it included tools, such as zoning review and bond issuance, that had been resisted for years. The agency Barnes would later introduce had both those tools.[114]

By the time Barnes took his inaugural oath in early January 1999, a bill to create a new regional planning agency had been drafted and was waiting in the wings. Supposedly written by Barnes himself, "the legislation require[d] all parties involved—

the state Department of Transportation, local governments, the Atlanta Regional Commission—to cede a little power."[115] Barnes planned to push the bill through the upcoming session of the General Assembly as quickly as possible to avoid questions and buildup of resistance. Drawing from his experience guiding the Georgia Planning Act through the legislature ten years earlier, Barnes understood that by emphasizing the urgency of the bill and striking early, most legislators would have little opportunity or even inclination to learn about the bill they were voting on, thereby greatly increasing its chances of passing.[116] Though Barnes was forced to include a few compromises, senate bill 57 moved from committee to floor vote to the governor's desk in only eight weeks.[117]

A powerful agency as described in its legislation, the Georgia Regional Transportation Authority (GRTA) promised to strengthen coordination of land-use and transportation planning across jurisdictions in metro Atlanta, serving as an intermediary between the state and ARC. Yet GRTA was "set up to be more than a transportation agency." Among other things, it "ha[d] the final say over millions of dollars in transportation spending," had the power to review (and reject) zoning decisions related to developments of regional impact, and was designated "as the governor's development council . . . with authority to decide whether local governments qualify for state assistance." Moreover, GRTA would have "final approval over metro Atlanta's official 20-year transportation spending plan," a power that allowed the authority to oversee how federal transportation dollars would be spent in the metropolitan area.[118] Finally, it could issue public bonds to raise capital funds to plan, build, and operate transit systems across the region.

Responses to GRTA and its broad array of powers ranged from glee to outright hostility.[119] Backed by the Atlanta business community and various environmental groups, GRTA was Barnes's vigorous response to out-of-control urban sprawl and traffic. Yet just a few days after the introduction of Barnes's bill to create GRTA, "talks between [the Roadblockers] and the Federal Highway Administration, Georgia Department of Transportation and the Atlanta Regional Commission" broke down, and the environmental advocacy groups "made good on their threat to file a lawsuit." Despite the promise Barnes's bill offered, ARC's insistence that the grandfathered road projects proceed had convinced the environmental coalition to move forward with a lawsuit. They reasoned that if the grandfathered projects were allowed to be constructed without challenge, the door would be thrown open for ARC and the state to finalize the long-range transportation plan, which included the Northern Arc, reestablishing the flow of federal road money without any significant changes to the regional planning process. As the lead attorney for the group remarked, "The goal of our lawsuit is to get the agencies to begin now to invest in transportation options that improve air quality."[120] With or without GRTA, the Roadblockers recognized that Atlanta could be a test case of the strength of the 1990 amendments to the Clean Air Act.

The lawsuit charged that ARC, the EPD, and GDOT, with tacit approval of USDOT, the Federal Highway Administration, and the EPA, had "improperly bent the rules to push the so-called 'grandfathered' projects through" the approval process and into an interim transportation plan. The suit claimed that ARC and the state, colluding with several federal agencies, had approved road projects for funding that were not under construction or did not have completed and approved environmental impact statements. The suit also alleged that ARC, GDOT, the EPA, and USDOT had violated federal statute by approving road-capacity-adding projects without a conforming state implementation plan or long-range regional transportation plan.[121]

Four weeks after the Roadblockers filed suit, the Court of Appeals for the District of Columbia Circuit "declared illegal the regulations that permit federal agencies to fund road projects in areas that violate Clean Air laws" in a case brought before it by the Environmental Defense Fund. The appeals court held that despite a grandfather clause being included in the Clean Air Act legislation, "Congress never envisioned that . . . dozens of such projects would be compiled into a new plan that was never tested for its effects on air quality." Because the Washington case was so similar to the dispute in Atlanta, state and regional leaders realized that, in the words of the president of the Metro Atlanta Chamber of Commerce, "the world as we knew it just ended in the business of transportation." Indeed, the attorney representing the Environmental Defense Fund said, "Atlanta . . . was the key test case cited in the suit."[122] Though the decision did not bear directly on Atlanta, the similarities indicated that the rationale used by the appeals court judges to reach their decision, that "just because a project had been part of a so-called conforming plan in the past did not mean it was good for air quality today," was probably a foreshadowing of the eventual outcome of the case between ARC and the Roadblockers. Fearing a similar outcome in Atlanta, ARC and the state sought to speed up negotiations toward an out-of-court settlement.[123]

The appeals court decision in Washington also indirectly underscored the importance of GRTA to solving Atlanta's transportation crisis. As the chamber of commerce president noted, "It puts even more at stake, and it reinforces the need to have a regional authority that can get a handle on these problems."[124] In the early summer of 1999, GRTA began setting up an administrative structure to carry out its charge, building a working relationship with ARC, and clarifying its role in the region. The opportunity to serve on its fifteen-member governing board drew nearly 150 applicants from across the state. Although state and local politicians lobbied hard for positions, the governor selected not one elected official. The list drew "heavily from the Metro Atlanta Chamber of Commerce and the Georgia Conservancy," along with other Atlanta business groups, still "[the] appointments surprised many observers for their relative lack of high-profile leaders."[125] Most of those selected were "politically connected" to Barnes, and "at least five of the 15 contributed to Barnes' campaign."[126] Barnes picked Joel Cowan, the local developer who had been a mainstay of Georgia's planning and development politics for nearly three decades, as inaugural chairman of the agency. A professor of city planning from the Georgia Institute of Technology would be hired later that year as the executive director. The charge for the board was to move metro Atlanta back into federal compliance by the spring of 2000.

In June, days after GRTA was constituted, "a truce in a long-running battle over road-building practices in metro Atlanta" materialized when ARC and the Roadblockers reached an out-of-court settlement that "allow[ed] 17 projects on 11 roads to proceed, while the other 44 [would] be ineligible for the 80 percent federal funding they would have received [if they had been grandfathered]."[127] The terms of the settlement called for "a comprehensive study of transportation needs in the north metro area . . . a panel of experts, monitored by the plaintiffs, to oversee the ARC's use of computer models to predict air quality and congestion as a result of its transportation plans," and "an analysis of whether billions in transportation spending is helping or hurting minority and poor populations."[128] The settlement also required GRTA to approve the state implementation and long-range regional transportation plans before they could be sent to the EPA for approval.

In the end, ARC and the state agreed to almost everything the Roadblockers had sought in their suit. Hence with almost no time standing on its new legs, GRTA was thrust directly into the center of the regional planning firestorm. By July 1999 ARC staff was working toward a March 2000 deadline on "a plan . . . that will enable the 13-county bad air region to meet federal ozone standards by 2003." Achieving this goal would require intensive collaboration between ARC and GRTA, since the governor expected that "the new board [would] play a key role in developing a transportation plan that gets and keeps the region in federal air quality compliance."[129] As the collaboration got under way a few minor skirmishes flared between the agencies, but they quickly settled into a stable relationship.[130]

The settlement required ARC to complete additional revisions to the long-range regional transportation plan, receive GRTA's approval, and then submit the plan to the EPA for air quality compliance evaluation. The regional transportation plan then had to be incorporated into the state implementation plan, which also had to be tested against the EPA's air quality standards. Both steps were necessary to lift the ban on using federal funds for capacity-adding projects. In December the EPA reminded state officials that the interim plan remained "too weak" to clean up Atlanta's air by the 2003 deadline. To bring the plan into compliance, the EPA suggested a few modifications to the mix of transportation projects, including adding counties to the every-other-year auto emissions testing program, instituting stricter pollution controls on point-source polluters in counties on the fringes of metro Atlanta, upgrading the pollution control systems of several major electric power plants close to Atlanta, and requiring lower-sulfur fuel to be sold in most northern Georgia counties. If state officials and ARC accepted the proposed changes, the EPA promised to work with state officials to ensure approval of the revised plans by the summer of 2000.[131]

Nevertheless, at the outset of the 2000 session of the Georgia General Assembly, Atlanta's transportation woes remained unresolved. While GRTA had provided a positive boost, ARC was not due to finalize the long-range regional transportation plan until March at the earliest, and EPD officials were not scheduled to complete their updates to the state implementation plan until early spring. Late winter brought a bit of good news, as the EPA informed state officials in February that, as they had promised, the revised implementation plan appeared likely to be approved.[132] In March ARC submitted the revised long-range regional transportation plan to GRTA, the EPA, and USDOT for review, anticipating approval. In early April, however, forward progress took a turn when the Roadblockers sent a letter to federal officials alleging that ARC's "promises of providing people with transportation choices, breathable air and improved communities are flimsy, and rest on hoped-for state and local government cooperation."[133] Questioning "the accuracy of data the Atlanta Regional Commission used to develop the plan, the availability of federal, state and local money to pay for it, and local government's commitment to it," the environmental groups urged USDOT to scrutinize the plan and threatened to sue if the plan as written was approved.[134] The Roadblockers also urged GRTA to take their concerns seriously in its review of the plan.

In late April, fearing that GRTA would be pressured to approve the regional transportation plan regardless of its shortcomings, the Roadblockers filed a suit against the EPA in federal district court in Atlanta to try to stop the review process, "charging [that] the agency acted illegally in extending metro Atlanta's deadline for meeting federal air quality standards. The lawsuit also charge[d] that the [long-range] transportation plan, designed to improve the region's air quality, [was] based on flawed data." The group sought to have the EPA's review of the plan delayed until these concerns were addressed. Despite the lawsuit, GRTA and the EPA approved the long-range transportation plan in July.[135] But mere hours after the EPA transmitted notification of its approval of the ARC plan to USDOT for final action, the Court of Appeals for the Eleventh Circuit in Atlanta granted the Roadblockers a stay in their lawsuit, preventing the EPA or USDOT approval from taking effect and suspending the review process until a full court hearing in September.[136]

However, a week after the appeals court stopped ARC's transportation plan from being approved by the EPA, "[USDOT] signed off on a [different version of the] plan . . . that says the region will make incremental progress toward complying with the Clean Air Act." USDOT's approval of an alternative plan, something of a surprise to the Roadblockers, was a result a special request ARC had made that asked "federal officials [to] consider an old [version of the] plan using the same transportation projects, but holding them to a different criteria." As approved, "the plan . . . holds the region to a more stringent level of air quality over the long term, but in the interim gives credit for making progress toward that goal." USDOT's assent to the old plan meant that ARC would be able to "start transportation projects contained in [its] 25-year, $36 billion blueprint for 13 metro counties."[137] Though the old plan suffered from the same flaws as the new one and promised significant emissions reductions, the ARC board reasoned that any bargain that would get federal road money restored as early as the upcoming fall was worth the trade-off.[138] With USDOT's approval of the old plan, the eleventh circuit's decision to stay the Roadblockers suit against the EPA was the only remaining impediment to lifting the now two-year-long suspension of federal road funds. Governor Barnes stepped into the fray in the early fall to negotiate a resolution. After the attorneys representing the Roadblockers indicated they would be willing to negotiate an out-of-court settlement rather than wait for the case to work its way through the courts, Barnes moved to strike a deal.[139]

By early December an agreement had been drafted and agreed to in principle by all parties. The basic settlement included accelerating "construction of high occupancy vehicle lanes north and south of the Perimeter on I-75," speeding up "a $4.5 million study of the health effects of metro Atlanta's air pollution," "pledg[ing] to make new reductions in ozone-causing air pollution during the next few years," and assisting "low-income residents who don't have cars or cab fare [to] find easier ways to get around."[140] On December 22, after "attorneys for the two sides reached a settlement to avoid a lawsuit against the state," the environmental groups formally dropped their case.[141]

Peace turned out to be fleeting. On January 2, 2001, state officials "asked federal agencies to release money for about a dozen metro Atlanta road projects, which had been on hold during negotiations," and end the road money drought.[142] A few days later, ARC and the Roadblockers both abruptly backed away from their settlement because of their inability to agree on how the settlement would be enforced and who would be responsible for monitoring progress once projects were under way. Amid allegations that Barnes, under intense political pressure, had rushed to get construction under way and tried to sidestep the terms of the settlement, the Southern Environmental Law Center filed a new lawsuit against the EPA to shut down the release of federal funds, "charg[ing] that the [agency] failed to reclassify metro Atlanta's air pollution status from serious to severe even though the region missed a 1999 deadline for complying with federal air quality laws."[143] The suit alleged that by not reclassifying Atlanta's air quality status, the EPA violated the federal law it was supposed to enforce. In early February attorneys at the Southern Environmental Law Center followed up with another lawsuit on behalf of the Roadblockers, this time naming ARC, GDOT, USDOT, the EPA, and the Federal Highway Administration as defendants and "charging that state and federal officials last year approved a $36 billion regional transportation plan based on faulty data and inaccurate funding assumptions." To permit time for the two lawsuits to move forward, in early April the attorneys requested an injunction to immediately stop construction on road projects included in the contested transportation plan, so as "to prevent irreparable harm to area residents and to preserve money for projects that would improve air quality."[144] In a hearing before a federal judge in early June, ARC, GDOT, and USDOT flatly denied the charges. Governor Barnes testified that the projects under way did not constitute an "environmental emergency" and that shutting them down while waiting for a trial would do far more harm than good.[145]

The lawsuits, the willingness of Governor Barnes to attempt a compromise, and the two-year-plus suspension of federal road money seemed to indicate that Atlanta's regional transportation planning program was headed for a major transformation. Indeed, the promise of using Atlanta as a test case of the Clean Air Act as a tool to reform regional planning processes nationwide appeared about to be fulfilled. But in June 2001 the tide once more turned. The federal court in Atlanta denied the Roadblockers' injunction request, allowing "road contractors [to] continue pouring concrete in metro Atlanta and Georgia DOT engineers [to] keep drawing lines." Moreover, the judge was evidently "not inclined to perform surgery on the region's transportation plan to allow transit projects to proceed while putting road projects on the shelf," an indication that the eventual ruling in the case would be in favor of the defendants.[146]

As the controversy surrounding the transportation crisis had dragged on, Barnes had quietly developed his own transportation plan. Sensing an opportunity in the wake of the judge's refusal to issue an injunction, Barnes, in a surprise move, unveiled the outline of his vision at the end of June. Initially heralded as both "bold" and "lacking proper balance," Barnes's five-year, $8.3 billion transportation plan for the state would accelerate completion of large-scale projects included in Atlanta's regional transportation plans without using federal funds and thus avoiding federal scrutiny.[147] The foundation of the plan was a new source of state funding and the short-listing of ostensibly air-quality-friendly transportation projects: new high-occupancy-vehicle lanes on Atlanta's freeways, new light-rail lines, a commuter rail system, improvements to congested intersections, and a region-wide express bus system. While the governor's proposal "galvanize[d] Georgia's transportation community" with its breadth and scope, the plan also drove a wedge into that community by including the Northern Arc.[148]

At the outset, Barnes's speeding up of the regional transportation planning process caught the attention of his supporters and adversaries.[149] By pushing major air-quality-friendly transportation infrastructure projects to the top of the funding list, Barnes hoped his plan would demonstrate to the EPA and USDOT the state's seriousness about confronting the detrimental environmental side effects of Atlanta's transportation plans. After the shock of the accelerated schedule passed, attention turned to the mechanism for funding so many major construction projects over such a short time. By revamping the State Road and Tollway Authority, including installation of GRTA's former chief transportation officer at the helm, Barnes proposed giving what had been a small state agency "unprecedented state bonding power—$8.5 billion worth."[150] Barnes had pushed a bill through the 2001 legislative session to reform the State Road and Tollway Authority, an agency originally established in 1953 to oversee a statewide system of toll roads that was never constructed.[151] The updated agency had a much broader scope. In its new form, the tollway authority could raise money for transportation projects by selling construction bonds backed by anticipated future federal transportation allocations and by redistributing funds collected from the state's two toll roads to support other projects.[152] As the director of the agency explained, "The plan's there. All we have to do now is execute."[153]

The bonds the tollway authority would issue to fund the governor's plan, known as Grant Anticipation Revenue Vehicles (GARVEEs), were a brand new type and mostly untested. They allowed the state to assume significant bond debt that was guaranteed only by future federal transportation allocations. Yet there was no assurance that future federal allocations would be sufficient to cover the cost of that debt, since federal transportation funds are subject to the winds of politics and can shift from year to year. Moreover, after the new infrastructure included in the plan was put up, the state would assume full responsibility for maintenance, a prospect that was almost certain to provoke backlash when local governments were asked to shoulder a share of this burden. Nevertheless, national bond markets were forecast to be strong, and most bond analysts expected Georgia to be able to manage any debt it took on.[154]

Bond problems aside, the issue in the governor's plan that received the most attention was his decision to include funding for the Northern Arc. By most measures, this iteration of the Northern Arc was basically the same one that had been debated before, except for one important difference: the Northern Arc in Barnes's plan would be limited to seven interchanges and have a permanent, thousand-foot-wide buffer along both sides.[155] Though the design change would minimize the aesthetic impact of the road, the Roadblockers were stunned that the governor's five-year plan would use the state's new bonding capacity to accelerate the construction of a major suburban freeway. That a massive new road would be included in a plan designed to reduce automobile emissions struck many observers as ridiculous.[156]

Though Barnes's decision to include the Northern Arc in his proposal appeared to surprise even his allies, his decision might have been anticipated. The Outer Perimeter had never been removed from the Governor's Road Improvement Program, which was controlled by GDOT, and many of Barnes's oldest legislative allies, many of whom had close connections to the construction industry, had long supported the idea of the road, including the man Barnes had appointed to lead GDOT. Despite perceptions to the contrary in Atlanta, big road projects remained an abiding interest of Georgia's rural legislators.

The projects included in Barnes's plan had been on regional wish lists for years, and the prospect of seeing those projects on a fast track to completion proved terribly enticing. While the pending lawsuits muddied the plan's prospects, at minimum Barnes offered a bold, if flawed, resolution to the impasse. As the *Atlanta Constitution* editorial page noted, Barnes's "proposed $8.3 billion, five-year bond initiative for transportation will not solve all the state's challenges, and it contains some projects of questionable value. However, viewed as a whole, it's a darn sight more preferable than the timid, incremental path the region has been on for too long."[157]

But by the end of the summer of 2002 Barnes's plan was doomed. The lawsuits filed by the Roadblockers had raised enduring questions about the state's willingness to pursue a transportation plan that honestly balanced expenditures on roads and transit and ensured regional equity in transportation expenditures, questions USDOT concurred with. The northern tilt of the governor's plan appeared to offer relatively few improvements to accessibility for the low-income, transit-dependent population of the region, "residents who have been paying taxes for public transportation for 30 years, but who sometimes find their work and school options limited by awkward or non-existent bus and train connections."[158] ARC studies had long shown that an Outer Loop or Northern Arc would do little to reduce congestion on the existing perimeter highway and even less to improve the region's air quality. Regional analyses had consistently questioned the road's ability to relieve congestion, noted its potential to push the urban fringe farther into the countryside, and argued that such a large investment in a single project would exacerbate an unfair balance in transportation spending in the region.

Rising tension between Barnes and members of the ARC board also appeared to threaten the governor's plan. Because the projects in the fast-track list were already included in ARC's approved long-range regional plan, control over when individual projects would be pushed into the design and construction phase remained in the hands of the ARC board. When the governor's plan was announced, ARC board members from Gwinnett and Cobb Counties "criticized [Barnes] for not consulting with counties when the program was developed" and claimed "participation at the local level ha[d] been ignored." In apparent retaliation for the governor's failing to seek ARC's input on his list of transportation projects, the commission board "threatened to stall" projects in the governor's plan unless their questions were answered.[159]

Accusations of ethical violations by members of the boards of ARC, GRTA, and GDOT further complicated the picture. Evidence had begun to accrue showing that several donors to Barnes's reelection campaign owned land near the route of the Northern Arc. When it became clear that members of the boards of GDOT and ARC were involved in decisions about the Northern Arc that would potentially benefit them, conflict of interest was too obvious to deny. In addition to its dubious environmental and financial impact, the Northern Arc looked corrupt.[160]

By the early fall, it had become clear that Barnes's transportation plan had divided the regional leadership in unexpected ways and not necessarily into cleanly separated groups. Among the governor's supporters, opinions about the plan, especially the Northern Arc, remained divided. Even GRTA's board, appointed by the governor himself, were split in their opinions about the feasibility of the plan. The ARC board reacted similarly. Having exercised primary control over the region's transportation planning for years, ARC members had been uneasy with the governor's plan since it was first revealed.[161] The editorial page of the *Journal-Constitution* had turned against the plan, too, reversing course from its cheerleading just a few months earlier.[162] It seemed now that everyone had a problem with the plan, and the revelation of corruption sealed its fate. The outlines of the final round of the fight, pitting the governor, GRTA, ARC, and the Roadblockers against each other, had emerged.

With lines drawn, the opposing sides settled into a brief standstill as the legal challenges to ARC's regional transportation plan were decided in two different federal courts in downtown Atlanta. In the background, the State Road and Tollway Authority, preparing for a ruling in the governor's favor, continued to prequalify engineering and construction firms interested in bidding on the projects in the governor's plan. ARC and GDOT received a temporary boost in mid-January 2002, when a "federal [district court] judge . . . ruled that metro Atlanta's $36 billion transportation plan is legal, rejecting arguments that state and federal agencies violated the Clean Air Act in approving the plan." As the executive director of ARC noted, the ruling upheld "the validity of the regional planning process in creating the long-range transportation plan" and allowed state and regional officials to continue moving forward with transportation projects in the plan while the Roadblockers appealed the decision.[163]

But in April ARC and Barnes experienced a significant setback, when the Roadblockers' suit against the EPA over the federal agency's decision not to downgrade metropolitan Atlanta's air quality "won a temporary victory that require[d] the region to meet a more stringent measure of air quality by 2005 in carrying out its proposed . . . transportation plan," in a ruling issued by the Eleventh Circuit Court of Appeals. The ruling required ARC's planners "to work on transportation strategies that include more alternatives to cars," and to "prepare models for both [more stringent and less stringent] air quality standards."[164] Fearing more court defeats, in early July the governor reversed course and asked ARC to remove the Northern Arc from all regional transportation plans, at least until the appeals court delivered a final ruling on the Roadblockers' suit against the EPA and a stronger conflict-of-interest law could be considered by the next session of the General Assembly. Thus began the collapse of Barnes's transportation plan.[165]

In late August yet another hurdle emerged when a group of suburban homeowners and urban environmental organizations (including the Roadblockers) united in their opposition to the Northern Arc and created the Northern Arc Task Force, devoted to stopping the road. This diverse antiroad coalition of upper-middle-class homeowners and environmental activists was able to muster significant resources (financial and organizational) in their fight against the Northern Arc. Events outside its control also aided the task force: residential developments continued to sprout in the proposed road corridor. With each new house, the price of the Northern Arc inched up just a little bit; several hundred high-priced houses could make a significant difference in the state's ability to buy land for a road right-of-way.

When the task force hired Georgia's former attorney general and filed a lawsuit in the Fulton County Superior Court against Barnes and GRTA, alleging that the GARVEE bond program for funding the road violated Georgia's constitution, Barnes was presented with an intractable situation.[166] The bond program itself had become an issue in Barnes's tough reelection campaign, as Republican challengers all claimed to object to using GARVEE bonds to fund transportation infrastructure and promised to kill the program if elected.[167] Because the controversial bond program would fund almost all the transportation projects in Barnes's plan, the lawsuit threatened even air-quality-friendly projects, like regional commuter bus service, intersection improvements, and rail transit expansion.

August also brought another ruling from the Court of Appeals for the Eleventh Circuit in favor of the Roadblockers. Agreeing that the EPA "illegally extended the 1999 deadline to meet federal smog standards," the court issued an emergency stay that "block[ed] Georgia from continuing to use a standard that allows the state to violate the Clean Air Act." Now ARC would be forced to evaluate transportation projects against "an old ozone standard that allow[ed] for less pollution."[168] In mid-September, the Fulton County Superior Court ruled that the governor's plan to sell GARVEE bonds was not unconstitutional on its face, but it left open the possibility of appeal to the Georgia Supreme Court, which the Northern Arc Task Force filed almost immediately.[169]

The November 2002 election brought a final, decisive end to the governor's plan, when Barnes was upset in his reelection bid by Sonny Perdue, a Republican state senator and veterinarian from central Georgia. Barnes's defeat not only ended the battle over the use of bonds to pay for transportation projects but squelched the entire plan. Sans Barnes, the motive force behind the accelerated transportation program and the Northern Arc was gone. Even before Barnes tried to pull the plug on the Northern Arc in a last-ditch effort to save his campaign, there were signs that ARC was likely turn against the governor's plan.[170] With the resignation of the chairman of the ARC board in mid-2002, a critical supporter for the Northern Arc on the commission was gone. Moreover, opposition to the Northern Arc among other ARC board members had hardened to the point of putting every part of the governor's plan in jeopardy.

Nevertheless, by May 2003 the new governor made it abundantly clear that he had no intention of allowing GARVEE bonds to be sold to support the remnants of Barnes's transportation plan. Ironically, in July 2003, six months after Barnes had left office and Perdue scrapped the GARVEE bond idea, the Georgia Supreme Court ruled against the Northern Arc Task Force, finding that the former governor's bond plan was constitutional.[171]

The Aftermath

The battle over the Northern Arc encapsulated the pressures that had produced a broader regional planning crisis in metro Atlanta. As a result of overinvestment in roads, underinvestment in transit, and tremendous population growth, when federal air quality regulations tightened in 1990 ARC and the state were faced with the difficult task of figuring out a way to reduce the total number of vehicle miles driven in the region. Doing this amid a period of heightened political divisions among regional leaders made the work that much more difficult. As the regional planning process broke down, the arrival of Governor Barnes promised a way out. Barnes's effort to transform the regional planning process ultimately failed, along with his bid for a second term.

During his single term as governor, Roy Barnes attempted to reform the regional planning process by executing another major expansion of state power over land development practices. Barnes expected to succeed, by virtue of his considerable political capital and his skills as a politician and because he was following a well-worn path established by his predecessors, Jimmy Carter and Joe Frank Harris. In a time of deep misgivings about the region's path forward, Barnes's efforts could have paved the way for a new era of state and regional coordination. Yet Barnes ran headlong into Atlanta and Georgia's changed political culture, in which his base was split and his opposition united. The governor's attempt to solve Atlanta's planning crisis fostered unexpected alliances that led to his defeat. On one side of the anti-Barnes alliance was a coalition of liberal, central-city environmental organizations that had been working for several years to push ARC, the state, and local politicians toward a more equitable form of regional planning that would aggressively address the externalities of sprawl and push Atlanta toward a more sustainable and equitable form of development. On the other side was a group of state and local politicians and their supporters, many new to Georgia's political scene. Based in the Republican-dominated suburban counties north of the city, motivated perhaps by the annoyance of traffic, they had a broader disagreement with the liberal governing coalition that had dominated Georgia's politics for nearly three decades and were decidedly opposed to giving the state more control over land-use decisions than it already had. Though coming from different ends of the political spectrum, the two groups agreed that the consequences of the governor's proposed reforms would have been more damaging to the region than any potential benefits.[172]

Caught between Barnes and his opposition was ARC. For nearly thirty years ARC had been at the center of the regional planning and development process. While Barnes and ARC had started on the same page, the relationship between them frayed quickly. Though GRTA was initially welcomed as a tool for getting Atlanta out of air-quality nonconformity, it was later perceived as a threat to ARC's position.[173] Barnes's "autocratic leadership" style only eroded his support.[174] These differences exploded any chance of easily reforming the regional planning process. GRTA, despite its power, got lost amid the fight for control over the regional planning process and never found a stable base of support. As the Metro Atlanta Chamber of Commerce president remarked a month before Barnes ultimately went down in defeat, "[GRTA] got us out of nonconformity. That's progress . . . [but] are we totally happy? No, we're not totally happy."[175] What started as a long-term solution to the short-term crisis, GRTA was quickly mothballed once Barnes was booted from office.

Barnes's defeat in the 2002 election ended an uninterrupted 130-year period of Democratic control of the state's executive and legislative branches and drew to a close a line of so-called New South governors in Georgia that dated back to Jimmy Carter.[176] More than anything, Barnes's spectacular failure stemmed from changing politics. When suburban homeowners joined urban environmentalists to challenge the governor, the battle turned into something more than just a dispute over regional transportation plans. The fight over the regional planning process was a manifestation of the competition for political control over the region and, by extension, the state. During the 1990s baby boomers living in Atlanta's affluent northern suburbs, many transplants from other states, had finally accumulated enough power to begin molding metropolitan politics in their image.[177] The rise of this voting bloc began at the local level, evidenced in the tumultuous county commission elections in the early 1990s, but later extended to the state legislature and Georgia's congressional delegation. As this new cohort of elected officials took control of county commissions and assumed seats on the ARC board, they attempted to reconfigure the regional planning process, rejecting the "regional statesmanship" that had characterized ARC for the first two decades of its existence. In its place, they installed a more confrontational style in which delivering spoils to their respective counties took precedence over regionally minded collaboration.[178]

Atlanta's planning crisis tested this new leadership, their ability to cooperate with each other, and their ability to negotiate with state and federal officials. It also tested their capacity to bend the regional planning process in ways that would allow the metro area to be able to meet federal air quality goals. Under the intense scrutiny the air quality crisis generated, the ability of Atlanta's new political leaders to manage the regional planning process and guide it toward compliance broke down. As a result, faith in their ability to lead the region waned, which sparked lawsuits by the environmental coalition and encouraged Barnes to create GRTA and pursue his own transportation plan. The transportation crisis temporarily turned Atlanta's regional planning agenda on its head, a situation that was not resolved until Barnes was defeated. In the end, the immediate battle to defeat the Northern Arc was won, but the cooperation that had long grounded the regional planning process was lost.

7
A Regional Story

This project set out to answer three questions. How have regional planning agencies supported and extended metropolitan decentralization? What role have regional planning agencies played in the expansion of federal and state power over land development decisions? Through what channels have regional planning agencies coordinated planning and development activity? By looking across three decades, from 1970 to 2002, of regional planning and exploring a series of planning events in Atlanta, I have attempted to sketch an answer. An unexpectedly coordinated regional planning process, managed by the Atlanta Regional Commission (ARC) and supported by the state of Georgia, lay behind the construction of Atlanta's notorious urban sprawl. The regional planning process reflected underlying political circumstances in the region, but it also operated according to an internal logic that changed the region's politics. The complexity of this relationship offers perspective on a larger question: to what extent has late twentieth-century urban sprawl been planned? Atlanta's experience suggests that regional planning should be considered one of the major factors that, along with demographic, technological, and economic changes, transformed American cities in the decades between the end of World War II and the end of the twentieth century. In short, ARC and the state did not create growth, but they had a major hand in allocating where growth happened.

From the late 1940s to the mid-1960s, discussion and debate about regional planning among Atlanta's politicians, businessmen, public administrators, and planners centered on who should have the authority to make development decisions and what kind of organizational structure would best facilitate those decisions. Whether publicly stated or not, the conclusion was consistently reached that the opinions of the men who ran Atlanta's downtown businesses should hold sway.[1] The tenor of this debate began to change in the late 1960s, though, and the stable leadership that had long governed the city, and by default most of its suburbs, faced new challenges. Changing demographics, shifting state politics, and expanding federal policy meant Atlanta's tight-knit governing coalition began to lose control over the regional planning process in the early 1970s. What emerged in its place was a broader coalition spread over a wider geography, in which the state and the regional planning commission came to occupy the seat of power. This expanded governing coalition, a group that also included increasingly powerful suburban politicians, displaced Atlanta's existing governing regime. Through a series of plans and legislation, ARC and the state slowly tightened control over land development across metropolitan Atlanta—control, however, that led not to more compact or sensitive forms of development but just the opposite: the rise of what might be called massive sprawl. Instead of softening the impact of growth, the new regional planning coalition accelerated it. Though ARC and the state could not and did not attempt to control the details of small development decisions within the region, they controlled the large decisions related to infrastructure and governance.

When it emerged from the Georgia General Assembly, the bill that created ARC in 1971 granted policy-making authority to a large governing board comprising elected officials, including county commissioners and mayors, and citizens. ARC's structure helped codify the changed politics of metropolitan Atlanta. The growth of the suburban belt that stretched around the city had given the politicians based there significant power within the region, which was reflected in the ARC board: every member had one vote regardless of geographic affiliation. While Atlanta's old elites had not entirely lost their place, the organization of ARC pointed to a future in which the regional power structure would increasingly bend to suburban concerns.[2] With so much federal infrastructure money at stake, suburban politicians recognized that gaining a voice in the regional planning process would ensure that a large portion of those funds benefited their districts. Politicians in Atlanta's suburbs were hungry for growth and development, and in their courting of new development they tended to pay little mind to the form that growth took. Despite significant changes in federal antipoverty and environmental policy, issues related to socioeconomic equity, affordable housing, or protecting fragile natural resources received little attention. The politics of development in the early 1970s instead remained focused on roads, water, transit, and airports, the placement of which would have enormous implications for land development.

As had been the case with the earlier Metropolitan Planning Commission and the Atlanta Region Metropolitan Planning Commission, the issues important to the regional political leadership helped shape many of ARC's substantive activities. Yet in the case of ARC, federal and state policy also dictated the commission's responsibilities.

The beginning of this period, at the end of the 1960s, saw state agencies become more aggressive in identifying and managing resources. This shift was one indicator that Atlanta's three decades of regime politics, the diffuse network of elected city officials and downtown Atlanta businessmen, had ceased to be the primary force shaping development in the region. By the end of 1971, regional planning in metropolitan Atlanta, driven partly by federal and state policy and partly by ARC's assertion of a strong identity, was set to take a different path. The work ARC would do over the course of the next two decades was strongly influenced by its early leaders, the organizational structure they established, and the network of relationships they created.[3] From this point forward, the reputation of ARC would grow because of the commission's support from the state, its ability to consistently communicate ideas about urban development, its facility in managing different sources of information, and its role in interpreting increasingly complex federal regulations.[4]

The three major functions identified in ARC's founding legislation stemmed almost equally from federal mandates, state needs, and the concerns of local governments. The first was review of and comment on local applications for state or federal financial assistance (according to requirements established by individual federal granting agencies). In Act 5 (1971), ARC was designated the contact point between federal and state funding agencies and local governments (in accordance with the requirements outlined in the 1962 Federal Aid Highway Act and Circular A-95 of the federal Office of Management and Budget). Shortly thereafter, ARC was designated the Section 208 agency in accordance with the Clean Water Act. Any local application for federal money had to pass through ARC, which read the application, compared it to the goals of existing regional plans and policies, and then made official comments as to the application's merit. ARC then forwarded a record of this review to the respective federal granting agency for a final decision. Working with other state agencies, ARC's comments served as the official comments of the state.

The second was review of plans with area-wide implications (a determination left to the ARC board). Area plan reviews were devised to give ARC formal entrée into cross-jurisdictional debates, for municipal and county plans as well as plans produced by utilities or other public commissions. If ARC deemed a planning project area-wide, it had to be submitted for review, which would allow the commission to alert affected public agencies and municipal governments and give them time to formally comment on the plan. If any proposal was judged inconsistent with regional plans or policies or questioned by affected public bodies, a conference was called to resolve the conflict. If a resolution could be found, the plan was returned to the submitting jurisdiction and the project could proceed. If no resolution emerged, the ARC board transmitted the board's official position on the proposal along with staff comments to the submitting jurisdiction, which could revise its original to address the review or attempt to push forward without approval.

Third was a set of more general tasks, defined as a "continuous program of research, study, and planning."[5] Subject areas included population forecasts, land use, transportation, solid waste, parks and open space, law enforcement, and health. Other less concrete but equally important tasks included providing a forum for cross-boundary discussions by public officials and managing channels for information dissemination. The sum total of these activities formed the base from which ARC grew.

From the time of its inaugural meeting in early 1972, ARC's influence across the region expanded almost continuously for the next twenty years. Explanations for how ARC, in the face of tremendous population growth and land development pressure, maintained its position as the nerve center of Atlanta's planning network include its administrative capacity, political connections, regionalist outlook, state support, and three major federal urban policy innovations: finding appropriate strategies to improve intergovernmental relations, connecting land development to water quality, and managing the relationship of transportation system planning to air quality.

First, by virtue of consistent and abundant financial support, the commission could afford to grow its staff quickly, deploy sophisticated data analysis, and undertake a wide variety of regional studies. Federal funds for mandated regional coordination activities, state support for data gathering and analysis, and local support for technical assistance filled ARC's coffers in its early days. ARC maintained this administrative capacity through its position as the central forum for regional development information and managing regional planning projects, interpreting federal regulations and policies, and disseminating critical information to its constituent local governments. Being an information-sorting facility shared by stakeholders was critical to the ability of the commission to maintain regional coordination. Divisions over the direction the region should take were managed by the commission, which until the mid-1990s, mostly turned away outside challenges to the existing planning agenda. In other words, throughout most of the period under study, ARC's administrative capacity normalized a form of regional development that had the appearance of received wisdom.[6] This is how ARC from early on helped structure many of the major development plans and policies that allowed Atlanta to grow in its remarkably decentralized fashion.

The second issue pertains to the politics of regional coordination, influenced by the Bureau of the Budget's Circular A-95, a result of the Model Cities Act of 1966 and the Intergovernmental Cooperation Act of 1968. With the beginning of the A-95 review program in 1969, regional planning agencies like ARC received a major boost in federal support. When Reagan rescinded the circular in 1982, a chief direct federal support for state and regional planning disappeared. I have argued that land development in Atlanta in the 1970s and 1980s was better coordinated, in part because of the A-95 review process, than often recognized and political fragmentation less pronounced than often suggested. During its first two decades, stable leadership allowed ARC's board to pursue a highly active role for the commission. Though regional planning agencies often operate in a politically treacherous climate, agreement among stakeholders within metro Atlanta remained fairly consistent. Tight connections between ARC's board and staff, the state executive branch, the state legislature, and key local politicians made regional relationships easy to create and maintain, at least until the mid-1990s. These agreements helped ARC manage the complicated character of regional planning but also controlled attempts to reconfigure the process. The wide and relatively even distribution of population across metro Atlanta meant no single municipality could dominate the process, a condition that undercut the city versus suburbs problem so common in many places. In this case, squabbles between municipalities concealed a deeper level of cooperation and consensus about how development should proceed. In three of the four planning events highlighted here, broad consensus among participants was the norm rather than the exception.

Third is the legacy of regionalist thinking as an intellectual pursuit but also as a form of planning practice. Five decades of publicly supported regional planning offered basic legitimacy to regional planning, which proved important to ARC's stability. During this period, regional planning in Atlanta adhered to neither Lewis Mumford's idealized notion of region as revolution nor the more pragmatic form of cooperative governing in line with the metropolitan growth model resident in *Plan of New York and Its Environs*.[7] Rather, Atlanta represented a combination of the two, mixed with Howard Odum's vision of using state and regional planning as a tool to develop the South.[8] The three decades covered here underscore how slowly the regional planning process moves. Plans took years to develop and years to implement and were subject to almost continuous negotiation. In Atlanta that process was the most important aspect of the plans, which meant that ideas often reemerged several times before becoming part of regional practice.

Fourth is the support of the state. During the early 1970s, Georgia's political leaders developed strong interest in intergovernmental coordination and planning, albeit toward ends that do not necessarily correspond to widely held notions of good (or progressive) planning. The state's engagement with regional development issues over the years demonstrated how deeply planning had become embedded in state politics, even if sprawling growth was the outcome. A band of state political leaders who embraced planning established ARC, supported legislation that empowered regional coordination, and worked to expand the legal framework for controlling development. Such consistent support helped maintain a stable governing environment in metropolitan Atlanta.

This environment began to unravel in the early 1990s, as Georgia's political landscape experienced a major shake-up when the long-ruling Democratic Party lost its grip on power.[9] In a process that began at the local level with a few county commission elections and quickly spread to state legislative races, by the early 2000s the Democrats had been relieved of their majority in the General Assembly and turned out of the governor's mansion for the first time in 130 years. During this transfer of power, ARC faced a serious challenge, its position threatened by a new cadre of politicians who showed little interest in cross-jurisdictional collaboration or "regional statesmanship."[10] The internecine fight that resulted shattered Atlanta's old regional governing coalition, ushering in a rocky transition to a new political order.

The conflict over the Northern Arc presented a real challenge to ARC and state leaders over control of the regional development process after nearly twenty-five years of relative stability. Changing local and state politics disrupted ARC's stable management structure. With several long-serving officials retiring or being ousted from office, the factors that had enabled ARC to maintain its position and legitimacy were swept away. As the crisis over Atlanta's transportation woes grew, ARC's leadership was unable to maintain control of the planning process. Internal fractures spilled into the public realm, jeopardizing the style of planning regional political leaders had long followed. Barnes's defeat in 2002 brought order back to the regional planning process. The Republicans took power at the statehouse and scaled back ambitions for change. With the George W. Bush administration's decision to relax urban air quality enforcement, the regional planning crisis began to abate.[11] Under new leadership, ARC was able to get back to work. But the problems that had emerged in the late 1990s did not vanish, and the commission's position in the regional planning process had been altered. Congestion on the region's roads continued to grow, and the interstate fight over water supply finally exploded.

The long-term actions of the state, ARC, and local politicians present a sharp contrast to the notion that regional planning necessarily leads toward one set of ends. In the case of Atlanta, coordinated region- and state-level planning was embraced as part of a process of negotiation, accommodation, and economic development. Jimmy Carter's single term as governor in the early 1970s gave prominence to the roles coordination, resource management, and administrative reform could play within metropolitan Atlanta and throughout the state. When Joe Frank Harris entered his second term as governor in 1986, he reinvigorated Carter's initiatives, leveraging water resource management and infrastructure funding to make local, regional, and state planning critical to governance. In 1998 Roy Barnes put land development near the center of his gubernatorial term and attempted to leverage the transportation crisis to transform Atlanta's planning milieu. Each of these moments reveals the importance of the state to the way decisions about Atlanta's development have unfolded. The details of Atlanta's regional planning process raise questions about the utility of the model of coordinated regional planning that has long served as an example to planners everywhere: Portland, Oregon. In the case of Portland, as in Atlanta, the state played a key role, creating a regional planning agency and then supporting it over time. But unlike Portland, Atlanta does not stand apart as a singular case. Rather, it may represent a more typical model of regional planning, one in which state and regional leaders worked together closely, in a highly coordinated fashion, but produced a sprawling urban region instead of a compact city.

The state's interest in supporting regional planning in Atlanta must be understood in the context of the region's influence on Georgia's economy and politics. The planning events highlighted here span a period of almost uninterrupted population and economic growth, which transformed Atlanta from a bounded city to an "unbound" metropolitan area.[12] By the early 1990s, Atlanta had been experiencing sustained population and economic growth for the better part of forty years. The influx of people and jobs brought both problems and opportunities. Housing, offices, and stores helped push the urban fringe outward from the core, overwhelming northern Georgia's small towns, farms, and forests with subdivisions, strip malls, and office parks. For many places swept into the urban fold, planning, understood as controlling what individuals do with their private land, became a necessary but confusing evil, one that most local governments knew little about. Atlanta's growth also steadily transferred political control from rural Georgia to the handful of counties composing the metropolitan core. Like other American big cities in the postwar period, Atlanta and its suburbs were transformed into a complex web of urban space that stretched across a vast area.[13] Changes in the national and global economy helped turn Atlanta into a center of corporate headquarters, transportation and logistics, and advanced business support activities, economic sectors somewhat more sensitive to the externalities of the absence of coordinated planning. State political leaders increasingly believed that not having the state involved in planning would undermine Atlanta's future success. Three issues dominated their concerns: intergovernmental relations, water, and air.

A tangle of federal policies supporting intergovernmental relations and cleaning up water and air pollution faced political conflict during long and convoluted attempts at implementation. The policies helped shape the state's involvement in ARC in ways that transcended the scope of local politics. The A-95 review program laid some of the groundwork for state governments and local governments to coordinate around key regional issues. Federal water pollution legislation, notably the Clean Water Act, provided a powerful new policy foundation for addressing the condition of watersheds, which brought new attention to land use and reinforced cross-jurisdictional cooperation. Similarly, the 1990 Clean Air Act amendments and the 1991 Intermodal Surface Transportation Efficiency Act (ISTEA) made combating declining air quality a high-profile national environmental issue with serious implications for regional planning.

An Open Secret

While the legacy of state, regional, and local planning policies working together to channel infrastructure funds to support regional growth is visible in the urban landscape, most of the time the deliberations that led to the policies that shaped development went mostly unnoticed. In a context in which regional planning was ongoing, routine, and somewhat "boring," small decisions went unchallenged.[14] The federal agencies responsible for overseeing Atlanta's regional planning activities, which might have been a moderating influence, were themselves deeply embedded in the local context and often sidestepped their responsibility to challenge decisions made by Atlanta's leaders. While regional planning in Atlanta has not always been visible, the public agencies overseeing planning have not been unimportant. The small decisions that structured the growth of the region accumulated over so many years that they were difficult for most observers to see.[15] Only at moments of extreme crisis did anyone pay much attention, and then the public took note only when an outside organization challenged the regional leadership in federal court. The public agencies influencing Atlanta's regional planning process were hiding in plain sight.[16]

Though receiving little attention, the regional planning process helped establish a basic set of parameters and paths that structured future development. Only on rare occasions did observers of the regional planning process in Atlanta grasp this or address it.[17] The creation of ARC, the *Chattahoochee Corridor Study*, the 1976 regional development plan, the Metropolitan Atlanta Water Resources Management Study (the Atlanta Study), and the Georgia Planning Act embodied Atlanta's regional planning process. Occasional challenges to the process, such as the transportation crisis and the Northern Arc battle, were actually part of the process. Regional planning was more than just a simple meeting among local governments to discuss the allocation of federal money. It was a critical component of the intergovernmental relationships that shaped decisions about development and the urbanization of Atlanta.

From the 1930s Atlanta's political leaders had engaged in an active public discourse about the importance of regional planning. Each of Atlanta's regional planning agencies—the Metropolitan Planning Commission, the Atlanta Region Metropolitan Planning Commission, and ARC—provided data analysis, training, technical service, and advice to local governments within their jurisdictions, practices that encouraged a greater understanding of the importance of planning. But devising and implementing policies could move no faster than the pace of politics. Georgia's essentially conservative approach to regulation meant that major regulatory changes could come only slowly. Following the huge wave of urbanization that moved outward from the central city beginning in the 1950s and the accompanying shift from rural to urban power in the General Assembly in the 1960s, the state's creation of ARC in 1971 acknowledged the importance of *metropolitan* Atlanta and pointed toward a future in which it would thoroughly and completely dominant the state.

The legislation that emerged in 1971 focused quite intensely on creating a predictable development process to make the state and local governments eligible for federal funding for infrastructure upgrades and to make land development easier. This process, however, did not attempt to dictate the form development would take.

Thus, environmental protection ensured water supply, not preservation of fragile ecosystems from development; coordination among governments supported economic investment, not compact development; and transportation plans permitted more automobiles, not better accessibility. Though ARC, and the regional planning process it supported, could be deemed a success by the state, protecting the environment and stopping sprawl were largely ignored.[18] In fact, when the legislation that created ARC was pushed through the General Assembly, the proposed agency had been weakened by a critical compromise (lack of zoning review) that would be made again and again. Read this way, questions about ARC's teeth, or the willingness of Atlanta's political establishment to develop and pursue a vision of compact, transit-oriented, and ecologically sensitive urban development, were beside the point, despite most observers seeing expressions of "despotic power"—the power (and willingness) to say no—as an indicator of the success of regional planning.[19] In retrospect, we see that a small group of politicians, planners, and public administrators recognized the value of regional planning and coordination for the predictability it could produce for governments, investors, property owners, and businesses. For thirty years the basic agreement about how regional planning should work that was forged out of this relationship—that regional policies should be oriented toward encouraging more growth, not restricting it—trumped most other disagreements.

Those thirty years also provide a close view of shifts in federal urban policy from the late 1960s through the late 1990s.[20] The development of comprehensive regional planning agencies was motivated by federal policies relating to transportation and intergovernmental relations in the 1960s, which were later joined by regulations that accompanied the environmental movement in the 1970s.[21] Jimmy Carter would rise to the presidency in 1976 and advocate "comprehensive" environmental and urban policy, but his single term in the White House was overwhelmed by inflation, energy supply disruptions, and unemployment.[22] A depressed economy effectively upended any push for new federal support for state and regional planning during the late 1970s. Under Reagan, federal support for state and regional planning activities dimmed, a result of the reluctance of his administration to embrace policies aimed at controlling growth. With the introduction of the Clean Air Act amendments and ISTEA in the early 1990s under President George H. W. Bush federal support for state and regional planning took a turn for the better. The new policies put greater emphasis on improving the relationship between transportation plans and land use and grappled with the environmental and social equity implications of federal urban policy.[23]

For the last thirty years, a chorus of scholars has argued that in the second half of the twentieth century federal policy lured (or pushed) a huge number of households to the urban fringe, a movement that simultaneously forced many of the nation's largest central cities into a state of decline. The commingling of policy, infrastructure, inexpensive land, a preference for single-family dwellings in a pastoral setting, racism, and global economic restructuring sped the process along.²⁴ The result has been a restructuring of urban space in the United States, a process that has been particularly intense across the Sunbelt.²⁵

Kick-starting this period of massive spatial restructuring was the changing geographic focus of federal expenditures. Beginning during World War II and intensifying in the Cold War, the federal government directed major defense-related investments toward Sunbelt states. Expanded military installations (e.g., Naval Air Station North Island in California and Eglin Air Force Base in Florida), research and development laboratories (e.g. Oak Ridge National Laboratory in Tennessee, Los Alamos National Laboratory in New Mexico, and the Centers for Disease Control and Prevention in Georgia), and related support facilities (e.g., NASA centers in Alabama, Florida, and Texas) were scattered across the southern half of the United States, with particular concentrations in California, Texas, Georgia, and Florida. Supported by the federal purse, these investments boosted the economy of the Sunbelt, spawned an array of supporting services, laid the groundwork for a skilled workforce, and attracted domestic migrants.²⁶ The combination of federal dollars, cheap labor, technology, and opportunities for expanding into new markets attracted branches of manufacturing firms based in the Northeast and Midwest and later the corporate headquarters themselves. The confluence of these two sets of distinct but related processes created a national pattern of decentralization of, housing and jobs. This marked the beginning of the relocation of the nation's political center, from small lots and small houses in dense northern cities to large lots and large houses in sprawling southern suburbs. Over the same period, the position of roads and the environment in the social and economic life of the country changed considerably.²⁷ Roads were transformed from chaotic public spaces to engines of economic development to critical infrastructure reserved for the sole purpose of moving as much motorized traffic as possible.²⁸ The environment went from a wild expanse for exploitation to a collection of places that should be preserved for inherent value to a complex ecological space in which humans play only one part.²⁹

Beginning in the 1940s, Atlanta started down a long growth trajectory. Yet unlike with urbanization in the decades before World War II, the city captured relatively little of the influx in the postwar period. Most newcomers to the region went straight to the suburbs. So much growth in the unincorporated sections of the suburban-exurban fringe made for a challenging governing environment.³⁰ In a region with only a few small suburban cities and no townships, county governments were forced to take responsibility for providing a full array of urban services, often over very large areas, many of which were quasi-rural. The resulting regulations could be described as necessarily loose. This was both advantageous and detrimental to the regional planning process. While the number of individual governments was limited, making coordination among neighbors potentially easier, county governments often used a light touch when it came to restricting land development. Moreover, county governments were just large enough to pursue investments in road and water infrastructure but not large enough to contain the spillover effects of these investments.

The greater Atlanta metropolitan region began a growth explosion in 1970, going from 1.5 million residents spread over fifteen counties to 4.1 million people in twenty-eight counties in 2000.[31] Migrants who originated in smaller towns in the South and urban counties in the Northeast and Midwest drove much of this growth, but from the mid-1980s immigrants from Latin America and south and east Asia made up an increasing proportion of the region's newcomers.[32] By the mid-1990s the region's relentless growth raised questions about the quality of planning and development regulations put in place in the 1970s, sparking a debate about the spatial and, implicitly, political future of Atlanta.[33] Though the benefits derived from federal, state, and regional policies that encouraged and supported urban decentralization were legion, by the late 1990s almost everyone had come to see the procession of Atlanta's sprawling landscape as problematic.[34]

The State Rules

The defeat of Governor Barnes and ousting of the Democratic majority in the General Assembly in the autumn of 2002 represented more than lost elections: it was also the end of a governing coalition that had held sway over state politics for thirty years. Barnes's loss was a sad end to the career of a politician who not only understood the importance of state and regional planning but also put efforts to transform it near the center of his political identity. With Barnes's booting from office, another expansion of state support for the regional planning process became less likely. With the GOP assuming the reins of power in the state, taking over not only the governor's mansion but both branches of the General Assembly and many county commissions, the prospects for a return to the old order seemed dim.

The new Republican governor, Sonny Perdue, opposed Barnes's prescription for solving the region's planning problems, and he also generally disagreed with the vision of the environmental organizations. Tightening development regulations, changing the terms of coordination among local governments, creating a stronger regional planning agency, and providing desperately needed investments to benefit the transit system were not part of his agenda.[35] The new Republican leadership acted quickly to stamp out the remains of the state's last Democratic administration.[36] Early in his term, Perdue and his legislative floor leaders pulled the plug on Barnes's infrastructure plans, shut down the GARVEE bond program, and defanged the Georgia Regional Transportation Authority (GRTA) by replacing the board with his supporters, including one of the leaders of the Northern Arc Task Force.[37] The lawsuits filed against ARC and the state were settled or dismissed. At the federal level, the

George W. Bush administration had recently relaxed the EPA's urban air quality rules, which took much of the pressure off ARC to immediately deal with the region's lingering air quality issues. The regional crisis settled down and briefly receded from view.

Yet Atlanta continued to add people apace. By early 2006 the census bureau estimated Atlanta's Metropolitan Statistical Area had topped five million, a substantial (25 percent) increase just since 2000. ARC estimated the population of its ten-county planning area at just over four million. While most of this growth, as in the previous four decades, occurred in unincorporated counties, four aspects are worth pointing out about the character of the region's very recent growth. One, the city of Atlanta saw a striking turnaround beginning in the mid-1990s, as its population began to grow for the first time since the 1970s. The majority of these newcomers were white and highly educated, signaling the potential for a major shift in the city's politics sometime in the early twenty-first century. Two, growth was beginning to be spread more evenly around the region, with counties to the south of the city showing surges in population. Three, the newcomers were even more ethnically diverse. While blacks and whites still composed the majority of in-migrants, the number of foreign-born immigrants greatly increased. By the end of 2005 there were nearly five hundred thousand Latinos in the region, a sevenfold increase from 1990, and just over two hundred thousand Asians, a fourfold increase. Most of these immigrants landed in the core suburban counties; few ended up in central-city neighborhoods. Four, the concentration of the region's population in the core urban counties remained high, though what could be considered the central urbanized area had expanded considerably. The total population in Cobb, Gwinnett, Dekalb, Clayton, and Fulton Counties was 65 percent of the population of the entire Atlanta Metropolitan Statistical Area, and most of the new growth continued to locate in those counties.[38]

Though the state's new leadership tried to put the transportation crisis behind it, the problems plaguing the region remained. In the early twenty-first century, ARC advanced two new planning programs in response. The first, the Livable Centers Initiative, was introduced in 2000 and laid out a strategy for structuring future development around the constellation of small-town centers and mass transit stations that were spread around the region.[39] Providing substantial initial funds for planning activities and then follow-up funds for infrastructure supporting the plans, the Livable Centers Initiative offered a glimpse of what strategic marginal changes could accomplish in reshaping the region's sprawl. Communities across the region wrote plans encouraging mixed land use, denser residential development, and more pedestrian-oriented infrastructure. At its inception, the initiative received $5 million for five years to support the development of plans and another $350 million for construction funds, no small achievement given Atlanta's reputation. As a result of the program's popularity and success, in 2005 another $5 million for planning and $150 million for construction were set aside. By 2003 projects planned as part of the Livable Centers Initiative had received $132 million in construction funds.[40]

The second new strategy came in 2006, aimed at a longer-term fix. Expanding the existing mass transit system and building new commuter rails continued to garner relatively high levels of support among the chamber of commerce crowd, regional planners, Atlanta-area legislators, and the public.[41] Assuming there would be little state or federal financial support for new infrastructure, ARC, the Metro Atlanta Chamber of Commerce, and a group of state legislators devised an alternative way to pay for major infrastructure improvements that the region still desperately needed (many left over from the days of Governor Barnes). The plan permitted groups of counties to band together to levy special local taxes for infrastructure development. Legislation to permit the special taxation was introduced in the General Assembly in 2008.[42] When the measure failed to pass, supporters went back to the drawing board and with Governor Perdue's support succeeded in getting a lightly modified version of the legislation through the General Assembly in 2010. The list of projects to be funded by the special tax, however, became engulfed in controversy.[43] The first public referendum on the new tax in July 2012 was overwhelmingly rejected. The plan's fate remains unknown.[44]

As the regional economy rebounds in the wake of the recent recession, the planning problems facing the region cannot continue to go unaddressed. In the absence of a major change in federal policy, only a renewed commitment by the state to support investment in transportation infrastructure can help solve the transportation problems facing the region. The outcome of the legal case between Georgia, Alabama, and Florida notwithstanding, adopting a more aggressive regional water management program could prevent another episode like the summer drought of 2007, when the region's water supply systems nearly ran dry. With the resurgence in Atlanta's population and a recession that crushed the market for new housing in the suburbs, the commonly assumed goal of regional planning—a denser population and less sprawl—may be achieved in unexpected ways (and not necessarily because of anything the planners did). Moreover, the problems of Atlanta's sprawl, as in other cities, are compounded by factors outside local or state (or even national) control. The rising cost of gasoline in an automobile-dependent metropolis could translate into serious hardship for a majority of the region's inhabitants, portending trouble for metro Atlanta's quality of life and the region's economic vitality. What will happen depends on the collective work of every level of government and every organization with a stake in the region.

Metropolitan Atlanta has come to represent one possible form of urban development, in which a diffuse network of city, suburb, and exurb, a collection of spaces that remain hard to differentiate, has replaced the city-suburb dichotomy. Understanding the details of how regional planning, as embodied by the relationship between ARC and the state, has fit into this broader context will aid planners and policy makers in their ability to manage the planning process that structures the relationship between transportation, the environment, and land use. Regional planning has been an important factor in metropolitan change in the United States during the twentieth century but has been conspicuously overlooked when researchers seek explanations for how and why urban change happens. Given the mounting problems associated with sprawl, better understanding of how regional planning functions should be a subject of intense scholarly and practical interest.

Notes

Chapter 1

1. Anthony Downs, "Urban Realities: Some Controversial Aspects of the Atlanta Region's Future," *Brookings Review*, Summer 1994, 27. Another version of the argument that Atlanta's sprawl is the result of unplanned growth is contained in Robert Bullard, Glenn Johnson, and Angel Torres, eds., *Sprawl City: Race, Politics, and Planning in Atlanta* (Washington, DC: Island Press, 2000).

2. Lewis Mumford, "The Plan of New York," in *Planning the Fourth Migration: The Neglected Vision of the Regional Planning Association of America*, ed. Carl Sussman (Cambridge, MA: MIT Press, 1976), 225. The history of regional planning in the United States has been covered by many authors. Among the important contributions are Gill C. Lim, ed., *Regional Planning: Evolution, Crisis, and Prospects* (Totowa, NJ: Allanheld, Osman, 1983); Robert Fishman, ed., *The American Planning Tradition* (Baltimore: Johns Hopkins University Press, 2000); John Friedmann and Clyde Weaver, *Territory and Function: The Evolution of Regional Planning* (Berkeley: University of California Press, 1979); Peter Hall, *Cities of Tomorrow: An Intellectual History of Urban Planning and Design in the Twentieth Century* (Malden, MA: Blackwell, 2002); Bruce Katz, ed., *Reflections on Regionalism* (Washington, DC: Brookings Institution Press, 2000); Roy Lubove, *Community Planning in the 1920s: The Contribution of the Regional Planning Association of America* (Pittsburgh, PA: University of Pittsburgh Press, 1963); Mark Luccarelli, *Lewis Mumford and the Ecological Region* (New York: Guilford, 1995); Ann Markusen, *Regions: The Economics and Politics of Territory* (Totowa, NJ: Rowman and Littlefield, 1987); Mel Scott, *American Planning since 1890* (Berkeley: University of California Press, 1969); Carl Sussman, ed., *Planning the Fourth Migration: The Neglected Vision of the Regional Planning Association of America* (Cambridge, MA: MIT Press, 1976); and Benton MacKaye, *The New Exploration: A Philosophy of Regional Planning* (New York: Harcourt, Brace, 1928).

3. Lewis Mumford has written more about regional planning than any other American intellectual. While his writings are far too vast to recite here, perhaps the most well-developed introductions to his ideas about regionalism and planning are *The Culture of Cities* (New York: Harcourt, Brace, 1938) and *The City in History* (New York: Harcourt, Brace, and World, 1961). Mumford's ideas about regional planning were perhaps most succinctly expressed in a public argument between him and Thomas Adams about the value of the *Plan of New York and Its Environs*, completed under the guidance of Adams in the early 1930s. Mumford criticized the plan as being metropolitan rather than regional. Adams took offense and defended the effort. For the details of the debate, see Sussman, *Planning the Fourth Migration*, especially chaps. 15 and 16, where the exchange between Mumford and Adams has been reprinted. Mumford's conceptualization of regional planning was inspired by the Englishman Ebenezer Howard, whose *A Path to Peaceful Reform: The City of To-morrow* (London: Swan Sonnenschein, 1902) provided the clearest enunciation of the idea of Garden City, and Scotsman Patrick Geddes, who spent years developing many ideas about regionalism. See, for example, Geddes's *City Development: A Study of Parks, Gardens, and Culture-Institutes, a Report to the Carnegie Dunfermline Trust* (Birmingham, UK: Saint George, 1904). Other relevant early works by American regional planners include MacKaye, *The New Exploration*; Catherine Bauer, *Modern Housing* (New York: Houghton, Mifflin, 1934); and Clarence Stein, *Toward New Towns for America* (New York: Reinhold, 1957). The sociologist Howard Odum represents yet another branch of American regional planning, one derived from Geddes's vision but usually associated with the South. For an introduction to Odum and his ideas, see Howard Odum, *The Regional Approach to National Social Planning* (New York: Foreign Policy Association, 1935); Howard Odum, *Southern Regions of the United States* (Chapel Hill: University of North Carolina Press, 1936); Howard Odum, ed., *In Search of the Regional Balance of America*, (Chapel Hill: University of North Carolina Press, 1945); and Pat Vernor, "The Missionaries of Chapel Hill," *Planning* 53, no. 6 (1987): 6–12.

4. Among the most influential advocates of regional planning and governance as a matter of public policy in the late 1930s in the United States was Thomas Harrison Reed. A political scientist by training, Reed published several books examining metropolitan governance and advocated the establishment of regional planning agencies in U.S. cities. As a consultant for the National Municipal League, Reed authored dozens of reports analyzing different cities, Atlanta being one of them. Reed's influence on postwar regional planning, though likely extensive, is largely undocumented. For an example of his writings, see Thomas Harrison Reed, *Municipal Government in the United States* (New York: Century, 1926).

5. Ideas about the benefits of planned urban decentralization date from at least the mid-nineteenth century and have been through a huge number of iterations and refinements. The message that humans are better off when they are within a short distance of the open countryside, however, persists. For examples, see Charles Fourier, *Design for Utopia: Selected Writings of Charles Fourier* (1901; repr., New York: Schocken, 1976); Geddes, *City Development*; Ebenezer Howard, *Garden Cities of To-morrow* (Cambridge, MA: MIT Press, 1965); Donald Leslie Johnson, "Observations on J.C. Loudon's Beau Ideal Town of 1829," *Journal of Planning History* 11, no. 3 (2012): 191–209; and Robert Owen, *A New Society and Other Writings* (1817; repr., New York: Dutton, 1972). For an intellectual history of the nineteenth- and twentieth-century utopians famous for advocating urban decentralization, see Robert Fishman, *Urban Utopias in the Twentieth Century: Ebenezer Howard, Frank Lloyd Wright, and Le Corbusier* (Cambridge, MA: MIT Press, 1982).

6. U.S. Congress, Housing Act of 1954, Pub. L. No. 560, 68 Stat. 590, Section 701. Section 701 of the Housing Act of 1954 provided federal financial aid to "facilitate urban planning

for smaller communities lacking adequate planning resources." Ibid. For a detailed, firsthand accounting of how federal support for regional planning was conceived, see Carl Feiss, "The Foundations of Federal Planning Assistance: A Personal Account of the 701 Program," *Journal of the American Planning Association* 51, no. 2 (1985): 175–184.

7. Richard White suggests that boredom helps planners avoid scrutiny. Richard White, *The Organic Machine: The Remaking of the Columbia River* (New York: Hill and Wang, 1995), chap. 3.

8. While I do not use the term "plan making," the regional plans and the regional planning process are the basic ingredients of plan making. For a discussion of plan making and its meaning, see Charles Hoch, "Making Plans: Representation and Intention, *Planning Theory* 6, no. 16 (2007): 16–35.

9. In making the case that postwar regional planning is a good example of the power of the state, I invoke recent work by William Novak, Robert Fishman, and Richard White. Novak characterizes the expression of state power as "the interpenetration of public and private spheres—the convergence of public and private authority in everyday policymaking." He draws from a range of sources in developing his argument but most notably from the sociologist Michael Mann's differentiation of "despotic" and "infrastructural" state power and the American Pragmatist philosophers who "eschewed the kind of abstract, formal definitions and typologies that dominate state theory . . . [and] recommended instead that one look in detail at what state officials of all kinds . . . actually did." William Novak, "The Myth of the 'Weak' American State," *American Historical Review*, June 2008, 770; see also Michael Mann, "The Autonomous Power of the State: Its Origins, Mechanisms, and Results," *European Journal of Sociology* 25, no. 2 (1984): 185–213. In *The Organic Machine*, Richard White explores an idea similar to Novak's, showing how federal plans and policies reshaped the Columbia River as a case study in state power. Robert Fishman also examines the power of pragmatic planning by the federal government, connecting the 1808 plan for canals and roads by Albert Gallatin, Thomas Jefferson's secretary of the Treasury, to the 1908 *Preliminary Report of the Inland Waterways Commission* produced under the administration of President Theodore Roosevelt. Robert Fishman, "1808–1908–2008: National Planning for America," paper presented at the meeting of the Regional Planning Association of America, July 8–13, 2007, available at http://www.rpa.org/pdf/temp/America%20 2050%20Website/Fishman%20National%20Planning%20Final.pdf.

10. Literature on the history of postwar regional planning commissions, public agencies sanctioned and supported by federal and state policy, rarely connects their work to the prewar intellectual tradition of regionalism. Sources that explore the history of these agencies include U.S. Advisory Commission on Intergovernmental Relations, *Metropolitan Councils of Government* (Washington, DC: Government Printing Office, 1966); U.S. Advisory Commission on Intergovernmental Relations, *Regional Decision Making: New Strategies for Substate Districts*, vol. 1 (Washington, DC: Government Printing Office, 1973); U.S. Advisory Commission on Intergovernmental Relations, *Toward More Balanced Transportation: New Intergovernmental Proposals* (Washington, DC: Government Printing Office, 1974); William Casella, "Regional Planning and Governance. History and Politics," in Lim, *Regional Planning*, 3–14; Bruce McDowell, "Substate Regionalism Matures Gradually," *Intergovernmental Perspective* 6, no. 4 (1980): 20–26; and Mark Solof, *History of Metropolitan Planning Organizations* (Newark, NJ: North Jersey Transportation Planning Authority, 1998). After the passage of the Intermodal Surface Transportation Efficiency Act (ISTEA) in 1991, the duties of regional planning agencies were substantially reshuffled. For details, see Robert Gage and Bruce McDowell, "ISTEA and the Role of MPOs in the New Transportation Environment: A Midterm Assessment," *Publius:*

The Journal of Federalism 25, no. 3 (1995): 133–154; and Judith Innes and Judith Gruber, *Bay Area Transportation Decision Making in the Wake of ISTEA: Planning Style in Conflict at the Metropolitan Planning Commission* (Berkeley: University of California Transportation Center, 2001). Criticism of metropolitan planning agencies has taken several forms but has focused most intensely on exposing bias (racial, economic, geographic, and transport mode) in their behavior. For examples, see Seth Benjamin, John Kinkaid, and Bruce McDowell, "MPOs and Weighted Voting," *Intergovernmental Perspective* 20, no. 2 (1994): 31–35; Paul Lewis, "Regionalism and Representation: Measuring and Assessing Representation in Metropolitan Planning Organizations," *Urban Affairs Review* 33, no. 6 (1998): 839–853; Arthur Nelson, Tom Sanchez, James Wolf, and Mary Beth Farquhar, "Metropolitan Planning Organization Voting Structure and Transit Investment Bias: Preliminary Analysis with Social Equity Implications," *Transportation Research Record: Journal of the Transportation Research Board*, no. 1895 (2004): 1–7; and Thomas Sanchez, "An Inherent Bias? Geographic and Racial-Ethnic Patterns of Metropolitan Planning Organization Boards," paper for Brookings Institution Series on Transportation Reform, January 2006.

11. Research on the influence of the Southern regionalists on state and regional planning in the twentieth century is limited. David Goldfield touches on the issue in "The Urban South: A Regional Framework," *American Historical Review* 86, no. 5 (1981): 1009–1034. Clyde Woods provides a little more insight in *Development Arrested: The Blues and Plantation Power in the Mississippi Delta* (New York: Verso, 1998). Robert Dorman addresses Odum and his followers in *Revolt of the Provinces: The Regionalist Movement in America, 1920–1945* (Chapel Hill: University of North Carolina Press, 1993) but does not consider their influence on regional development policy. However, much has been written about the South's modernization and urbanization. Important works in this literature include James Cobb, *The Selling of the South: The Southern Crusade for Industrial Development, 1936–1980* (Baton Rouge: Louisiana State University Press, 1982); David Goldfield, *Cotton Fields and Skyscrapers: Southern City and Region, 1607–1980* (Baton Rouge: Louisiana State University Press, 1982); George Tindall, *Emergence of the New South, 1913–1945* (Baton Rouge: Louisiana State University Press, 1967); and Bruce Schulman, *From Cottonbelt to Sun Belt: Federal Policy, Economic Development, and the Transformation of the South, 1938–1980* (New York: Oxford University Press, 1991). Most scholarly work on the region's development over the last sixty years owes a deep debt to W. J. Cash, *The Mind of the South* (New York: Knopf, 1941).

12. See Floyd Hunter, *Community Power Structure: A Study of Decision Makers* (Chapel Hill: University of North Carolina Press, 1969); Floyd Hunter, *Community Power Succession: Atlanta's Policy Makers Revisited* (Chapel Hill: University of North Carolina Press, 1980); and M. Kent Jennings, *Community Influentials: The Elites of Atlanta* (Glencoe, IL: Free Press, 1964).

13. Clarence Stone played an important role in developing urban regime theory, which he applied to Atlanta. He developed these ideas in "Atlanta: Protests and Elections Are Not Enough," *PS* 19, no. 3 (1986): 618–625; "Partnership New South Style: Central Atlanta Progress," *Proceedings of the Academy of Political Science* 36, no. 2 (1986): 100–110; *Regime Politics: Governing Atlanta, 1946–1988* (Lawrence: University Press of Kansas, 1989); and "The Atlanta Experience Re-examined: The Link between Agenda and Regime Change," *International Journal of Urban and Regional Research* 25, no. 1 (2001): 20–34. A more general expression of regime theory can be found in Stephen Elkin, "Twentieth Century Urban Regimes," *Journal of Urban Affairs* 7, no. 2 (1985): 11–28; and Stephen Elkin, *City and Regime in the American Republic* (Chicago: University of Chicago Press, 1987).

14. Scholarship considering Atlanta's physical development is extensive. The best examples of this literature include Ronald Bayor, *Race and the Shaping of Twentieth-Century Atlanta*

(Chapel Hill: University of North Carolina Press, 1996); Georgina Hickey, *Hope and Danger in the New South City: Working-Class Women and Urban Development in Atlanta, 1890–1940* (Athens: University of Georgia Press, 2003); Larry Keating, *Atlanta: Race, Class, and Urban Expansion* (Philadelphia: Temple University Press, 2001); Kevin Kruse, *White Flight: Atlanta and the Making of Modern Conservatism* (Princeton, NJ: Princeton University Press, 2005); LeeAnn Lands, *The Culture of Property: Race, Class, and Housing Landscapes in Atlanta, 1880–1950* (Athens: University of Georgia Press, 2009); Matthew Lassiter, *The Silent Majority: Suburban Politics in the Sunbelt South* (Princeton, NJ: Princeton University Press, 2006); Harvey Newman, *Southern Hospitality: Tourism and the Growth of Atlanta* (Tuscaloosa: University of Alabama Press, 1999); Gary Pomerantz, *Where Peachtree Meets Sweet Auburn: The Saga of Two Families and the Making of Atlanta* (New York: Scribner, 1996); Howard Preston, *Automobile Age Atlanta: The Making of a Southern Metropolis, 1900–1935* (Athens: University of Georgia Press, 1979); and Charles Rutheiser, *Imagineering Atlanta: The Politics of Place in the City of Dreams* (New York: Verso, 1996). The relationship between race and urban development in contemporary Atlanta is explored in Bullard, Johnson, and Torres, *Sprawl City*; and David Sjoquist, ed., *The Atlanta Paradox* (New York: Russell Sage Foundation, 2000).

15. See David Harvey, *Limits to Capital* (New York: Verso, 1984); John Logan and Harvey Molotch, *Urban Fortunes: The Political Economy of Place* (Los Angeles: University of California Press, 1987); Rutheiser, *Imagineering Atlanta*; Drew Whitelegg, "A Battle on Two Fronts: Competitive Urges 'Inside' Atlanta," *Area*, June 2002, 128–138; and Jason Henderson, "Contesting the Spaces of the Automobile: The Politics of Mobility and the Sprawl Debate in Atlanta, Georgia" (Ph.D. diss., University of Georgia, 2004).

16. The primary examples of this literature are Arnold Hirsch, *Making the Second Ghetto: Race and Housing in Chicago, 1940–1960* (Chicago: University of Chicago Press, 1982); Thomas Sugrue, *Origins of the Urban Crisis: Race and Inequality in Postwar Detroit* (Princeton, NJ: Princeton University Press, 1996); and Robert Self, *American Babylon: Race and the Struggle for Postwar Oakland* (Princeton, NJ: Princeton University Press, 2003).

17. Robert Fishman, "The American Metropolis at Century's End: Past and Future Influences," *Housing Policy Debate* 11, no. 1 (2000): 208.

18. In discussing the development of early Boston suburbs, Sam Bass Warner argues that "a kind of partnership" between individuals and institutions gave the suburbs their physical shape and that "common ideas and attitudes created the partnership," "color[ing] every decision, whether it was a decision made by the director of a large corporation or by a mortgage-pressed carpenter." I suggest that regional planning and development in Atlanta happened in a similar way, with the Atlanta Regional Commission (ARC) serving as the key institution in promulgating partnership and a consistent style of planning in the region. See Sam Bass Warner Jr., *Streetcar Suburbs: The Process of Growth in Boston, 1870–1900* (Cambridge, MA: Harvard University Press, 1978), 4.

19. These figures are calculated from data from the 2000 Census of Population and Housing. The Bureau of the Census defines "urban" and "rural." See *Federal Register* 67, no. 51 (March 15, 2002): 11663–11670. The Office of Management and Budget defines "Metropolitan Statistical Area" (MSA), which is used by the census bureau. See Office of Management and Budget, "Standards for Defining Metropolitan and Micropolitan Statistical Areas," *Federal Register* 69, no. 249 (December 27, 2000): 82228–82238.

20. According to Michel Foucault, "Excessive insistence on [state power] playing an exclusive role leads to the risk of overlooking all the mechanisms and effects of power which don't pass directly via the State apparatus, yet often sustain the State more effectively than its own institutions, enlarging and maximizing its effectiveness." Michel Foucault, "Questions on Geography,"

in *Power/Knowledge: Selected Interviews and Other Writings, 1972–1977*, ed. Colin Gordon (New York: Pantheon, 1980), 72. Richard White wryly notes a similar idea, arguing that "planning is an exercise of power, and in a modern state much real power is suffused with boredom. The agents of planning are usually boring; the planning process is boring; the implementation of plans is always boring. . . . Power does not have to be exercised behind the scenes. It can be open. The audience is asleep." White, *The Organic Machine*, 64.

21. For a good example of this kind of evaluation, see Leora Waldner, "Regional Plans, Local Fates? The Influence of the 1976 and 1985 Atlanta Regional Development Plans on Local Government Policy" (Ph.D. diss., University of California, Berkeley, 2003).

22. Hunter, *Community Power Structure*, 24.

23. Hall, *Cities of Tomorrow*, 88–97.

24. The most influential regionalist organizations were the Regional Planning Association of America, whose members wrote widely about the role regional planning could play in correcting the iniquities of American-style capitalism, and the *Plan of New York and Its Environs*, a planning effort that evolved into a nonprofit regional planning agency that continues to advocate for regional planning issues in New York City (the Regional Plan Association). See Robert Fishman, "The Death and Life of American Regional Planning," in Katz, *Reflections on Regionalism*, 107–123; David Johnson, *Planning the Great Metropolis: The 1929 Plan of New York and Its Environs* (New York: Taylor and Francis, 1995); Andrew Meyers, "Invisible Cities: Lewis Mumford, Thomas Adams, and the Invention of the Regional City, 1923–1929," *Business and Economic History*, 27, no. 2 (1998): 292–306; Kermit Parsons, "Collaborative Genius: The Regional Planning Association of America," *Journal of the American Planning Association* 60, no. 4 (1994): 462–482; and Sussman, *Planning the Fourth Migration*.

25. Some scholars suggest that Charles Eliot's 1892 plan for the metropolitan park system of Boston might be the first regional plan for a U.S. urban area, but the sharply limited scope of the plan makes it more of a proto-regional plan. For a discussion of this period, see Jon Peterson, *The Birth of City Planning, 1840–1917* (Baltimore: Johns Hopkins University Press, 2003). Daniel Burnham and Edward Bennett's 1909 *Plan of Chicago* stands as the most famous urban development plan of the early twentieth century, but it had a decidedly physical orientation (buildings and streets and parks) and, with a few exceptions, was mostly confined to the city. Therefore, the plan should be considered a precursor to the *Plan of New York* but not a comprehensive regional plan itself. See Daniel Burnham and Edward Bennett, *Plan of Chicago*, ed. Charles Moore (New York: Princeton Architectural Press, 1993). Among the well-known writers who contributed to the *Plan of New York* were Clarence Perry, Thomas Adams, Frederick Law Olmsted Jr., Robert Murray Haig, and Edward Bassett. For finer details about the plan and the process behind its production, see Johnson, *Planning the Great Metropolis*. Los Angeles also experienced early and extensive regional planning. See Greg Hise, *Magnetic Los Angeles: Planning the Twentieth Century Metropolis* (Baltimore: Johns Hopkins University Press, 1999); and Greg Hise and William Francis Deverell, *Eden by Design: The 1930 Olmsted-Bartholomew Plan for the Los Angeles Region* (Berkeley: University of California Press, 2000).

26. The problems with the New York plan, specifically its failure to acknowledge the difference between "regional" and "metropolitan," were vehemently argued by Mumford in "The Plan of New York," published in *New Republic* in 1930 and reprinted in Sussman, *Planning the Fourth Migration*. Over a dozen pages, he takes the authors of the plan to task for "fail[ing] to demonstrate valid principles and useful methods of procedure" (226). Mumford makes this same distinction in "The Regional Framework of Civilization," first published in 1925 and reprinted in both Sussman, *Planning the Fourth Migration*, and Donald Miller, ed., *The Lewis Mumford Reader* (1952; repr., New York: Pantheon, 1986). Robert Fishman also recounts the debate in

"The Death and Life of American Regional Planning," suggesting that regionalism and metropolitanism diverged in the postwar period and declaring metropolitanism the clear winner. For a different perspective on the conflicting visions, in which the apparent disagreements between the writers of the *Plan of New York* and the Regional Planning Association of America masked a common vision, see Meyers, "Invisible Cities."

27. Federal support for regional and national planning was most visible in the Tennessee Valley Authority, the National Resettlement Administration, and the National Resources Planning Board. These agencies widely employed planners and landscape architects. See Marion Clawson, *New Deal Planning: The National Resources Planning Board* (Baltimore: Johns Hopkins University Press, 1981); Paul Conkin, *Tomorrow a New World: The New Deal Community Program* (Ithaca, NY: Cornell University Press, 1959); Erwin Hargrove and Paul Conkin, eds., *TVA: Fifty Years of Grass-Roots Bureaucracy* (Champaign: University of Illinois Press, 1983); Daniel Schaffer, "Ideal and Reality in 1930s Regional Planning: The Case of the Tennessee Valley Authority," *Planning Perspectives* 1, no. 1 (1986): 27–44; and Philip Warken, *A History of the National Resources Planning Board, 1933–1943* (New York: Garland, 1979).

28. See Fishman, "The Death and Life of American Regional Planning"; Clawson, *New Deal Planning*; MacKaye, *The New Exploration*; and Robert Fishman, "The Fifth Migration," *Journal of the American Planning Association* 71, no. 4 (2005): 357–366.

29. See Burnham and Bennett, *Plan of Chicago*.

30. See Solof, *History of Metropolitan Planning Organizations*. Perhaps the most complete and thoughtful statement about how planning should be incorporated in municipal government is T. J. Kent's *The Urban General Plan* (San Francisco: Chandler, 1965). In this influential book, Kent discusses the history of "urban general plans" and the "place of city planning in the structure of local government," concluding that the "city council should be the principal client of the general plan" because "every important physical-development policy . . . must eventually come before the city council for final determination and action" (23).

31. John Mollenkopf, *The Contested City* (Princeton, NJ: Princeton University Press, 1983).

32. See Carl Feiss, "The Foundations of Federal Planning Assistance"; and Richard Flanagan, "The Housing Act of 1954: The Sea Change in National Urban Policy," *Urban Affairs Review* 33, no. 2 (1997): 265–286.

33. Under the 1962 Federal Aid Highway Act, the Bureau of Public Roads developed a program called 3Cs (comprehensive, cooperative, and continuing). The program encouraged metropolitan planning organizations to connect transportation plans to land-use and economic issues. See Edward Weiner, *Urban Transportation Planning in the United States: An Historical Overview* (Washington, DC: Greenwood, 1999), 50. For an overview of the history of metropolitan planning organizations, see Solof, *History of Metropolitan Planning Organizations*.

34. Major federal legislation with regional planning implications include the 1964 Highway Act, 1964 Civil Rights Act, 1966 Historic Preservation Act, 1966 Metropolitan Development Act, 1968 Intergovernmental Cooperation Act, 1969 National Environmental Policy Act, 1970 Clean Air Act Amendment revisions, and 1972 Clean Water Act.

35. For a sampling of different versions of the history of the modern environmental movement in the United States, see Samuel Hays, *Beauty, Health, and Permanence: Environmental Politics in the United States, 1955–1985* (New York: Cambridge University Press, 1987); Adam Rome, *The Bulldozer in the Countryside* (New York: Cambridge University Press, 2001); Hal Rothman, *The Greening of a Nation? Environmentalism in the United States since 1945* (Forth Worth, TX: Harcourt, Brace, 1997); and Ted Steinberg, *Down to Earth: Nature's Role in American History* (New York: Oxford University Press, 2002).

36. See Cliff Ellis, "Interstate Highways, Regional Planning, and the Reshaping of Metropolitan America," *Planning Practice and Research* 16, nos. 3–4 (2001): 247–269; Kenneth Jackson, *Crabgrass Frontier* (New York: Oxford University Press, 1985); Hays, *Beauty, Health, and Permanence*; Mollenkopf, *The Contested City*; Official Code of Georgia, 50-32-11, 1971; and Yale Rabin, "Federal Urban Transportation Policy and the Highway Planning Process in Metropolitan Areas," *Annals of the American Academy of Political and Social Science* 451, no. 1 (1980): 21–35.

37. See Ellis, "Interstate Highways"; Jackson, *Crabgrass Frontier*; Hays, *Beauty, Health, and Permanence*; Mollenkopf, *The Contested City*; Official Code of Georgia, 50-32-11, 1971; and Rabin, "Federal Urban Transportation Policy."

38. The literature on this subject is voluminous and constantly growing. Its foundations were laid by Sam Bass Warner Jr., *Urban Wilderness: A History of the American City* (Berkeley: University of California Press, 1972); Jackson, *Crabgrass Frontier*; and Robert Fishman, *Bourgeois Utopias* (New York: Basic Books, 1987). More recent work has situated the origins of suburban history in the context of the postwar urban crisis, revealing details about how federal policies, local politics, and demographic shifts played out on the ground. For examples of this literature, see Dolores Hayden, *Greenfields and Urban Growth, 1820–2000* (New York: Vintage, 2004); Howard Gillette, *Camden after the Fall: Decline and Renewal in a Post-industrial City* (Philadelphia: University of Pennsylvania Press, 2005); Lassiter, *Silent Majority*; Lisa McGirr, *Suburban Warriors: The Origins of the New American Right* (Princeton, NJ: Princeton University Press, 2001); and Becky Nicolaides, *My Blue Heaven: Life and Politics in Working Class Los Angeles, 1920 to 1965* (Chicago: University of Chicago Press, 2002).

39. See Bayor, *Race and the Shaping of Twentieth-Century Atlanta*, and Kruse, *White Flight*.

40. U.S. Department of Commerce, Bureau of the Census, *Census of Population and Housing* (Washington, DC: Government Printing Office, 1901, 1961, 2001).

41. Frank Popper, "Understanding American Land Use Regulation since 1970: A Revisionist Interpretation," *Journal of the America Planning Association* 54, no. 3 (1988): 291–301.

42. In the last few years, a group of researchers has been advocating a new regionalism to deal with the complicated problems urban development has created. Representative publications include Peter Dreier, Todd Swanstrom, and John Mollenkopf, *Place Matters: Metropolitics for the Twenty-First Century* (Lawrence: University Press of Kansas, 2005); and Myron Orfield, *Metropolitics: A Regional Agenda for Community and Stability* (Washington, DC: Brookings Institution Press, 1997).

43. Downs, "Urban Realities," 28.

44. For an overview and introduction to the struggle to coordinate federal domestic programs, see Melvin Mogulof, *Governing Metropolitan Areas: A Critical Review of Council of Governments and the Federal Role* (Washington, DC: Urban Institute, 1971).

45. Orfield, *Metropolitics*.

Chapter 2

1. Between 1971 and 1979 ARC's annual operating budget grew from $1.7 million to $3.1 million. ARC, "Annual Report," 1972, 1980, Atlanta Regional Commission Collection (ARCC), Kenan Research Center (KRC), Atlanta History Center (AHC). Regarding the issue of convening governments to foster coordination, see William Davis, "From the Director," *Intergovernmental Perspective* 20, no. 3 (1994): 4–5. ARC's legislation also conveyed the power to coordinate and convene. See "A Matter of Much Importance," 1967, MSS 619, Box 117, ARCC, KRC, AHC; "The Planning Process, Narrative by Tom Roberts," 1972, ARCC, KRC, AHC; "Review Manual," 1980, ARCC, KRC, AHC; and "The Unique Role of the Regional Council

Administrator, by Harry West, Executive Director of the Atlanta Regional Commission," 1981, ARCC, KRC, AHC.

2. The local administrators who wrote the legislation that created ARC saw the new commission as a response to new federal urban policies adopted in the 1960s, as part of Governor Jimmy Carter's modernization of state bureaucracy, and as a more robust regional planning agency desired by some politicians. Letter from Jas Aldredge to Nelson Severinghaus, January 6, 1971, ARCC, KRC, AHC.

3. Dana White and Tim Crimmins, "How Atlanta Grew: Cool Heads, Hot Air, and Hard Work," *Atlanta Economic Review*, January–February 1978, 7–15.

4. See Floyd Hunter, *Community Power Structure: A Study of Decision Makers* (Chapel Hill: University of North Carolina Press, 1969); Floyd Hunter, *Community Power Succession: Atlanta's Policy Makers* (Chapel Hill: University of North Carolina Press, 1980), chap. 2; and Clarence Stone, *Regime Politics: Governing Atlanta, 1946–1988* (Lawrence: University Press of Kansas, 1989).

5. Jack Spalding, "Where Now, Atlanta?" *Atlanta Journal-Constitution*, September 5, 1971.

6. David Goldfield's understanding of urbanization through a "regional framework" draws in part from the work of Howard Odum and Lewis Mumford in the 1930s. See David Goldfield, "The Urban South: A Regional Framework," *American Historical Review* 86, no. 5 (1981): 1009–1034; and Raymond Mohl, "City and Region: The Missing Dimension in U.S. Urban History," *Journal of Urban History* 25, no. 4 (1998): 3–21.

7. Frank Popper, "Understanding Land Use Regulation since 1970: A Revisionist Interpretation," *Journal of the American Planning Association* 54, no. 3 (1988): 291–301.

8. The subject of intergovernmental relations was relatively new at the time. In many ways, it was fostered by the Advisory Commission on Intergovernmental Relations. For a short overview of ACIR's founding, see Bruce McDowell, "Advisory Commission on Intergovernmental Relations in 1996: The End of an Era," *Publius: The Journal of Federalism* 27, no. 2 (1997): 111–127.

9. See Melvin Mogulof, "Regional Planning, Clearance, and Evaluation: A Look at the A-95 Review Process," *American Institute of Planners Journal* 37, no. 6 (1971): 418–422; and Rochelle Stanfield, "The Development of Carter's Urban Policy: One Small Step for Federalism," *Publius: The Journal of Federalism* 8, no. 1 (1978): 39–53.

10. Section 701 of the 1954 Housing Act provided the most direct and stable source of funding for postwar regional planning agencies. See John Friedmann and Robin Bloch, "American Exceptionalism in Regional Planning, 1933–2000," *International Journal of Urban and Regional Research* 14, no. 4 (1990): 576–601; Mark Solof, *History of Metropolitan Planning Organizations* (Newark, NJ: North Jersey Transportation Planning Authority, 1998).

11. Edward Weiner, *Urban Transportation Planning in the United States: An Historical Overview* (Washington, DC: Greenwood, 1999), 31.

12. See McDowell, "Advisory Commission on Intergovernmental Relations in 1996."

13. For a discussion of the creation of ACIR, see William Coleman and Delphis Goldberg, "The Eisenhower Years and the Creation of ACIR," *Intergovernmental Perspective* 16, no. 3 (1990): 19–23.

14. For a brief discussion of the commission's history, see McDowell, "Advisory Commission on Intergovernmental Relations in 1996," 111–114; and "ACIR at 35: Achievements in Perspective," *Intergovernmental Perspective* 20, no. 3 (1994): 31–33.

15. Reports and studies published by the commission include *The Problem of Special Districts in American Government* (May 1964), *Metropolitan Social and Economic Disparities: Implications for Intergovernmental Relations in Central Cities and Suburbs* (January 1965), and *Building Codes: A Program of Intergovernmental Reform* (January 1966).

16. Judson James, "Federalism and the Model Cities Experiment," *Publius: The Journal of Federalism* 2, no. 1 (1972): 69–94.

17. Lyndon B. Johnson, "Remarks upon Signing the Intergovernmental Cooperation Act," October 16, 1968, *American Presidency Project*, available at http://www.presidency.ucsb.edu/ws/?pid=29181.

18. Along with 701 housing funds, the A-95 review process provided substantial federal support for regional-planning-related activities in urban areas across the country. See Mogulof, "Regional Planning, Clearance, and Evaluation," 418–422.

19. *Report of the National Advisory Commission on Civil Disorders* (Washington, DC: Government Printing Office, 1968).

20. National Commission on Urban Problems, *Building the American City: Report of the National Commission on Urban Problems* (New York: Praeger, 1969), 7.

21. Scholarship documenting race and its role in urban decline, suburban growth, and metropolitan restructuring in the postwar period is voluminous (and growing). Perhaps the most interesting are Arnold Hirsch, *Making the Second Ghetto: Race and Housing in Chicago, 1940–1960* (Chicago: University of Chicago Press, 1982); Thomas Sugrue, *Origins of the Urban Crisis: Race and Inequality in Postwar Detroit* (Princeton, NJ: Princeton University Press, 1996); and William J. Wilson, *The Truly Disadvantaged: The Inner City, the Underclass, and Public Policy* (Chicago: University of Chicago Press, 1987). Others include Howard Gillette Jr., *Camden after the Fall: Decline and Renewal in a Post-industrial City* (Philadelphia: University of Pennsylvania Press, 2005); Paul Jargowsky, *Poverty and Place: Ghettos, Barrios, and the American City* (New York: Russell Sage Foundation, 1997); Kevin Kruse, *White Flight: Atlanta and the Making of Modern Conservatism* (Princeton, NJ: Princeton University Press, 2005); Matthew Lassiter, *Silent Majority: Suburban Politics in the Sunbelt South* (Princeton, NJ: Princeton University Press, 2006); Nicholas Lemann, *The Promised Land: The Great Black Migration and How It Changed America* (New York: Random House, 1991); Douglas Massey and Nancy Denton, *American Apartheid: Segregation and the Making of the Underclass* (Cambridge, MA: Harvard University, 1993); and Robert Self, *American Babylon: Race and the Struggle for Postwar Oakland* (Princeton, NJ: Princeton University Press, 2003).

22. The Douglas Commission report describes the relationship of minority neighborhoods in central cities and surrounding white neighborhoods using the metaphor of a "white noose." National Commission on Urban Problems, *Building the American City*, 1.

23. One example is the Metropolitan Council in Minneapolis–St. Paul. Created in 1967 to counteract political fragmentation, the council oversees regional planning and development and remains surprisingly underresearched. A comprehensive history of the organization has yet to be written. One of the few significant studies of the council is John Harrigan and William Johnson, *Governing the Twin Cities Region: The Metropolitan Council in Comparative Perspective* (Minneapolis: University of Minnesota Press, 1978). A more recent evaluation of the Metropolitan Council, including a short history, is Myron Orfield and Thomas Luce Jr., *Region: Planning the Future of the Twin Cities* (Minneapolis: University of Minnesota Press, 2009).

24. National Commission on Urban Problems, *Building the American City*, 31.

25. For the most extensive historical account of Atlanta's founding and early history, see Franklin Garrett, *Atlanta and Environs* (Athens: University of Georgia Press, 1969).

26. See Joel Chandler Harris, *Joel Chandler Harris' Life of Henry W. Grady Including His Writings and Speeches* (New York: Cassell, 1890).

27. Garrett, *Atlanta and Environs*; Frederick Allen, *Secret Formula: How Brilliant Marketing and Relentless Salesmanship Made Coca-Cola the Best-Known Product in the World* (New York: Harper Collins, 1995).

28. See Howard Preston, *Automobile Age Atlanta: The Making of a Southern Metropolis, 1900–1935* (Athens: University of Georgia Press, 1979), 110–112. The reconfiguration of Atlanta's residential geography in the late nineteenth and early twentieth centuries is covered in LeeAnn Lands, *The Culture of Property: Race, Class, and Housing Landscapes in Atlanta, 1880–1950* (Athens: University of Georgia Press, 2009), chap. 1.

29. Atlanta in the nineteenth and early twentieth centuries was a moderate-sized urban area, not much larger than Birmingham or Dallas and considerably smaller than New Orleans. See David Goldfield, *Cotton Fields and Skyscrapers: Southern City and Region, 1607–1980* (Baton Rouge: Louisiana State University Press, 1982), chap. 3.

30. Atlanta had the largest concentration of federal offices outside Washington, D.C., a legacy of long-term federal investment in the region. ARC, "Regional Agenda for the Atlanta Region," February 1998, ARCC, KRC, AHC.

31. For an excellent discussion of the role of federal jobs in securing middle-class status for blacks in the early twentieth century in Atlanta, see David Pomerantz, *Where Peachtree Meets Sweet Auburn* (New York: Scribner, 1996).

32. See Kruse, *White Flight*, chap. 9; and Preston, *Automobile Age Atlanta*, chap. 6.

33. Robert Lang draws an interesting distinction between lower-density sprawl in wet places like Atlanta and higher-density sprawl in dry places like Phoenix. Robert Lang, "Open Spaces, Bounded Places: Does the American West's Arid Landscape Yield Dense Metropolitan Growth?" *Housing Policy Debate* 13, no. 4 (2003): 755–778.

34. Interview with Walter Douglas, August 5, 1977, From Mule to MARTA Collection, Box 124, Folder 3, KRC, AHC.

35. Thomas Reed, *Report: The Governments of Atlanta and Fulton County, Georgia* (Philadelphia: National Municipal League, 1938).

36. Ronald Bayor, *Race and the Shaping of Twentieth-Century Atlanta* (Chapel Hill: University of North Carolina Press, 1996), 86–87. See also Preston, *Automobile Age Atlanta*, 153. The city made this last annexation in 1952 to bring in a large, and largely white, area of unincorporated Fulton County directly north of the city known as Buckhead, a move that not only expanded the city's footprint but solidified a white electoral majority for the next twenty years.

37. Two companion documents published in 1959 by the Metropolitan Planning Commission explained the connection between the freeway routes the Lochner report identified in the mid-1940s: *Access to Central Atlanta* and *Crosstown and By-Pass Expressways*, ARCC, KRC, AHC.

38. Fulton and Dekalb Metropolitan Planning District and Commission, Act 230, Acts and Resolutions of the State of Georgia (1947), pp. 849–854.

39. The two plans the Metropolitan Planning Commission wrote were *Up Ahead: A Regional Land Use Plan for Metropolitan Atlanta* (February 1952), and *Now . . . for Tomorrow: A Master Planning Program for the Dekalb-Fulton Metropolitan Area* (September 1954), ARCC, KRC, AHC.

40. Metropolitan Planning Commission, *Up Ahead*, 2.

41. Atlanta Region Metropolitan Planning Commission, "Regional Planning for Metropolitan Atlanta: A Fresh Start," March 1971, MSS 619, Box 44, ARCC. See also Marco Amati and Makoto Yokohari, "The Establishment of the London Greenbelt: Reaching Consensus over Purchasing Land," *Journal of Planning History* 6, no. 4 (2007): 311–337.

42. For a detailed description of the Neighborhood Unit concept, see Clarence Perry, *Housing for the Machine Age* (New York: Russell Sage, 1939).

43. Metropolitan Planning Commission, *Up Ahead*, 14.

44. See Bayor, *Race and the Shaping of Twentieth-Century Atlanta*, especially 69–76; Christopher Silver, *Twentieth-Century Richmond: Planning Politics and Race* (Knoxville: University of Tennessee Press, 1985); and Charles Connerly, *The Most Segregated City in America: City Planning and Civil Rights in Birmingham, 1920–1980* (Charlottesville: University of Virginia Press, 2005).

45. Bayor, *Race and the Shaping of Twentieth-Century Atlanta*, 59–60.

46. Atlanta Region Metropolitan Planning Commission, "Regional Planning for Metropolitan Atlanta: A Fresh Start," March 1971, MSS 619, Box 44, Folder 9, ARCC, KRC, AHC. In *Automobile Age Atlanta*, Howard Preston notes that during the 1920s "demand for residential land in suburban areas of Atlanta was indeed booming," and by 1930 nearly one-third of metro Atlanta's population resided outside the city limits (152–153). This emerging spatial form had induced concern that the city's "narrow municipal boundaries" meant that "those who worked in Atlanta were, to a greater and greater extent, living on the outside" and thus not paying taxes to support the city's infrastructure (151).

47. Weiner, *Urban Transportation Planning in the United States*, 25. Section 701 provided funding for planning activities at the state, regional, and local levels from 1954 to 1981 and was a significant means of federal support for planning for state and local governments. For a longer explication of Section 701, see Carl Feiss, "The Foundations of Federal Planning Assistance: A Personal Account of the 701 Program," *APA Journal* 51, no. 2 (1985): 175–184.

48. See Alan Black, "The Chicago Area Transportation Study: A Case of Rational Planning," *Journal of Planning Education and Research* 10, no. 1 (1990): 27–37.

49. A survey of development regulations in metropolitan Atlanta in 1974 provides a snapshot of codes adopted by governments around the region. ARC, *Construction Codes in the Atlanta Metropolitan Area: A Survey of Current Practices*, July 1974, ARCC, KRC, AHC.

50. Metropolitan Planning Commission, "Summary Report: North Georgia Conference for Planning and Development," September 19, 1957, ARCC, KRC, AHC.

51. Goldfield, *Cotton Fields and Skyscrapers*, chap. 4; Larry Keating, *Atlanta: Race, Class, and Urban Expansion* (Philadelphia: Temple University Press, 2001), chap. 3; Lands, *Culture of Property*, chap 1. For a broader perspective on black suburbs in the United States, see Andrew Wiese, *Places of Their Own: African American Suburbanization in the Twentieth Century* (Chicago: University of Chicago Press, 2004).

52. See Preston, *Automobile Age Atlanta*, chap. 6.

53. Charles Pyles, "S. Ernest Vandiver and the Politics of Change," in *Georgia Governors in an Age of Change*, ed. Harold Henderson and Gary Roberts (Athens: University of Georgia Press, 1988), 143–156.

54. Resolution 158, Acts and Resolutions of the State of Georgia (1960); Atlanta Regional Metropolitan Planning District, Act 847, Acts and Resolutions of the State of Georgia (1960), 12.

55. For a very brief overview of Metropolitan Statistical Area (MSA) and SMSA designations, see Office of Management and Budget, "Standards for Defining Metropolitan and Micropolitan Statistical Areas," *Federal Register* 69, no. 249, (December 7, 2000): 82228–82238.

56. Weiner, *Urban Transportation Planning in the United States*, 50.

57. Atlanta Regional Metropolitan Planning District, Act 847, Acts and Resolutions of the State of Georgia (1960).

58. Legislation that created the Metropolitan Atlanta Rapid Transit Authority (MARTA) was an outcome of ARMPC's lobbying the General Assembly. See *Atlanta Case Study*, vol. 2 of *An Assessment of Community Planning for Mass Transit*, March 1976, Congress, Office of

Technology Assessment (Washington, DC: Government Printing Office, 1976). For a brief overview of the Urban Mass Transit Administration, see Weiner, *Urban Transportation Planning in the United States*, 42–43.

59. ARMPC, "Summary of Findings and Recommendations," 1964, ARCC, KRC, AHC; ARMPC, "Strategy for the Seventies, 1967, MSS 616, Box 117, ARCC, KRC, AHC.

60. The 1962 Federal Aid Highway Act mandated regional coordinated planning in conjunction with receiving federal highway funds. See Weiner, *Urban Transportation Planning in the United States*, 34–37.

61. Jennifer Pinson, "Atlanta Hartsfield International Airport: A Case Study of Urban Public Policy Conflicts" (master's thesis, Emory University, 1982).

62. ARC, "Profile of Local Governments Served by the Atlanta Regional Commission," 1974, ARCC, KRC, AHC.

63. ARC, "Construction Codes in the Atlanta Metropolitan Area: A Survey of Current Practices, Section D: Housing Codes," 1974, ARCC, KRC, AHC.

64. See Keating, *Atlanta*, chap. 2.

65. Campbell Gibson and Kay Jung, "Historical Census Statistics on Population Totals by Race, 1790 to 1990, and by Hispanic Origin, 1970 to 1990, for Large Cities and Other Urban Places in the United States" (Population Division working paper no. 76, U.S. Bureau of the Census, 2005). For a much more in-depth discussion of the role of race in the politics of the city in the postwar period, see Stone, *Regime Politics*; Bayor, *Race and the Shaping of Twentieth-Century Atlanta*; and Pomerantz, *Where Peachtree Meets Sweet Auburn*. In his book *White Flight*, Kruse explores the details of neighborhood level racial politics. In *Atlanta*, Keating writes about the influence of race from the perspective of city-suburb relations.

66. ARC, "Expressways," 1978, MSS 619, Box 117, ARCC, KRC, AHC.

67. For in-depth discussion of the multiyear process of creating MARTA, see Konrad, *Transporting Atlanta*, chap. 3; Keating, *Atlanta*, chap. 6; and Kruse, *White Flight*, 248–251.

68. See Chapter 3 for a detailed discussion of Atlanta's water supply issues.

69. ARC, "Growth and Development of the Atlanta Region," *Commission Working Session*, vol. 2, 1985, ARCC, KRC, AHC.

70. For example, "CAP Warns of Crime Fears," *Atlanta Constitution*, September 21, 1974.

71. For an overview, see Irene Holliman, "From Crackertown to the ATL: Race, Urban Renewal, and the Re-making of Downtown Atlanta" (Ph.D. diss., University of Georgia, 2010); and Charles Rutheiser, *Imagineering Atlanta: The Politics of Place in the City of Dreams* (New York: Verso, 1996), chap. 4. For a broader view of the cause and effect of postwar urban decline, see Robert Beauregard, *Voices of Decline: The Postwar Fate of U.S. Cities* (Oxford, UK: Blackwell, 1993).

72. See William Fulton, *The Reluctant Metropolis: The Politics of Urban Growth in Los Angeles* (Baltimore: Johns Hopkins University Press, 1997), chap. 6; Melvin Mogulof, "A Modest Proposal for the Governance of America's Metropolitan Areas," *Journal of the American Institute of Planners*, July 1975, 252–253; and Weiner, *Urban Transportation Planning in the United States*, 46.

73. Mogulof, "Regional Planning, Clearance, and Evaluation," 418–422.

74. For an overview of the Model Cities program by two Department of Housing and Urban Development administrators, see H. Ralph Taylor and George Williams, "Comments on the Demonstration Cities Program," *Journal of the American Institute of Planners* 32, no. 6 (1966): 366–376.

75. See Weiner, *Urban Transportation Planning in the United States*, 51. Though a master plan for a system of limited-access expressways had appeared in the Lochner plan in 1946,

Atlanta's highway system had subsequently been planned and built piecemeal, the result of the work of a loose affiliation of Atlanta's regional planning agencies (the MPC and ARMPC), the state highway commission, and the federal Bureau of Public Roads. While these agencies were supposed to work together through a technical coordinating committee, they had been unable to reach a consensus. "Diagram of Regional Transportation Planning in Atlanta, 1964," shows the different agencies involved in the Atlanta Area Transportation Study and their relationships. MSS 619, Box 44, ARCC, KRC, AHC.

76. *The Atlanta Area Transportation Study*, 1968, MSS 619, Box 77, ARCC, KRC, AHC.

77. ARC, Memo from William Maynard to Citizens Transportation Advisory Committee, November 23, 1970, ARCC, KRC, AHC.

78. "Diagram of Regional Transportation Planning in Atlanta, 1964," shows the different agencies involved in the Atlanta Area Transportation Study and their relationships. MSS 619, Box 44, ARCC, KRC, AHC.

79. Ibid. See also "In 20 Years, We Are the Oldest," MSS 619, Box 117, Folder 1, ARCC, KRC, AHC.

80. "Summary of Recommendations of American Society of Planning Officials and Summary of Response of Atlanta Region Metropolitan Planning Commission," June 1967, MSS 619, Box 1, ARCC, KRC, AHC.

81. Ibid., 2–3.

82. Ibid., 3.

83. Ibid.

84. Ibid.

85. "Atlanta Region Metropolitan Planning Commission and Atlanta Area Transportation Study Policy Committee Minutes of Joint Meeting, January 6, 1971," MSS 619, Box 1, Folder 6, ARCC, KRC, AHC.

86. Ibid., 3. The failure of the MARTA referendum in 1968 was cited as evidence that the transportation staff was not heeding community priorities or listening to each other.

87. The text of Georgia Senate Bill 298, creating the Bureau of State Planning and Community Affairs, noted that the act was written "to implement the requirements of the Federal Intergovernmental Cooperation Act of 1968." Bureau of State Planning and Community Affairs, General Acts and Resolutions, Georgia Laws, 1970 Session, p. 321.

88. Ibid., 3201.

89. Ibid., 3199–3200.

90. "Report of the Department of Community Affairs Study Committee," *Journal of the House of Representatives of the State of Georgia*, December 1969, 3200. The 1970 census revealed that the five counties of metro Atlanta contained over 30 percent of Georgia's population.

91. Bureau of State Planning and Community Affairs, General Acts and Resolutions, Georgia Laws, 1970 Session, p. 323.

92. "House Resolution 663-1368," *Journal of the House of Representatives of the State of Georgia*, 1970; Minutes of Joint Meeting of Atlanta Region Metropolitan Planning Commission and Atlanta Area Transportation Study Policy Committee, January 6, 1971, MSS 619, Box 1, ARCC, KRC, AHC.

93. "House Resolution 1003," *Journal of the House of Representatives of the State of Georgia*, 1970, 2785.

94. Another factor pushing state-level discussions of regional planning was the national land-use debates in Congress. See Noreen Lyday, *The Law of the Land: Debating National Land Use Legislation, 1970–1975* (Washington, DC: Urban Institute, 1976).

95. "Outline for Presentation to Staff of Atlanta Regional Commission," April 26, 1972, Dan Sweat Papers, Box 2, Folder 2, Georgia Government Documentation Projection (GGDP), Special Collections, Georgia State University.

96. "Regional Planning for Metropolitan Atlanta: A Fresh Start," prepared by the staff of the ARMPC, March 1971, MSS 619, Box 44, ARCC, KRC, AHC.

97. "Wade Lashes Council Plan," *Atlanta Journal*, February 11, 1971.

98. "Metropolitan Area Planning and Development Commissions Created," General Acts and Resolutions, Georgia Laws, 1971 Session.

99. "Regional Policy Development Process, Summary of Recommendations of ARMPC," n.d., ARCC, KRC, AHC.

100. There had been several attacks on the rational-comprehensive model of planning by 1971. The most famous were Alan Altshuler, *The City Planning Process: A Political Analysis* (Ithaca, NY: Cornell University Press, 1965); Paul Davidoff, "Advocacy and Pluralism in Planning," *Journal of the American Institute of Planners* 31, no. 4 (1965): 331–338; and Jane Jacobs, *The Death and Life of Great American Cities* (New York: Random House, 1961). For a broader and more recent discussion of the power of rational planning in urban governance, see James Scott, *Seeing Like a State* (New Haven, CT: Yale University Press, 1999), chap. 2. For more discussion of how planning theory had shifted by the early 1970s, see Peter Hall, *Cities of Tomorrow: An Intellectual History of Urban Planning and Design in the Twentieth Century* (Malden, MA: Blackwell, 2002), chap. 10.

101. "Metropolitan Area Planning and Development Commissions Created," p. 19.

102. Ibid., Section 18.

103. ARMPC and Atlanta Area Transportation Study Policy Committee Minutes of Joint Meeting, January 6, 1971, MSS 619, Box 1, Folder 6, ARCC, KRC, AHC.

104. "Metropolitan Area Planning and Development Commissions Created," p. 24.

105. Ibid., 18.

106. Letter from H. Aldredge to Nelson Severinghaus, January 6, 1971, ARCC, KRC, AHC.

107. In the 1990s the commission's role in the regional planning process would be challenged from different directions. ARC managed to flex without breaking as the politics around the commission significantly changed, seriously undercutting its influence among local elected officials. This period is detailed in Chapter 6.

108. In an interview with Cliff Kuhn and Shep Barbash, Dan Sweat discusses the role of career public administrators in developing the concept for ARC and pushing it through the legislative process. Dan Sweat, interview by Cliff Kuhn and Shep Barbash, December 2, 1996, Dan Sweat Papers, Box P-1, GGDP, Special Collections, Georgia State University, p. 40.

109. Dan Sweat, interview by Cliff Kuhn and Shep Barbash, November 20, 1996, Dan Sweat Papers, Box P-1, GGDP, Special Collections, Georgia State University, pp. 45–50.

110. Sweat's effort to establish ARC's legitimacy is covered more in depth in Chapter 3.

111. Dan Sweat, interview, December 2, 1996, p. 18.

112. Dan Sweat, interview, November 20, 1996, p. 48.

113. Jerry Weitz, *Sprawl Busting: State Programs to Guide Growth* (Chicago: Planners Press, 1999), chap. 2.

114. Ibid., 40.

115. ARC, "Annual Report of the Atlanta Regional Commission," 1976, ARCC, KRC, AHC.

116. *Baker v. Carr* upended the county-unit system of apportionment of state elected officials. See Phil Neal, "*Baker v. Carr*: Politics in Search of Law," *Supreme Court Review* 1962:

252–327. As the historian Gary Fink noted, "Carter found himself being projected nationally as the vanguard of yet another 'New South.'" Gary Fink, "Jimmy Carter and the Politics of Transition," in *Georgia Governors in an Age of Change: From Ellis Arnall to George Busbee*, ed. Harold Henderson and Gary Roberts (Athens: University of Georgia Press, 1988), 237. For an introduction to the vast and expanding Sunbelt literature, see Carl Abbott, *The New Urban America: Growth and Politics in Sunbelt Cities* (Chapel Hill: University of North Carolina Press, 1981); Raymond Mohl, ed., *Searching for the Sunbelt: Historical Perspectives on a Region* (Knoxville: University of Tennessee Press, 1990); and Bruce Schulman, *From Cotton Belt to Sunbelt: Federal Policy, Economic Development, and the Transformation of the South, 1938–1980* (Oxford: Oxford University Press, 1991).

117. For a more general discussion of the Office of Management and Budget's role in setting the framework for federal data collection, see Julius Shiskin, "Recent Developments in Federal Statistics," *American Statistician*, December 1971: 18–21.

118. See Bruce Lindeman, "The Future of Atlanta," *Atlanta Economic Review*, August 1971, 8–13.

119. For a discussion of white flight and public schools, see Lassiter, *The Silent Majority*, chaps. 3 and 5; and Kruse, *White Flight*, chaps. 5 and 6.

120. ARC, "Growth and Development of the Atlanta Region."

121. Evidence of Atlanta's boom was still abundant. By the end of 1971 a dozen large buildings in downtown and midtown were under construction or had been approved. "City's Appetite for Office Space Growing," *Atlanta Journal-Constitution*, February 22, 1970; "Atlanta's Real Estate: Poised, but for What?" *Atlanta Journal-Constitution*, November 21, 1971.

122. For the best discussion of this phenomenon, see Stone, *Regime Politics*, chap. 3. Stone documents the way the downtown business elites were preoccupied with insulating downtown Atlanta from black intrusion. They used a variety of methods, including most cleverly building with federal money infrastructure barriers between the central business district and the black neighborhoods that surrounded it on three sides. Stone, however, does not address regional events outside the boundaries of the central city.

123. For an example of criticism of the ways metropolitan planning organizations operate, including the way representation is established, see Thomas Sanchez, "An Inherent Bias? Geographic and Racial-Ethnic Patterns of Metropolitan Planning Organization Boards," paper for Brookings Institution Series on Transportation Reform, January 2006.

Chapter 3

1. For a general history of the Chattahoochee River, see Lynn Willoughby, *Flowing through Time: A History of the Lower Chattahoochee Valley* (Tuscaloosa: University of Alabama Press, 1999). A discussion of the Chattahoochee in the nineteenth century also forms a backdrop in John Lupold and Thomas French Jr., *Bridging Deep South Rivers: The Life and Legend of Horace King* (Athens: University of Georgia Press, 2004). The high-profile dispute between Georgia, Alabama, and Florida over water in the Apalachicola-Chattahoochee-Flint (ACF) system has received limited attention by planners and political scientists. For examples, see David Feldman, "Barriers to Adaptive Management: Lessons from the Apalachicola-Chattahoochee-Flint Compact," *Society and Natural Resources*, 21, no. 6 (2008): 512–525; and James Newman, "Examining Interest Group Conflict in River Basin Interstate Compacts in the Southeastern United States" (Ph.D. diss., Mississippi State University, 2006). The conflict has been extensively covered in the environmental law literature. See Robert Abrams, "Water Federalism and the Army Corps of Engineers' Role in Eastern States Water Allocation," *University of Arkansas Little Rock*

Law Review 31 (2009): 395–426; Robert Abrams, "Settlement of the ACF Controversy: Sisyphus at the Dawn of the 21st Century," *Hamline Law Review* 31 (2008): 679–702; Charles DuMars and David Seeley, "The Failure of the Apalachicola-Chattahoochee-Flint River Basin and Alabama-Coosa-Tallapoosa River Basin Compacts and a Guide to the Successful Establishment of Interstate Water Compacts," *Georgia State University Law Review* 21, no. 2 (2004): 373–400; Dustin Stephenson, "The Tri-State Compact: Falling Waters and Fading Opportunities," *Journal of Land Use and Environmental Law* 16 (2000): 83–109; C. Hansell Watt IV, "Who Gets the 'Hooch'? Georgia, Florida, and Alabama Battle for Water from the Apalachicola-Chattahoochee-Flint River Basin," *Mercer Law Review* 55 (2004): 1453–1487. One edited volume provides an overview of recent ACF conflict but no historical depth. Jeffrey Jordan and Aaron Wolf, eds., *Interstate Water Allocation in Alabama, Florida, and Georgia: New Issues, New Methods, New Models* (Gainesville: University Press of Florida, 2006). On the history of water resource planning in the United States, see David Feldman, *Water Resources Management: In Search of an Environmental Ethic* (Baltimore: Johns Hopkins University Press, 1991); Robert Gottlieb, *A Life of Its Own: The Politics and Power of Water* (San Diego, CA: Harcourt, Brace, Jovanovich, 1988); Beatrice Holmes, *History of Federal Water Resources Programs and Policies, 1961–1970* (Washington, DC: Department of Agriculture, 1979); Susan Marks, *Aqua Shock: The Water Crisis in America* (New York: Bloomberg, 2009); Paul Milazzo, *Unlikely Environmentalists: Congress and Clean Water, 1945–1972* (Lawrence: University Press of Kansas, 2006); Karen O'Neill, *Rivers by Design: State Power and the Origins of U.S. Flood Control* (Durham, NC: Duke University, 2006); and Peter Rogers, *America's Water: Federal Roles and Responsibilities* (Cambridge, MA: MIT Press, 1993). Discussions of water infrastructure projects specific to major U.S. river systems or regions include Donald Pisani, *Water and American Government: The Reclamation Bureau, National Water Policy, and the West, 1902–1935* (Berkeley: University of California Press, 2002); Marc Reisner, *Cadillac Desert: The American West and Its Disappearing Water* (New York: Viking, 1986); Richard White, *The Organic Machine: The Remaking of the Columbia River* (New York: Hill and Wang, 1995); and Donald Worster, *Rivers of Empire: Water, Aridity, and the Growth of the American West* (New York: Pantheon, 1986).

2. Letter from William B. Hartsfield to Colonel A. C. Boatner, April 18, 1947, Box 2, Tri-State Water Compact Commission Negotiation Files, Government Records Series, Georgia Archives, Morrow, Georgia; letter from William B. Hartsfield to Colonel P. A. Feringa, July 24, 1947, Box 2, Tri-State Water Compact Commission Negotiation Files, Government Records Series, Georgia Archives; "The Buford Dam," *Atlanta Constitution*, July 23, 1947.

3. Lake Sidney Lanier begins thirty-five miles northeast of downtown Atlanta and snakes its way north across Hall, Dawson, and Forsyth Counties for another twenty miles. As the metropolitan region grew northward, eventually surrounding the lake, use of the impounded water evolved from electricity generation for the Southeastern Power Administration and control of downstream floods to recreation for the thousands of single-family houses that mushroomed along the lake's shores to a critical source of municipal water. This progression of uses increased both withdrawal by Atlanta-area municipalities and discharge of pollution downstream. For a very brief overview, see "Lake Lanier Blame Game Brews," *Atlanta Journal-Constitution*, July 26, 2009; "Decades before Water Wars, Buford Dam Won City Support, Not Finances," *Atlanta Journal-Constitution*, July 25, 2009.

4. Dan Sweat, interview by Clifford Kuhn and Shep Barbash, January 22, 1997, Georgia Government Documentation Project (GGDP), Special Collections, Oral History Collection Series P: Dan Sweat, Georgia State University.

5. Lucy Justus, "The Banks of Georgia's Most Famous River Will Become a Park or Commercial Area," *Atlanta Journal and Constitution Magazine*, March 14, 1971, 8, 28–31.

6. See R. Harold Brown, *The Greening of Georgia: The Improvement of the Environment in the Twentieth Century* (Macon, GA: Mercer University Press, 2002), 129; and "River Basin Fight Pits Atlanta against Neighbors," *New York Times*, August 15, 2009.

7. Atlanta Regional Commission (ARC), *Chattahoochee River Corridor: A Case Study*, 1972, Atlanta Regional Commission Collection (ARCC), Kenan Research Center (KRC), Atlanta History Center (AHC).

8. ARC, *Chattahoochee Corridor Study*, 1972, State of Georgia Program and Budget Office Records, Planning Studies Folder, Box 1, Georgia Archives.

9. By suggesting that Atlanta had a distinctly regional vision for water, I mean to contrast that vision with the argument that cities and suburbs battle each other for access to valuable natural resources.

10. Bill Rankin, "Atlanta a Loser in Water Wars," *Atlanta Journal-Constitution*, July 18, 2009, p. 1A; George Sherk, "The Management of Interstate Water Conflicts in the Twenty-First Century: Is It Time to Call Uncle?" *New York University Environmental Law Journal* 12 (2005): 764–827.

11. As an example of this wisdom, see one of the most popular textbooks on growth management, Douglas Porter, *Managing Growth in America's Communities* (Washington, DC: Island Press, 2008), chap. 8.

12. Clarence Velz, *Apalachicola Basin, Apalachicola-Chattahoochee-Flint Rivers Water Resources Background Facts* (National Council for Stream Improvement, University of Michigan, School of Public Health, 1953).

13. "Apalachicola, Chattahoochee, and Flint Rivers, Ga. and Fla. Letter from the Secretary of War transmitting a letter from the Chief of Engineers, United States Army, dated April 20, 1939, submitting a report, together with accompanying papers and an illustration, on a reexamination of Apalachicola, Chattahoochee, and Flint Rivers, Ga and Fla, June, 16, 1939," Government Records Series, Tri-State Water Compact Commission Negotiation Files, Box 2, Georgia Archives, p. 25.

14. Ibid., 26.

15. Ibid., S27–S28.

16. For a discussion of the history of the Rural Electrification Administration and the goals set for the program, see D. Clayton Brown, *Electricity for Rural America: The Fight for the REA* (Westport, CT: Greenwood Press, 1980).

17. "Letter from the Secretary of War Transmitting a Letter from the Chief of Engineers, United States Army, Dated April 20, 1939, Submitting a Report, Together with Accompanying Papers and an Illustration, on a Reexamination of Apalachicola, Chattahoochee, and Flint Rivers, Ga and Fla, Requested by Resolution of the Committee on Rivers and Harbors, House of Representatives, Adopted April 28, 1936," Government Records Series, Tri-State Water Compact Commission Negotiation Files, Executive Coordinating Committee, Water Supply as an Authorized Purpose for Buford Dam/Lake Lanier Folder, Georgia Archives. See also Marion Clawson, *New Deal Planning: The National Resources Planning Board* (Baltimore: Johns Hopkins University Press, 1981), 111–119.

18. Memorandum from P. A. Feringa, Corps of Engineers, to the chief of engineers, U.S. Army, October 28, 1943, Government Records Series, Tri-State Water Compact Commission Negotiation Files, Box 2, Georgia Archives.

19. Eightieth Congress, First Session, House Document No. 300, 1947, Government Records Series, Tri-State Water Compact Commission Negotiation Files, Box 2, Georgia Archives, p. vii.

20. Hartsfield to Boatner, April 18, 1947; Hartsfield to Feringa, July 24, 1947; "The Buford Dam."

21. Linda Broderson, "Cobb Success Partly 'Growing with the Flow,'" *Atlanta Journal and Constitution Magazine*, October 24, 1988, 10–11.

22. W. W. Horner and H. G. Shifrin for Atlanta Region Metropolitan Planning Commission (ARMPC), "Summary of Preliminary Findings: Comprehensive Water and Sewerage Planning Atlanta Metropolitan Area," January 1968, ARCC, KRC, AHC, p. 5.

23. For example, the Dekalb County Water Authority sold water wholesale to Rockdale County (which had no intake system of its own), and Atlanta's Water Resources Commission sold water to the Fayette County Water System (which had a severely limited intake capacity). ARC, *Regional Water Supply Plan*, 1976, ARCC, KRC, AHC; Willoughby, *Flowing through Time*, 168.

24. Fayette and Rockdale Counties processed wastewater themselves and returned it to much smaller rivers and streams outside the Chattahoochee watershed. Before 1980, selling water between municipal systems that spanned different river basins was legally dubious, though the practice was long standing and mostly overlooked. In 1980 the Georgia Supreme Court ruling in *Pyle v. Gilbert* legitimized the practice. This ruling potentially "opened the legality to interbasin transfers, at least between adjacent watersheds." Stephen Draper, "Sharing Water through Interbasin Transfer and Basin of Origin Protection in Georgia: Issues for Evaluation in Comprehensive State Water Planning for Georgia's Surface Water Rivers and Goundwater Aquifers," *Georgia State University Law Review* 21 (2004): 354.

25. ARC, *Chattahoochee Corridor Study*, 1972.

26. Brown, *The Greening of Georgia*, 130. The southernmost trout hatchery in North America, the Chattahoochee Forest National Fish Hatchery, sits along the Chattahoochee near Suches, Georgia.

27. The U.S. Study Commission, Southeastern River Basins, sponsored regional pollution enforcement conferences in the 1960s that called attention to the problems of the Chattahoochee and also voiced concern with the future allocation of the river's water between the three states laying claim to it. U.S. Study Commission, Southeast River Basins, *Plan for Development of the Land and Water Resources of the Southeast River Basins* (Washington, DC: Government Printing Office, 1963). The commission itself was inspired by the water studies compiled by the National Resources Planning Board in the 1930s. For details on those water studies, see Clawson, *New Deal Planning*, 116. He describes a report published in 1936 that explored water problems in the major drainage areas of the United States, including rivers in the southeast.

28. See Clawson, *New Deal Planning*, 112.

29. *Report by the Presidential Advisory Committee on Water Resources Policy* (Washington, DC: Government Printing Office, 1956) summed up the problem of national water management policy in 1956: "Because the problems are nationwide, it is appropriate that the Federal Government take cognizance of them and provide leadership for solving them by establishing sound nationwide policies" (1–2).

30. Forming the first wave of federal commissions and advisory committees that addressed water in the early postwar years, the Hoover Commission (which issued its initial report in 1949 and a second report in 1955), Cooke Commission (1950), Presidential Advisory Committee on Water Resources Policy (1956), and Kerr Commission (1961) had ambitions to evaluate the overall condition of federal water policy, offer suggestions for reforming policy-making mechanisms, address the issue of scarcity, and clear up lingering jurisdictional conflicts among federal agencies and between levels of government. The early commissions consistently encouraged a broad shift in the focus of federal water planning "away from regional development to the apportionment of an increasingly scarce resource," yet they consistently failed to ameliorate interagency conflicts over water management. This failure would disrupt attempts to make water scarcity

central to national policy. Rogers, *America's Water*, 10, 56. See also Advisory Commission on Intergovernmental Relations, *Intergovernmental Responsibilities for Water Supply and Sewage Disposal in Metropolitan Areas* (Washington, DC: Government Printing Office, 1962).

31. Inspired by the 1922 Colorado Compact, the first interstate compact allocating water from the Colorado River to the states it flows through, and the work of the Tennessee Valley Authority in the 1930s, Kerr's proposed legislation would have established several study commissions to collect hard evidence about existing watershed conditions, produced plans for watershed protection, and encouraged more collaboration across political boundaries. The Senate Select Committee on National Water Resources, known as the Kerr Commission, reviewed federal water policy and issued recommendations that were taken up by Congress. One of those recommendations led to formation of the U.S. Study Commission, which focused on specific regional watersheds, including the ACF basin in the southeastern United States.

32. Hartsfield to Boatner, April 18, 1947.

33. U.S. Study Commission, Southeast River Basins, *Plan for Development*. For an extended discussion of the work of the commission after delivering its report, see C. E. Kindsvater, ed., *Organization and Methodology for River Basin Planning: Proceedings of a Seminar Based on the U.S. Study Commission–Southeast River Basins* (Atlanta: Water Resource Center, Georgia Institute of Technology, 1964).

34. "The Atlanta metropolitan area complex presents a difficult problem in the pollution abatement field. The cities in the Atlanta group are so located that drainage from the urbanized area is divided among the Chattahoochee, Flint, and Altamaha River basins. The metropolitan area is currently diverting about 200 cubic feet per second from the Chattahoochee, about 70 second-feet of which finds its way into the Altamaha and Flint basins as return flow or sewage-plant effluent." U.S. Study Commission, Southeast River Basins, *Plan for Development*, 4–35.

35. Ibid., 4–5.

36. Ibid., 179.

37. Municipal wastewater systems that contain CSOs allow mixed sewage, industrial wastewater, and storm water runoff to flow directly into a public water body. For an overview of the problems CSOs present to water quality, see Environmental Protection Agency, "Combined Sewer Overflow Policy," *Federal Register* 59, no. 75 April 19, 1994: 18688–18698. For a historical overview of wastewater treatment systems in general, including CSOs, see Steven Burian, Stephan Nix, S. Rocky Durrans, Robert Pitt, Chi-Yuan Fan, and Richard Field, "The Historical Development of Wet-Weather Flow Management," Environmental Protection Agency Document No. EPA/600/JA-99/275 (1999).

38. Horner and Shifrin, "Summary of Preliminary Findings," p. 2.

39. The only contemporary evaluation of the work of the commission lauded its administrative structure, which allowed it to straddle the divide between different federal agencies and the states. The evaluation noted that the bureaucratic staff had a strong voice, vis-à-vis the politically appointed commissioners, in the ideas that found their way into the plan, which relied on empirical data and technical analysis. By quantifying policies and establishing variables that could be precisely measured, the staff could provide apparently neutral, authoritative information to the commissioners at critical moments during their policy discussions. Kindsvater, *Organization and Methodology for River Basin Planning*, 500, 517. See also U.S. Study Commission, Southeast River Basins, *Plan for Development*, 3–5.

40. Richard N. L. Andrews, *Managing the Environment, Managing Ourselves: A History of American Environmental Policy*, 2nd ed. (New Haven, CT: Yale University Press, 2006), chap. 11.

41. Before the 1964 act, water quality in Georgia had been the responsibility of the Board of Public Health, an agency with a vast array of duties. Needless to say, water pollution was often overlooked.

42. *Proceedings: A Conference in the Matter of Pollution of the Interstate Waters of the Chattahoochee River and Its Tributaries, from Atlanta, Georgia to Fort Gaines, Georgia*, U.S. Department of the Interior, Federal Water Pollution Control Administration, July 14–15, 1966.

43. Federal authority over water pollution derived from the 1948 Water Pollution Control Act. Pollution policy was expanded by amendments that provided construction grants to local governments in 1956, 1961, 1965, and 1966. See Clinton Shinn, "The Federal Grant Program to Aid Construction of Municipal Sewage Treatment Plants: A Survey of the 1972 FWPCA Amendments," *Tulane Law Review* 48 (1973): 85–104.

44. The Water Resources Council was to comprise the "Secretaries of Interior, Agriculture, Army, Health, Education and Welfare, and the Chairman of the Federal Power Commission, with the heads of other agencies participating on matters affecting their responsibilities . . . to be considered by the Council. The Chairman of the Council is to be designated by the President." U.S. Congress, Water Resources Planning Act, Pub. L. No. 89-90, 42 U.S.C. 1962.

45. Lyndon B. Johnson, "Remarks at the Signing of the Water Quality Act of 1965," October 2, 1965, *American Presidency Project*, available at http://www.presidency.ucsb.edu/ws/?pid=27289.

46. U.S. Congress, Water Pollution Control Act, Pub. L. No. 89-753, 33 U.S.C. 466.

47. With the 1948 Water Pollution Control Act, the federal government had signaled its interest in managing interstate water quality issues, which had particular salience for rivers like the Chattahoochee that crossed or formed state boundaries. The 1965 Water Quality Act significantly boosted federal oversight of surface water quality, created water quality standards, and established the Federal Water Pollution Control Administration. See William Andreen, "The Evolution of Water Pollution Control in the United States: State, Local, and Federal Efforts, 1789–1972, Part 2," *Stanford Environmental Law Journal* 22:215–294.

48. Letter from Gordon Warren to Newt Creekmore (city engineer, Apalachicola), March 21, 1966, State Water Quality Control Board, Executive Secretary's Subject Files, Folder 3, Georgia Environmental Protection Division, Georgia Archives.

49. "Official Wants Public Hearing," *Eufaula Tribune*, December 7, 1965.

50. "Billions to Clean Up the Rivers," *Business Week*, April 24, 1965, p. 60.

51. *Second Session of the Conference in the Matter of Pollution of the Chattahoochee River and Its Tributaries in the States of Georgia and Alabama*, U.S. Department of the Interior, Federal Water Pollution Control Administration, February 17, 1970.

52. Ibid., 210.

53. Ibid., 226.

54. Letter from W. W. Horner and H. G. Shifrin to Glenn Bennett, executive director of the Atlanta Region Metropolitan Planning Commission, January 24, 1968, ARCC, KRC, AHC; Horner and Shifrin, "Summary of Preliminary Findings," 5.

55. ARMPC, *Preliminary Water and Sewer Report*, December 1968, ARCC, KRC, AHC; "Northern Chattahoochee Water and Sewer Authority," prepared by Alston, Miller, and Gaines, December 1968, ARCC, KRC, AHC. The Metropolitan North Georgia Water Planning District was finally established in 2001 and had much of the power and responsibility first recommended in the 1968 Regional Development plan. Metropolitan North Georgia Water Planning District Act, *Annotated Code of Georgia* 12, chap. 5, art. 10 (2001).

56. Letter from R. S. Howard to James Quigley, December 23, 1966, Water Quality Control Board, Executive Secretary's Subject Files, 1965–1970, Georgia Environmental Protection Division, Correspondence—Washington Folder, Box 3, Georgia Archives.

57. Letter from R. S. Howard to J. L. Crockett, February 27, 1968, Water Quality Control Board, Executive Secretary's Subject Files, 1965–1970, Georgia Environmental Protection Division, Correspondence—Washington Folder, Box 3, Georgia Archives.

58. Letter from Paula Young to Whom It May Concern, April 13, 1973, Water Quality Control Board, Executive Secretary's Subject Files, 1966–1975, Georgia Environmental Protection Division, Georgia Archives.

59. "River Zoning Is a Hot Potato Not Likely to Cool for Awhile," *Atlanta Constitution*, July 26, 1971.

60. The commissioners also neutralized an existing agreement to set aside a different part of the parcel for a future public-use area (part of an ongoing but separate effort to create a national recreation area along part of the river). "River Land Developer Old Friend, Cates Says," *Atlanta Constitution*, July 17, 1971.

61. Betsy Cody and Nicole Carter, "35 Years of Water Policy: The 1973 National Water Commission and Present Challenges," Congressional Research Service Report for Congress R40573, May 11, 2009.

62. The National Water Commission produced a report in 1973 that contained a long list of specific recommendations for restructuring federal water policy to deal with the growing pollution problem. Seven major themes tied the recommendations of the water commission together: refocusing water policy to be more engaged in determining future demand, rather than the other way around; prioritizing water quality enhancement over development of resources; recognizing the critical role of land use in water planning; crafting national water conservation policies; improving cost-benefit calculations used in water project accounting; updating riparian water laws; and devolving much of the responsibility for water protection from the federal government to state governments and regional planning agencies. National Water Commission, *Water Policies for the Future: Final Report to the President and to the Congress of the United States by the National Water Commission* (Washington, DC: Government Printing Office, 1973). See also Rogers, *America's Water*, 58.

63. Gwinnett County created a water authority in the mid-1960s, but because of funds mismanagement by the county commission, a county supply system was only partially constructed. In 1970 the county commission created a replacement water and sewer authority that completed construction of the system, which included two additional intakes in Lake Lanier. Over time, these intakes would become the primary sources of water withdrawals for the county's water system. Horner and Shifrin, "Summary of Preliminary Findings," p. A-49.

64. The transfer agreements reduced the Chattahoochee's downstream flow and resulted in the dumping of large volumes of effluent into watersheds too small to handle the load.

65. ARC, *Metropolitan Atlanta Water Resources Study*, 1978, ARCC, KRC, AHC.

66. "Act on Area River Plan," *Atlanta Constitution*, July 7, 1971; "Zoning on the River," *Atlanta Constitution*, July 21, 1971.

67. Since the Metropolitan Planning Commission's first regional development plan in 1952 the value of maintaining a permanent natural buffer along the Chattahoochee to limit pollution discharges had been stressed. That early regional plan, *Up Ahead*, as well as *Now . . . for Tomorrow* in 1954, identified water resource protection as a high priority. The analytic sophistication of watershed planning received a major boost in the 1960s with the emergence of environmental science and ecology as formal academic disciplines. It was not until the 1970s, though, that state legislation protecting the Chattahoochee became law.

68. "River Zoning Is a Hot Potato."

69. ARC, *Chattahoochee Corridor Study*, 3. Atlanta Regional Commission, State of Georgia Program and Budget Office Records, Planning Studies Folder, Box 1, Georgia Archives. For recent indications of the public recognition of the importance of access to the Chattahoochee, see "Alabama Governor Agrees to Water Talks," *Atlanta Journal-Constitution*, August 17, 2009.

70. "ARC Criticized for Opposing River Bill," *Atlanta Constitution*, January 29, 1972.

71. Minutes of Conference on Regionalism, remarks by Dan Sweat, ARC, June 1985, ARCC, KRC, AHC.

72. ARC opposition ended the Walling bill's chances of passage during the 1972 session (the bill was channeled to the natural resources committee in the senate and died there), but with the zoning controversy continuing, prospects for a state-level river bill remained bright. See "Zoning on the River"; "Fulton Lobbyist Fights River Control Bill," *Atlanta Constitution*, July 28, 1971.

73. "Fulton-ARC Court Test Seen on Zones," *Atlanta Constitution*, September 7, 1972.

74. "ARC Wins a River Plan Battle," *Atlanta Constitution*, September 14, 1972; Memo from Dan Sweat to ARC Board, ARC, September 22, 1972, ARCC, KRC, AHC. Fulton County is the largest, most urbanized county in Georgia.

75. The vulnerability categories were subcategorized into flood plains, flood hazard areas, and vegetative buffers. Permanent structures within the flood plain were largely prohibited. Within the vegetative buffer, trees and plants within fifty feet of the Chattahoochee's banks and within thirty-five feet of tributaries' banks were to remain undisturbed, and the only structures allowed were bridges, water supply infrastructure, utility lines, and footpaths. Flood hazard zones permitted permanent structures, provided floors were two feet above the adjacent flood plain elevation and structural height was limited to thirty-five feet. ARC, *Chattahoochee Corridor Study*.

76. See Michel Foucault, *Power/Knowledge: Selected Interviews and Other Writings, 1972–1977*, ed. Colin Gordon (New York: Pantheon Books, 1980), 74–75.

77. ARC, *Chattahoochee Corridor Plan Update*, 1981, ARCC, KRC, AHC.

78. Memorandum from Joe Tanner to Jimmy Carter, "Adoption of ARC Plan by the Mayor of Roswell," October 26, 1972, Director's Office, Director's Subject Files, 1965–1977, Government Records Series, Georgia Environmental Protection Division, Georgia Archives.

79. For a discussion of land-based versus unit process wastewater treatment technologies, see William Jewell and Belford Seabrook, *A History of Land Application as a Treatment Alternative*, Environmental Protection Agency Technical Report MCD-40 (Washington, DC: EPA Office of Water Program Operations, 1979).

80. Between 1972 and 1976, as many as two thousand wastewater treatment facilities were built in the United States. See Jewell and Seabrook, *A History of Land Application*, 1.

81. See Milazzo, *Unlikely Environmentalists*, chap. 8.

82. The Office of Management and Budget's Circular A-95 set guidelines for interactions of federal agencies with local governments in metropolitan regions. Similarly, Section 208 of the 1972 Clean Water Act required states to designate a regional agency to manage area-wide wastewater management plans in all metropolitan statistical areas. Demonstration Cities and Metropolitan Development Act, Pub. L. No. 89-754, 80 Stat. 1255; Intergovernmental Cooperation Act, Pub. L. No. 90-577, 82 Stat. 1102; Federal Water Pollution Control Act, Pub. L. No. 92-500, 86 Stat. 816; Bureau of the Budget, Circular A-95, July 24, 1969; George Gordon, "Office of Management and Budget Circular A-95: Perspectives and Implications," *Publius: The Journal of Federalism* 4, no. 1 (1974): 45–68.

83. Section 208 of the Clean Water Act required that the "Governor of each State . . . shall identify each area within the State which, as a result of urban-industrial concentrations or other factors, has substantial water quality control problems. . . . The Governor shall designate (A) the boundaries of each such area, and (B) a single representative organization . . . capable of developing effective areawide waste treatment management plans for such an area." Federal Water Pollution Control Act, Pub. L. No. 92-500, 33 U.S.C. 1251.

210 | Notes to Chapter 3

84. Research concerning the A-95 review process and its successes, failures, and implications for regional planning is extensive, but at this point most of this work is twenty years old or more and largely forgotten. For examples, see Advisory Commission on Intergovernmental Relations, *Regionalism Revisited: Recent Areawide and Local Responses* (Washington, DC: Government Printing Office, 1977); Gordon, "Office of Management and Budget Circular A-95"; George Gordon and Irene Rothenberg, "Regional Coordination of Federal Categorical Grants: Change and Continuity under the New Federalism," *Journal of the American Planning Association* 51, no. 2 (1985): 200–208; Melvin Mogulof, *Governing Metropolitan Areas: A Critical Review of Council of Governments and the Federal Role* (Washington, DC: Urban Institute, 1971); Melvin Mogulof, "Regional Planning, Clearance, and Evaluation: A Look at the A-95 Process," *Journal of the American Institute of Planners*, November 1971, 418–422; Michael Steinman, "The A-95 Review Process: Suggestions for a New Perspective," *State and Local Government Review* 14, no. 1 (1982): 32–36.

85. Memorandum from Dan Sweat, executive director, to members of the Atlanta Regional Commission, "Metropolitan Sewer Plans and Policies: Background," July 20, 1972, State Water Quality Control Board, Executive Secretary's Subject Files, Box 3, Georgia Environmental Protection Division, Georgia Archives; letter from D. A. Raymond, Major General, Department of the Army, South Atlantic Division, Corps of Engineers, to Ernest Barrett, chairman, ARC, May 12, 1972, State Water Quality Control Board, Executive Secretary's Subject Files, Box 3, Georgia Environmental Protection Division, Georgia Archives.

86. *New Directions in US Water Policy: Summary, Conclusions, and Recommendations from the Final Report of the National Water Commission* (Washington, DC: Government Printing Office, 1973), 8.

87. Letter from Burt Bell to Senator David Gambrell, July 28, 1971, Director's Office, Director's Subject Files, Box 2, Georgia Environmental Protection Division, Georgia Archives.

88. *A Resolution by the Atlanta Regional Commission Urging Early Congressional Approval of Appropriations for a Metropolitan Atlanta Urban Wastewater Management Study by the U.S. Corps of Engineers in Cooperation with the Atlanta Regional Commission*, 1972, State Water Quality Control Board, Executive Secretary's Subject Files, Box 2, Georgia Environmental Protection Division, Georgia Archives. For a discussion of the Corps of Engineers efforts to pursue more pollution- and policy-oriented projects, see Milazzo, *Unlikely Environmentalists*, chap. 7.

89. Press Release from the Office of Herman Talmadge of Georgia, U.S. Senate, September 24, 1971, Atlanta Water Resources Study 1980 Folder 1, Director's Office, Director's Subject Files, 1980–1981, Box 37, Georgia Environmental Protection Division, Georgia Archives.

90. Letter from D. A. Raymond to Ernest Barrett, May 12, 1972, Atlanta Water Resources Study 1980 Folder 1, Director's Office, Director's Subject Files, Box 27, Georgia Environmental Protection Division, Georgia Archives.

91. "ARC Plan for River Gaining," *Atlanta Journal*, December 25, 1972; letter from Joe Tanner (Department of Natural Resources) to Jimmy Carter (governor), October 26, 1972, Governor's Subject Files, 1971–1974, Georgia Governor's Office, Box 2, Georgia Archives.

92. The final report of the Atlanta Study recommended building the long-delayed reregulation dam on the Chattahoochee at Roswell. Later, the Corps revised this recommendation, suggesting that reallocating water in Lake Lanier could serve the same purpose as an additional dam. See DuMars and Seeley, "River Basin Compacts," 373–400.

93. Minutes of Conference on Regionalism, remarks by Dan Sweat, ARC, June 1985, ARCC, KRC, AHC; Memorandum from Joe Tanner to Jimmy Carter, "Adoption of ARC Plan by the Mayor of Roswell."

94. During the 1973 General Assembly session, only two amendments were proposed by assembly members to weaken the bill. The first, to reduce the width of the protection corridor from two thousand to one thousand feet, failed by a wide margin. But the second passed. It tempers ARC's regulatory authority by allowing local governments with land under the jurisdiction of the corridor plan to override ARC recommendations for modifying a development proposal with a simple majority vote of the elected body rather than a supermajority, as had been originally proposed. Another successful amendment clarifies the right of a person or corporation to dredge sand from the watercourse provided no effluent discharge or erosion occurs as a result. "HB 1093 Discussion," *Journal of the Senate of the State of Georgia*, March 16, 1973, 2215–2225.

95. See Metropolitan River Protection Act, Acts and Resolutions of the General Assembly of the State of Georgia, vol. 1, 1973 Session, Section 10 (Milledgeville, GA: Clark and Hines).

96. Metropolitan River Protection Act, Acts and Resolutions of the General Assembly of the State of Georgia, vol. 1, 1973 Session (Milledgeville, GA: Clark and Hines), 129.

97. Memorandum to Jody Powell (governor's office) from Chuck Parrish (Department of Natural Resources), June 20, 1973, Director's Office, Director's Subject Files, Box 13, Georgia Environmental Protection Division, Georgia Archives.

98. The law also required that proposals be accompanied by detailed site, grading, and landscaping plans that included the location of vulnerability categories, existing vegetation, topography, and structural footprints and other associated land-disturbing activities. ARC, *Chattahoochee Corridor Study*.

99. "River Protection Lagging, Study Says," *Atlanta Constitution*, November 21, 1973.

100. Letter from R. S. Howard Jr. to John Biggs, September 13, 1973, Director's Office, Director's Subject Files, Box 2, Georgia Environmental Protection Division, Georgia Archives.

101. Letter from Jack Ravan (EPA) to Harry West (ARC), January 30, 1974, Director's Office, Director's Subject Files, ARC, Environmental Policy Subcommittee, 1972–1977 Folder, Box 7, Georgia Environmental Protection Division, Georgia Archives.

102. Letter from Ernest Barrett to Jimmy Carter, March 1, 1974, Director's Office, Director's Subject Files, ARC, Environmental Policy Subcommittee, 1972–1977 Folder, Box 7, Georgia Environmental Protection Division, Georgia Archives.

103. Ibid.

104. Letter from Jimmy Carter (governor) to Russell Train (EPA), March 11, 1974, Director's Office, Director's Subject Files, Box 39, Georgia Environmental Protection Division, Georgia Archives.

105. Memorandum from J. Leonard Ledbetter (Environmental Protection Division) to Jimmy Carter (governor), March 18, 1974, Director's Office, Director's Subject Files, Box 37, Georgia Environmental Protection Division, Georgia Archives.

106. In 1974 members of the Land Use Planning Subcommittee of the State Planning and Community Affairs Committee in the Georgia House of Representatives sponsored the Vital Areas bill, which would have instituted erosion control measures along the state's waterways. The bill failed to gain much support in Georgia's house or senate. "Report of the State Planning and Community Affairs Committee," *Journal of the House of Representatives of the State of Georgia*, December 1974, 4379–4403.

107. Georgia's first major erosion control legislation was introduced in 1964 as the Water Quality Control Act. The law set up an independent water quality control board responsible for investigating water quality problems but with limited formal power to enforce water quality standards. The new law replaced the old law. See Erosion and Sedimentation Act of 1975, Acts

and Resolutions of the General Assembly of the State of Georgia, vol. 1, 1975 Session (Milledgeville, GA: Clark and Hines, 1975), 994–1001.

108. Ibid., 995.

109. Ibid., 999.

110. Ibid., 994–1001. Georgia's Soil Conservation Service was a by-product of New Deal–era legislation to reduce soil erosion caused by agricultural practices. Into the 1970s the service was still an important part of the state's efforts to manage water quality.

111. Changes to the river protection act meant that local governing bodies that could previously evade ARC review of a development proposal now had to obtain a statement from the director of the state's Environmental Protection Division certifying that the alternative development plan would provide protection equivalent to or better than what would be expected if the regulations in the Chattahoochee corridor plan were followed to the letter. ARC, *Summary Steps in Metro River Review Process*, 1982, ARCC, KRC, AHC.

112. Brown, *The Greening of Georgia*, 141, 156, 186.

113. "10 Years, $100 Million Later, Rivers Cleaner Here," *Atlanta Journal-Constitution*, March 31, 1974; Brown, *The Greening of Georgia*, 141, 156, 186. Atlanta's two major news dailies, the *Atlanta Constitution* (founded 1868) and *Atlanta Journal* (founded 1883) came under the same owner in 1950 but maintained separate editorial offices. From 1950 to 1976, the papers were published in a combined edition on Sundays (sometimes called the *Atlanta Journal-Constitution* and at other times called the *Sunday Journal-Constitution* or the *Atlanta Journal and Constitution*). From 1976 to 2001, Saturday editions were also combined. In late 2001 they became a single paper, the *Atlanta Journal-Constitution*. For ease of reference in this book, all the combined papers are called the *Atlanta Journal-Constitution*.

114. "Clean Water: Lot Left to Do," *Atlanta Constitution*, November 10, 1975; Brown, *The Greening of Georgia*, 131–132.

115. Michael Jungman, "Areawide Planning under the Federal Water Pollution Control Act Amendments of 1972: Intergovernmental and Land Use Implications," *University of Texas Law Review* 54 (1976): 1047–1080.

116. ARC, *Water Supply Plan for the Atlanta Region*, June 1976, ARCC, KRC, AHC, pp. 25–28; ARC, *Atlanta Region Areawide Wastewater Management Plan*, June 1976, ARCC, KRC, AHC, p. 24. At the time ARC's wastewater plan was published, point-source pollution was the primary front in the war on water pollution and, accordingly, the plan's focus. But non-point-source pollution remained as a major contributor to degradation of urban watersheds in part because of a lack of reliable data to measure or evaluate runoff. Only later, in the 1980s, would techniques sophisticated enough to measure the extent of non-point-source pollution be deployed on a regional scale.

117. "Clean Water: Lot Left to Do"; ARC, *Water Supply Plan for the Atlanta Region*, 38–43.

118. Letter from Michael Trotter (Alston, Miller, and Gaines) to Glenn Bennett (ARMPC), December 16, 1968, Director's Office, Director's Subject Files, Box 2, Georgia Environmental Protection Division, Georgia Archives.

119. Letter from J. Leonard Ledbetter (Environmental Protection Division [EPD]) to Harry West (ARC), September 7, 1976, Director's Office, Director's Subject Files, Memorandum of Agreement between EPD and Environmental Protection Agency Folder, Box 7, Georgia Environmental Protection Division, Georgia Archives.

120. "Who Controls State Water?" *Atlanta Journal*, January 16, 1977.

121. Richard Ausness, "Water Rights Legislation in the East: A Program for Reform," *William and Mary Law Review* 24 (1983): 547–590.

122. Letter from J. Leonard Ledbetter to Harry West, September 21, 1977, Director's Office, Director's Subject Files, Box 7, Georgia Environmental Protection Division, Georgia Archives.

123. Letter from Kay McKenzie, Friends of the River, to Honorable Jimmy Carter, Governor of Georgia, August 25, 1972, Water Quality Control Board, Executive Secretary's Subject Files, 1966–1975, Box 2, Georgia Environmental Protection Division, Georgia Archives.

124. Letter from Dan Sweat (ARC) to Senator Sam Nunn (D-GA), January 18, 1973, Governor's Subject Files, 1971–1974, Natural Resources Folder, Georgia Governor's Office, Box 62, Georgia Archives.

125. Memorandum from Joe Tanner (Department of Natural Resources) to Jimmy Carter (governor), February 7, 1973, Governor's Subject Files, 1971–1974, Natural Resources Folder, Georgia Governor's Office, Box 62, Georgia Archives.

126. ARC, *Chattahoochee River Corridor: A Case Study*; memorandum from Harvey Young to Jack Crockford and Leon Kirkland, "Trout Hatchery Site Land Owned by Mrs. Causie Wood," December 1, 1972, Water Quality Control Board, Executive Secretary's Subject Files, Box 3, Georgia Environmental Protection Division, Georgia Archives.

127. "River Park Bill Hopes Vanish," *Atlanta Constitution*, October 1, 1976.

128. In 1978 Congress allocated $72.9 million for acquisition of land for the national recreation area. In 1979 another $35 million was appropriated. ARC, *Areawide Capital Improvements Program, 1980–1984*, Program and Budget Office Files, Planning Studies Box, Georgia Archives.

129. "The Chattahoochee River and Metro Atlanta Water Supply, prepared by Nancy Wiley, Natural Resources Commission, August 1980," Director's Office, Director's Subject Files, Box 27, Georgia Environmental Protection Division, Georgia Archives.

130. "Chattahoochee Dam Plan Creates Uproar," *Atlanta Journal*, September 10, 1980. Local environmental, civic, and recreation groups commenting during one of the public meetings included the Sierra Club, League of Women Voters, Trout Unlimited, Friends of the River, Georgia Conservancy, Georgia Clean Water Coalition, Georgia Canoeing Association, and Chattahoochee River Coalition.

131. Letter from Elmer Butler (Atlanta Audubon Society) to Rebecca Hanmer (EPA), October 17, 1980, Director's Office, Director's Subject Files, Box 27, Georgia Environmental Protection Division, Georgia Archives.

132. Letter from Robert Hice to Department of the Army, Corps of Engineers, Savannah District, September 8, 1980, Director's Office, Director's Subject Files, Atlanta Metro Water Study, Atlanta Metro Water Resources Study Folder 1, Box 27, Georgia Environmental Protection Division, Georgia Archives.

133. Letter from Jacob Varn (Florida Department of Environmental Regulation) to Colonel Tilford Creel (Corps of Engineers), December 16, 1980, Director's Office, Director's Subject Files, Atlanta Metro Water Study, Atlanta Metro Water Resources Study Folder 1, Box 27, Georgia Environmental Protection Division, Georgia Archives.

134. Letter from Larry Goldman (Fish and Wildlife Service area manager) to district engineer, Corps of Engineers, October 20, 1980, Director's Office, Director's Subject Files, Atlanta Metro Water Study, Atlanta Metro Water Resources Study Folder 1, Box 27, Georgia Environmental Protection Division, Georgia Archives.

135. Letter from James Rathlesberger (DOI) to Creel, October 26, 1980, Director's Office, Director's Subject Files, Atlanta Metro Water Study, Atlanta Metro Water Resources Study Folder 1, Box 27, Georgia Environmental Protection Division, Georgia Archives.

136. Letter from John Hagan (EPA Region 6) to Creel, October 7, 1980, Director's Office, Director's Subject Files, Atlanta Metro Water Study, Atlanta Metro Water Resources Study Folder 1, Box 27, Georgia Environmental Protection Division, Georgia Archives (emphasis in the original).

137. Letter from Harry Wright (Department of Energy) to Creel, September 5, 1980, Director's Office, Director's Subject Files, Atlanta Metro Water Study, Atlanta Metro Water Resources Study Folder 1, Box 27, Georgia Environmental Protection Division, Georgia Archives.

138. Letter from Edward Jenkins (D-GA, Ninth District) to Creel, September 9, 1980, Director's Office, Director's Subject Files, Atlanta Metro Water Study, Atlanta Metro Water Resources Study Folder 1, Box 27, Georgia Environmental Protection Division, Georgia Archives.

139. Letter from George Busbee, Maynard Jackson, Ernest Barrett, Walter Russell, Milton Farris, and Wayne Mason to Creel, October 10, 1980, Director's Office, Director's Subject Files, Atlanta Metro Water Study, Atlanta Metro Water Resources Study Folder 1, Box 27, Georgia Environmental Protection Division, Georgia Archives.

140. Letter from S. H. Gardner (Henry County Water and Sewerage Authority) to Creel, September 29, 1980, Director's Office, Director's Subject Files, Atlanta Metro Water Study, Atlanta Metro Water Resources Study Folder 1, Box 27, Georgia Environmental Protection Division, Georgia Archives; letter from Harry West (ARC) to Creel, October 29, 1980, Director's Office, Director's Subject Files, Atlanta Metro Water Study, Atlanta Metro Water Resources Study Folder 1, Box 27, Georgia Environmental Protection Division, Georgia Archives; letter from Wayne Mason (Gwinnett County Water and Sewerage Authority) to Creel, November 6, 1980, Director's Office, Director's Subject Files, Atlanta Metro Water Study, Atlanta Metro Water Resources Study Folder 1, Box 27, Georgia Environmental Protection Division, Georgia Archives; letter from Ernest Barrett (Cobb County–Marietta Water Authority) to Creel, December 4, 1980, Director's Office, Director's Subject Files, Atlanta Metro Water Study, Atlanta Metro Water Resources Study Folder 1, Box 27, Georgia Environmental Protection Division, Georgia Archives.

141. Letter from Robert Scherer (Georgia Power) to Creel, October 7, 1980, Director's Office, Director's Subject Files, Atlanta Metro Water Study, Atlanta Metro Water Resources Study Folder 1, Box 27, Georgia Environmental Protection Division, Georgia Archives.

142. The state and ARC had very recently funded the construction of the trout hatchery and thus were concerned about its fate. Memorandum from Charles Badger (Georgia Office of Planning and Budget) to Creel, October 10, 1980, Director's Office, Director's Subject Files, Atlanta Metro Water Study, Atlanta Metro Water Resources Study Folder 1, Box 27, Georgia Environmental Protection Division, Georgia Archives.

143. "Lake Lanier Area Residents Favor New Dam," *Atlanta Journal*, September 9, 1980.

144. "Notes from Public Hearing, September 10, 1980," Director's Office, Director's Subject Files, Atlanta Metro Water Study, Atlanta Metro Water Resources Study Folder 1, Box 27, Georgia Environmental Protection Division, Georgia Archives.

145. DuMars and Seeley, "River Basin Compacts," 373–400.

146. Originally constructed to help manage flood control, Lake Lanier by the mid-1960s had begun to be transformed into a recreational amenity for the region and was increasingly viewed as a potential drinking water source. Convincing the Corps to designate the lake for recreational purposes would stem water releases obligated to maintain power generation and downstream agriculture. *Metropolitan Atlanta Water Resources Study Summary Report*, U.S. Army Corps of Engineers, Savannah District, February 1981, Director's Office, Director's Subject Files, 1980–1981, Atlanta Water Resources Study 1980 Folder 1, Georgia Environmental

Protection Division, Georgia Archives, p. 2; "Report Concedes Lanier Is Lake for Recreation," *Atlanta Journal*, May 23, 1979.

147. In addition to the forty-eight-mile section of the Chattahoochee between Atlanta and Buford Dam, the study also looked at water issues facing several downstream counties on the verge of being sucked into Atlanta's metropolitan fold. U.S. Army Corps of Engineers, Savannah District, *Metropolitan Atlanta Area Water Resources Management Study, Summary Report*, February 1981, Director's Office, Director's Subject Files, 1981 Folder, Box 27, Georgia Environmental Protection Division, Georgia Archives, pp. 9, 14–15.

148. "Study: Chattahoochee Can Meet Water Need," *Atlanta Constitution*, May 24, 1979; *Metropolitan Atlanta Area Water Resources Management Study*, 11.

149. Testimony before the U.S. House Subcommittee on Water Resources by Michael Lomax, Chairman, Fulton County Commission, Atlanta, Georgia, and Member, Atlanta Regional Commission, July 23, 1982, Director's Office, Director's Subject Files, 1981 Folder, Box 27, Georgia Environmental Protection Division, Georgia Archives.

150. Letter from Bo Ginn (D-GA, First District) to Michael Lomax (Fulton County), August 6, 1982, Director's Office, Director's Subject Files, 1981 Folder, Box 27, Georgia Environmental Protection Division, Georgia Archives.

151. Memorandum and Order, July 17, 2009, Case No. 3:07-md-01 (PAM/JRK), U.S. District Court, Middle District of Florida, pp. 43–44.

152. Less well known than the Atlanta Study was a corollary study of water resources for four counties south of Atlanta (Coweta, Fayette, Henry, and Spalding) that highlighted a subset of water supply issues and offered strategies (several of which were implemented) for dealing with a possible wave of population growth. A separate flood reduction study for Peachtree Creek and Nancy Creek, both of which flow through the most densely built parts of the region, provided guidance for evacuation and flood-proofing requirements for structures near the floodplain. *Metropolitan Atlanta Area Water Resources Management Study*.

153. ARC, *Chattahoochee River/Lake Lanier Management System Report*, 1992, ARCC, KRC, AHC; ARC, "Reduction in Routine Water Demand through Water Conservation," *Metropolitan Atlanta Water Resources Study*, February 1980, ARCC, KRC, AHC.

154. *Atlanta Wastewater Management Planning Process: Plan of Study*, December 1976, ARCC, KRC, AHC, p. 1.

155. "Lake Lanier Blame Game Brews," *Atlanta Journal-Constitution*, July 26, 2009; "National Solution to Water Dispute? Georgia Delegation May Propose Legislation in Tri-state Controversy," *Atlanta Journal-Constitution*, August 13, 2009; Abrams, "Settlement of the ACF Controversy," 7; U.S. Army Corps of Engineers, Mobile District, *1989 Draft Post Authorization Change Notification Report for the Reallocation of Storage from Hydropower to Water Supply at Lake Lanier, Georgia* (Mobile, AL: Mobile District Engineers Office, USACE).

156. Dan Sweat, interview by Clifford Kuhn and Shep Barbash, January 22, 1997, Georgia Government Documentation Project (GGDP), Oral History Collection Series P: Dan Sweat, Box P-1, Special Collections and Archives, Georgia State University, Atlanta.

157. Benjamin Snowden, "Bargaining in the Shadow of Uncertainty: Understanding the Failure of the ACF and ACT Compacts," *New York University Environmental Law Review* 13 (2005): 134–196.

158. Joseph Dellapenna, "Interstate Struggles over Rivers: The Southeastern States and the Struggle over the 'Hooch,'" *New York University Environmental Law Journal* 12 (2005): 828–900.

159. Ibid.; "ACT/ACF River Basins," Tri-State Water Compact Commission, Negotiation Files, January 1997 Folder, Georgia Governor's Office, Box 2, Georgia Archives.

160. Between 1970 and 1990, the population of the five counties that form the core of metropolitan Atlanta—Clayton, Cobb, Dekalb, Fulton, and Gwinnett—grew by nearly 70 percent.

161. In the late 1980s, ARC developed a conservation pricing policy for water supply systems, including peak-use surcharges. Most metro-area water suppliers adopted the conservation pricing structure and seven suppliers adopted surcharges. The commission also adopted a policy mandating ultra-low-flow water fixtures for new construction and major renovations. This policy was put into law by the state legislature in 1992. *Water Conservation Activities in the Atlanta Region*, June 9, 1993, ARCC, KRC, AHC, p. 1.

162. By 2000 metro Atlanta's water use (measured in per capita gallons per day) was lower than just about every other major Sunbelt city, including Los Angeles, Dallas, Phoenix, and Las Vegas. Water Contingency Planning Task Force, *Findings and Recommendations, Appendix 2*, Office of the Governor, State of Georgia, December 2009, p. 6.

163. See, for example, letter from McKenzie to Carter, August 25, 1972, Georgia Archives; letter from Elmer Butler (Audubon Society) to Rebecca Hanmer (EPA), October 17, 1980, Director's Office, Director's Subject Files, Box 27, Georgia Environmental Protection Division, Georgia Archives.

164. The difficulty of predicting drought and modeling water supply is outlined by Shannon Peterson and Rose Wallick, "Water Allocation during Scarcity: Reservoir Modeling and Drought Protection in the ACT Basin," chap. 10 in Jordan and Wolf, *Interstate Water Allocation in Alabama, Florida, and Georgia*.

165. Attempts to build new reservoirs in northern Georgia were legion, but most failed. An effort in the mid-1970s to construct a major reservoir on the Flint River south of Atlanta failed, after meeting significant resistance from metro-area environmental organizations, the EPA, and Governor Jimmy Carter. "Carter Keeps Tough Stance on Flint Dam," *Albany Herald*, February 21, 1974. Georgia's 1989 growth management legislation included a major water supply bill that authorized the Department of Natural Resources to identify sites for future reservoirs and issue bonds for land acquisition, planning, and construction. From the moment the water supply bill was introduced, it experienced significant resistance. Ultimately, the water war between Georgia, Alabama, and Florida, in addition to the cost of building reservoirs and the difficulty of getting an environmental impact statement approved, killed most of the planned reservoirs. "Governor's Reservoir Plan Having Run of Dry Luck," *Savannah Morning News*, January 11, 1989; "Reservoirs Can Wait a Year; Examine Alternatives," *Atlanta Journal*, February 27, 1989; "Reservoirs Plan Just Won't Wash, Sierra Club Says," *Marietta Daily Journal*, March 2, 1989; "Partial Peace Treaty Signed in Tri-state War over Water," *Atlanta Constitution*, May 2, 1991; "Supply and Demand: Water's the Coin of the Realm in Growing Suburbs; Prolonged Dry Spells Can Play Havoc with Even the Best Laid Plans," *Atlanta Journal-Constitution*, June 9, 1996.

166. Snowden, "Bargaining in the Shadow of Uncertainty," 3.

167. That nearly $400 million had been spent on modernizing wastewater treatment facilities in metro Atlanta between 1972 and 1984 certainly helped this support. "Workshop on Regionalism in Atlanta," May 17, 1985, ARCC, KRC, AHC, p. 121.

168. Reagan hoped to force state and local governments to cosponsor water projects and assume a much greater overall greater share of total project costs. The passage of the 1986 Water Resources Development Act, a major legislative effort backed by the Reagan administration that allocated $16 billion for water projects and planning, represented an attempt to implement cost-sharing ideas. To get the federal government off the hook for 75 percent of the cost of building wastewater treatment infrastructure, Reagan also vetoed renewal of the Clean Water Act in 1987. Congress overrode his veto, a move that limited the decentralizing effect of the Water

Resources Development Act and maintained significant federal funding for wastewater treatment infrastructure for years to come. See Rogers, *America's Water*, 65–66.

169. By the late 1990s, as the water war between Georgia, Alabama, and Florida was heating up, accusations flew from Georgia communities downstream of Atlanta that the state was "primarily interested in metro Atlanta efforts to gain additional access to surface water" and was willing to "compromise and restrict" their access to water to ensure Atlanta's success. The fight was devolving into an Atlanta-versus-everyone ordeal. Letter from Sam Griffin (*Bainbridge Post-Searchlight*) to Mac Collins (R-GA, Eighth District), January 10, 1997, Tri-state Water Compact Commission, Negotiation Files, January 1997 Folder, Georgia Governor's Office, Box 2, Georgia Archives.

170. Memorandum and Order, July 17, 2009.

171. The view of Georgia's and Atlanta's leaders as to their rights to the water of the ACF system was noted in 1995, when Georgia, Alabama, and Florida were attempting to negotiate a formal agreement (a process that had broken down and restarted several times). Charles DuMars, a well-known attorney and professor at the University of New Mexico who specializes in water law, was hired to advise Georgia in the negotiations. DuMars noted that "Georgia wants the biggest amount of water retained in Georgia with the least amount of constraints," a statement that captures the essence of what Atlanta and the state had been doing since the 1950s: trying to take every possible drop of water. Letter from Charles DuMars to Harold Reheis, August 17, 1995, Tri-state Water Compact Commission, Negotiation Files, Executive Coordinating Committee, November 1995 Folder, Georgia Archives, p. 1. In an article analyzing the ACF controversy, DuMars and a coauthor argue that "Georgia has the high ground in this controversy. It has the legal capacity to divert water directly from any of its river systems so long as those diversions do not violate specific federal laws." DuMars and Seeley, "River Basin Compacts," 373–400.

Chapter 4

1. ARC's founding legislation stated that the commission would produce "development guides . . . based upon . . . physical, economic, and health needs of the Area and shall take into consideration future development which may have an impact on the Area." ARC, *Regional Development Plan of Metropolitan Atlanta*, 1976, Atlanta Regional Commission Collection (ARCC), Kenan Research Center (KRC), Atlanta History Center (AHC), p. 6.

2. Later in the 1970s, federal policy would require regional review of local policies on the aging population, policing practices, and public hospital administration.

3. ARC, *Regional Development Plan*, 6.

4. In a series of meetings between ARC staff and planners working for constituent local governments, candid opinions about the influence of the urban model were aired. For example, planners for Atlanta complained that the 1976 RDP had "resulted in projects which tend to encourage a spreading of growth throughout the region," and they cautioned ARC about the dominating influence of the urban model. Planners in suburban Gwinnett County worried that the model had underestimated growth at the urban edge. ARC, 1981 Meetings with Local Planning Departments to Discuss the RDP Update, April 1982, ARCC, KRC, AHC.

5. For background reports on early use by regional planners of urban models, see two special issues of the *Journal of the American Institute of Planners* devoted to urban models: "The Nature and Uses of Models in City Planning" *Journal of the American Institute of Planners* 25, no. 2 (1959), and "New Tools For Planning," *Journal of the American Institute of Planners* 31, no. 2 (1965). For an early comparison of several leading urban models, including the one ARC adapted

for the 1976 RDP, EMPIRIC, see Ira Lowry, "Seven Models of Urban Development: A Structural Comparison," paper presented at the National Research Council Highway Research Board, Conference on Urban Development Models, Hanover, NH, June 26–30, 1967. The difficulty of using large-scale models like EMPIRIC was aptly described by the U.S. Department of Transportation in the 1970s: "The effective calibration and application of EMPIRIC requires a significant degree of familiarity with . . . the development process, and particularly with the fundamental principles of econometric techniques. The model can very easily be misapplied." U.S. Department of Transportation, *An Introduction to Urban Development Models and Guidelines for Their Use in Urban Transportation Planning* (Washington, DC: Government Printing Office, 1975), 66.

6. For one of the few examinations of specific cases of how and why models were adopted, see Howard Pack and Janet Pack, "Urban Land Use Models: The Determinants of Adoption and Use," *Policy Sciences* 8, no. 1 (1977): 79–101. For a quick overview of some of the issues and consequences of using large-scale urban models over the years, see Sheryl Burling-Wolf and Jiangua Wu, "Modeling Urban Landscape Dynamics: A Review," *Ecological Research* 19, no. 1 (2004): 119–129; Michael Iacono, David Levinson, and Ahmed El-Geneidy, "Models of Transportation and Land Use Change: A Guide to the Territory," *Journal of Planning Literature* 22, no. 4 (2008): 323–340; and Richard Klosterman, "An Introduction to the Literature on Large-Scale Urban Models," *Journal of the American Planning Association* 60, no. 1 (1994): 3–6. The accuracy of projection techniques used in planning models has been studied independently. For examples of this scholarship, see Andrew Isserman, "The Accuracy of Population Projections for Subcounty Areas," *Journal of the American Institute of Planners*, 43, no. 3 (1977): 247–259; Andrew Isserman, "Projection, Forecast, and Plan: On the Future of Population Forecasting," *Journal of the American Planning Association* 50, no. 2 (1984): 208–221; Andrew Isserman, "The Right People, the Right Rates," *Journal of the American Planning Association* 59, no. 1 (1993): 45–64; Steve Murdock, Rita Hamm, Paul Voss, Darrell Fanin, and Beverly Pecotte, "Evaluating Small Area Population Projections," *Journal of the American Planning Association* 57, no. 4 (1991): 432–443; Dowell Myers and Alicia Kitsuse, "Constructing the Future in Planning," *Journal of Planning Education and Research* 19, no. 3 (2000): 221–231; and Jeff Tayman, "The Accuracy of Small Area Population Forecasts Based on a Spatial-Interaction Land Use Modeling System," *Journal of the American Planning Association* 62, no. 1 (1996): 85–98. More recently, projection models have been examined in conjunction with studies of the politics of major infrastructure projects. See Alan Altshuler and David Luberoff, *Mega-Projects: The Changing Politics of Urban Public Investment* (Washington, DC: Brookings Institution Press, 2003); and Bent Flyvbjerg, Nils Bruzelis, and Werner Rothengatter, *Megaprojects and Risk: An Anatomy of Ambition* (New York: Cambridge University Press, 2003).

7. ARC, Memorandum from Bart Lewis to Connie Blackmon, September 3, 1981, ARCC, KRC, AHC; ARC, Memorandum from Bart Lewis to Connie Blackmon, October 2, 1981, ARCC, KRC, AHC; ARC, Memorandum from Bart Lewis to Connie Blackmon, December 31, 1982, ARCC, KRC, AHC.

8. See Ronald Bayor, *Race and the Shaping of Twentieth-Century Atlanta* (Chapel Hill: University of North Carolina Press, 1996); Larry Keating, *Atlanta: Race, Class, and Urban Expansion* (Philadelphia: Temple University Press, 2001); and Clarence Stone, *Regime Politics: Governing Atlanta, 1946–1988* (Lawrence: University Press of Kansas, 1989). Each grounded his analysis in the relationship between the city's political and business leadership and its black voters.

9. For the tenor of this coverage, see "The Flight to Suburbia" and "A Decade of Drive," *Atlanta Journal-Constitution*, January 18, 1970.

10. See Richard White, *The Organic Machine: The Remaking of the Columbia River* (New York: Hill and Wang, 1995), 64.

11. ARC, *Atlanta Region: Area Development Profile Update, 1985*, MSS 619, Box 44, Folder 9, ARCC, KRC, AHC, p. 9.

12. Robert Fishman, "The Death and Life of American Regional Planning," in *Reflections on Regionalism*, ed. Bruce Katz (Washington, DC: Brookings Institution Press, 2000), 107, 115.

13. Scholarly writing about the growth of Atlanta has followed relatively consistent themes of boosterism and race, but the role of regional planning has not been well explored. For studies of Atlanta's history, see Bayor, *Race and the Shaping of Twentieth-Century Atlanta*; Ronald Bayor, "Roads to Racial Segregation: Atlanta in the Twentieth Century," *Journal of Urban History* 15, no. 1 (1988): 3–21; Robert Bullard, Glenn Johnson, and Angel Torres, eds., *Sprawl City: Race, Politics, and Planning in Atlanta* (Washington, DC: Island Press, 2000); Keating, *Atlanta*; Kevin Kruse, *White Flight: Atlanta and the Making of Modern Conservatism* (Princeton, NJ: Princeton University Press, 2005); Charles Rutheiser, *Imagineering Atlanta: The Politics of Place in the City of Dreams* (New York: Verso, 1996); and Dana White and Tim Crimmins, "How Atlanta Grew: Cool Heads, Hot Air, and Hard Work," *Atlanta Economic Review*, January–February 1978, 7–15.

14. The role of regional planning agencies in the late 1960s and 1970s has been described but remains only partially explored. For a few examples, see Robert Fishman, "The Metropolitan Tradition in American Planning," and Margaret Weir, "Planning Environmentalism and Urban Poverty: The Political Failure of National Land-Use Planning Legislation, 1970–1975," both chapters in *The American Planning Tradition*, ed. Robert Fishman (Washington, DC: Brookings Press, 2000). Scholars have recently begun to explore how federal interest in regional solutions for urban problems evolved in the 1960s and early 1970s. See Wendall Pritchett, "Which Urban Crisis? Regionalism, Race, and Urban Policy 1960–1974," *Journal of Urban History* 34, no. 2 (2008): 266–286.

15. See ARC, *Regional Snapshot: The Changing Atlanta Region*, 2003, ARCC, KRC, AHC; ARC, *Regional Snapshot: Density vs. Sprawl*, 2004, ARCC, KRC, AHC; and Brookings Institution Center on Urban and Metropolitan Policy, *Moving beyond Sprawl: The Challenge for Metropolitan Atlanta* (Washington, DC: Brookings Institution Press, 2000). The power ARC derived from the federal government enabled it to influence the major infrastructure investments that shaped Atlanta's footprint. The idea of a self-fulfilling prophecy was developed by Robert Merton, "The Self-Fulfilling Prophecy," *Antioch Review* 8, no. 2 (Summer 1948): 193–210.

16. In *Regime Politics*, Clarence Stone discusses the interweaving of the downtown interests and Atlanta's two daily papers, the *Journal* and the *Constitution*, into the governance of the city in the two decades after World War II (chap. 3). See also Stone's discussion of the newspapers as key sources of information about politics and business in Atlanta (259).

17. Stone, *Regime Politics*, 77.

18. John Pennington, "What Atlanta May Be like in the Year 2000," *Atlanta Journal and Constitution Magazine*, October 12, 1969, p. 10; see also "Magic Number: 51 Pct," *Atlanta Journal*, October 30, 1971.

19. Jack Spalding, "Where Now, Atlanta?" *Atlanta Journal-Constitution*, September 5, 1971.

20. "Gwinnett's Growing Pains Have Resulted in Progress," *Atlanta Constitution*, January 14, 1970; "Urban Sprawl Jarring Forsyth," *Atlanta Journal-Constitution*, March 21, 1971.

21. As Keating in *Atlanta* argues, "The growth of the north metro region has had a profound effect on the city. One of the main consequences has been the dispersal of employment" (8).

22. "Atlanta's Real Estate: Poised, but for What?" *Atlanta Journal*, November 21, 1973; "8 of the 10 Municipalities in Fulton Grew in Decade," *Atlanta Journal*, July 16, 1970; "Atlanta Boom—No End in Sight," *Atlanta Journal-Constitution*, May 19, 1974.

23. "Atlanta like Seven-Legged Octopus," *Atlanta Journal-Constitution*, January 18, 1970, p. 8J.

24. ARC, "Strategy for the Seventies," 1970, ARCC, KRC, AHC; "Metropolitan Area Planning and Development Commissions Created," *Acts and Resolutions of the General Assembly of the State of Georgia*, vol. 1, 1971 Session.

25. Examples of the emerging regional emphasis in federal policy were the Model Cities Act of 1966 and the Intergovernmental Cooperation Act of 1968. Both signed into law during Lyndon Johnson's second term, the acts sought to reduce federal urban policy overlaps by channeling federal funding programs through a regional review process to increase coordination between local governments. Circular A-95, issued by the Office of Management and Budget in early 1969, implemented the acts. For details, see Office of Management and Budget, *Circular No. A-95: What It Is—How It Works* (Washington, DC: Government Printing Office, 1976). Early criticism of the A-95 program's effectiveness was summarized in a report, *The Use of Land*. Task Force on Land Use and Urban Growth, *The Use of Land: A Citizen's Policy Guide to Urban Growth* (New York: Thomas Crowell, 1973).

26. ARC, Board Meeting Minutes, March 26, 1975, ARCC, KRC, AHS.

27. The drawing of analogies between the plans of the 1950s and 1970s came from recommendations in the 1967 report by the American Society of Planning Officials that had laid out a strategy for reformulating Atlanta's regional planning agency. "Metropolitan Regional Planning Commission," Acts and Resolutions of the General Assembly of the State of Georgia (1971).

28. The local political climate presented a challenge at times. Though ARC benefited from a legacy of state support for publicly funded regional planning, its existence had not escaped public debate. As the legislation that would establish the commission wound its way through the General Assembly, a handful of legislators, county commissions, and a few vocal citizens raised questions about the legality of a significantly expanded regional agency. Under Georgia law, they asked, did such an agency have a constitutional right to exist? More critically, was the agency a supergovernment that would supplant locally elected commissions? A few even asked if ARC were a toehold in an effort to introduce a Marxist government. Though both daily papers, the *Atlanta Journal* and the *Atlanta Constitution*, supported the creation of ARC, their writers consistently referred to the new agency as an umbrella government, an awkward choice of phrase that likely exacerbated local suspicion. The ARC board duly answered accusations to alleviate fears but carried on with its duties. See "A View from Atlanta-in-Dekalb," *Atlanta Journal-Constitution*, January 18, 1970; "And Now an Umbrella," *Atlanta Journal-Constitution*, February 1, 1970; "Regional Council: 3 Views," *Atlanta Journal*, January 2, 1971; "Atlanta 'Umbrella' to Spread?" *Atlanta Journal-Constitution*, February 7, 1971; "Cobb Residents Tear into ARC at Hearing," *Atlanta Constitution*, February 8, 1973.

29. ARC, *Regional Development Plan*.

30. ARC, "Staff Recommendation Report, RDP," June 1975, ARCC, KRC, AHC.

31. ARC, *The Atlanta Region: Framework for the Future*, 1975, ARCC, KRC, AHC, p. 2.

32. Metropolitan Planning Commission, "Transportation Policy Project, Reports 1–4," 1956, ARCC, KRC, AHC. The phrase "a continuous planning process" would appear again and again during the 1976 RDP process. For more details about urban models, see the published symposium on large-scale models in the *Journal of the American Planning Association* 60, no. 1 (1994).

33. Alan Black, "The Chicago Area Transportation Study: A Case Study of Rational Planning," *Journal of Planning Education and Research* 10, no. 1 (1990): 27–37.

34. See Edward Weiner, *Urban Transportation Planning in the United States: An Historical Overview* (Washington, DC: Greenwood, 1999), chap. 5.

35. U.S. Department of Transportation, *Urban Development Models and Guidelines*, 1.

36. For discussion of the features and merits of urban models written in their early years, see Britton Harris, "New Tools for Planning," *Journal of the American Institute of Planners* 31, no. 2 (1965): 90–95; Alan Vorhees, "The Nature and Uses of Models in City Planning," *Journal of the American Institute of Planners* 25, no. 2 (1959): 57–60; and U.S. Department of Transportation, *Urban Development Models and Guidelines*, chap. 1. For a description of the grandfather of large-scale urban models, see Black, "The Chicago Area Transportation Study."

37. Richard Klosterman, *Community Analysis and Planning Techniques* (Savage, MD: Rowman and Littlefield, 1990), xv. General remarks regarding how "it happens that urban metropolitan phenomena are so complex and so resistant to abstraction in any simple terms that computer solutions to them come to have an appealing simplicity" are provided by Harris, "New Tools for Planning," 90.

38. The idea of putting science in the service of regional planning, a replacement for the philosophical regionalism of Mumford, MacKaye, and Odum, was ushered along by Walter Isard and his many students. See John Thomas, "Holding the Middle Ground," chap. 2 in Robert Fishman, *The American Planning Tradition*. The persistence of a systems approach to planning and its expression in popular urban models is described by Michael Batty, in "A Chronicle of Scientific Planning," *Journal of the American Planning Association* 60, no. 1 (1994): 7–16. T. J. Kent's *The Urban General Plan* (San Francisco: Chandler, 1965) presents a thoughtful argument for the utility of the comprehensive plan in municipal governance. Standard planning textbooks of the period include Mary Maclean, *Local Planning Administration* (Chicago: International City Managers Association, 1959); F. Stuart Chapin, *Urban Land Use Planning* (Champaign: University of Illinois Press, 1965); and Kevin Lynch, *Site Planning* (Cambridge, MA: MIT Press, 1960). All present the rational-comprehensive plan as standard and give variations.

39. For a broad discussion of the tradition of policy analysis in planning, see John Friedmann, *Planning in the Public Domain: From Knowledge to Action* (Princeton, NJ: Princeton University Press, 1987), chap. 4.

40. The history of large-scale urban models begins with the entry of computers into planning practice in the 1950s. The most famous of these was CATS, which began in 1955 and set a standard for metropolitan-level allocation models. See Black, "The Chicago Area Transportation Study." For a general overview of early urban models, see Highway Research Board, *Urban Development Models: Proceedings of a Conference* (Washington, DC: National Research Council, 1968); Douglas Lee, "Requiem for Large-Scale Models," *Journal of the American Institute of Planners* 39, no. 3 (1973): 163–178; and Peter Stopher and Arnim Meyburg, *Urban Transportation Modeling and Planning* (New York: Lexington Books, 1975). A more recent appraisal of urban models can be found in "Large Scale Urban Models: Twenty Years Later," a special issue of the *Journal of the American Planning Association* 60, no. 1 (1994).

41. White, *The Organic Machine*, 64.

42. ARC, *Study Design for Development and Application of EMPIRIC Activity Allocation Model*, prepared by Peat, Marwick, Mitchell, and Co., December 1972, ARCC, KRC, AHC, p. i. The EMPIRIC model, originally developed by Traffic Research Corp., was acquired by Peat, Marwick, Mitchell, and Co., which eventually became the global accounting firm KPMG.

43. The accuracy of projections used in planning has been studied independently and more recently in conjunction with the politics of major infrastructure projects. For examples of this scholarship, see Alan Altshuler and David Luberoff, *Mega-Projects: The Changing Politics of Urban Public Investment* (Washington, DC: Brookings Institution Press, 2003); Flyvberg, Bruzelis, and Rothengatter, *Megaprojects and Risk*; Isserman, "The Accuracy of Population Projections for Subcounty Areas"; Isserman, "Projection, Forecast, and Plan"; Isserman, "The Right People, the

Right Rates"; Steve Murdock et al., "Evaluating Small Area Population Projections"; and Tayman, "Accuracy of Small Area Population Forecasts."

44. ARC, *Regional Development Plan*, 20. Other North American cities that adopted EMPIRIC for regional modeling included Boston, Washington, and Minneapolis–St. Paul in the United States and Winnipeg and Toronto in Canada. See U.S. Department of Transportation, *Urban Development Models and Guidelines*, 55.

45. ARC, "Development and Initial Application of the Empiric Activity Allocation Model for the Atlanta Region: Final Report," 1974, ARCC, KRC, AHC, p. i.

46. ARC, "ARC Working Paper: Development of a Data Inventory Reference System and Regional Information System Design," December 1975, ARCC, KRC, AHC.

47. Atlanta Regional Metropolitan Planning Commission, *Atlanta Silhouettes: People, Jobs, and Land*, 1962, From Mule to MARTA Collection, MSS 619, KRC, AHC; Metropolitan Planning Commission, *Up Ahead*, 1952, ARCC, KRC, AHC; Metropolitan Planning Commission, *Now . . . for Tomorrow*, 1954, ARCC, KRC, AHC.

48. The EMPIRIC urban model was well traveled among regional planning agencies in the late 1960s and early 1970s. First developed in 1963 for the Eastern Massachusetts Regional Planning Project, EMPIRIC was applied in several cities over the next decade. The model was designed to (1) allocate regional projections of population, employment, and land use; (2) assess the impact of planning policies on growth distribution; and (3) help evaluate policy decisions. A simultaneous-equation module sits at the center of the model. For a detailed description of the model, see U.S. Department of Transportation, *Urban Development Models and Guidelines*, 55–66.

49. ARC, *Study Design for Development and Application of EMPIRIC*, p. VII-30.

50. "ARC Forecasters Pose Questions," *Atlanta Journal-Constitution*, October 28, 1973, p. E1.

51. Projections are usually defined as mere extrapolations of past trends, whether linear or exponential. They do not take into account external factors, like migration rates, or attempt to account for contextual nuance. Projections are considered simplistic and formulaic. Forecasts, on the other hand, do account for contextual nuance, moving from the basic information provided in a projection to a more sustained consideration of likely future scenarios. Forecasts often use data from different sources to enhance accuracy and plausibility. Because of this, they are considered more sophisticated. But small-area projections and forecasts, the kind used in a regional planning process, both possess well-documented problems with accuracy. The smaller the geographic area, the more difficult it is to use rates of change derived from national data to measure in-migration and out-migration, births and deaths. Accordingly, most research has tended to study projections and forecasts for accuracy and performance. But whether defined as a projection or forecast, its role in the planning process tends to be similar. In fact, in practice, the terms often have been interchanged. The inaccuracy of small-area forecasts and projections need not be problematic for planning, but because they have come to occupy a significant place in the process, their accuracy (real or perceived) has become important. Forecasts are subject to political manipulation, particularly by powerful actors interested in using the numbers for their own gain. Yet research on this problem has been limited to overviews and theoretical generalizations; detailed case studies of the ways projections operate are virtually nonexistent. And investigations of how projections and forecasts are positioned in a concrete case of a planning process are lacking. See Myers and Kitsuse, "Constructing the Future in Planning."

52. For a recent overview of traffic analysis zones, see Luis Martinez, Jose Manuel Viegas, and Elisabete Silva, "A Traffic Analysis Zone Definition: A New Methodology and Algorithm," *Transportation* 36, no. 5 (2009): 581–599.

53. In 1970 only part of the Atlanta metro area had been divided into census tracts or traffic analysis zones, which limited the amount of historical data for EMPIRIC. After the 1970 census,

ARC was contracted by the Office of Management and Budget to help establish future census tract boundaries in metropolitan Atlanta. ARC, "1974 Action Program Element Summary Descriptions," 1974, ARCC, KRC, AHC. In the early 1980s, in a series of memos on how input data for EMPIRIC had been selected, ARC staff noted that 1961 and 1970 had been picked as baseline years for the model because of limited data, particularly information about land use. Lack of good data introduced an additional source of error into the model. ARC, Memorandum from Bart Lewis to Connie Blackmon, "Need to Recalibrate EMPIRIC," December 31, 1982, ARCC, KRC, AHC, p. 3.

54. Atlanta's future regional population was calculated from an economic base study that projected future employment on the basis of the region's share of total U.S. employment. Once future employment was established, total population was calculated according to the population the future labor force would be expected to support. ARC, *Regional Development Plan*, 26.

55. In the final step of the model, each superdistrict served as reference area for calculating the population of each district. See ARC, *Study Design for Development and Application of EMPIRIC*; and ARC, *EMPIRIC Activity Allocation Model*.

56. ARC, *Regional Development Plan*, 17.

57. The decision to bundle development policies set limitations on the number of possible outcomes of the modeling process, even before the process got started. Decisions about which policies to include in each bundle were the result of collaboration by staff and the board.

58. ARC, *Development and Initial Application of the EMPIRIC Activity Allocation Model for the Atlanta Region*, 1975, ARCC, KRC, AHC, pp. vii–17.

59. ARC, *Study Design for Development and Application of EMPIRIC*; U.S. Department of Transportation, *Urban Development Models and Guidelines*, 61.

60. "The 'trend-based' approach of the model is commonly recognized. One resulting problem is the difficulty in representing a situation that is not supported by adequate historical data." U.S. Department of Transportation, *Urban Development Models and Guidelines*, 65.

61. ARC, *EMPIRIC Activity Allocation Model*, vii–30.

62. ARC staff fully acknowledged EMPIRIC's error only when the update to the 1975 RDP began in the early 1980s. See ARC, Memorandum from Bart Lewis to Connie Blackmon, "Regarding 1980 EMPIRIC Forecast Errors," December 31, 1982, ARCC, KRC, AHC, p. 1; and ARC, Memorandum from Bart Lewis to Connie Blackmon, "Need to Recalibrate EMPIRIC," December 31, 1982, p. 3. See also ARC, *EMPIRIC Activity Allocation Model*, ii–22; ARC, *Regional Development Plan Small Area Forecast*, 1975, ARCC, KRC, AHC.

63. ARC, *Study Design for Development and Application of EMPIRIC*; ARC, *Framework for the Future*. The first EMPIRIC projections were released in early 1975.

64. In fact, EMPIRIC by design did not have a "strong, unique theoretical foundation," which put a "heavy burden on the ability of the analyst to develop his own conceptual structure and to translate [it] into a set of meaningful, valid statistical relationships." U.S. Department of Transportation, *Urban Development Models and Guidelines*, 66.

65. ARC, *EMPIRIC Activity Allocation Model*; ARC, *Regional Development Plan*, 8, 26.

66. ARC, *Trends in Land Use Planning Law for the Atlanta Region*, June 1976, ARCC, KRC, AHC.

67. ARC, *Study Design for Development and Application of EMPIRIC*, vii–29.

68. ARC, *Framework for the Future*, 5.

69. John Logan and Harvey Molotch, *Urban Fortunes: The Political Economy of Place* (Berkeley: University of California Press, 1987), 50.

70. As Floyd Hunter and Clarence Stone argue, many of Atlanta's most powerful elites were chief executives who ran the city's major companies. Floyd Hunter, *Community Power*

Structure: A Study of Decision Makers (Chapel Hill: University of North Carolina Press, 1969); Floyd Hunter, *Community Power Succession: Atlanta's Policy Makers* (Chapel Hill: University of North Carolina Press, 1980); Stone, *Regime Politics*. These elites were not land developers, at least not directly. Yet by the beginning of the 1970s, they had begun to diversify and included developers and construction company owners. The *Atlanta Journal-Constitution* reminded readers that the real estate industry "has always assumed major dimensions within the overall framework of Atlanta's business community." "Young Talent Led Atlanta's Go-Go Decade," January 18, 1970.

71. Growth has been at the center of planning since the early nineteenth century or earlier. One might go back to Ebenezer Howard's *Garden Cities of To-morrow* (Cambridge, MA: MIT Press, 1965) to see how growth was conceptualized as a necessary precondition for the realization of Garden City.

72. The second regional development plan written for Atlanta, 1954's *Now . . . for Tomorrow*, eschewed the idea of "decid[ing] ahead of time the limits of future expansion" of the region, which had been suggested just two years earlier in *Up Ahead*. Metropolitan Planning Commission, *Now . . . for Tomorrow*, 54. Instead it "suggest[ed] unlimited but planned incremental, concentric growth for the region." ARMPC, "Regional Planning for Metropolitan Atlanta: A Fresh Start," March 1971, MSS 619, Box 44, Folder 9, ARCC, AHC, KRC. Two decades later, the 1976 RDP did essentially the same thing, this time basing the plan on a mixture of fashionable planning ideas, which included assuming that "the concept known as 'design with nature' is sound" and that quality of life in the region "can be improved through increased and more innovative use of open space, sensitive redevelopment, neighborhood preservation, and planned new communities." ARC, Staff Recommendation Report, Regional Development Plan, 1975, ARCC, KRC, AHC, p. 3.

73. ARC, *EMPIRIC Activity Allocation Model*, v.

74. ARC, *Annual Report*, 1972, ARCC, KRC, AHC, pp. 9, 17, 22. See also "Metropolitan Regional Planning Commission."

75. ARC, *Regional Development Plan*, 26.

76. Ibid., 47.

77. For descriptions of what good regional planning should entail, as advocated by the Regional Planning Association of America, see Mumford, "The Ideal Form of the Modern City," in *The Lewis Mumford Reader*, ed. Donald Miller (1952; repr., New York: Pantheon, 1986); and Clarence Stein, *Toward New Towns for America* (New York: Reinhold, 1957), especially the introduction penned by Mumford. Ian L. McHarg's *Design with Nature* (Garden City, NY: Natural History Press, 1969) introduced suggestions for how to design regions by noting that "it is not a choice of either the city or the countryside" but rather a blending of the two that makes for good places (5).

78. That the RDP presented water quality as an important issue reflected Governor Jimmy Carter's push to make environmental management a higher state priority and the pending implementation of the federal Clean Water Act, which made cleaning up surface water a high federal priority. "Inaugural Address by James Carter," *Journal of the Senate of the State of Georgia*, January 12, 1971; Peter Rogers, *America's Water: Federal Roles and Responsibilities* (Cambridge, MA: MIT Press, 1993); Paul Milazzo, *Unlikely Environmentalists: Congress and Clean Water, 1945–1972* (Lawrence: University Press of Kansas, 2006), chap. 8.

79. ARC, *Framework for the Future*.

80. ARC, *Staff Recommendations Report: Regional Development Plan*, June 1975, ARCC, KRC, AHC, pp. 3–9; ARC, *Regional Development Plan*, 20, 36.

81. For an interesting contribution to the discussion of the role of population projections in planning and public policy, see Martin Wachs, "Ethical Dilemmas in Forecasting for Public Policy," *Public Administration Review* 42, no. 6 (November–December 1982): 562–567; see also Andrejs Skaburskis and Michael Teitz, "Forecasts and Outcomes," *Planning Theory and Practice* 4, no. 4 (2003): 429–442.

82. ARC, Board Meeting Minutes, December 13, 1972, ARCC, KRC, AHC, p. 3.

83. Letter from Atlanta Chapter American Institute of Architects to ARC, September 8, 1975, ARCC, KRC, AHC.

84. Letter from Virginia Taylor to Harry West, July 25, 1974, ARCC, KRC, AHC; letter from Taylor to L. D. Lacy, May 31, 1974, ARCC, KRC, AHC.

85. ARC, Georgia Conservancy Statement regarding the Proposed ARC Regional Development Plan, September 3, 1975, ARCC, KRC, AHC.

86. ARC, Board Meeting Minutes, January 13, 1975, ARCC, KRC, AHC.

87. ARC, Memorandum from Thomas D. Hills to Community Development Advisory Council, Atlanta Regional Commission, June 5, 1975, ARCC, KRC, AHC.

88. "Chief Defends ARC's Population Estimates," *Atlanta Constitution*, June 30, 1978, p. 1C.

89. Regional population projections were required by the EPA under the aegis of Section 208. As the designated regional planning agency for metropolitan Atlanta, ARC was responsible for producing the projections. Memorandum to Members of the Atlanta Regional Commission Executive Committee, October 19, 1977, Caution Collection, Box 51, Emory University Manuscripts, Archives, and Rare Book Library.

90. Memorandum from Bart Lewis to Connie Blackmon, December 31, 1982, ARCC, KRC, AHC.

91. In retrospective discussions about the 1976 RDP, ARC board members commented that the next "RDP should be more goal oriented. The current plan appears to be too project specific, particularly in the area of transportation." ARC, Working Session, October 31, 1983, ARCC, KRC, AHC.

92. A good example of the differences in the way soft infrastructure like land use and hard infrastructure like highways were debated in the planning process can be found in ARC, *Staff Recommendations Report—Regional Development Plan*, 1975, ARCC, KRC, AHC, pp. 3–25.

93. The major environmental policies included restricting development in flood plains, in areas where the water table was high, in areas with impermeable subsurface rock, on steep slopes, and on soils with a high shrink-swell rate. The major transportation policies advocated road improvements, downtown accessibility, rapid-rail and bus infrastructure, bicycle facilities, and transportation for the elderly. ARC, *Regional Development Plan of Metropolitan Atlanta*, pp. 11–13. Several of the policy areas ARC included in the RDP were there likely because of the influence of the American Law Institute's model land-use code published in 1974. American Law Institute, *A Model Land Development Code* (Philadelphia: American Law Institute, 1974).

94. Memorandum from Wilbur Smith Associates to ARC staff, "Regional Development Plan Update: Study Design Considerations," February 1981, ARCC, KRC, AHC, pp. 4–7.

95. Memorandum from Bart Lewis to Connie Blackmon, September 3, 1984, ARCC, KRC, AHC.

96. A good example is the case of water and sewer system infrastructure. A pattern of altering plans for constructing mains and treatment plants had emerged by the time the RDP process was concluding. Federal funds for constructing infrastructure, increased as a result of the 1972 Clean Water Act, were distributed on the basis of projected demand, which was in turn based on population and employment projections. Hence plans written in the early 1970s to guide

through 1988 the expansion of water transmission lines and build new wastewater treatment capacity in Gwinnett County, one of the jurisdictions in the ARC region, were revised as the RDP projections were developed and adopted. This allowed the county to take advantage of available money but at the same time lay the infrastructure that would support and encourage development in outlying areas. This happened repeatedly in the region. In each instance, existing policies were changed or replaced according to projections (or revisions to projections).

97. Memorandum from Bart Lewis to Connie Blackmon, October 2, 1981, ARCC, KRC, AHC.

98. Memorandum from Bart Lewis to Connie Blackmon, September 3, 1981, ARCC, KRC, AHC.

99. Federal programs that required projections as part of awarding funds included the Federal Aid Highway Act of 1962, Urban Mass Transit Act of 1964, Clean Air Act amendments of 1970, and Clean Water Act of 1972.

100. "Metropolitan Area Planning and Development Commissions Created," Acts and Resolutions of the General Assembly of the State of Georgia (1971).

101. "ARC Forecasters Pose Questions," *Atlanta Journal-Constitution*, October 28, 1973.

102. In the early 1980s, ARC began the process of updating the 1976 RDP. Finally acknowledging that much of the output from EMPIRIC had been of relatively poor quality, commission staff picked a new model for the new RDP. See ARC, "Area Development Plan for the Atlanta Region: 1981–1982," 1981, ARCC, KRC, AHC; ARC, "Briefing on New Forecasts for the Atlanta Region, 1990, 2000, 2010," 1983, ARCC, KRC, AHC; ARC, *Final Technical Report: Atlanta Region Forecasts*, 1983, ARCC, KRC, AHC; and Memorandum from Bart Lewis to Connie Blackmon, December 31, 1982, "Regarding Need to Recalibrate EMPIRIC," ARCC, KRC, AHC, p. 3.

103. The effect of regional planning in postwar metropolitan development has received precious little attention. Examples of recent work that attempts to address regional planning activities and institutions include Ray Bromley, "Metropolitan Regional Planning: Enigmatic History, Global Future," *Planning Practice and Research* 16, nos. 3–4 (2001): 233–245; Cliff Ellis, "Interstate Highways, Regional Planning and the Reshaping of Metropolitan America," *Planning Practice and Research* 16, nos. 3–4:247–269; and Robert Fishman, ed., *The American Planning Tradition* (Washington, DC: Brookings Press, 2000).

104. Atlanta Region Metropolitan Planning Commission, "Regional Planning for Metropolitan Atlanta: A Fresh Start," March 1971, ARCC, KRC, AHC.

105. Beginning in the early 1980s, urban models grew larger and more sophisticated, capable of handling a greater variety of data inputs and providing planners more precise control over outputs. The models also became much more spatially explicit as the power and accessibility of geographic information systems increased, allowing geographically crosscutting themes to be displayed and analyzed with more accuracy. Greater cognizance of the connections between urban infrastructure and environmental quality helped keep projections and forecasts close to the center of the regional planning process. As Richard Klosterman noted in 1994, "Large-scale urban models are likely to be much more important for future planning practice than they have been in the past twenty years. . . . The Clean Air Act Amendments of 1990 and the Intermodal Surface Transportation Efficiency Act of 1991 both require a consideration of the long range effect of land use–transportation interactions that only large-scale urban models can provide." Richard Klosterman, Large-Scale Urban Models: Retrospect and Prospect," *Journal of the American Planning Association* 60, no. 1 (1994): 5. For an example of this change, see ARC, "A Community's Vision Takes Flight: Vision 2020: Key Initiatives for the Future," 1995, ARCC, KRC, AHC.

Chapter 5

1. John Sibley III, "How the Georgia Growth Management Plan Enhances Local Preservation," *Preservation Forum* 4, no. 2 (Summer 1990): 14–15.

2. E. Stanly Godbold Jr., *Jimmy and Rosalynn Carter: The Georgia Years, 1924–1974* (New York: Oxford University Press, 2010), 140; Ronald Reagan, "Inaugural Address," January 20, 1981, *American Presidency Project*, available at http://www.presidency.ucsb.edu/ws/?pid=43130. For more context on the origins of Reagan's New Federalism, see Timothy Conlan, *From New Federalism to Devolution: Twenty-Five Years of Intergovernmental Reform* (Washington, DC: Brookings Institution Press, 1998); and John Mollenkopf, *The Contested City* (Princeton, NJ: Princeton University Press, 1983), chap. 3. For a broader discussion of the rise of the political right of which Reagan was the flag bearer, see, for example, Rick Perlstein, *Nixonland: The Rise of a President and the Fracturing of America* (New York: Scribner, 2010); and Bruce Schulman and Julian Zelizer, eds., *Rightward Bound: Making America Conservative in the 1970s* (Cambridge, MA: Harvard University Press, 2008). For an introductory discussion of 1970s political culture, see Bruce Schulman, *The Seventies: The Great Shift in American Culture, Society, and Politics* (New York: Da Capo, 2002).

3. See Mollenkopf, *The Contested City*, chap. 6.

4. For a detailed discussion of the history of the Interstate Highway System, see Owen Gutfreund, *20th-Century Sprawl: Highways and the Reshaping of the American Landscape* (New York: Oxford University Press, 2004); and Mark Rose, *Interstate: Express Highway Politics, 1939–1989* (Knoxville: University of Tennessee Press, 1990). See also Jane Kay Holtz, *Asphalt Nation: How the Automobile Took Over America and How We Can Take It Back* (Berkeley: University of California Press, 1998).

5. The cost of commuting has been the subject of a vast amount of research. While there is consensus that the daily commute has economic and opportunity costs associated with it, research about the benefits of commuting has complicated the picture. See William Alonso, *Location and Land Use: Toward a General Theory of Land Rent* (Cambridge, MA: Harvard University Press, 1964); Alex Anas, *Residential Location Markets and Urban Transportation* (New York: Academic Press, 1982); William Clark and James Burt, "The Impact of Workplace on Residential Relocation," *Annals of the Association of American Geographers* 70 (1980): 59–66; Randall Crane, "The Influence of Urban Form on Travel, An Interpretative Review," *Journal of Planning Literature* 15 (2000): 3–23; Peter Gordon, Harry Richardson, and Myung-Jin Jun, "The Community Paradox: Evidence from the Top Twenty," *Journal of the American Planning Association* 57, no. 4 (1991): 416–420; Richard Muth, *Cities and Housing: The Spatial Pattern of Urban Residential Land Use* (Chicago: University of Chicago Press, 1969); David Ory, Patricia Mokhtarian, Lothlorien Redmond, Ilan Salomon, Gustavo Collantes, and Sangho Choo, "When Is Commuting Desirable to the Individual?" *Growth and Change* 35 (2004): 334–359; and Lothlorien Redmond and Patricia Mokhtarian, "The Positive Utility of the Commute: Modeling Ideal Commute Time and Relative Desired Commute Amount," *Transportation* 28 (2001): 179–205.

6. See Kenneth Jackson, *Crabgrass Frontier* (New York: Oxford University Press, 1985); and Robert Fishman, *Bourgeois Utopias* (New York: Basic, 1987).

7. For details about the Intergovernmental Cooperation Act and the A-95 program, see Office of Management and Budget, *Circular No. A-95: What It Is—How It Works* (Washington, DC: Government Printing Office, 1976).

8. Along with significant funds for infrastructure, the 1972 Clean Water Act designated regional water planning agencies and required jurisdictions applying for funds to complete A-95

coordination through these agencies. See Federal Water Pollution Control Act of 1972, Pub. L. No. 92-500, 33 U.S.C. 1251, Section 205.

9. For more discussion of Clean Air Act amendments, see Samuel Hayes, *Beauty, Health, and Permanence: Environmental Politics in the United States, 1955–1985* (New York: Cambridge University Press, 1989), 773–776.

10. See Edward Weiner, *Urban Transportation Planning in the United States: An Historical Overview* (Washington, DC: Greenwood, 1999), 56–62.

11. Case studies of state growth management programs that include some historical framing include Carl Abbott, "The Politics of Land Use Law in Oregon: Senate Bill 100, Twenty Years Later," *Oregon Historical Quarterly* 94 (Spring 1993): 4–35; Carl Abbott, Deborah Howe, and Sy Adler, eds., *Planning the Oregon Way: A Twenty-Year Evaluation* (Corvallis: Oregon State University Press, 1994); David Callies, *Regulating Paradise* (Honolulu: University of Hawaii Press, 1984); Donald Chance, "A Behavioral Theory of Planning" (Ph.D. diss., Virginia Polytechnic Institute and State University, 2007); Timothy Chapin, Charles Connerly, and Harrison Higgins, eds., *Growth Management in Florida: Planning for Paradise* (Burlington, VT: Ashgate, 2007); George Cooper and Gavan Davis, *Land and Power in Hawaii: The Democratic Years* (Honolulu: University of Hawaii Press, 1990); John DeGrove, *Land, Growth, and Politics* (Chicago: Planners Press, 1984); John DeGrove and Julian Juergensmeyer, eds., *Perspectives on Florida's Growth Management Act of 1985* (Cambridge, MA: Lincoln Institute of Land Policy, 1986); John DeGrove and Deborah Miness, *The New Frontier for Land Policy: Planning and Growth Management in the States* (Cambridge, MA: Lincoln Institute of Land Policy, 1992); John Dykman, "State Development Planning: The California Case," *Journal of the American Institute of Planners* 30 (1964): 144–152; Arnold Howitt and James D'Amicis, *Growth Management in Maine* (Cambridge, MA: Lincoln Institute of Land Policy, 1993); Thomas Pelham, "The Florida Experience: Creating a State, Regional, and Local Comprehensive Planning Process," in *State and Regional Comprehensive Planning: Implementing New Methods for Growth Management*, ed. Peter Buchsbaum and Larry Smith (Chicago: American Bar Association, 1993), 95–119; Richard Settle and Charles Gavigan, "The Growth Management Revolution in Washington: Past, Present, and Future," *University of Puget Sound Law Review* 16 (1992–1993): 867–948; and Alan Wallis, *Growth Management in Florida* (Cambridge, MA: Lincoln Institute of Land Policy, 1993).

12. Fred Bosselman and David Callies coined the term "quiet revolution" in a 1971 report for the Council on Environmental Quality, *The Quiet Revolution in Land Use Control* (Washington, DC: Government Printing Office, 1972). Detailing new restrictions and controls on land development that arose during the 1960s, they conclude that the revolution had been driven by the "realization that local zoning is inadequate to cope with problems that are statewide or regionwide in scope" (14). Assessments of the aftermath of the quiet revolution include Daniel Mandelkar, "The Quiet Revolution—Success and Failure," *Journal of the American Planning Association* 55, no. 2 (1989): 204–205; Frank Popper, "Understanding American Land Use Regulation since 1970: A Revisionist Interpretation," *Journal of the American Planning Association* 54, no. 3 (1988): 291–301; and Richard Walker and Michael Heiman, "Quiet Revolution for Whom?" *Annals of the American Association of Geographers* 71, no. 1 (1981): 67–83.

13. Committee on Interior and Insular Affairs, U.S. Senate, *National Land Use Policy: Background Paper on Past and Pending Legislation and the Roles of the Executive Branch, Congress, and the States in Land Use Policy and Planning* (Washington, DC: Government Printing Office, 1972).

14. The literature on growth management is substantial. For an overview of the literature in annotated bibliography form, see Jerry Weitz, "From Quiet Revolution to Smart Growth: State Growth Management Programs, 1960 to 1999," *Journal of Planning Literature* 14, no. 2 (1999):

266–337. Analyses in greater depth include Benjamin Chinitz, "Growth Management: Good for the Town, Bad for the Nation?" *Journal of the American Planning Association* 56, no. 1 (1990): 3–8; Raymond J. Burby and Peter J. May, *Making Governments Plan: State Experiments in Managing Land Use* (Baltimore: Johns Hopkins University Press, 1997); Callies, *Regulating Paradise*; DeGrove, *Land, Growth, and Politics*; John DeGrove, *Planning Policy and Politics: Smart Growth and the States* (Cambridge, MA: Lincoln Institute of Land Policy, 2005); DeGrove and Miness, *The New Frontier of Land Policy*; Robert Healy, *Land Use and the States* (Washington, DC: Resources for the Future Press, 1976); Arthur Nelson and James Duncan, *Growth Management Principles and Practices* (Chicago: Planners Press, 1995); Douglas Porter, *Managing Growth in America's Communities* (Washington, DC: Island Press, 1997); and Jerry Weitz, *Sprawl Busting: State Programs to Guide Growth* (Chicago: Planners Press, 1999). Other influential works include David Godschalk, D. Brower, and Vestal McBennett, *Constitutional Issues of Growth Management* (Chicago: Planners Press, 1979); Randall W. Scott, ed., *Management and Control of Growth* (Washington, DC: Urban Land Institute, 1975); and American Law Institute, *Model Land Development Code* (Philadelphia: ALI Press, 1976). A sampling of the literature that evaluates different aspects of state growth management programs includes Jerry Anthony, "Do State Growth Management Regulations Reduce Sprawl?" *Urban Affairs Review* 39, no. 3 (2004): 376–397; Scott Bollens, "State Growth Management: Intergovernmental Frameworks and Policy Objectives, *Journal of the American Planning Association* 58, no. 4 (1992): 454–466; John Carruthers, "The Impacts of State Growth Management Programs: A Comparative Analysis," *Urban Studies* 39, no. 11 (2002): 1959–1982; Dennis Gale, "Eight State-Sponsored Growth Management Programs: A Comparative Analysis," *Journal of the American Planning Association* 58, no. 4 (1992): 425–439; and Arthur Nelson, "Comparing States with and without Growth Management: Analysis Based on Indicators with Policy Implications," *Land Use Policy* 16, no. 2 (1999): 121–127.

15. See Weitz, *Sprawl Busting*, chap. 3; American Law Institute, *Model Land Development Code*. For an overview of the national land-use debates in the early 1970s, see Noreen Lyday, *The Law of the Land: Debating National Land Use Legislation, 1970–1975* (Washington, DC: Urban Institute, 1976); and Margaret Weir, "Planning, Environmentalism, and Urban Poverty: The Political Failure of National Land-Use Planning Legislation, 1970–1975," in *The American Planning Tradition: Culture and Policy*, ed. Robert Fishman (Washington, DC: Woodrow Wilson Center Press, 2000), 193–215.

16. For years, planners have debated what does and does not count as a statewide growth management program. See Nelson, "Comparing States with and without Growth Management." Examples of evaluations of state growth management programs are numerous. See Jerry Anthony, "Do State Growth Management Regulations Reduce Sprawl?" *Urban Affairs Review* 39, no. 3 (2004): 376–397; John Carruthers, "Evaluating the Effectiveness of Regulatory Growth Management Programs: An Analytic Framework," *Journal of Planning Education and Research* 21, no. 4 (2002): 391–405; and Tom Daniels and Mark Lapping, "Has Vermont's Land Use Control Program Failed? Evaluating Act 250," *Journal of the American Planning Association* 50, no. 4 (1984): 502–508.

17. For a longer discussion of the connections between the popular environmental movement, suburbanization, and local planning issues, see Adam Rome, *The Bulldozer in the Countryside* (New York: Cambridge University Press, 2001), chap. 6. The chief theoretical statement on how states adopt policy innovations in general is Jack Walker, "The Diffusion of Innovations among the American States," *American Political Science Review* 63, no. 3 (1969): 880–899. Specific to growth management, David Rusk and others have asserted that states must become the innovators of new land-use controls. See David Rusk, *Inside Game/Outside Game* (Washington,

DC: Brookings Institution Press, 1999), chap. 14; David Rusk, "Growth Management: The Core Regional Issue," in *Reflections on Regionalism*, ed. Bruce Katz (Washington, DC: Brookings Institution Press, 2000), 78–106; Andres Duany, Elizabeth Plater-Zyberk, and Jeff Speck, *Suburban Nation: The Rise of Sprawl and the Decline of the American Dream* (New York: North Point Press, 2000); and Juliet Gainsborough, "Bridging the City-Suburb Divide: States and the Politics of Regional Cooperation," *Journal of Urban Affairs* 23, no. 5 (2001): 497–512.

18. For an extended discussion of the development of Oregon's growth management law as it applied to Portland specifically, see Carl Abbott, *Portland: Planning, Politics, and Growth in a Twentieth-Century City* (Lincoln: University of Nebraska Press, 1983).

19. Carter's major public mention of a commission for planning came during his 1974 State of the State address, when he said he would be requesting additional funding for a "planned growth commission." Jimmy Carter, "State of the State Address," *Journal of the Senate of the State of Georgia*, January 14, 1974.

20. See Arthur Nelson, "Growth Strategies: The New Planning Game in Georgia," *Carolina Planning* 16, no. 1 (1990): 1–6. Characterizing sprawl according to climate suggests distinct differences in physical form between, for example, Phoenix and Atlanta. See Robert Lang, "Open Spaces, Bounded Places: Does the American West's Arid Landscape Yield Dense Metropolitan Growth?" *Housing Policy Debate* 13, no. 4 (2003): 755–778.

21. Governor's Growth Strategies Commission, "Quality Growth Partnership: The Bridge to Georgia's Future," November 2, 1988, Governor, Legal Division Subject Files, 1984–1990, Growth Strategies Commission Folder, Georgia Archives, Morrow, Georgia.

22. Ibid.; "Governors Commission on Planned Growth Status Report," November 1973, Governor, Legal Division Subject Files, 1971–1975, Governors Commission on Planned Growth Folder, Georgia Archives. See also Joseph Whorton, "Innovative Strategic Planning: The Georgia Model," *Environmental and Urban Issues* 17, no. 1 (1989): 15–23; and Harry West, "The Evolution of Growth Management in Georgia," *Environmental and Urban Issues* 18, no. 3 (1992): 15–27.

23. "Inaugural Address by James Carter," *Journal of the Senate of the State of Georgia*, January 12, 1971.

24. Carter organized the West Central Georgia Planning Commission and later "helped to organize and became the first president of the Georgia Planning Association, which sought to accomplish on the state level what the west central commission had attempted regionally." Gary Fink, *Prelude to the Presidency: The Political Character and Legislative Leadership Style of Governor Jimmy Carter* (Westport, CT: Greenwood Press, 1980), 11–12.

25. See Gary Fink, "Jimmy Carter and the Politics of Transition," in *Georgia Governors in an Age of Change: From Ellis Arnall to George Busbee*, ed. Harold Henderson and Gary Roberts (Athens: University of Georgia Press, 1988), 238–240.

26. Carter had put administrative reform near the center of his unsuccessful 1966 gubernatorial run, an issue that he would reengage in the early 1970s. See Robert Behn, "Leadership Counts," *Journal of Policy Analysis and Management* 8, no. 3 (1989): 494–500; and Fink, *Prelude to the Presidency*.

27. It is worth noting that Carter's administrative changes came amid a period of tumult in the state, symbolized by the last of the old demagogic segregationists, Lester Maddox, leaving the governor's mansion in 1971. For an overview of this transition, see Fink, "Jimmy Carter and the Politics of Transition."

28. Executive Order, August 21, 1973, Governor, Public Officials Commissions, Executive Appointees Recommendations Files, 1971–1974, Jimmy Carter, Governors Commission on Planned Growth Folder, Georgia Archives.

29. For an extended discussion of postwar planned new towns, see Ann Forsyth, *Reforming Suburbia: The Planned Communities of Irvine, Columbia, and The Woodlands* (Los Angeles: University of California Press, 2005); see also Richard Oliver Brooks, *New Towns and Communal Values: A Case Study of Columbia, Maryland* (New York: Praeger, 1974).

30. "Report of the Governors Commission on Planned Growth," December 1973, Governor, Legal Division Subject Files, 1971–1975, Governors Commission on Planned Growth Folder, Georgia Archives, p. 1.

31. "Commission Could Cause Detrimental Delay in Legislative Zoning Measures," *Fulton County Daily Report*, December 1, 1987.

32. "Report of the Governors Commission on Planned Growth," December 1973, p. 2.

33. Ibid.

34. Durwood McAlister, "State Must Build Consensus to Solve Its Problems," *Atlanta Constitution*, June 18, 1987.

35. "Governors Commission on Planned Growth Status Report," November 1973.

36. "Report of the Governors Commission on Planned Growth," December 1973.

37. See Lyday, *The Law of the Land*.

38. Enthusiasm that had initially accompanied the A-95 review process was waning. Evidence of the policy's effectiveness was hard to discern in cooperation among local governments, and the hoped-for regional intelligence seemed fleeting. The zeal to ensure that every valuable penny of federal infrastructure funding flowed into local government coffers encouraged regional planning agencies to green-light virtually every application for aid. The near completion of the Interstate Highway System signaled a looming decrease in federal funding for road building, as the focus of federal transportation planning shifted toward system maintenance and demand management rather than construction. Congress's failure to pass a national land-use bill in 1974 reduced the pressure on states to pass comprehensive growth management legislation. See Melvin Mogulof, "Regional Planning, Clearances and Evaluation: A Look at the A-95 Process," *American Institute of Planners Journal* 37, no. 6 (November 1971): 418–422.

39. Perhaps the highlight of Busbee's tenure was a change in the state's constitution that allowed governors to serve two consecutive terms. See Eleanor Main and Gerard Gryski, "George Busbee and the Politics of Consensus," in *Georgia Governors in an Age of Change: From Ellis Arnall to George Busbee*, ed. Harold Henderson and Gary Roberts (Athens: University of Georgia Press, 1988), 261–278.

40. Similar in name to North Carolina's law, the 1978 Balanced Growth Act signed into law by President Carter sought to codify full employment and foreign trade balance, among other issues, in federal law. For a very brief introduction, see Stephen Cimbala and Robert Stout, "The Economic Report of the President: Before and After the Full Employment and Balanced Growth Act of 1978," *Presidential Studies Quarterly* 13, no. 1 (1983): 50–61.

41. Memorandum from Joe Parker, cochairman for State Goals and Policy Board, and Claud O'Shields, cochairman for Local Government Advocacy Council, to fellow board and commission members, North Carolina Department of Administration, June 7, 1979, Governor Public Officials Commissions, Executive Appointees Recommendation Files, 1975–1983, Georgia Commission on State Growth Policy Folder, Georgia Archives.

42. Explanations and evaluations of North Carolina's balanced growth policy include Brad Stuart, *Making North Carolina Prosper: A Critique of Balanced Growth and Regional Planning* (Raleigh: North Carolina Center for Public Policy Research, 1979); and Deil Wright, *North Carolina's Balanced Growth Strategy* (Washington, DC: Government Printing Office, 1980).

43. A background report on the North Carolina act was forwarded to Governor Busbee by his chief of staff in late 1981. Griff Doyle, "A Proposal for a Procedure to Establish a State

Growth Policy," n.d., Governor Public Officials Commissions, Executive Appointees Recommendation Files, 1975–1983, George Busbee, Georgia Commission on State Growth Policy Folder, Georgia Archives.

44. Conlan, *From New Federalism to Devolution*, 95–96.

45. Ronald Reagan, "Executive Order 12372—Intergovernmental Review of Federal Programs," July 14, 1982, *American Presidency Project*, available at http://www.presidency.ucsb.edu/ws/?pid=42735.

46. Mogulof, "Regional Planning, Clearances and Evaluation," 418; see also Irene Rothenberg, "National Support for Regional Review: Federal Compliance and the Future of Intergovernmental Coordination," *Publius: The Journal of Federalism* 13, no. 4 (1983): 43–58.

47. For a discussion of the Reagan rollbacks on federal transportation policy, see Weiner, *Urban Transportation Planning in the United States*, chaps. 10 and 11.

48. Executive Department of the State of Georgia, "Executive Order by the Governor," August 31, 1982, Governor Public Officials Commissions, Executive Appointees Recommendation Files, 1975–1983, George Busbee, Georgia Commission on State Growth Policy Folder, Georgia Archives. A sunset clause inserted in the legislation would dissolve the commission in mid-1984 if no further action were taken. See Senate Bill 601, Georgia General Assembly 1982, Governor Public Officials Commissions, Executive Appointees Recommendation Files, 1975–1983, George Busbee, Georgia Commission on State Growth Policy Folder, Georgia Archives.

49. Remarks by Joe Frank Harris, Prelegislative Forum, November 9, 1988, Governor, Legal Division Subject Files, 1984–1990, Growth Strategies Commission Folder, Georgia Archives.

50. "Harris Urged to Form State 'Growth Strategy' Commission," *Atlanta Constitution*, November 24, 1986.

51. "Why Florida Is Getting a Growth-Management Watchdog," *Florida Trend*, December 1986, 83–84. See also Weitz, *Sprawl Busting*, 69.

52. Another important influence on Harris was Roy Barnes, at the time a young representative from suburban Cobb County who served as Harris's legislative floor leader in the middle to late 1980s. Barnes was a strong voice for growth management and likely contributed to the state planning bill that passed the General Assembly in 1989. See "Governor's Vision: Barnes Building Growth Legacy," *Atlanta Journal-Constitution*, November 26, 2001.

53. Letter from Steve Rieck to Walt Sessoms, December 19, 1983, Governor, Public Officials Commissions, Executive Appointments Recommendations Files, 1983–1990, Joe Frank Harris, Georgia Commission on State Growth Policy Act Folder, Georgia Archives.

54. Memorandum from Gracie Phillips to Steve Rieck, February 7, 1983, Governor, Public Officials Commissions, Executive Appointments Recommendations Files, 1983–1990, Joe Frank Harris, Georgia Commission on State Growth Policy Act Folder, Georgia Archives.

55. Memorandum from Jim Higdon (DCA [Department of Community Affairs] commissioner) to Tom Perdue, "Regarding: Commission on State Growth Policy," June 7, 1984, Governor, Public Officials Commissions, Executive Appointments Recommendations Files, 1983–1990, Joe Frank Harris, Georgia Commission on State Growth Policy Act Folder, Georgia Archives.

56. Ibid., 1 (emphasis in the original).

57. Memorandum from Jim Higdon (DCA commissioner) to Tom Perdue, "Regarding: Commission on State Growth Policy."

58. Joe Frank Harris, "Inaugural Address," *Journal of the House of Representatives of the State of Georgia*, January 13, 1987, pp. 70–72.

59. "Governor Shows Courage by Aiming to Control Growth," *Atlanta Journal-Constitution*, November 1, 1987.

60. "A Resolution Urging the Governor to Create a Governor's Commission on Growth Strategy," *Journal of the House of Representatives of the State of Georgia*, March 12, 1987.

61. "Growth Strategy Pushed: Project May Force Zoning on Counties," *Savannah Morning News*, November 1, 1987.

62. Ibid.

63. Weitz, *Sprawl Busting*, 26.

64. See Carlton Basmajian, "Projecting Sprawl? The Atlanta Regional Commission and the 1975 Regional Development Plan of Metropolitan Atlanta," *Journal of Planning History* 9, no. 2 (2010): 95–121.

65. "Report of the Governor's Commission on Planned Growth," December 1973, p. 1.

66. "Unless Georgia Manages Growth, We're in Trouble," *Atlanta Journal-Constitution*, February 1, 1987; memorandum from John Sibley to Joel Cowan, July 22, 1987, Governor, Intergovernmental Relations, Subject Files, 1983–1991, Joe Frank Harris, Growth Strategies Commission, Correspondence, July 1987 Folder, Georgia Archives.

67. For a detailed look at the Sibley commission and school desegregation in Georgia, see Jeff Roche, *Restructured Resistance: The Sibley Commission and the Politics of Desegregation in Georgia* (Athens: University of Georgia Press, 1998).

68. Memorandum from John Sibley to Joe Frank Harris, Subject: Growth Strategies Commission, May 13, 1987, Governor, Chief of Staff, Subject Files, 1983–1991, Joe Frank Harris, Growth Strategies Commission 87–88 Folder, Georgia Archives.

69. Ibid.

70. Executive Order, June 16, 1987, Governor, Executive Department, Executive Department Minutes, February–October 1987, Joe Frank Harris, Governor's Growth Strategies Commission 87–88 Folder, Georgia Archives.

71. Ibid.

72. "Harris to Swear in 36 on Commission to Map 'Quality Growth' Plan for State," *Atlanta Constitution*, June 1, 1987. Along with a partner, Cowan had founded Peachtree City in 1958, a planned suburb on the southern outskirts of metro Atlanta. Since his time as chairman of Jimmy Carter's planning growth commission, Cowan had built a real estate investment firm in Atlanta that underwrote several high-profile development ventures.

73. Letter from Johnny Isakson to Joe Frank Harris, January 5, 1987, Governor, Public Officials Commission, Executive Appointees Recommendations Files, 1983–1990, Joe Frank Harris, Governor's Growth Strategies Commission General Folder, Georgia Archives, p. 1; see also letter from Jeanne Ferst (Chairman Fulton Economic Development Advisory Board) to Grace Phillips (Office of the Governor), March 10, 1987, Governor, Public Officials Commission, Executive Appointees Recommendations Files, 1983–1990, Joe Frank Harris, Governor's Growth Strategies Commission General Folder, Georgia Archives; letter from Charles Hatcher (D-GA) to Joe Frank Harris, May 11, 1987, Governor, Public Officials Commission, Executive Appointees Recommendations Files, 1983–1990, Joe Frank Harris, Governor's Growth Strategies Commission General Folder, Georgia Archives; and letter from Dorothy Felton to Joe Frank Harris, January 8, 1987, Governor, Public Officials Commission, Executive Appointees Recommendations Files, 1983–1990, Joe Frank Harris, Governor's Growth Strategies Commission General Folder, Georgia Archives.

74. Letter from Harry Whitehead (Dahlonega-Lumpkin County Chamber of Commerce) to Joe Frank Harris, June 29, 1987, Governor, Intergovernmental Relations, Subject Files, 1983–1991, Joe Frank Harris, Growth Strategies Commission Folder, Georgia Archives.

75. "Steinberg Fumes over Not Being Put on Growth Panel," *Atlanta Constitution*, June 17, 1987. A few days later Steinberg wrote to Harris to apologize, explaining that her anger was a

result of "being denied the opportunity to participate in something which means so much to [her]" but admitting that her comments had been "disrespectful and inappropriate." Letter from Kathy Steinberg (Representative, Georgia General Assembly) to Joe Frank Harris, June 30, 1987, Governor, Public Officials Commission, Executive Appointees Recommendations Files, 1983–1990, Joe Frank Harris, Governor's Growth Strategies Commission General Folder, Georgia Archives.

76. Memorandum from Gracie Phillips to Governor Harris, August 26, 1987, Governor, Public Officials Commission, Executive Appointees Recommendations Files, 1983–1990, Joe Frank Harris, Governor's Growth Strategies Commission General Folder, Georgia Archives.

77. "Governor's Charge to Growth Strategy Commission," n.d., Governor, Public Officials Commission, Executive Appointees Recommendations Files, 1983–1990, Joe Frank Harris, Governor's Growth Strategies Commission General Folder, Georgia Archives.

78. "State Must Build Consensus to Solve Its Problems," *Atlanta Journal*, June 18, 1987.

79. "New Growth Panel Starts off Brainstorming," *Atlanta Constitution*, July 14, 1987; "New Planning Group Headed to Dispute over Priorities?" *Creative Loafing*, July 25, 1987.

80. "Yes, to State Land-Use Planning," *Atlanta Constitution*, July 24, 1987.

81. Sibley worried that the "expertise of a core staff" would unduly shape the commission's decisions. Memorandum from John Sibley (Staff Director) to Members of the Growth Strategies Commission, "Subject: Process for Developing Growth Strategies," June 16, 1987, Governor, Executive Department, Executive Department Minutes, February–October 1987, Joe Frank Harris, Governor's Growth Strategies Commission Folder, Georgia Archives.

82. Memorandum from John Sibley to Gracie Phillips regarding Growth Strategies Commission, June 19, 1987, Governor, Public Officials Commission, Executive Appointees Recommendations Files, 1983–1990, Joe Frank Harris, Governor's Growth Strategies Commission General Folder, Georgia Archives.

83. Memorandum from Rick Campbell (UGA, Vinson Institute) to John Sibley, September 22, 1987, Governor, Intergovernmental Relations, Subject Files, 1983–1991, Joe Frank Harris, Growth Strategies Commission, Commission Proceedings June 87–November 88 Folders, Georgia Archives, p. 1. See also Memorandum from David Sawicki to Lynn Thornton (asst. commissioner DCA), "Re: Briefing Facts for the Task Forces," September 21, 1987, Governor, Intergovernmental Relations, Subject Files, 1983–1991, Joe Frank Harris, Growth Strategies Commission, Commission Proceedings June 87–November 88 Folders, Georgia Archives; letter from Howard Zeller (Department of Natural Resources) to Lynn Thornton, September 24, 1987, Governor, Intergovernmental Relations, Subject Files, 1983–1991, Joe Frank Harris, Growth Strategies Commission, Commission Proceedings June 87–November 88 Folders, Georgia Archives; and memorandum from Floyd Hardey (GDOT Engineer) to John Sibley, September 22, 1987, Governor, Intergovernmental Relations, Subject Files, 1983–1991, Joe Frank Harris, Growth Strategies Commission, Commission Proceedings June 87–November 88 Folders, Georgia Archives.

84. Natural Resources Task Force, Governor's Growth Strategies Commission, "Draft Results of the December 10 Meeting," n.d., Governor, Intergovernmental Relations, Subject Files, 1983–1991, Joe Frank Harris, Growth Strategies Commission, Commission Proceedings June 87–November 88 Folders, Georgia Archives.

85. Memorandum from Joel Cowan to Growth Issues Resources Council, "Subject: Land Use Task Force," January 12, 1988, Governor, Intergovernmental Relations, Subject Files, 1983–1991, Joe Frank Harris, Growth Strategies Commission, Commission Proceedings June 87–November 88 Folders, Georgia Archives.

86. Minutes of the Economic Development Task Force Meeting, January 13, 1988, Governor, Intergovernmental Relations, Subject Files, 1983–1991, Joe Frank Harris, Growth

Strategies Commission, Commission Proceedings June 87–November 88 Folders, Georgia Archives.

87. *Interim Report*, Governor's Growth Strategies Commission, Governor, Chief of Staff, Subject Files, 1983–1991, Governor Joe Frank Harris, Growth Strategies Commission 87–88 Folder, Georgia Archives, p. 17.

88. Memorandum from John Sibley to Joe Frank Harris, "Subject: Governor's Growth Strategies Commission," February 25, 1988, Governor, Legal Division Subject Files, 1984–1990, Growth Strategies Commission Folder, Georgia Archives.

89. "How to Manage Georgia's Growth," *Georgia Trend Magazine*, March 1988, pp. 75–76.

90. "Governor's Growth Strategies Commission Interim Report," June 1988, Governor, Intergovernmental Relations, Subject Files, 1983–1991, Joe Frank Harris, Growth Strategies Commission, Georgia Archives.

91. "Conceptual Outline, Public Hearing Process," n.d., Governor, Intergovermental Relations, Subject Files, 1983–1991, Joe Frank Harris, Growth Strategies Commission Folder, Georgia Archives.

92. "Analysis of the Transcripts of Public Meetings Held by the Governor's Growth Strategies Commission," DCA, May 1988, Governor, Intergovernmental Relations, Subject Files, 1983–1991, Joe Frank Harris, Growth Strategies Commission Folder, Georgia Archives, pp. 12–14, 19–20.

93. "Analysis of the Transcripts of Public Meetings," 2.

94. "Growth Report Boggles Mind," *Gainesville Times*, May 12, 1988; "Growth Panel's Proposals Met with Mixed Reaction," *Atlanta Constitution*, April 12, 1988.

95. Jim Wooten, "Consolidation? What Does That Dirty Word Mean?" *Atlanta Journal-Constitution*, April 3, 1988.

96. "Growth Panel's Proposals Met with Mixed Reaction."

97. "Dream State: A Maverick Commission Presses Its Agenda," *Southline*, April 6, 1988.

98. Memorandum from John Sibley to Joe Frank Harris, May 9, 1988, Governor, Intergovernmental Relations, Subject Files, 1983–1991, Joe Frank Harris, Growth Strategies Commission Folder, Georgia Archives.

99. Memorandum from John Sibley to Joe Frank Harris, June 24, 1988, Governor, Chief of Staff, Subject Files, 1983–1991, Governor Joe Frank Harris, Growth Strategies Commission 87–88 Folder, Georgia Archives; letter from Hal Rives (GDOT commissioner) to Joel Cowan, August 30, 1988, Governor, Chief of Staff, Subject Files, 1983–1991, Governor Joe Frank Harris, Growth Strategies Commission 87–88 Folder, Georgia Archives.

100. Memorandum from John Sibley to Joe Frank Harris, June 30, 1988, Governor, Chief of Staff, Subject Files, 1983–1991, Governor Joe Frank Harris, Growth Strategies Commission 87–88 Folder, Georgia Archives; "A Resolution Supporting the Recommendations of the Governor's Growth Strategies Commission to Establish a Comprehensive, Continuous and Coordinated Planning Growth Management System for Georgia," n.d., Governor, Chief of Staff, Subject Files, 1983–1991, Governor Joe Frank Harris, Growth Strategies Commission 87–88 Folder, Georgia Archives.

101. Memorandum from John Sibley to Joe Frank Harris, July 29, 1988, Governor, Chief of Staff, Subject Files, 1983–1991, Governor Joe Frank Harris, Growth Strategies Commission 87–88 Folder, Georgia Archives, p. 1; see also "Governor's Growth Strategies Commission Interim Report," 13.

102. Memorandum from John Sibley to Joe Frank Harris, July 29, 1988, p. 1; see also *Coordinated Planning Policy Implementation Draft Report*, State of Georgia Governor's Growth

Strategy Commission, July 1988, Governor, Chief of Staff, Subject Files, 1983–1991, Governor Joe Frank Harris, Growth Strategies Commission 87–88 Folder, Georgia Archives.

103. Memorandum from John Sibley to Work Group on Coordinated Planning, August 11, 1988, Governor, Intergovernmental Relations, Subject Files, 1983–1991, Joe Frank Harris, Growth Strategies Commission, Commission Proceedings June 87–November 88 Folders, Georgia Archives.

104. "Financing Mechanisms and Incentives for Economic Development," Report of Governor's Growth Strategies Commission Work Group on Financing Economic Development, August 22, 1988, Governor, Intergovernmental Relations, Subject Files, 1983–1991, Joe Frank Harris, Growth Strategies Commission, Commission Proceedings June 87–November 88 Folders, Georgia Archives.

105. Memorandum from Myles Smith (Finance Team Chairman) to Staff Advisory Team on Finance Issues, "Re: List of Potential New or Enhanced Financing Tools," August 8, 1988, Governor, Intergovernmental Relations, Subject Files, 1983–1991, Joe Frank Harris, Growth Strategies Commission, Commission Proceedings June 87–November 88 Folders, Georgia Archives.

106. Memorandum from Thomas Hamall (Arbor Gate Group) to E. Milton Bevington and members of the Marketing Committee of the Governor's Growth Strategies Commission, "Subject: Proposed Videotape and Executive Summary," June 29, 1988, Governor, Intergovernmental Relations, Subject Files, 1983–1991, Joe Frank Harris, Growth Strategies Commission, Commission Proceedings June 87–November 88 Folders, Georgia Archives, p. 1. See also Public Information Committee Meeting Minutes, May 25, 1988, Governor, Intergovernmental Relations, Subject Files, 1983–1991, Joe Frank Harris, Growth Strategies Commission, Commission Proceedings June 87–November 88 Folders, Georgia Archives.

107. "Growth Commission's Recommendations Parallel Georgia Conservancy Direction," *Georgia Conservancy Panorama*, July–August 1988; letter from Alan Toney (Georgia Sierra Club) to the Governor's Growth Strategy Commission, September 24, 1988, Governor, Intergovernmental Relations, Subject Files, 1983–1991, Joe Frank Harris, Growth Strategies Commission, Growth Strategies Commission Hearing Statements Folder, March–May, 1988, Georgia Archives.

108. Letter from James Burgess to Durwood McAlister, July 29, 1988, Governor, Intergovernmental Relations, Subject Files, 1983–1991, Joe Frank Harris, Growth Strategies Commission, Commission Proceedings June 87–November 88 Folder, Georgia Archives; see also letter from Jerry Griffin to Durwood McAlister, July 29, 1988, Governor, Intergovernmental Relations, Subject Files, 1983–1991, Joe Frank Harris, Growth Strategies Commission, Commission Proceedings June 87–November 88 Folder, Georgia Archives; and letter from Alan Toney to Governor's Growth Strategies Commission, September 24, 1988, Governor, Intergovernmental Relations, Subject Files, 1983–1991, Joe Frank Harris, Growth Strategies Commission, Commission Proceedings June 87–November 88 Folder, Georgia Archives.

109. Memorandum from John Sibley to Joe Frank Harris, September 21, 1988, Governor, Chief of Staff, Subject Files, 1983–1991, Governor Joe Frank Harris, Growth Strategies Commission 87–88 Folder, Georgia Archives.

110. Letter from Jim Higdon to Zell Miller, October 7, 1988, Governor, Legal Division Subject Files, 1984–1990, Growth Strategies Commission Folder, Georgia Archives.

111. "Enforcement Power Needed to Make Planning Work," *Atlanta Journal*, November 1, 1988; see also "Land Use Plan May Change Face of Rural Georgia," *Atlanta Journal-Constitution*, October 30, 1988.

112. Governor's Growth Strategies Commission, *Quality Growth Partnership: The Bridge to Georgia's Future*, November 2, 1988, pp. 4, 13; memorandum from John Sibley to Joe Frank

Harris, "Subject: Governor's Growth Strategies Commission," October 5, 1988, Governor, Legal Division Subject Files, 1984–1990, Growth Strategies Commission Folder, Georgia Archives.

113. "Harris Begins Bid for State Land-Use Plan," *Atlanta Constitution*, November 3, 1988.

114. "State's Growth Agency Hit as Duplicating Effort," *Florida Times-Union*, November 17, 1988.

115. John DeGrove, "Implementation, Funding Needed to Make Planning System Success," *Atlanta Journal-Constitution*, November 6, 1988.

116. "Enforcement Power Needed to Make Planning Work," *Atlanta Journal*, November 1, 1988.

117. "Will the Governor Prove Critics Wrong?" *Atlanta Constitution*, November 14, 1988.

118. "An Uphill Fight for Growth Planning," *Georgia Trend Magazine*, July 1988, pp. 23–24.

119. Memorandum from Jim Higdon to Joe Frank Harris, October 28, 1988, Governor, Legal Division Subject Files, 1984–1990, Growth Strategies Commission Folder, Georgia Archives, p. 1.

120. "Referendum on Land Use Not a Must," *Atlanta Journal-Constitution*, December 3, 1988.

121. "Harris's Land-Use Planning Bill Will Lack Enforcement Provision," *Atlanta Constitution*, December 28, 1988.

122. Ibid.; "It's Too Early to Compromise on Growth Planning," *Atlanta Journal*, December 30, 1988; "Governor's Game Plan: Capitulation," *Atlanta Constitution*, December 30, 1988; "Governor Wrong to Drop Stick," *Columbus Ledger-Enquirer*, January 4, 1989.

123. "Carrot with Teeth," *Rome Times-Tribune*, January 4, 1989.

124. "Who Wants More Government Planning?" *Georgia Trend Magazine*, January 1989, p. 66.

125. Joel Cowan, "Georgia Now Poised for New Economic Development Initiatives," submitted for publication in the January 8, 1989, edition of the *Atlanta Journal-Constitution* but never published; see also letter from John Sibley to Paul Bernstein, January 6, 1989, Governor, Intergovernmental Relations, Subject Files, 1983–1991, Joe Frank Harris, Growth Strategies Commission, Correspondence Folders, Georgia Archives.

126. "Growth Proposal Is Revolutionary," *Augusta Chronicle*, January 2, 1989.

127. Memorandum from Rusty Sewell and Stan Gunter (Office of the Governor) to Administration Floor Leaders (General Assembly), "Subject 1989 Legislative Package," January 3, 1989, Governor, Intergovernmental Relations, Subject Files, 1983–1991, Joe Frank Harris, Growth Strategies Commission, Correspondence Folders, Georgia Archives.

128. "Governor's Growth Strategies Plan Gains Momentum, Possible Support of Murphy," *Columbus Ledger-Enquirer*, January 9, 1989.

129. "House Panel Ready to OK Land Use Planning," *Atlanta Constitution*, January 18, 1989. The committee hearing brought a few minor changes to the bill, notably a request for legislative oversight of future changes to regional planning boundaries, an oversight that Sibley told Governor Harris could "cause a problem" though in the end did not. Memorandum from John Sibley to Joe Frank Harris, January 19, 1989, Governor, Intergovernmental Relations, Subject Files, 1983–1991, Joe Frank Harris, Growth Strategies Commission, Correspondence Folders, Georgia Archives.

130. Joe Frank Harris, "Supplying Water to a Growing Georgia, *Urban Georgia*, October 1988.

131. "Governor's Reservoir Plan Having Run of Dry Luck," *Savannah Morning News*, January 11, 1989.

132. "State Senate Bill Creates Horrifying Water Monster," *Atlanta Journal*, January 30, 1989.

133. For a foreshadowing of the trouble the reservoir plan would meet, see "Reservoirs Can Wait a Year, Examine Alternatives," *Atlanta Journal*, February 27, 1989; and "Reservoirs Plan Just Won't Wash, Sierra Club Says," *Marietta Daily Journal*, March 2, 1989. The proposed system of reservoirs ultimately proved untenable, for reasons financial, environmental, and political, though a few reservoirs were eventually permitted. See "To Dam or Not to Dam—State Reservoir Plan Could Bog Down," *Atlanta Constitution*, January 23, 1990; "Alabama Protests Georgia Reservoir—Tallapoosa Plan Called Part of a 'Water War,'" *Atlanta Constitution*, November 29, 1990; "Georgia Withdrawing Plan to Build Reservoir Near Alabama," *Atlanta Constitution*, March 22, 1991; and "Towaliga Basin Reservoir OK'd," *Atlanta Journal*, November 26, 1992.

134. "House Panel Ready to OK Land Use Planning," *Atlanta Journal*, January 18, 1989.

135. "Weakened Version of Governor's Land Use Planning Clears House," *Atlanta Journal*, February 10, 1989.

136. Memorandum from John Sibley to All Commission Members, March 16, 1989, Governor, Intergovernmental Relations, Subject Files, 1983–1991, Joe Frank Harris, Growth Strategies Commission, Correspondence Folders, Georgia Archives, p. 1.

137. As part of the signing ceremony, Harris revealed that he had hired Sibley to direct the newly created Governor's Development Council, the executive branch body responsible for implementing the new laws. Remarks by Governor Joe Frank Harris, Growth Strategies Bill Signing Ceremony, April 18, 1989, Governor, Intergovernmental Relations, Subject Files, 1983–1991, Joe Frank Harris, Growth Strategies Commission Folder, Georgia Archives.

138. "Growth Panel Produces Hard to Decipher Blueprint," *Atlanta Journal*, February 15, 1989.

139. "Harris Approves 4 Bills on Growth Strategies," *Augusta Chronicle*, April 19, 1989; see also letter from Robert Knox to Joe Frank Harris, March 20, 1989, Governor, Intergovernmental Relations, Subject Files, 1983–1991, Joe Frank Harris, Growth Strategies Commission Folder, Georgia Archives.

140. "Effect of Growth Strategies Planning Bill Uncertain, Other Expense, Trouble," *Athens Daily News*, March 27, 1989.

141. Sibley, "How the Georgia Growth Management Plan Enhances Local Preservation," 15; see also letter from John Sibley to Barbara Morgan, June 27, 1989, Governor, Intergovernmental Relations, Subject Files, 1983–1991, Joe Frank Harris, Growth Strategies Commission, Correspondence Folders, Georgia Archives; William Fulton, "In Land-Use Planning, a Second Revolution Shifts Control to the States," *Governing Magazine*, March 1989; and Whorton, "Innovative Strategic Planning."

142. American Planning Association, "Planners Honor Georgia with National Award," n.d., Governor, Intergovernmental Relations Subject Files, 1983–1991, Joe Frank Harris, Growth Strategies Commission, Georgia Archives, p. 1. See also 1990 National Planning Board, "Governor Joe Frank Harris's Contribution to Planning," Application for American Planning Association Award, September 29, 1989, Governor, Intergovernmental Relations Subject Files, 1983–1991, Joe Frank Harris, Growth Strategies Commission, Georgia Archives.

143. *State-wide Planning and Development—Governor's Development Council Created; Regional Development Centers; Local Governments; Department of Community Affairs; Department of Natural Resources; Powers and Duties*, General Acts and Resolutions, Georgia Laws, 1989 Session, vol. 1, no. 634, part 1.

144. "Bureau of State Planning and Community Affairs," Act 1066, Georgia Laws, 1970 Session.

145. The local plans were to analyze housing, land use (existing and future), transportation, human services, natural resources, historic resources, infrastructure, vital areas, economy, recreation facilities, and other substantive topics.

146. *State-wide Planning and Development*, part 2.

147. Ibid. The new regional development commissions (RDCs) replaced the system of area planning and development commissions (APDCs) that had been in existence for almost twenty years. While nominally involved with planning, the APDCs had long been cash poor, which limited their activities.

148. Ibid., part 3.

149. Ibid., part 4.

150. Ibid., part 5.

151. Ibid., part 6.

152. "State Land-Use Plan: 'Hardest Part Is Yet to Come' as Georgia Localities Likely to Fight Growth Rules," *Atlanta Constitution*, April 17, 1989.

153. Barnes went on to win the governor's office as a Democrat in 1998, and Isakson (who had lost a 1990 bid for governor) won the heavily Republican Sixth District seat in the U.S. House of Representatives vacated by Newt Gingrich in 2000. In 2004 Isakson was elected to replace Zell Miller as one of Georgia's U.S. senators.

Chapter 6

1. ARC, *1992 Population and Housing* (Atlanta: Atlanta Regional Commission, 1992), p. 4.

2. In 1993 ARC added one county, Cherokee, to its jurisdiction. But as a result of population growth and commuting patterns revealed in the 1990 Census of Population, the federal Office of Management and Budget expanded the boundaries of Atlanta's Metropolitan Statistical Area to eighteen counties in 1992. For an overview of the OMB procedures for reclassification of counties during the 1990 census, see Bureau of the Census, *Supplementary Reports: Metropolitan Areas as Defined by the Office of Management and Budget* (U.S. Department of Commerce, June 30, 1993).

3. Data for nonwhite population were taken from the Summary File 1 of Bureau of the Census, *1990 Census of Population: General Population Characteristics (CP-1)*, 1992.

4. "The tracts with the highest share of the region's black and other races population [are] in south Fulton, south and central Dekalb, and north Clayton counties." ARC, *1992 Population and Housing*, 10.

5. A 1994 publication detailing ARC's forecasts for Atlanta's population growth suggested that growth would continue to be strongest north of Interstate 20, reinforcing an existing pattern. ARC, "Vision 2020 Baseline Forecasts," June 1994, Atlanta Regional Commission Collection (ARCC), Kenan Research Center (KRC), Atlanta History Center (AHC), p. 12.

6. ARC, *1992 Population and Housing*, 27.

7. See Larry Keating and Carol Flores, "Sixty and Out: Techwood Homes Transformed by Enemies and Friends," *Journal of Urban History* 26, no. 3 (2000): 275–311; Larry Keating, "Redeveloping Public Housing: Relearning Urban Renewal's Immutable Lessons," *Journal of the American Planning Association* 66, no. 4 (2000): 384–397.

8. See Larry Keating, *Atlanta: Race, Class, and Urban Expansion* (Philadelphia: Temple University Press, 2001), chaps. 7 and 8.

9. "Tensions of Transition; North Clayton Adapts to Racial Shifts, Growing Pains," *Atlanta Journal-Constitution*, April 5, 1998.

10. The 2010 Census of Population and Housing revealed that the non-Hispanic white populations of Cobb and Gwinnett were less than 50 percent of the total. Bureau of the Census, *Census of Population and Housing, 2010: CPH-1, Summary of Population and Housing Characteristics*, 2012.

11. In 1990 the population density of the ten counties in ARC's jurisdiction was 837 persons per square mile.

12. For an example of the steps involved in the air quality conformity process, see ARC, "Air Quality Interim Conformity Determination for the Regional Transportation Plan, 1987–2010," October 1991, ARCC, KRC, AHC. For an extended discussion and analysis of the process of regional transportation planning in the post-ISTEA period, see Judith Innes and Judy Gruber, "Bay Area Transportation Decision Making in the Wake of ISTEA" (Berkeley: University of California Transportation Center, 2000).

13. Between 1990 and 1996 the Clear Air Act amendments and ISTEA required a reduction in measurable hydrocarbons of 15 percent across metro Atlanta. ARC, "Amendments to the Atlanta Region's Regional Transportation Plan, 1987–2010, September 1993, ARCC, KRC, AHC, p. 3.

14. Ambient air quality is determined from the concentration of widespread air pollutants considered harmful to public health and the environment. The 1970 amendments to the Clean Air Act required the EPA to establish National Ambient Air Quality Standards. The agency identified seven air pollutants for measurement and regulation: carbon monoxide, lead, nitrogen dioxide, two types of particulates, ozone, and sulfur dioxide. Clean Air Act, 1990, Title 1, Part A, Section 109, and Title III, Section 302.

15. For details about the ISTEA legislation, see Robert Jay Dilger, *American Transportation Policy* (Westport, CT: Praeger, 2003), especially chap. 3.

16. For a detailed recounting of the evolution of federal highway policy, see Edward Weiner, *Urban Transportation Planning in the United States: An Historical Overview* (Washington, DC: Greenwood, 1999), especially chap. 4.

17. See Raymond Mohl, "Stop the Road: Freeway Revolts in American Cities," *Journal of Urban History* 30, no. 5 (2004): 674–706.

18. See Robert Caro, *The Power Broker* (New York: Knopf, 1974), chap. 34.

19. Road-building controversies in Atlanta, not thoroughly documented, include a stretch of Interstate 75 and Interstate 85 in the 1950s, Interstate 485 (a proposed segment of the interstate system that would have cut through several neighborhoods east of downtown), the Presidential Parkway in the early 1980s (connecting the Carter Center to downtown), and Georgia 400 in the late 1980s (a toll road through the upscale Buckhead neighborhood). For brief mention of these controversies, see Jason Henderson, "Contesting the Spaces of the Automobile: The Politics of Mobility and the Sprawl Debate in Atlanta, Georgia," (Ph.D. diss., University of Georgia, 2004), chap. 4; and Keating, *Atlanta*, chaps. 4 and 6. Bayor, in chapter 3 of *Race and the Building of Twentieth-Century Atlanta*, discusses at length the controversy over the downtown segments of Interstates 75 and 85.

20. For critiques of the practice and politics of freeway planning, see Alan Altshuler, *The City Planning Process: A Political Analysis* (Ithaca, NY: Cornell University Press, 1965); Herbert Gans, *People and Plans: Essays on Urban Problems and Solutions* (New York: Basic Books, 1968); Mohl, "Stop the Road"; and Zachary Schrag, "The Freeway Fight in Washington, D.C.: The Three Sisters Bridge in Three Administrations," *Journal of Urban History* 30, no. 5 (2004): 648–673.

21. Conflict over control of land development has been quite pronounced in the postwar period and intensified after 1970 as regulations increased. For an overview, see Harvey Jacobs,

"Fighting over Land: America's Legacy . . . America's Future?" *Journal of the American Planning Association* 65, no. 2 (1999): 141–149; Harvey Jacobs and Kurt Paulsen, "Property Rights: The Neglected Theme of 20th-Century American Planning, *Journal of the American Planning Association* 75, no. 2 (2009): 134–143; Frank Popper, "Understanding American Land Use Regulation since 1970: A Revisionist Interpretation," *Journal of the American Planning Association* 54, no. 3 (1988): 291–301.

22. Los Angeles and Atlanta constructed their regional freeway systems during roughly the same period, but Los Angeles's network was more distributed, like a grid, while Atlanta's resembled the spokes of a wheel. As origins and destinations of trips changed over the years, crosstown mobility was severely compromised in Atlanta. Hence though both regions are paragons of automobility, Los Angeles's freeway network has helped maintain a much denser urban fabric. For more about the Los Angeles situation, see William Fulton, *The Reluctant Metropolis: The Politics of Urban Growth in Los Angeles* (Baltimore: Johns Hopkins University Press, 1997), 133–134.

23. "1946 Lochner Plan," CAUTION Collection, Box 51, Manuscript, Archives, and Rare Book Library, Emory University; "Expressways," Manuscript 619, Box 117, 1978, ARCC, KRC, AHC.

24. For an overview of this phenomenon, see Robert Cervero, *America's Suburban Centers: The Land Use Transportation Link* (New York: Routledge, 1989).

25. The literature on travel behavior is far too vast to list here. For an overview of issues related to travel behavior and road congestion, see Anthony Downs, *Still Stuck in Traffic: Coping with Peak-Hour Traffic Congestion* (Washington, DC: Brookings Institution Press, 2004).

26. "Shifting Work Patterns Weaken City's Center; Suburbanites Are Sticking Closer to Home," *Atlanta Journal-Constitution*, June 16, 1991, p. 1H.

27. ARC, *Atlanta Region Development Area Profile*, 1983, ARCC, KRC, AHC.

28. "Road Building Naysayers Ignore the Problem," *Atlanta Journal-Constitution*, March 24, 2002.

29. Metropolitan Planning Commission, "Metropolitan Planning Commission Preliminary Outline for a Local Transit Study," 1952, Mule to MARTA Collection, Box 1, Folder 7, ARCC, KRC, AHC; Metropolitan Planning Commission, *Now . . . for Tomorrow*, 1954, ARCC, KRC, AHC, p. 16; Metropolitan Planning Commission, "Mapped Streets Fact Book: A Survey Concerning Right-of-Way Protection in Metro Atlanta," November 1956, ARCC, KRC, AHC.

30. Weiner, *Urban Transportation Planning in the United States*, 128.

31. Metropolitan Planning Commission, "Access to Central Atlanta," 1959, ARCC, KRC, AHC; M. John Moskaluk and James Marks, "Final Report: Evaluation of HUD-USDOT 1975–76 Atlanta Region Travel to Work Survey," March 1980, ARCC, KRC, AHC.

32. See R. Shep Melnick, *Regulation and the Courts: The Case of the Clean Air Act* (Washington, DC: Brookings Institution Press, 1983), especially chap. 2.

33. April 22, 1970, was the inaugural Earth Day.

34. For more discussion of amendments to the Clean Air Act, see Samuel Hayes, *Beauty, Health, and Permanence: Environmental Politics in the United States, 1955–1985* (New York: Cambridge University Press, 1987), 773–776.

35. The 1977 amendments set up a graduated scale into which counties would be slotted according to their air levels of ozone, carbon monoxide, and particulate matter. Each pollutant's scale was slightly different from the others, but all generally stepped from marginal concentration to extreme. The values of each step were modified in 1990. For more details and an example of how the categories work for measurements of ozone, see Clean Air Act, 1990, Part D, Subpart 2, Section 181.

36. "Shifting Transportation Gears ARC Expected to Address Air Quality Concerns, "*Atlanta Constitution*, September 22, 1993. For background on the Clean Air Act amendments of 1977, see David Currie, "The Mobile Source Provisions of the Clean Air Act," *University of Chicago Law Review* 46, no. 4 (Summer 1979): 811–909.

37. ARC, "Exhibit Three: Conformity Documentation Atlanta Regional Transportation Plan, 1987–2010," in *Outer Loop Study*, 1994, ARCC, KRC, AHC, p. 4; "Ozone Increased Slightly Here in Past 10 Years," *Atlanta Constitution*, March 7, 1991.

38. For an overview, see David Currie, "Relaxation of Implementation Plans under the 1977 Clean Air Act Amendments," *Michigan Law Review* 78, no. 2 (1979): 155–203.

39. "EPA Finds Quality of Air in Southeast Much Improved, Atlanta Fails to Meet Smog Standard," *Atlanta Constitution*, October 20, 1992.

40. "Atlanta's Dirty Air Due Close Scrutiny," *Atlanta Constitution*, July 22, 1992.

41. "Shifting Transportation Gears"; "Atlanta Reaches Roads' End," *Atlanta Constitution*, June 14, 1996; "Growing a New Atlanta," *Atlanta Journal-Constitution*, June 8, 1997.

42. The Atlanta Region Metropolitan Planning Commission and the state highway commission decided to scrap the Outer Perimeter because of its excessive cost, though the road was never permanently deleted from long-range regional transportation plans. ARC, "The Outer Loop Background, March 25, 1994," in *Outer Loop Study*.

43. Beginning in 1972, the agency responsible for "technical aspects and day-to-day conduct of the region's transportation planning process [was] the Transportation Coordinating Committee," a committee housed within ARC that consisted of planners from ARC's seven member counties, the city of Atlanta, GDOT, ARC, and the Department of Natural Resources. ARC, "Prospectus for Urban Transportation Planning in the Atlanta Region," January 1980, ARCC, KRC, AHC, p. 5.

44. The Appalachian Regional Commission, created by Congress in 1965, included thirty-five counties in northern Georgia, several of which the Outer Loop would have passed through. An important part of the Appalachian Regional Commission program included funding economic development projects in Appalachian counties, and infrastructure (e.g., roads) was a popular target. A small part of the Outer Loop might have been eligible for Appalachian Regional Commission funds, which undoubtedly boosted the road's popularity among certain public officials.

45. ARC, *Outer Loop Study*, 1.

46. *The Governor's Road Improvement Program for Georgia's Continued Economic Growth and Safety*, 1989, Governor, Legal Division, Legal Division Subject Files, 1984–1990, Growth Strategies Commission Folder, Georgia Archives, Morrow, Georgia.

47. "Barnes and Perdue on the Issues: To Arc or Not To Arc? That Is One Question," *Atlanta Journal-Constitution*, October 6, 2002. See also Eleanor Main and Gerard Gryski, "George Busbee and the Politics of Consensus," in *Georgia Governors in an Age of Change: From Ellis Arnall to George Busbee*, ed. Harold Henderson and Gary Roberts (Athens: University of Georgia Press, 1988), 261–278.

48. "Smog's Still 'Serious' in Atlanta, EPA Says," *Atlanta Constitution*, October 22, 1992. See also Governor's Growth Strategies Commission, *Quality Growth Partnership: The Bridge to Georgia's Future*, November 2, 1988, Governor, Legal Division, Legal Division Subject Files, 1984–1990, Growth Strategies Commission Folder, Georgia Archives.

49. "Atlanta Officials Fear Loop Idea Still Has Too Much Life Left in It," *Atlanta Constitution*, December 8, 1994; "Highway Officials Want a Loop around the Loop," *Atlanta Journal-Constitution*, October 12, 1986; "New Highway Loop outside Present Perimeter Is Seen," *Atlanta Constitution*, August 12, 1971.

50. "Shifting Transportation Gears."

51. ARC, "Exhibit Three," in *Outer Loop Study*, 1.

52. "Governor's Vision: Barnes Building Growth Legacy; Land-Use Initiatives Applauded, but Road-Building Plans Draw Criticism," *Atlanta Journal-Constitution*, November 26, 2001, p. 1E.

53. "Gridshock: Atlanta's Trouble with Traffic," *Atlanta Constitution*, December 30, 1996, p. 4B.

54. "On Transportation, Barnes Bound by Political Reality," *Atlanta Constitution*, June 8, 2001, p. 22A.

55. "Election-Year Turnover Could Take Toll on Farsighted ARC," *Atlanta Constitution*, September 3, 1992, p. 2H.

56. "Voters Have Almost Wiped Out Region's Leaders," *Atlanta Journal*, August 12, 1992, p. 8A.

57. "Election-Year Turnover," p. 2H.

58. "On Transportation, Barnes Bound by Political Reality"; "Looking into the Crystal Ball: Traffic, Air Quality Top List," *Atlanta Journal-Constitution*, September 22, 1991.

59. ARC, *Draft Regional Transportation Plan*, 1996, ARCC, KRC, AHC; "The Outer Perimeter: Readers Split on Merits of Road," *Atlanta Journal-Constitution*, June 19, 1994, p. 7J.

60. "DOT Wants vs. Metro Needs," *Atlanta Constitution*, March 19, 1997.

61. ARC, *Outer Loop Study*.

62. "Public Speaks Up about Outer Loop," *Atlanta Journal-Constitution*, October 1, 1994, p. 12B.

63. "The Outer Perimeter: Readers Split on Merits of Road," p. 7J; see also "The Outer Loop: Other Voices; The Only Way," *Atlanta Journal-Constitution*, November 20, 1994.

64. "Regional planners spent months and more than $200,000 on a recently completed study that found an array of pitfalls to building the second highway around Atlanta, 20 miles outside I-285. Staff of the Atlanta Regional Commission predicted only little or no gains over current gridlock." "Commissioners Unwilling to Give Up on Loop," *Atlanta Journal*, November 15, 1994, p. 1J.

65. ARC, "Questions and Answers on the Outer Loop," in *Outer Loop Study*.

66. ARC, "Outer Loop Study and Summary of Focus Seminar, January 19, 1994," in *Outer Loop Study*; ARC, Meeting Minutes, November 23, 1994, ARCC, KRC, AHC.

67. ARC, "The Outer Loop Background, March 25, 1994," in *Outer Loop Study*; ARC, News Release, December 2, 1994, ARCC, KRC, AHC.

68. ARC, Atlanta Regional Commission Meeting Minutes, November 23, 1994, ARCC, KRC, AHC, p. 4.

69. "Commissioners Unwilling to Give Up on Loop," p. 1J.

70. See Jason Henderson, "Secessionist Automobility: Racism, Anti-urbanism, and the Politics of Automobility in Atlanta, Georgia," *International Journal of Urban and Regional Research* 30, no. 2 (2006): 293–307.

71. "The Outer Loop: A Special *Constitution* Editorial; The Fast Lane to Suburban Sprawl," *Atlanta Journal-Constitution*, November 20, 1994, p. 8H; see also "In Unusual Move, Business Groups Cool on Highway," *Atlanta Constitution*, November 22, 1994, p. 1D.

72. "Outer Loop Vote: Power of DOT Evident in Decision," *Atlanta Constitution*, November 24, 1994.

73. "Atlanta Officials Fear Loop Idea Still Has Too Much Life Left in It."

74. "Loop Comes around Again," *Atlanta Constitution*, November 11, 1994.

75. "The Road That Will Not Die," *Atlanta Journal-Constitution*, November 27, 1994. See also Truman Hartshorn, *The Northern Arc: The Outer Perimeter Reincarnated?* (Atlanta: Research Atlanta, 2000).

76. "Limited by Air Quality Standards, Officials Seek Projects That Can Get Federal Funding," *Atlanta Constitution*, September 10, 1996.

77. "Building of Roads Hits Snag," *Atlanta Constitution*, June 13, 1996, p. 1A.

78. "EPA Road Ban Jeopardizes Growth, Metro Leaders Say," *Atlanta Constitution*, August 16, 1996, p. 11E.

79. "DOT Mapping Plans for Outer Loop's Northern Arc," *Atlanta Constitution*, September 5, 1996, p. 1A.

80. "Atlanta Reaches Roads' End," p. 20A.

81. "Limited by Air Quality Standards, Officials Seek Projects That Can Get Federal Funding."

82. "Gridshock: Atlanta's Trouble with Traffic."

83. "DOT Wants vs. Metro Needs," p. 14A.

84. "EPA Road Ban Jeopardizes Growth."

85. These deliberations were carried out in an environment of mutual blame over which organization was most responsible for the air quality predicament. "Gridshock: Proposed Gwinnett Mega-mall Could Turn 'Growth' into a Fighting Word," *Atlanta Constitution*, December 29, 1996.

86. "Gridshock: Atlanta's Trouble with Traffic," p. 4B.

87. "With state agencies doing little more than pointing fingers at each other, and with powerful development interests loathe to slow the growth engine, virtually every knowledgeable observer points to Gov. Zell Miller as the one official with the power to demand a coherent state strategy. But Miller doesn't want to touch this one." "Atlanta's Bad Air: A Crisis Top Leaders Won't Touch," *Atlanta Journal-Constitution*, March 8, 1998; "Air: Area Has Driven into a Dangerous Corner," *Atlanta Journal-Constitution*, March 8, 1998; "Choked to a Standstill," *Atlanta Journal-Constitution*, March 15, 1998.

88. "Road Plans Place Air Quality at Risk," *Atlanta Journal*, March 13, 1997, p. 5B.

89. Ibid.

90. "Six Road Projects May Be Cleared," *Atlanta Journal-Constitution*, April 13, 1997, p. 1J.

91. "The Race Is On," *Atlanta Journal-Constitution*, June 28, 1997.

92. Ibid., p. 1D.

93. "Tricky Solution," *Atlanta Journal-Constitution*, July 26, 1997.

94. "ARC Agenda on the Roads," *Atlanta Constitution*, July 11, 1997, p. 1D.

95. Ibid.

96. See, for example, "Time to Clear the Air," *Atlanta Constitution*, July 15, 1997, p. 10A.

97. "DOT Faces Air Quality Challenge," *Atlanta Journal*, November, 20, 1997, p. 1F.

98. "54 Road Plans Get Go-Ahead under ARC's Spending Plan," *Atlanta Constitution*, November 25, 1997, p. 1B.

99. "Camps Divided over Road Rulings," *Atlanta Journal-Constitution*, January 18, 1998.

100. "Sprawl Confounds Planners," *Atlanta Constitution*, March 11, 1998, p. 1A.

101. "Path-Friendly Plan Wins ARC Approval," *Atlanta Constitution*, July 23, 1998.

102. "Interim ARC Plan Lacks Pollution Data," *Atlanta Journal*, July 6, 1998, p. 8A.

103. "Traffic Problems Dominate New Panel," *Atlanta Constitution*, July 2, 1998, p. 1C.

104. "Traffic's Real Culprits," *Atlanta Constitution*, September 11, 1998, p. 26A.

105. "Election '98; Barnes' Priorities," *Atlanta Constitution*, October 27, 1998, p. 7C.

106. "Latest Fear: Atlanta Leaders Say Traffic May Stall Economic Boom," *Atlanta Constitution*, June 19, 1998.

107. "61 Road Projects Opposed by Groups," *Atlanta Constitution*, November 10, 1998, p. 1C. One of the durable features of the Clean Air Act legislation, and indeed federal environmental regulations in general, is a door left open for lawsuits against federal, state, and local governments for failure to follow the letter of the laws. Beginning with the 1970 amendments and continuing with every subsequent amendment, the act authorizes legal action as a check on the regulation and enforcement process. Environmental organizations can take advantage of this opening to force government to take action in cases where action is needed but government has failed. Clean Air Act, 1990, Title III, Section 304.

108. Clinton, "Executive Order 12898—Federal Actions to Address Environmental Justice in Minority Populations and Low-Income Populations." For more on the issue of regional planning agency structure and transportation investment patterns, see Arthur Nelson, Thomas Sanchez, James Wolf, and Mary Beth Farquhar, "Metropolitan Planning Organization Voting Structure and Transit Investment Bias: Preliminary Analysis with Social Equity Implications," *Transportation Research Record: Journal of the Transportation Research Board*, no. 1895 (2004): 1–7.

109. "61 Road Projects"; "Three Advocacy Groups Sue over Projects," *Atlanta Constitution*, January 21, 1999, p. 4B.

110. "Barnes to Crack Down on Grants," *Atlanta Constitution*, November, 20, 1998.

111. "United States: To Traffic Hell and Back," *The Economist*, May 8, 1999; "Is Traffic-Clogged Atlanta the New Los Angeles?" *Wall Street Journal*, June 18, 1998.

112. ARC, "Workshop on Regionalism in Atlanta," May 17, 1985, ARCC, KRC, AHC.

113. "Traffic's Real Culprits," p. 26A.

114. "Governor's Slate of GRTA Members Is a Head-Scratcher," *Atlanta Constitution*, June 4, 1999, p. 2H.

115. "Transit Authority Gives Region Hope," *Atlanta Journal*, January 26, 1999, p. 14A.

116. "GRTA Has Its Work Cut out for It," *Atlanta Journal-Constitution*, March 28, 1999, p. 4R.

117. The main compromise in the bill required federal transportation money to be equally distributed among Georgia's eleven congressional districts. "A Myth Disproven," *Atlanta Constitution*, June 25, 1999.

118. "Can GRTA Put Us on Road to a Better Life?," *Atlanta Constitution*, March 28, 1999, p. 6D.

119. In March the *Atlanta Journal Constitution* offered a hopeful editorial on the future of the transportation authority, "On Tuesday, what had once seemed impossible was accomplished with surprising ease when the '99 General Assembly overwhelmingly approved creation of the Georgia Regional Transportation Authority. That 15-member board, still to be appointed by the governor, has the potential to first create and then implement a much-needed regional vision for Atlanta. It gives us the tools we need to tackle the problems confronting us." "GRTA Has Its Work Cut Out for It," p. 4R. But by July the newspaper was reporting that the public was not convinced that GRTA would be able to solve the region's problems. "So far, according to a recent poll of metro Atlanta residents, there's plenty of skepticism about whether it will accomplish anything. The poll conducted this spring for the *Atlanta Journal-Constitution* shows nearly two-thirds of those who responded were 'not very confident' GRTA would help solve metro Atlanta's air quality and congestion problems." "Public Still Skeptical about Transportation Board," *Atlanta Constitution*, June 7, 1999, p. 1E.

120. "3 Advocacy Groups Sue over Highway Projects," *Atlanta Constitution*, January 21, 1999, p. 4B.

121. Ibid.

122. "Court Ruling a Threat to Local Roads," *Atlanta Journal*, March 4, 1999, p. 1D; see also Environmental Defense Fund v. EPA et al., 167 F.3d 641 (D.C. Cir. 1999).

123. "Court Ruling a Threat to Local Roads," p. 1D.

124. Ibid.

125. "GRTA Members Face Great Expectations," *Atlanta Journal*, June 4, 1999, p. 1A.

126. Ibid.

127. "Road Case Settled with 17 Projects Approved," *Atlanta Journal*, June 22, 1999, p. 1C.

128. Ibid.

129. "Atlanta Moves Closer to Air Quality Goals," *Atlanta Constitution*, July 16, 1999, p. 1C.

130. "ARC Miffed at GRTA's Failure to Communicate," *Atlanta Constitution*, August 13, 1999, p. 3C.

131. "EPA Rejects Battle Plan for Metro Smog," *Atlanta Constitution*, December 2, 1999.

132. "Emissions Bill May Endanger Federal Funding," *Atlanta Journal*, March 21, 2000.

133. "New Obstacle for Clean Air Plan," *Atlanta Constitution*, April 10, 2000, p. 3D.

134. Ibid.

135. "GRTA OKs Three-Year Traffic Plan," *Atlanta Constitution*, June 16, 2000, p. 3H; see also "DOT Ready to Resume Road Work after Ban," *Atlanta Constitution*, December 18, 2000.

136. "Court Halts Regional Transportation Plan," *Atlanta Constitution*, July 19, 2000.

137. "Region Is 'One Step Closer' to Road Funds," *Atlanta Constitution*, July 26, 2000, p. 1C.

138. "Flawed ARC Plan Will Haunt Us All," *Atlanta Journal*, July 28, 2000.

139. "Environmental Groups Conditionally Accept State Plan on Roads," *Atlanta Constitution*, December 12, 2000.

140. Ibid., 3D.

141. "Air Let out of Lawsuit," *Atlanta Journal-Constitution*, December 23, 2000, p. 1D.

142. "War on Atlanta Air Goes Back to Court," *Atlanta Constitution*, January 18, 2001, p. 1B.

143. Ibid.; see also "Environmentalist Plaintiffs Are Only Hope for Clean Air," *Atlanta Constitution*, April 9, 2001, p. 8A.

144. "Environmental Groups Sue over Road Building," *Atlanta Constitution*, February 14, 2001, p. 3C; see also "Road Plans Face Barrier," *Atlanta Journal*, April 6, 2001.

145. "On Transportation, Barnes Bound by Political Reality," 22A.

146. "Roadwork Goes On," *Atlanta Constitution*, June 18, 2001, p. 1E.

147. "Transit Plan Moves to Fast Lane," *Atlanta Constitution*, June 28, 2001, p. 1A; see also "No Road Relief in Sight," *Atlanta Constitution*, June 29, 2001.

148. "Transit Plan Moves to Fast Lane," 1A.

149. "Transportation Plan Offers Only Questions," *Atlanta Constitution*, July 17, 2001; "Northern Arc Must Justify Itself," *Atlanta Constitution*, July 9, 2001; "Partners Left in the Dark, with the Tab," *Atlanta Journal-Constitution*, July 29, 2001; "State Transit Plan Seen as Little Help inside Perimeter," *Atlanta Constitution*, August 20, 2001.

150. "State Finally Ready to Give $8.5 Billion to Transit Projects," *Atlanta Constitution*, July 16, 2001, p. 3C.

151. "State Road and Tollway Authority," *Official Code of Georgia Annotated*, Title 32, Chapter 10, 2007.

152. In 1995 the Federal Highway Administration expanded the number and type of debt-financing mechanisms for states seeking funding for transportation projects eligible for federal aid. Several states had used or attempted to use bonds that would be retired by using anticipated future federal highway funds (out of the yearly highway funding bill approved by Congress). Georgia was one of these states, and many of the projects in Barnes's transportation plan would have been the first to use Grant Anticipation Revenue Vehicle (GARVEE) bonds to expedite planning and construction. For information on the GARVEE program, see "Tools and Programs: Federal Debt Financing Tools," USDOT, n.d., available at http://www.fhwa.dot.gov/ipd/finance/tools_programs/federal_debt_financing/garvees/index.htm.

153. "State Finally Ready to Give $8.5 Billion to Transit Projects," p. 3C.

154. "Major Transit Plans Ahead; State to Rely on Feds' Coffers to Fund Project," *Atlanta Constitution*, August 6, 2001.

155. In its deliberations about including the Northern Arc in a long-range transportation plan, ARC had put limits on the design to minimize the road's impact. Barnes supported this version of the road, though up until the project was canceled, GDOT maintained a plan that called for more intersections and a much smaller buffer. "Northern Arc Design Adds Exits, Slims Buffer," *Atlanta Journal-Constitution*, April 18, 2002.

156. Hartshorn, *The Northern Arc*.

157. "Transportation Plan Offers Bold Ambitions for State," *Atlanta Constitution*, June 29, 2001, p. 18A.

158. "State Transit Plan Seen as Little Help inside Perimeter," p. 1B.

159. "ARC Feels Left Behind in Regional Transit Plans," *Atlanta Constitution*, July 26, 2001, p. 1C.

160. "Judgment Day for Transportation Plan," *Atlanta Constitution*, April 17, 2000; "Barnes Gets Road Tying Arc to Park," *Atlanta Business Chronicle*, May 24, 2002; "More Officials Tied to Northern Arc Land," *Atlanta Business Chronicle*, June 7, 2002.

161. "Commissioners Divided over Road," *Atlanta Journal-Constitution*, July 11, 2002.

162. "ARC Transportation Plan Far from Intended Goal," *Atlanta Constitution*, October 30, 2001.

163. "Metro Transportation Plan Gets Court OK," *Atlanta Journal-Constitution*, January 19, 2002, p. 5H.

164. "Court Reinstates Stricter Atlanta Air Standards," *Atlanta Journal-Constitution*, April 19, 2002, p. 1C.

165. "Northern Arc Czar Wants Recusals," *Atlanta Business Chronicle*, June 14, 2002; "Legal Assault against Northern Arc Tempered by Barnes' Bombshell," *Atlanta Business Chronicle*, July 19, 2002; "DOT Family Owns Property Near Arc," *Atlanta Journal-Constitution*, July 5, 2002.

166. "Arc Related Lawsuits Delays Transportation Projects," *Atlanta Business Chronicle*, August 19, 2002.

167. "ARC's Out, GOP Hopefuls Agree," *Atlanta Journal-Constitution*, August 13, 2002.

168. "State's Clean-Air Plan Blocked," *Atlanta Journal-Constitution*, August 23, 2002, p. 10D.

169. "Bonds Lawsuit Costly for DOT," *Atlanta Journal-Constitution*, September 4, 2002; "Northern Arc Challenge Will Go to Ga. Supreme Court," *Atlanta Business Chronicle*, October 11, 2002; "Northern Va. Politics Carry Lesson about Traffic," *Atlanta Journal-Constitution*, April 28, 2003.

170. "Commissioners Divided over Road," *Atlanta Journal-Constitution*, July 11, 2002.

171. "Barnes' Road, Transit Plan Will Be Killed," *Atlanta Journal-Constitution*, May 14, 2003; "Court Upholds Innovative Loans for Roads, Rail," *Atlanta Journal-Constitution*, July 1, 2003.

172. As one of the leaders of the Northern Arc Task Force remarked, "When you let bonds . . . cover [other] bonds, it's kind of like getting a new credit card to pay off debt from the old one. How responsible are these kinds of actions?" "Bonds Lawsuit Costly for DOT," *Atlanta Journal-Constitution*, September 4, 2002, p. 1D.

173. "Partners Left in the Dark, with the Tab," *Atlanta Journal-Constitution*, July 29, 2001.

174. "GRTA Requires Perdue's Attention," *Atlanta Journal-Constitution*, January 30, 2003, p. 14A.

175. "Barnes and Perdue on the Issues: To ARC or Not to ARC? That Is One Question," *Atlanta Journal-Constitution*, October 6, 2002, p. 1F.

176. For an overview of the 1970 gubernatorial elections in the South, see Randy Sanders, *Mighty Peculiar Elections: The New South Gubernatorial Elections of 1970 and the Changing Politics of Race* (Gainesville: University Press of Florida, 2002).

177. Hartshorn, *The Northern Arc*; Henderson, "Secessionist Automobility"; Drew Whitelegg, "A Battle on Two Fronts: Competitive Urges 'Inside' Atlanta," *Area* 34, no. 2 (2002): 128–138.

178. "Should Voters Have Their Say in ARC?" *Atlanta Constitution*, December 15, 1997; "Two ARC Leaders Reject Stronger Role in Planning," *Atlanta Constitution*, September 10, 1998; Cynthia Tucker, "Off the Map: Gwinnett Commission Chair Needs Growth Lessons," *Atlanta Constitution*, May 12, 1999; "Rifts Rise to Surface during ARC Meeting," *Atlanta Constitution*, July 16, 2001; "ARC Feels Left Behind in Regional Transit Plans," *Atlanta Constitution*, July 26, 2001; "Finger-Pointing Won't Fund Transportation Alternatives," *Atlanta Constitution*, July 27, 2001.

Chapter 7

1. See Floyd Hunter, *Community Power Structure: A Study of Decision Makers* (Chapel Hill: University of North Carolina Press, 1969); *Community Power Succession: Atlanta's Policy Makers* (Chapel Hill: University of North Carolina Press, 1980), and Clarence Stone, *Regime Politics: Governing Atlanta, 1946–1988* (Lawrence: University Press of Kansas, 1989). Similar patterns in other places, Chicago, for example, have been detailed by Edward C. Banfield, *Political Influence* (Glencoe, IL: Free Press, 1961), and Alan Altshuler, *The City Planning Process: A Political Analysis* (Ithaca, NY: Cornell University Press, 1965). For a more theoretical discussion of community power, see C. Wright Mills, *The Power Elite* (New York: Oxford University Press, 1956).

2. For example, see Jack Spalding, "Where Now, Atlanta?" *Atlanta Journal-Constitution*, September 5, 1971; and ARC, "Growth and Development of the Atlanta Region," Atlanta Regional Commission Working Session, vol. 2, 1985, Atlanta Regional Commission Collection (ARCC), Kenan Research Center (KRC), Atlanta History Center (AHC).

3. Dan Sweat, participant in the four years of negotiations and discussions that led to ARC's creation and executive director in its first two years, left a permanent imprint on the way the commission would function in the coming decades. Sweat was both a public administrator and a political operator. He bridged the old central-city regime, the downtown businesses that governed Atlanta between the end of World War II and the late 1960s, and the new regional commission, one of the large public agencies that would guide the region beginning in the early 1970s. See Stone, *Regime Politics*, chap. 8.

4. Dan Sweat, interview by Clifford Kuhn and Shep Barbash, November 20, 1996, Dan Sweat Papers, Box P-1, Georgia Government Documentation Project (GGDP), Special Collections, Georgia State University.

5. "Metropolitan Area Planning and Development Commissions Created," General Acts and Resolutions, Georgia Laws, 1971 Session.

6. See William Fulton's *Reluctant Metropolis: The Politics of Urban Growth in Los Angeles* (Baltimore: Johns Hopkins University Press, 1997) for an extended description of the regional planning process in metro Los Angeles, specifically, how it consistently failed.

7. See Robert Fishman, "The Death and Life of American Regional Planning," in *Reflections on Regionalism*, ed. Bruce Katz (Washington, DC: Brookings Institution Press, 2000), 107–123; Lewis Mumford, "The Plan of New York," in *Planning the Fourth Migration: The Neglected Vision of the Regional Planning Association of America*, ed. Carl Sussman (Cambridge, MA: MIT Press, 1976), 224–259; Thomas Adams, "A Communication: In Defense of the Regional Plan," in Sussman, *Planning the Fourth Migration*, 260–267; and Ethan Seltzer and Armando Carbonell, *Regional Planning in America, Practice and Prospect* (Cambridge, MA: Lincoln Land Institute Press, 2011), chaps. 3 and 7.

8. See Howard Odum, "A Southern Promise," in *Folk, Region, and Society: Selected Papers of Howard W. Odum*, ed. Katharine Jocher, Guy Johnson, George Simpson, and Rupert Vance (Chapel Hill: University of North Carolina Press, 1964), 113–127.

9. The shift in political power in Georgia mirrored events across the South that unfolded in the 1980s and 1990s. A few examples of work that details aspects of this shift include Earl Black and Merle Black, *Politics and Society in the South* (Cambridge, MA: Harvard University Press, 1987); Matthew Lassiter, *The Silent Majority: Suburban Politics in the Sunbelt South* (Princeton, NJ: Princeton University Press, 2006); and Byron E. Shaffer and Richard Johnston, *The End of Southern Exceptionalism: Class, Race, and Partisan Change in the Postwar South* (Cambridge, MA: Harvard University Press), chap. 1.

10. ARC, "Draft Strategy, 1979–1983 Commission Work Program Goals, 5 Year Objectives, and 1979 Work Program," September 1979, ARCC, KRC, AHC, pp. 11–20.

11. "Bush Backs Off Carbon Dioxide Rules," *Atlanta Constitution*, March 14, 2001.

12. See Robert Fishman, "Metropolis Unbound: The New City of the Twentieth Century," *Flux* 6, no. 1 (1990): 43–55.

13. Henri Lefebvre suggests that the transition from the industrial city to the urban city entails a transformation of social, economic, and political concern from the production and management of goods or things, separate inanimate objects, to the production and management of space. Beginning with the establishment of agricultural production and ending with what he calls "the urban problematic," Lefebvre works through the meaning of this latest phase in the evolution of human settlements. He argues that the concept of the bounded city no longer adequately captures the scale and complexity of life, that the totality of human life has been subsumed by the unfolding experiences of urban development, "which becomes a productive force." The essential feature of "the urban" is not "as an accomplished reality . . . but . . . as a horizon," therefore it is the "analyst's responsibility to identify and describe the various forms of urbanization and explain what happens to the forms, functions, and urban structures that are transformed by . . . the process of generalized urbanization." Henri Lefebvre, *The Urban Revolution* (Minneapolis: University of Minnesota, 1970), pp. 15–17.

14. In *The Organic Machine: The Remaking of the Columbia River* (New York: Hill and Wang, 1995), Richard White wryly notes that "planning is an exercise of power, and in a modern state much real power is suffused with boredom. The agents of planning are usually boring; the planning process is boring; the implementation of plans is always boring. In a democracy boredom works for bureaucracies and corporations as smell works for a skunk. It keeps danger away" (64).

15. Fred Bosselman and David Callies, *The Quiet Revolution in Land Use Control* (Washington, DC: Government Printing Office, 1972); Frank Popper "Understanding American Land Use Regulation since 1970: A Revisionist Interpretation," *Journal of the America Planning Association* 54, no. 3 (1988): 291–301; Richard Walker and Kevin Heiman, "Quiet Revolution for Whom?" *Annals of the Association of American Geographers* 71, no. 1 (1981): 67–83.

16. See Wilson Barmeyer, "The Problem of Reallocation in a Regulated Riparian System: Examining the Law in Georgia," *Georgia Law Review* 40 (2005): 207–251.

17. Two editorials by Jim Wooten in back-to-back Sunday editions of the *Atlanta Journal-Constitution* highlighted the hidden role of the federal, state, and regional planning bureaucracy in determining how GRTA might regulate development. "Untouchables' Agendas Steer GRTA," *Atlanta Journal-Constitution*, May 7, 2000; and "High Priests Direct GRTA Off Course," *Atlanta Journal-Constitution*, May 14, 2000.

18. Georgia Department of Community Affairs, "Georgia's Growth Strategies Experiment: A Five Year Status Report," *Georgia Planner* 1 (February 1996): 5–9. For a different perspective, see Arthur Nelson, "Comparing States with and without Growth Management: Analysis Based on Indicators with Policy Implications," *Land Use Policy* 16 (1999): 121–127.

19. William Novak, "The Myth of the 'Weak' American State," *American Historical Review*, June 2008, 763.

20. See Timothy Conlan, *From New Federalism to Devolution: Twenty-Five Years of Intergovernmental Reform*; Timothy Conlan, *New Federalism: Intergovernmental Reform from Nixon to Reagan* (Washington, DC: Brookings Institution Press, 1988); James Lester, "New Federalism and Environmental Policy," *Publius: The Journal of Federalism* 16, no. 1 (1986): 149–166; Richard Cole and Delbert Taebel, "The New Federalism: Promises, Programs, and Performance," *Publius: The Journal of Federalism* 16, no. 1 (1986): 3–10.

21. See Jerry Weitz, *Sprawl Busting: State Programs to Guide Growth* (Chicago: Planners Press, 1999), chap. 2.

22. For an overview of Carter's troubles, see Bruce Schulman, *The Seventies: The Great Shift in American Culture, Society, and Politics* (New York: Free Press, 2001), chap. 5.

23. See Ann Bowman and James Franke, "The Decline of Substate Regionalism," *Journal of Urban Affairs* 6, no. 4 (1984): 51–63; Robert Jay Dilger, *American Transportation Policy* (Westport, CT: Praeger, 2003), chap. 3; Robert Gage, "Key Issues in Intergovernmental Relations in the Post-Reagan Era: Implications for Change," *American Review of Public Administration* 44, no. 2 (1990): 134–144.

24. For the broadest overviews, see Robert Fishman, *Bourgeois Utopias* (New York: Basic Books, 1987); Dolores Hayden, *Building Suburbia: Green Fields and Urban Growth* (New York: Vintage, 2004); and Kenneth Jackson, *Crabgrass Frontier* (New York: Oxford University Press, 1985).

25. See Robert Lang, "Open Spaces, Bounded Places: Does the American West's Arid Landscape Yield Dense Metropolitan Growth?" *Housing Policy Debate* 13, no. 4 (2003): 755–778.

26. See William Tabb, "Urban Development and Regional Restructuring, an Overview," in *Sunbelt/Snowbelt: Urban Development and Regional Restructuring*, ed. Larry Sawers and William Tabb (New York: Oxford University Press, 1984), 3–15; Bruce Schulman, *From Cotton Belt to Sunbelt: Federal Policy, Economic Development, and the Transformation of the South, 1938–1980* (Oxford: Oxford University Press, 1991); and Ann Markusen, Peter Hall, Scott Campbell, and Sabrina Dietrick, *The Rise of the Gunbelt: The Military Remapping of Industrial America* (New York: Oxford University, 1991).

27. See John Rae, *The Road and the Car in American Life* (Cambridge, MA: MIT Press, 1970); Robert Cervero, *America's Suburban Centers: The Land Use–Transportation Link* (Boston:

Unwin Hyman, 1989); Martin Wachs and Margaret Crawford, eds., *The Car and the City* (Ann Arbor: University of Michigan, 1992); Clay McShane, *Down the Asphalt Path: The Automobile and the American City* (New York: Columbia University Press, 1995); John Urry, "The 'System' of Automobility," *Theory, Culture, and Society* 21, nos. 4–5 (2004): 25–39.

28. See McShane, *Down the Asphalt Path*.

29. For a very brief review of the changing notion of the environment in the United States, see Donald Worster, "Introduction," in *American Environmentalism: The Formative Period, 1860–1915* (New York: John Wiley, 1973), 1–12; Hal Rothman, *The Greening of a Nation? Environmentalism in the United States since 1945* (Forth Worth, TX: Harcourt, Brace, 1997); and Theodore Steinberg, *Down to Earth: Nature's Role in American History* (New York: Oxford University Press, 2002).

30. After 1951 Georgia law restrained large-scale annexations, which meant that Atlanta's boundaries grew as those of most other Sunbelt cities grew. See David Rusk, *Cities without Suburbs* (Washington, DC: Woodrow Wilson Center Press, 1993).

31. For an overview of how the Office of Management and Budget periodically redefines Metropolitan Statistical Areas, see U.S. General Accounting Office, *Metropolitan Statistical Areas: New Standards and Their Impact on Selected Federal Programs* (Report to the Subcommittee on Technology, Information Policy, Intergovernmental Relations and the Census, Committee on Government Reform, House of Representatives, June 2004). For more general information regarding their definition, see *Metropolitan and Nonmetropolitan Areas: New Approaches to Geographical Definition* (Population Division working paper no. 12, Bureau of the Census, September 1995); Brian Berry, *Metropolitan Area Definition: A Re-evaluation of Concept and Statistical Practice* (working paper no. 28, Bureau of the Census, June 1968).

32. See Charles Rutheiser, *Imagineering Atlanta: The Politics of Place in the City of Dreams* (New York: Verso, 1996), chap. 2.

33. See Raymond Mohl, "The Interstates and the Cities: Highways, Housing, and the Freeway Revolt," Research Report for Poverty and Race Research Action Council, 2002, for a general discussion of highway conflicts in several U.S. cities.

34. For overviews of the environmental movement in the postwar period, see Rothman, *The Greening of a Nation?*; and Adam Rome, *Bulldozer in the Countryside* (New York: Cambridge University Press, 2001).

35. Perdue put forth a few regional transportation proposals, including a $500 million plan to build two rapid transit bus lines (which were later dropped), create a network of suburban commuter buses, and add more high-occupancy-vehicle lanes. "Mass Transit in Atlanta Disgraceful," *Atlanta Journal-Constitution*, October 18, 2004.

36. "Lopsided Transportation Plan Ignores Rail, Favors Buses," *Atlanta Journal-Constitution*, May 19, 2003.

37. "Two New Members to Join GRTA Board," *Atlanta Journal-Constitution*, September 1, 2003; "Stancil May Head Agency He Opposed," *Atlanta Journal-Constitution*, October 8, 2003; "Perdue Takes Wrong Turn with Choice to Lead GRTA," *Atlanta Journal-Constitution*, October 9, 2003; and "Steve Stancil: GRTA Executive Director," *Atlanta Journal-Constitution*, December 8, 2003.

38. U.S. Bureau of the Census, *American Community Survey*, 2006.

39. Livable centers were identified in the mid-1990s as a potential regional housing policy. Later the idea was broadened. ARC, "Regional Agenda for the Atlanta Region," December 1997, ARCC, KRC, AHC, p. H-62.

40. ARC, "Community Design and Smart Growth: The LCI Experience," presentation to Seventh-Annual New Partners for Smart Growth Conference, February 2008.

41. "Regional Leaders Face Key Road, Transit Decisions," *Atlanta Journal-Constitution*, August 10, 2011.

42. "ARC to Advise State on Funding," *Atlanta Journal-Constitution*, August 23, 2007; "With the GREAT Plan Gone, It's Time to Talk Roads," *Atlanta Journal-Constitution*, March 6, 2008.

43. "Transportation Package Set, Now It's up to Voters," *Atlanta Journal-Constitution*, October 14, 2011; "Transportation, Tax Reform on Deal Slate," *Atlanta Journal-Constitution*, January 10, 2012; "A Loud and Clear No," *Atlanta-Journal Constitution*, August 1, 2012.

44. "Defeat Gives Deal More Control, Few Options," *Atlanta Journal-Constitution*, August 2, 2012; "Few Transit Funding Options," *Atlanta Journal-Constitution*, August 5, 2012.

Index

Italic page numbers indicate material in figures.

A-95. *See* Circular A-95 (Bureau of the Budget)
AATS (Atlanta Area Transportation Study), 33–35
ACF (Apalachicola-Chattahoochee-Flint) Rivers basin, 47, *48*, 50–57
ACIR (Advisory Commission on Intergovernmental Relations), 17–19
Act 5, 39–40
Act 1066, 36–37
Adams, Thomas, 188n3
Advisory Commission on Intergovernmental Relations (ACIR), 17–19
Air Pollution Control Act (U.S., 1955), 142
airport planning, 31–32
air quality crisis: ARC, EPD, GDOT and, 75, 133–134, 143; federal requirements involved in, 9, 142, 178, 184; noncompliance leading to, 139, 143–144, 147, 153–157, 162; state implementation plans addressing, 142–143, 147, 149–151, 153, 161–163. *See also* lawsuits
Alabama, 47, 50, 56, 185, 216n165, 217n169
Aldredge, James, 37–38
Alexander, Doug, 137
Allen, Ivan, Jr., 30–31, 89
allocation models, 226n105
ambient air quality, 240n14

American Institute of Architects, 105
annexation of land, 23
APA (American Planning Association), 133
Apalachicola, Florida, 56
Apalachicola Bay, 47
Apalachicola-Chattahoochee-Flint (ACF) Rivers basin, 47, *48*, 50–57
Appalachian Regional Commission, 242n44
ARC (Atlanta Regional Commission): and air quality crisis, 139, 143–144, 147, 153–157, 162; and area plan reviews, 175–176; *Chattahoochee Corridor Study* by, *49*, 61, 68–69; and Circular A-95, 112, 177; consolidation of ARMPC, AATS, MACLOG into, 15, 40; counties covered by, 5; creation of, 12, 15, 20, 38–41, 120; development-review powers of, 60–61, 71–72; dissent within, over Outer Loop, 150–151, 169; and elimination of slow-growth scenario, 99; and EMPIRIC model, 92–98, *94*, *95*, *96*, 100; and enabling sprawl, 173–174; EPA and Section 208 status for, 70–71, *72*; federal financial support for, 176; and forecasting growth and water demand, 81–82; *Framework for the Future* by, 90, 93, 98; governing structure of, 40, 87, 89; and grandfathering of transportation

ARC (Atlanta Regional Commission) (*continued*) projects, 155–159, 160–162; influence of, 11, 45, 85, 87, 176; as information-sorting facility, 176; and invoking 1950s grand plans, 89–90; lack of zoning oversight by, 39; lawsuit against, by Roadblockers, 158–159, 160–163, 164–165, 167, 183; and loss of members in 1992, 148; naming of, 41; organizational structure of, *42*; power of, derived from process managing, 108; regional wastewater and water supply plans by, 73–74; in relationship with federal, state, local entities, 11, 15–16, 72–73, 82, 175; responsibilities of, 15, 40, 176; role of, under Metropolitan River Protection Act, 70; state support for, 177–178; *Study Design for Development and Application of EMPIRIC Activity Allocation Model* by, 93–*94*, *95*, *96*; and support of reregulation dam, 79; Sweat on, 43; use of Atlanta Study by, 69; use of scenarios by, 94–96, *95*, 99; and water supply security, 49; and working with GDOT and EPD on air quality, 143–144, 147–149, 153–157. *See also* RDP (regional development plan)

ARMPC (Atlanta Region Metropolitan Planning Commission): ASPO suggesting improvements for, 35; creation of, 29–30; erosion of support for, 33; and planning waste and supply systems together, 74; and regional transit authority, 31; reorganization plan for, 37; as replacing MPC, 29; and reporting on water infrastructure, 57, 59; and reviewing government applications, 31; voluntary nature of, 30

Army Corps of Engineers, 47, 49–51, 67, 79–82

Asians, 138, 183

ASPO (American Society of Planning Officials), 34–35

Association of County Commissioners of Georgia, 127

Atherton, Howard, 35–38, 115

Atlanta, Georgia. *See* metropolitan Atlanta

Atlanta Area Transportation Study (AATS), 33–35

Atlanta Journal and *Atlanta Constitution*: on air quality issue, 153–154, 156–157; on ARC, 148, 157, 159, 220n28; on Barnes's bond plan, 167–168; on Governor Harris, 120, 123; on Governor Miller, 244n87; on GRTA, 245n119; on GRTA proposal, 168; on Gwinnett county, 150; on history of Atlanta, 87–89; on influence in Atlanta, 16; on Manuel Maloof, 148; on need for planned growth, 120; on New South, 20; on Northern Arc/transportation, 137, 151, 157; on Outer Loop, 243n64; on Quality Growth Commission, 125, 127, 129, 131–132; on river pollution, 73; on upside of growth, 88–89

Atlanta Regional Commission (ARC). *See* ARC (Atlanta Regional Commission)

Atlanta Region Areawide Wastewater Management Plan, 74

Atlanta Region Metropolitan Planning Commission (ARMPC). *See* ARMPC (Atlanta Region Metropolitan Planning Commission)

Atlanta Silhouettes (Atlanta Region MPC), 92–93

Atlanta Study, 68–69, 77–81, 180

Atlanta Urban League, 38

Augusta Chronicle, 131

auto emissions: and Atlanta's air quality, 143–144, 150, 153–158, 162–166; under Clean Air Act, 142–143, 147; regional testing of, 154, 162

baby boomers, 10, 171

Baker v. Carr, 43

Balanced Growth Act (U.S., 1979), 231n40

Balanced Growth Policy Act (NC, 1979), 116–117

Barnes, Roy: conflict-of-interest charges against, 167; as elected governor, 158; electoral defeat of, 169, 171, 183; and environmental lawsuits, 158, 164, 168; and GRTA proposal, 159–161, 165–168, 178; as Harris's floor leader, 232n52; political roots of, 135–136, 158; and promotion of Northern Arc, 165–166, 168; and relationship with ARC, 171

Barrett, Ernest, 41

Bennett, Edward, 7, 192n25

Bennett, Glenn, 30–31, 33, 34, 37

bistate enforcement conferences, 56–57

bond issuance, 159, 166, 169 170

Bosselman, Fred, 228n12

Boston metropolitan park plan, 7

"The Bridge to Georgia's Future," 128, *129*

Brown, Charles, 41

Buckhead neighborhood, 44, 97, 141, 197n36

Buford Dam, *52*; and Atlanta Study Plan A, 78, 80; and Chattahoochee plan, 49; construction of, 47, 51–52; trout hatchery near, 76

Building the American City (National Commission on Urban Problems), 18–20

Bull Sluice Lake dredging (Plan C), 78

Bureau of State Planning and Community Affairs, 36

Bureau of the Budget, 30. *See also* Circular A-95

Burnham, Daniel, 7, 192n25

Busbee, George, 71, 75, 116–117

Bush, George H. W., 139, 181

Bush, George W., 178, 184

business community. *See* corporate leaders

Business Council of Georgia, 131

Byrne, Bill, 156

Callies, David, 228n12
Candler, Asa, 20
capitalism, 3, 8
carbon monoxide levels, 147, 241n35
Carroll, J. Douglas, 90
Carter, Jimmy: and Commission on Planned Growth, 115–116, 118; and consolidating power, 114; and defeat by Reagan, 111; and environmental policies as president, 181; and interpretation of Section 208, 70–71; and Metropolitan River Protection Act, 69; and modernization of state bureaucracy, 114, 195n2; and moratorium on river property rezoning, 60; and planned growth commission, 113; and prioritizing administrative reform, 38, 178; and push for state planning, 114–118; and support for ARC, 15; and support for Atlanta water supply efforts, 75–76
Cassandra Society, 148
CATS (Chicago Area Transportation Study), 90–92, 221n40
Centers for Disease Control and Prevention, 21, 182
Central Atlanta Progress, 44
central business district, 20, 26–27, 32–33, 44, 88, 202n122
Central Expressway Program, 22
chambers of commerce. *See* corporate leaders
Chattahoochee Corridor Study: areas covered by, 58; authority of, 69; land-use schematic diagram, 64; land vulnerability analysis, 63, 209n75; management mechanisms of, 66–67; maps of, 49, 58; model subdivision design, 65; and proposed national park, 76; "River Corridor Plan" diagram, 66; summary of land use plan, 62; Sweat's advocacy for, 76
Chattahoochee National Recreation Area, 75–79
Chattahoochee Palisades State Park, 76
Chattahoochee River, 50; 1963 report on pollution in, 54; as Atlanta's primary water source, 50, 53; and Atlanta Study, 68–69; biggest polluters of, 57; complaints about "gunk" in, 57; intergovernmental coordination of, 83; jurisdictional tensions over, 53; need for regulation of, 48, 79; northern waters of, 53; overreliance on, 82–83; regional development plans for, 11; takeover of, 81–82; traditional free use of, 47
Cherokee County, 88, 150
Circular A-95 (Bureau of the Budget): ARC and, 175; and Bureau of State Planning and Community Affairs, 36–37; impact of, 35, 87, 112, 179, 231n38; and mandate of regional planning for grants, 18–19, 114; rescinding of, 117, 176–177; and water planning, 67–68

Citizens and Southern Bank, 122
city-county consolidations, 36
city planning, birth of, 7
civil rights, 9, 17, 18, 114. *See also* race (generally); race in metro Atlanta
Clarke, Harold, 35
Clayton-Cobb Development Area, *28*
Clayton County, *28*; and ARC, 41; mandatory Act 5 contributions by, 40; population growth in, 21, 27, 184, 216n160; residential subdivisions in, 32; and support of ARMPC, 29
Clean Air Act (U.S., 1963), 142, 163; 1970 amendments to, 112, 143, 240n14, 245n107; 1977 amendments to, 112, 143, 144; 1990 amendments to, 139–140, 147–149, 153, 155, 160–161, 179, 181; and grandfathering of projects, 155; Roadblockers test case against, 142, 163, 168–169
Clean Water Act (U.S., 1972): amendments to, 148; ARC and, 73; and Army Corps of Engineers, 67; Carter's response to, 114–115, 224n78; complexity of water management planning under, 82; effect of, 179; and EPA, 59, 67; federal funding through, 67, 75, 99, 225–226n96; pilot studies for, 68; Reagan vetoing renewal of, 217; and requirement of A-95 coordination, 227–228n8. *See also* Section 208 (Clean Water Act of 1972)
Clinton, Bill, 155, 158
Cobb County: and 1951 water authority, 52–53; and 1969 report on Atlanta, 35–36; and ARC, 41; Clayton-Cobb Development Area, *28*; employment in, 141; growth of diversity in, 138; letter to Corps of Engineers from, 79; mandatory Act 5 contributions by, 40; and objection to Barnes proposal, 167; on Outer Loop and Northern Arc, 150; population growth in, 21, 27, 137–138, 184; residential subdivisions in, 32; and scuttling of river protection bill, 77; and support of ARMPC, 29; and support of greater state role, 35–36; water supply of, 57
COGs (councils of governments), 33
College Park, Georgia, 20, 26
Colorado Compact, 54
Commission on Planned Growth, 115–116, 118
Commission on State Growth Policy, 117, 118–119
Community Development Advisory Council, 105–106
commuting, 21, 111–112, 165, 227n5
coordinated planning, 12, 16
corporate leaders: and backing of GRTA, 160; and central business district, 20, 26–27, 32–33, 44, 88, 202n122; and chambers of commerce, 8, 16, 161; and concern about air quality, 148, 153, 156; and concern about water pollution, 56;

corporate leaders (*continued*)
  degree of influence of, 3; and Metropolitan Atlanta Transportation Initiative, 157, 159; on Northern Arc, 151; as "persons of dominance," 6; and power shift away from downtown, 12, 16, 174; and support of growth management bill, 122, 131
councils of governments (COGs), 33
counties: commissioners as part of governing coalition, 6; and end of county-unit system, 43; as expected to provide urban services, 23, 44, 53, 88, 182; and home rule, 128–130, 156; population of, 27; and use of water supply to finance growth, 53. *See also* unincorporated counties
County Commissioners Association, 36
Court of Appeals, D.C. Circuit, 161
Court of Appeals, Eleventh Circuit, 21, 169
Coverdell, Paul, 69, 115
Cowan, Joel, 115, 122, 124–125, 130–131, 161
Coweta County, 215n152
CSOs (combined sewer overflows), 54–55
cul-de-sacs, 11

Dahlonega-Lumpkin County, 122
Decatur, Georgia, 20, 26, 36
decentralization. *See* sprawl/urban decentralization
Dekalb County: and 1969 report on Atlanta, 35–36; and ARC, 41; Dekalb-Fulton Development Area, *28*; general fund support for MPC by, 23; mandatory Act 5 contributions by, 40–41; and opposition to Outer Loop, 150; as percentage of metro Atlanta, 32; population growth in, 10, 21, 27, 41, 44, 184; and post-treatment plant effluent, 73; and proposal of consolidation with Decatur, 36; and support of ARMPC, 29; and support of greater state role, 35–36; as water supplier, 50, 52–53, 57, 205n23
Dekalb-Fulton Development Area, *28*
DeMars, Charles, 217n171
Democratic Party: and Busbee, George, 71, 74, 116–117; and loss of power in Georgia, 6, 171, 177, 183; and Miller, Zell, 147–148, 155, 158. *See also* Barnes, Roy; Carter, Jimmy; Harris, Joe Frank
Demonstration Cities and Metropolitan Development (Model Cities) Act (U.S., 1966), 17, 18, 33, 176, 220n25
Department of Community Affairs (Georgia), 131–134, 137
Department of Housing and Urban Development, 31, 138
Department of Natural Resources (Georgia), 133–134, 143

Department of Transportation (USDOT), 155–156
Depression, Great, 21, 22, 51, 53
Detroit Metropolitan Area Traffic Study, 90
developers: erosion act and, 72–73; impact of Chattahoochee plan on, 67; impact of river protection act on, 69; and opposition to national park, 76; and planning and construction of roads, 142; and water supply plan, 73
development areas, 24
discourse of regional planning process, 5, 13
DOI (U.S. Department of the Interior), 78
"doughnut" calibration issue, 97, 100
Douglas, Paul, 18
Douglas, Walter, 21–22
Douglas Commission, 17–20, 88
Douglas County, 43
Downs, Anthony, 1–2, 4, 10, 11, 13
Downtown Connector, 21
drought, 83, 118, 185
Dunwoody, Georgia, 44

East Point, Georgia, 26
Edinburgh, Scotland, 7
Eglin Air Force Base (Florida), 182
Eisenhower, Dwight, 17, 54
electric power plants, 162
Eliot, Charles, 7, 192n25
empirical approach to regionalism, 7–8, 27
EMPIRIC model: and adoption by ARC, 92; constraints built into, 98; criticism of, 100, 105; and "doughnut" calibration issue, 97, 100; staff review of, 106; *Study Design* explaining, 93, 94, 95, 96; uses of, 93–97
employment patterns, 27, 32, 88, 140–141, 148
employment projections, 91–100
enforcement conferences (water), 56–57
environmentalists, 7; early legislation of, 9; Environmental Defense Fund, 156, 161; Georgia coalition of, 158, 170; Northern Arc Task Force, 169–170, 183, 248n172; Roadblockers, 158, 160–163, 166–168; Southern Environmental Law Center, 158; and support for GRTA, 160; and water quality, 55. *See also* Clean Air Act (U.S., 1963); Clean Water Act (U.S., 1972)
Environmental Protection Division (Georgia), 75
EPA (Environmental Protection Agency): and 1994–1996 extensions to ARC for air compliance, 153; and 1996 rejection of revised air quality plan, 153; and 2000 approval of ARC plan, 163; and challenge to RDP population projections, 106; and Clean Water Act (1972), 59, 67–68; grandfathering of road projects by, 155–159, 161–162; and partial funding freeze in Georgia, 156, 162; Roadblockers' lawsuit

against, 160–161; and support for reregulation dam, 78
EPD (Environmental Protection Division), Department of Natural Resources (Georgia), 75, 143–144, 147–149, 153–157
Erosion and Sedimentation Act (GA, 1975), 71
erosion control measures, 67, 71, 110, 211–212n107

Farrar, Robert, 35
Fayette County, 24, 205n24, 215n152
Federal Aid Highway Act (U.S., 1956), 8–9, 27, 140
Federal Aid Highway Act (U.S., 1962), 9, 17, 30–31, 33, 90–91
Federal Aid Highway Act (U.S., 1970, 1973, 1975), 112
Federal Highway Administration, 160–161, 164
federal housing acts, 17
Federal Power Commission, 51
Federal Reserve Bank, 21
federal role in regional planning: 1960s growth of, 16; 1980s pullback from, 12; 1990s reinvigoration of, 12; and branch offices, 21; as financing source, 8, 35, 43, 56, 225–226n96; and funding tied to population projections, 100, 109, 225–226n96; and funding tied to regional agencies, 2, 8–9, 17, 33, 67–68, 71, 112; sprawl following increase in, 22; and suburbanization, 10; and urban air quality, 142–143, 151; and use of SMSAs for allocations, 30
Fink, Gary, 201–202n116
first-wave land-use programs, 112–113
Fish and Wildlife Service (U.S.), 79
Fishman, Robert, 87
Five Points, 32
Flint River, 51
Florida: Department of Environmental Regulation in, 78; and filing of formal complaints about interstate water pollution, 56; growth management legislation in, 134–135
forecasts versus projections, 222n51
Foucault, Michel, 191–192n20
Framework for the Future, 90, 93, 98
Fulton County, 10, 21; and 1969 report on Atlanta, 35–36; and Atlanta Regional Commission, 41; Carter temporary moratorium in, 60; and consolidation with Atlanta, 36; and dispute of ARC review authority, 61; employment in, 141; environmentalist injunction against, 60; general fund support for MPC by, 23; growth in, 10, 27, 32, 184; land donated to, by Georgia Power, 76; mandatory Act 5 contributions by, 40–41; need for city services in, 23; and rezoning of protected river land, 59–60; and support for Atlanta Study report, 80; and support for greater state role, 35–36
FWPCA (Federal Water Pollution Control Administration), 56–57

Garden City concept, 7, 24
GARVEEs (Grant Anticipation Revenue Vehicles), 166, 169, 183, 247n152
GDOT (Georgia Department of Transportation): conflict-of-interest allegations against, 167; and grandfathering of transportation projects, 155–156, 158–159, 160–162; lawsuits against, 160–161, 164–165, 168; and objection to Quality Growth Commission, 126; and Outer Perimeter/Northern Arc, 147, 149–150, 153–154, 166–167; as responsible for state arterial highways, 142; and work with ARC and EPD on air quality, 143–144, 147–149, 153–157
Geddes, Patrick, 7
Georgia: Bureau of Outdoor Recreation, 76; Department of Community Affairs, 119; Department of Natural Resources, 74, 75, 79, 131; Environmental Facilities Authority, 131–132; FWPCA criticism of, 57; Highway Commission, 23; independent water quality control board, 55; military installations in, 182; R&D labs in, 182; State Capitol, 4; and state implementation plans (air quality), 142–143, 147, 149–151, 153, 161–163; as trying to avoid federal water intervention, 55; as an urban state, 88
Georgia Conservancy, 105, 127, 132, 158, 161
Georgia General Assembly: and Act 1066, 36–37; and allowing of special taxation (2010), 185; and Commission on Planned Growth, 115–116, 118; and debate over demographic changes (1968–1970), 88; and Erosion and Sedimentation Act (1975), 71; and establishment of AATS (1964), 33; and establishment of ARC (1971), 15, 20, 60, 120, 159, 174, 181; and establishment of ARMPC (1960), 29; and establishment of Cobb County water authority (1951), 52; and establishment of Commission on State Growth Policy (1982), 117; and establishment of MACLOG (1964), 33; and establishment of MPC (1947), 23; and Georgia Planning Act/State-Wide Planning and Development Act (1989), 113, 133–136, 137, 145, 180; and House Bill 84 (Act 5), 38–40; and House Bill 215 (land-use bill), 132; and Metropolitan River Protection Act (1973), 69–71; and overhaul of public education, 118; and permitting of constitutional referendum on transit authority, 31; Quality Growth Commission report to, 128–129; and Surface Water Management Act (1977),

Georgia General Assembly (*continued*) 75; and transition to Republican rule, 177–178, 183; and Walling river protection bill (1972, 1973), 60–61, 69; and Water Quality Control Act (1964), 55
Georgia Heritage Trust, 114
Georgia Municipal Association, 36, 127
Georgians for Transportation Alternatives, 158
Georgia Planning Act/State-Wide Planning and Development Act (1989), 133–136, 137, 145, 180
Georgia Power, 27, 76, 79–80
Georgia Trend Magazine, 124, 131
Ginn, Bo, 81
goals of regional planners, 5
governmental structure, 1, 19
Governor's Development Council, 131, 133
Governor's Road Improvement Program, 145–147, *146*
Grady, Henry, 20
grandfathered transportation projects, 155–158, 160–162
grant application review, 18
greenbelt, 24
groundwater, 74, 82, 135
growth: 1957 projections of, 27; accommodating versus guiding, 105; adjusting to, 87–90; despite environmental costs, 81–82; as key policy trigger, 26; as leading to suspension of federal road money, 159; planning for unlimited, 26; as predetermined in ARC/RDP model, 98–99, 107–108. *See also* sprawl/urban decentralization
GRTA (Georgia Regional Transportation Authority), 160–163, 183
Gwinnett County, 21, 27; and adapting plans to RDP projections, 225–226n96; and Atlanta Regional Commission, 41; growth of diversity in, 138; letter to Corps of Engineers from, 79; mandatory Act 5 contributions by, 40; and objection to Barnes proposal, 167; and Outer Loop/Northern Arc, 150, 155; population growth in, 88, 137–138, 184; residential subdivisions in, 32; water authority in, 59, 208n63; water intakes into Lake Lanier for, 81. *See also* Buford Dam

Hamilton, Grace, 38
hard-infrastructure policies, 107
Harris, Joe Frank: on Commission on Planned Growth, 115; and extension of Commission on State Growth Policy, 119; first term and reelection of, 117–118, 178–179; and Georgia Planning Act, 137; and hiring of Sibley, 238n137; and inaugural comments on state planning, 119–120; and land-use policy, 83; and Quality Growth Commission, 118–123, 126–*129*, 132–133, 145, 158
Hartsfield, William, 23, 51, 54
Henry County, 215n152
Higdon, Jim, 118–119, 121–122, 124, 126, 130
high-occupancy-vehicle lanes, 164, 165
highways: Atlanta freeway system, 23; evolution of Atlanta's roadways, 140–142; MPC facsimile map, *29*; schematic in Lochner Report, 26; state arterials, 142. *See also* Federal Aid Highway Act; Interstate Highway System; Outer Perimeter/Outer Loop/Northern Arc
Highway Trust Fund, 112
Hill, Wayne, 150
historians, 3
home rule, 128–130, 156
Hope VI program, 138
Horton, Gerald, 35–38
House Bill 84, 38–39
House Bill 215, 133–136, 137
House State Planning and Community Affairs Committee, 132
housing: and expansion of home size, 10; and high-end development, 44; and Housing Act (1954), 8, 27, 33; and lack of regulation outside urban area, 31; and lot sizes, 19; multiple jurisdictions governing, 19; and planned unit developments, 44; and proposed neighborhood design, *25*; single-family, 3, 11, 21
Howard, Ebenezer, 7, 24
hub-and-spoke transit system, 11
HUD (Department of Housing and Urban Development), 31, 138
Hunt, James, 116
Hunter, Floyd, 6
H. W. Lochner Co., 23, 26

"infrastructural power," 215n152
infrastructure systems: as bases of planning scenarios, 95–96; hard and soft policies on, 107; policy scenarios based on, 95–96, 105–106; as product of negotiated agreement, 11; and projections of driving development, 89, 92
interbasin transfers, 60, 205n24
Intergovernmental Cooperation Act (U.S., 1968), 17, 18, 35, 176, 220n25
interjurisdictional water contracts, 53
Interstate Highway System: Atlanta regional interstates, 32, 140, 151; completion of, 111, 231n38; development along, 32; federal

funding of, 8–9; and Lochner report, 23; public protests over, 140
interstate waters, 56
Introduction to Urban Development Models and Guidelines for the Use in Urban Transportation Planning (USDOT), 97
Isakson, Johnny, 135–136, 239n153
Island Ford Natural Area, 76
ISTEA (Intermodal Surface Transportation Efficiency Act), 139, 149, 153, 156, 179

Jacobs, Jane, 87, 140
Jenkins, Ed, 79
Johnson, Lyndon, 9, 18
Jonesboro Road, 21
jurisdiction(s): ACIR created to address, 17; for building permits, 13; and interjurisdictional water contracts, 53; problem of multiple, 19; for zoning, 13, 30, 120

Kent, T. J., 193n30
Kerner Commission, 17, 18, 88
Kerr, Robert, 54, 205–206n30
Klosterman, Richard, 226n105

Lake Lanier, 203n3; and Atlanta Study Plan B, 78; and Buford Dam, 47; direct water intakes into, 81; purpose of, 69, 80, 214–215n146; resident support for reregulation dam near, 80
Lake Seminole fish kills, 56
Lakewood Freeway, 140
Land and Water Conservation Fund, 76
land-disturbing activities, 69, 71, 131, 211n98
land-use plans: and Carter's planned growth commission, 113; first and second waves of, 112–113; and lack of accurate forecasting, 97; and Metropolitan River Protection Act, 69; in Oregon, 112–113; in RDP, 107; in *Up Ahead* (MPC), *22*, 23–29
land-use projections. *See* urban models
land vulnerability ratings, 66–67
Latinos, 138, 183
Lawler, Terry, 120
lawsuits, 180, 245n107; by ARC, 61; by Environmental Defense Fund, 156, 161, 183; by Northern Arc Task Force, 169–170; by Roadblockers, 158, 160–163, 164–165, 167, 183; by Southern Environmental Law Center, 164–165
League of Women Voters, 105
Lefebvre, Henri, 249n13
Levitas, Elliott, 35–37, 69, 71, 73, 77
light-rail lines, 165
Livable Centers Initiative, 184–185

lobbying: by ARMPC of General Assembly, 30; on behalf of reregulation dam, 80; against FWPCA, 56; and Quality Growth Commission, 131
local government: and attempts to mandate land-use planning, 120–121; as forced to deal with regional authorities, 9; and fragmentation, 19; as having zoning jurisdiction, 13, 30–31, 120; and home rule, 128–130, 156. *See also* unincorporated counties
Lochner report, 23, 26, 32
Logan, John, 99
Lomax, Michael, 80–81
London, England, 7, 24
Los Alamos National Laboratory (New Mexico), 182
Los Angeles freeway network, 241n22
low-density growth concept, 1, 4, 12–13, 22, 86, 99–100. *See also* sprawl/urban decentralization
lower-flow water fixtures, 83
Lower Manhattan Expressway, 140
lower-sulfur fuel, 162

MACLOG (Metropolitan Atlanta Council of Local Governments), 33–35
Maddox, Lester, 230n27
Maine, 112
Malaria Control Lab, 21
Maloof, Manuel, 148
mandates for regional planning: federal funding tied to, 2, 9, 17, 33, 67, 71, 112; by states, 19, 113, 125, 128, 130–131
maps: Atlanta "208 Planning Area," *72*; *Chattahoochee Corridor Study*, *49*, *58*, *62–65*; and generating control over issues, 61; by MPC, *24*, *28*, *29*
March to the Sea, 20
Marcus, Sidney, 35–38
Marietta, Georgia, 20, 26
Marietta Boulevard, 21
MARTA (Metropolitan Atlanta Rapid Transit Authority), 21, 32, 200n86
mature areas, 24
McDonald, Larry, 77
McHarg, Ian, 87
media: and anticipation of improvements in water quality, 73; and concern over demographic changes, 86; lack of reporting on RDP by, 108; and reaction to Atlanta's growth, 43, 88–89; and reaction to EPA rejection of air quality plan, 153–154; and reaction to polluted waters, 56, 60; and reaction to Quality Growth Commission, 125–128. *See also Atlanta Journal* and *Atlanta Constitution*

Memorial Drive, 21
Mendonsa, Don, 37
Metro Atlanta Chamber of Commerce, 157, 159, 161, 171, 185
metropolitan Atlanta: central business district, 20, 26–27, 32–33, 44, 88, 202n122; and consolidation with Fulton County, 36; expansion of, 12; and Georgia change from rural to urban, 43; governing structure of, 85; as lacking natural boundaries, 21–22; migration to, 21, 27; origins of, 12, 20–21; population density of, 10, 94, 139, 240n11; population of, 20, 27, 32, 43–44, 183–184; spatial inequality in, 88; as state capital and largest city, 4; suburbanization of, 10, 44; water supply for, 47. *See also* corporate leaders; race in metro Atlanta
Metropolitan Atlanta Council of Local Governments (MACLOG), 33–35
Metropolitan Atlanta Transportation Initiative, 157, 159
Metropolitan Atlanta Water Resources Management Study, 68–69, 77–81, 180
Metropolitan Planning Commission (MPC), 23, 90
Metropolitan Regional Council Study Committee, 37
Metropolitan River Protection Act (GA, 1973), 69–72, 134
Metropolitan Statistical Area, 184
Midtown neighborhood, 44
military installations, 182
Milledgeville, Georgia, 20
Miller, Zell, 147–148, 155, 158
Minneapolis–St. Paul, Minnesota, 13, 196n23
Model Cities Act (U.S., 1966), 17, 18, 33, 176, 220n25
model ordinances, ASPO encouragement of, 35
Molotch, Harvey, 99
Moses, Robert, 140
MPC (Metropolitan Planning Commission), *22*, 23–29
multifamily housing, 19, 59
Mumford, Lewis, 7, 177, 188n3, 192–193n26
municipal water treatment plants, water pollution from, 56

NASA centers (Alabama, Florida, Texas), 182
National Advisory Commission on Civil Disorders (Kerner Commission), 17, 18, 88
National Ambient Air Quality Standards, 143
National Commission on Urban Problems (Douglas Commission), 17–20, 88
national land use, 112, 143
National Park Service, 76, 79
national recreation area, 75–77
National Water Commission, 59, 68, 208n62
National Water Resources Planning Act (1965), 55–56
natural regions, 7
Naval Air Station North Island (California), 182
Neely, Douglas, 153
neighborhood design (*Up Ahead*), *25*
Neighborhood Units, 24
New Deal programs, 51
New Federalism, 111
New Jersey, 112
New Orleans–Apalachicola Inland Waterway, 51
New South, 20, 171, 201–202n116
New York, 8
non-point-source pollution, 212n116
North Carolina, 116
Northern Arc. *See* Outer Perimeter/Outer Loop/Northern Arc
Northern Arc Task Force, 169–170, 183, 248n172
Now . . . for Tomorrow plan for future growth, 26, *29*, 89
Nunn, Sam, 76

Oak Ridge National Laboratory (Tennessee), 182
Ocmulgee River, 73
Odum, Howard, 7, 177, 188n3, 190n11, 195n6, 221n38
off-stream water storage capacity, 74
Olympic Games (1996), 138
Oregon, 112–113
Outer Perimeter/Outer Loop/Northern Arc, 140, *152*, 1960s original concept of, 145–147; and 1993 public meetings and study by ARC, 149–*152*, 167; and 1994 Northern Arc compromise, 150–154; and 1997 long list and short list, 155, 160; and 2001 inclusion in governor's plan, 165–168; 2002 lawsuit over, 169–170, 183; as causing EPA to fail 1993 draft plan, 149; Doug Alexander on, 137
ozone levels, 147, 155, 164, 241n35

particulate matter, 241n35
Peachtree City, 115
Peachtree Trail, 20
peak-use surcharges, water, 216n161
Perdue, Sonny, 169, 183–185
Perimeter (Interstate 285), 140–141
Perry, Clarence, 24
personnel advice, ASPO encouragement of, 35
pilot study list for Clean Water Act, 68. *See also* Atlanta Study
"plan making," 189n8
Plan of Chicago (Burnham and Bennett), 7

Plan of Improvement (1952), 23
Plan of New York and Its Environs (Russell Sage Foundation), 8, 177
point-source discharges, 83
point-source pollution, 162, 212n116
population: density of, 10, 94, 139, 240n11; distribution of, 137–138, 177; of metro Atlanta, 20, 27; projections of, 90–91, 106. *See also* race in metro Atlanta; urban models
Portland, Oregon, 13, 178
Poytner, Randy, 151
Preston, Howard, 198n46
projections versus forecasts, 222n51. *See also* urban models
public: and anger over water pollution, 48; and citizen groups, 83; and forums on RDP, 105–106; and reaction to Atlanta Study Plan B, 77, 79; and referenda on regional transit authority, 31. *See also* environmentalists
public administrators, 6
public housing, 138
public sector planning to contain capitalism, 8
public transit systems, 10
Pyle v. Gilbert, 205n24

Quality Growth Commission: deliberations of, 122–124; final "bridge" report of, 128–*129*; General Assembly debate regarding, 131–133; and home rule issue, 128–131; initial plans for, 120–121; membership of, 122; public hearings and lobbying regarding, 125–127; and State-Wide Planning and Development Act (Georgia Planning Act), 133–136
Quality Growth Partnership, 128, *129*
quantitative tools for social problems, 91
"quiet revolution," 228n12

race (generally): Douglas Commission on, 19; and pattern of black migration in 1980, 111; and pattern of black migration in mid 2000s, 138; and redrawing of school boundaries, 19; and urban unrest in 1960s, 17, 18
race in metro Atlanta: 1920s distribution of, 20–21; 1950s distribution of, 24, 26–27; and 1950s urban renewal, 24, 26; 1960s distribution of, 88; 1970s distribution of, 32, 43–44; 1990s distribution of, 138; 2000s distribution of, 138, 184; and achieving black majority and black mayor, 3, 43–44; Asians, 138, 183; and civil rights and downtown abandonment, 33; and downtown infrastructure barriers, 202n122; Latinos, 138, 183; and progrowth politics, 86; and residential segregation, 26; unwillingness to address, 86

R&D labs, 182
RDP (regional development plan): as accommodating not guiding growth, 105; and citizen input process, 105–106; and emphasis on infrastructure, 107; final draft of, *98*; initial purpose of, 85; lack of public scrutiny of, 108; legacy of, 107–109; as manipulated for political purposes, 106–107; and projecting sprawl, 100, *101–104*; relationships cemented by process of, 106–107; as urban model, 85
Reagan, Ronald: and curtailing of federal funding, 111–112, 116–117, 142, 181; G. W. Bush partial reversal of, 139; and opposition to reregulation dam, 80–81; and rescinding of Circular A-95, 117, 177; and undermining of federal planning and regulation, 12, 83; and veto of Clean Water Act, 216–217n168; and Water Resources Development Act (1986), 216–217n168
redistricting, 88
redundancy in water supply systems, 74
Reed Report, 22–23, 26
regime theorists, 3
regional development plan. *See* RDP (regional development plan)
regionalism, 7–9, 11–13, 177, 192n24
regional planning (generally): adding predictability to process of, 181; and changing balance of power, 12; considered irrelevant and boring, 2, 180; in Decatur, College Park, East Point, Marietta, 27; discourse of, 5, 13; early history of, 2; and effect of accumulating over time, 107; as engine of economic growth, 8; and focus on ends versus means, 11, 13; and grant application review, 18; influence of, through plan making, 2–3; intellectual legacy of, 11–12; as mandated for federal funding, 2, 8–9, 17, 33, 67–68, 71, 112; previous research of, 5–6, 11; private versus public financing of, 8, 17; and Reed Report recommendations, 23; and region as unit of analysis, 4, 7–9; Robert Fishman on, 87; role of agencies in, 45; and sprawl, 10, 179; versus statewide commissions, 67–68; and surveys as tools, 7–8
regional planning process in Atlanta: and ARC-state relationship, 6, 11; birth of, 21–33; circular logic of, 107; Douglas Commission promotion of, 19; as growth strategy, 13; importance of, 180; maps for, *24*, *28*, *29*; and MPC (Metropolitan Planning Commission), 22, 23–29; and *Now . . . for Tomorrow* plan for future growth, 26, *29*, 89; and power shifting from businesses, 16; prior to ARC, 23; and regional transportation plans, 139–140, 158, 159–163, 184; and *Up Ahead* plan to limit growth, 24–26; USDOT

regional planning process in Atlanta (*continued*) evaluation of, 35. *See also* ARC (Atlanta Regional Commission)
"Regional Policy Development Process" (ARMPC), 39
regional rail systems, 10
"regional statesmanship," 41, 171, 178
renewal areas, 24
Republican Party: and Bush, George H. W., 139, 181; and Bush, George W., 178, 184; and McDonald, Larry, 76; in northern suburbs, 170; and Perdue, Sonny, 169, 183–185. *See also* Reagan, Ronald
reregulation dams, 51, 77–81
reservoirs, water, 51, 82–83, 124, 128, 131–132, 216n165, 238n133
residential program districts, *28*
Rhode Island, 112
rights-of-way, public, 142
riparian rights, 47, 55
river basin commissions, 55
Rivers and Harbors Act (U.S., 1945), 51
R. M. Clayton wastewater treatment plant, 50, 57
Roadblockers, 158, 160–163, 166–168
Road Improvement Program, Governor's, 145–147, *146*
Rockdale County, 24, 43, 150–151, 205n23
Roosevelt, Franklin, 8
Roswell, Georgia, 51
Rural Electrification Administration, 51
Russell, Richard B., 54
Russell Sage Foundation, 8

Sanders, Carl, 114
Sandy Creek wastewater treatment plant, 57
Sandy Springs, Georgia, 44
"Schematic Water Management System" (ARC), *80*
school boundaries, 19
second-wave land-use programs, 112
Section 208 (Clean Water Act of 1972), 209n83; ARC as agency for, 70–71, 175; effect of, 112, 114–115; and EMPIRIC, 106; and mandate of regional planning agencies, 67, 112; and state acceptance of ARC regional plan, 75; and "208 Planning Area," *72*, 209n83
Section 701 (Housing Act of 1954), 8, 26, 33, 87, 188–189n6
share-of-growth projections methods, 94–95, 97
Sherman, William T., 20
shopping malls: Lenox Square shopping mall, 27; regional, 44; strip malls, 3, 21; as taking business from downtown, 32–33

Sibley, John, III: and abandonment of constitutional amendment, 130; and "carrot with teeth" compromise, 131, 134; and creation of process plan, 123–124; and final "bridge" report, 127–*129*; and General Assembly debate, 131–133; on growth management in Georgia, 111; and home rule issue, 128–131; as picked to direct Quality Growth Commission, 120–123; and public hearings and lobbying, 125–127; and State-Wide Planning and Development Act (Georgia Planning Act), 133–136
Sierra Club, 127, 158
slow-growth scenario, 99
SMSA (Standard Metropolitan Statistical Area), 30, 40
sociologists, 3
soft-infrastructure policies, 107
soil conservation/erosion control, 67, 71, 211–212n107, 212n110
solid waste, 128, 132, 176
Southeastern Power Administration, 79
Southern Bell, 122
Southern Environmental Law Center, 158
South River, 73
Spalding, Jack, 16
Spalding County, 215n152
special taxation concept, 185
sprawl/urban decentralization: as assumed to be unplanned, 4; Barnes's attempts to control, 160, 170; as both policy and vision, 99; and climate, 197n33, 230n20; from desirable to undesirable, 99, 183, 185; in EMPIRIC projections, 100; General Assembly debates over, 88; Higdon opposition to regulation of, 119; and land-use planning in Atlanta, 113, 115; Livable Centers Initiative to curb, 184–185; and low-density growth concept, 1, 4, 12–13, 22, 86, 99–100; Miller opposition to regulation of, 148; Northern Arc and concerns over, 151; Oregon constraint of, 113; perceived benefits of, 5, 99, 188n5; and *Plan of New York and Its Environs*, 8; post-1970 development of, 10, 21–22; as product of regional planning, 3, 12, 50, 173–174, 177, 179; regional water plans encouraging, 50; as self-fulfilling prophecy, 86–87, 105; into unincorporated areas, 138–139
Standard Metropolitan Statistical Area (SMSA), 30, 40
State Biennial Development Program, 36
State Road and Tollway Authority, 166, 168
state(s): and air quality implementation plans, 142–144, 147, 149–151, 153, 161–163; and Georgia arterial highways, 142; influence of, on

regional planning, 3–4; legislature of, as part of governing coalition, 6; and mandate of regional planning, 113, 125, 128, 130–131; after Reagan pullback, 12; as unit of analysis, 4. *See also* Georgia; Georgia General Assembly

State-Wide Planning and Development Act (GA, 1989), 113, 133–136, 137

Steinberg, Kathy, 122, 233–234n75

Stewart Avenue, 21

Study Design for Development and Application of EMPIRIC Activity Allocation Model, 93–94, *95*, *96*

subdivision regulations, 26–27

suburbs: 1960s boom in, 18; evolution of, 10; and freeways, 6, 12; and hunger for development, 174; number of, 19; voting power of, 26; water supply for, 47, 52. *See also* highways; Outer Perimeter/Outer Loop/Northern Arc; unincorporated counties

Sunbelt growth pattern, 182–183

superdistricts, 94–95

Surface Water Management Act (GA, 1977), 75

surface water permits, 74–75

surveys as tools, 7–8

Sweat, Dan, Jr., 248n3; and ARC, 41–43, 85; and ARC development review authority, 60–61; and ASPO report, 34; on *Chattahoochee Corridor Study*, 82; and filing of lawsuit in Fulton Superior Court, 61; and objection to federal water legislation, 76; personal connections of, 89; work on Act 5 by, 37–38

Taft, Robert, 17

Talmadge, Herman, 68

3Cs highway planning process, 30–31

Train, Russell, 71

transportation: AATS and, 33; ARMPC plan for, 30; and decrease in mass transit (1970s), 10; as driving growth beyond capacity, 11; and evolution of Atlanta's roadways, 140–142; expansion versus mitigation of, 9; and gasoline, 157, 162, 185; heavy-rail, 23, 26, 31; and increase in traffic congestion, 141; and Livable Centers Initiative, 184–185; and Lochner report, 23, 26; and MARTA, 22, 32, 200n86; planning programs for, 68; post–World War II, 21; and public referendum on regional transit authority, 31; and traffic plans, *28*, *29*. *See also* air quality crisis; Outer Perimeter/Outer Loop/Northern Arc

Transportation Coordinating Committee, 242n43

trout fishing and hatcheries, 53, 76, 77, 79

"two Georgias" problem, 116, 123

ultra-low-flow water fixtures, 216n161

unincorporated counties, 20–21; delivery of city services to, 23, 44, 53, 88, 182; developers controlling placement of roads in, 142; and Fulton development controversy, 59–60; lack of planning by, 27; low density in, 138–139; and racial divide, 39, 44, 138. *See also individual counties*

University of Georgia, 123

"unlimited low-density" growth, 1

Up Ahead (Metropolitan Planning Commission), 22, 23–26

urban decentralization. *See* sprawl/urban decentralization

urban edge/fringe, 3; air quality in, 139; commuting and, 111–112; development of, 10–11; expectation of city services in, 23, 44, 53, 88, 182; and housing codes, 31; as leading to urban decline, 181–182; as requiring planning, 179

Urban Fortunes (Logan and Molotch), 99

Urban Land Institute, 1

Urban Mass Transit Administration, 30–31

Urban Mass Transportation Act (1964), 33, 35

urban models: apparent precision, objectivity, sophistication of, 91; and *Atlanta Silhouettes*, 92–93; and aura of legitimacy, 86; based on population, employment, land use, 94, 99–100; defined, 85; and "doughnut" calibration issue, 97, 100; and emphasis on transportation data, 86; EMPIRIC model, 92–98, *94*, *95*, *96*, 100; growing reliance on, 92–93, 217n4; high degree of error in, 97; history of, 86, 90–92; and population growth projections, 90–91, 106; and share-of-growth projections methods, 94–95, 97

urban region as unit of analysis, 4, 7–9

urban renewal, 9, 26

urban runoff, 55

Urban Studies Program, 68

urban unrest in 1960s, 17, 18

U.S. Department of the Interior (DOI), 78

USDOT (U.S. Department of Transportation), 35, 160–161, 163–164

U.S. Senate Public Works Committee, 68

U.S. Study Commission, Southeast River Basins, 54–55

Utoy Creek wastewater treatment plant, 57

Vandiver, Ernest, 27, 29–30, 114

vehicle emissions: and Atlanta's air quality, 143–144, 150, 153–158, 162–166; under Clean Air Act, 142–143, 147; and regional auto emissions testing, 154, 162. *See also* air quality crisis

Vital Areas Council, 115

Walling, Robert, 60–61, 69, 73
Warner, Sam Bass, 191n18
Washington, 112
water issues: in 1940s and 1950s, 54; complaints about federal directives, 57; conservation, 74, 83; efficiency gains and improved building standards, 83; exceeding release schedule, 82; federal interest in, 53–54; in Georgia Planning Act, 124; municipal water supply systems, 32; natural resource protection and Atlanta water supply, 113; pollution legislation, 9; relying on short-term adjustments, 81–84; runoff and siltation, 60; scope of urban water management, 56–57; wastewater, 48–50, 55, 57, 67–68, 70–75, 81–82, 106. *See also* Buford dam; Chattahoochee River; Lake Lanier
Water Pollution Control Act/Clean Water Restoration Act (U.S., 1966), 55–56, 207n47
Water Quality Act (U.S., 1965), 55
Water Quality Control Act (GA, 1964), 55
Water Resources Council, 55–56
Water Resources Development Act (U.S., 1986), 81

Water Supply Plan for the Atlanta Region, 74
water war (Georgia, Alabama, Florida), 216n165, 217n169
West, Harry, 37–38
Western and Atlantic of the State of Georgia railroad, 20
White, Richard, 191–192n20
"white noose," 196n22. *See also* race in metro Atlanta
white supremacy culture, 20. *See also* race (generally)
World War II–era support for public sector planning, 8

Young, Andrew, 77

zoning: ARC loss of zoning review, 181; and Georgia Planning Act, 123–124, 130; GRTA proposed power over, 159–160; local jurisdiction for, 13, 30, 120; Metropolitan River Protection Act loss of, 69–70, 73; Senator Walling bill on, 60–61

Carlton Wade Basmajian is Associate Professor of Community and Regional Planning at Iowa State University.